C000101640

family handyman

WHOLE HOUSE REPAIR GUIDE

family handyman

Whole House Repair Guide

Project Editor Mary Flanagan
Cover Photography Tom Fenenga
Cover Art Direction Vern Johnson
Page Layout David Farr

Text, photography and illustrations for *Whole House Repair Guide* are based on articles previously published in *Family Handyman* magazine (2915 Commers Dr., Suite 700, Eagan, MN 55121, familyhandyman.com). For information on advertising in *Family Handyman* magazine, call (646) 518-4215.

Hardcover, dated: 978-1-62145-538-7
Hardcover, undated: 978-1-62145-554-7
Trade: 978-1-62145-539-4

A NOTE TO OUR READERS: All do-it-yourself activities involve a degree of risk. Skills, materials, tools and site conditions vary widely. Although the editors have made every effort to ensure accuracy, the reader remains responsible for the selection and use of tools, materials and methods. Always obey local codes and laws, follow manufacturer instructions and observe safety precautions.

Family Handyman

Chief Content Officer Nick Grzechowiak
Editor-in-Chief Gary Wentz
Managing Editor Donna Bierbach
Associate Editors Bill Bergmann, Mike Berner, Jay Cork, Brad Holden
Creative Director Vern Johnson
Design and Production Mariah Cates, Jenny Mahoney, Andrea Sorensen
Photography Tom Fenenga
Illustrations Steve Björkman, Ron Chamberlain, Ken Clubb, Jeff Gorton, John Hartman, Trevor Johnston, Don Mannes, Christopher Mills, Frank Rohrbach
Set Builder Josh Risberg
Editorial Services Associate Peggy McDermott
Production Manager Aracely Lopez

Trusted Media Brands, Inc.

President & Chief Executive Officer Bonnie Kintzer

PRINTED IN CHINA
1 3 5 7 9 10 8 6 4 2

Safety first–**always!**

Tackling home improvement projects and repairs can be endlessly rewarding. But as most of us know, with the rewards come risks. DIYers use chain saws, climb ladders and tear into walls that can contain big and hazardous surprises.

The good news is, armed with the right knowledge, tools and procedures, homeowners can minimize risk. As you go about your projects and repairs, stay alert for these hazards:

Aluminum wiring

Aluminum wiring, installed in about 7 million homes between 1965 and 1973, requires special techniques and materials to make safe connections. This wiring is dull gray, not the dull orange characteristic of copper. Hire a licensed electrician certified to work with it. For more information go to cpsc.gov and search for "aluminum wiring."

Spontaneous combustion

Rags saturated with oil finishes like Danish oil and linseed oil, and oil-based paints and stains can spontaneously combust if left bunched up. Always dry them outdoors, spread out loosely. When the oil has thoroughly dried, you can safely throw them in the trash.

Vision and hearing protection

Safety glasses or goggles should be worn whenever you're working on DIY projects that involve chemicals, dust and anything that could shatter or chip off and hit your eye. Sounds louder than 80 decibels (dB) are considered potentially dangerous. Sound levels from a lawn mower can be 90 dB, and shop tools and chain saws can be 90 to 100 dB.

Lead paint

If your home was built before 1979, it may contain lead paint, which is a serious health hazard, especially for children six and under. Take precautions when you scrape or remove it. Contact your public health department for detailed safety information or call (800) 424-LEAD (5323) to receive an information pamphlet. Or visit epa.gov/lead.

Buried utilities

A few days before you dig in your yard, have your underground water, gas and electrical lines marked. Just call 811 or go to call811.com.

Smoke and carbon monoxide (CO) alarms

The risk of dying in reported home structure fires is cut in half in homes with working smoke alarms. Test your smoke alarms every month, replace batteries as necessary and replace units that are more than 10 years old. As you make your home more energy-efficient and airtight, existing ducts and chimneys can't always successfully vent combustion gases, including potentially deadly carbon monoxide (CO). Install a UL-listed CO detector, and test your CO and smoke alarms at the same time.

Five-gallon buckets and window covering cords

Anywhere from 10 to 40 children a year drown in 5-gallon buckets, according to the U.S. Consumer Products Safety Commission. Always store them upside down and store ones containing liquid with the covers securely snapped.

According to Parents for Window Blind Safety, hundreds of children in the United States are injured every year after becoming entangled in looped window treatment cords. For more information, visit pfwbs.org.

Working up high

If you have to get up on your roof to do a repair or installation, always install roof brackets and wear a roof harness.

Asbestos

Texture sprayed on ceilings before 1978, adhesives and tiles for vinyl and asphalt floors before 1980, and vermiculite insulation (with gray granules) all may contain asbestos. Other building materials, made between 1940 and 1980, could also contain asbestos. If you suspect that materials you're removing or working around contain asbestos, contact your health department or visit epa.gov/asbestos for information.

For additional information about home safety, visit homesafetycouncil.org. This site offers helpful information about dozens of home safety issues.

Contents

Chapter **one**
EXTERIOR

Chapter **two**
CONCRETE & ASPHALT

Chapter **three**
ELECTRICAL

Chapter **four**
PLUMBING

Chapter **five**
APPLIANCES

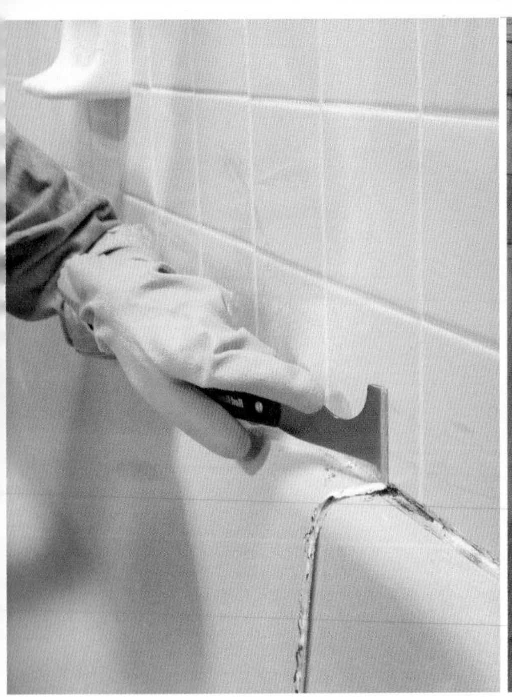

Chapter **six**

WALLS & CEILINGS

Chapter **seven**

DOORS & WINDOWS

Chapter **eight**

FLOORS & FLOOR COVERINGS

Chapter **nine**

FURNITURE & CABINETS

Chapter **ten**

SOLUTIONS FOR TOUGH CLEANING JOBS

Bonus **section**

GET RID OF PESTS!

Chapter **one**

EXTERIOR

Instant fixes for roof leaks

If you have water stains that extend across ceilings or run down walls, the cause is probably a roof leak. Tracking down the leak is the hard part; the fixes are usually pretty easy. We'll show you some simple tricks for finding and repairing most of the common types of roof leaks. But if you live in the Snow Belt and in the winter you have leaks only on warm or sunny days, you probably have ice dams.

If running water doesn't reveal the exact location of the leak, don't be timid. Start removing shingles in the suspect area. With them removed, there'll be evidence of the leak and you'll be able to track it down right to the source. You'll see discolored felt paper or water-stained or even rotted wood directly below and around it.

Finding the leaks

When you're trying to track down a leak, start by looking at the roof uphill from the stains. The first thing to look for is any roof penetrations. Items that penetrate the roof are by far the most common source of leaks. In fact, it's rare for leaks to develop in open areas of uninterrupted shingles, even on older roofs. Penetrations can include plumbing and roof vents, chimneys, dormers or anything else that projects through the roof. They can be several feet above the leak or to the right or left of it.

If you have attic access, the easiest way to track down a leak is to go up there with a flashlight and look for the evidence. There will be water stains, black marks or mold. But if access is a problem or you have a vaulted ceiling, you'll have to go up onto the roof and examine the suspect(s). The photos on the following pages will show you what to look for.

If the problem still isn't obvious, enlist a helper and go up on the roof with a garden hose. Start low, soaking the area just above where the leak appears in the house. Isolate areas when you run the hose. For example, soak the downhill side of a chimney first, then each side, then the top on both sides. Have your helper stay inside the house waiting for the drip to appear. Let the hose run for several minutes in one area before moving it up the roof a little farther. Tell your helper to yell when a drip becomes visible. You'll be in the neighborhood of the leak. This process can take well over an hour, so be patient and don't move the hose too soon. Buy your helper dinner.

1 Plumbing vent boots

Plumbing vent boots can be all plastic, plastic and metal, or even two-piece metal units. Check plastic bases for cracks and metal bases for broken seams. Then examine the rubber boot surrounding the pipe. That can be rotted away or torn, allowing water to work its way into the house along the pipe. With any of these problems, you should buy a new vent boot to replace the old one. But if the nails at the base are missing or pulled free and the boot is in good shape, replace them with the rubber-washered screws used for metal roofing systems. You'll find them at any home center with the rest of the screws. You'll have to work neighboring shingles free on both sides. If you don't have extra shingles, be careful when you remove shingles so they can be reused. Use a flat bar to separate the sealant between the layers. Then you'll be able to drive the flat bar under the nail heads to pop out the nails.

Problem: **When gasket-type plumbing vent flashing leaks, the culprit is usually a cracked gasket or missing or loose nails.**

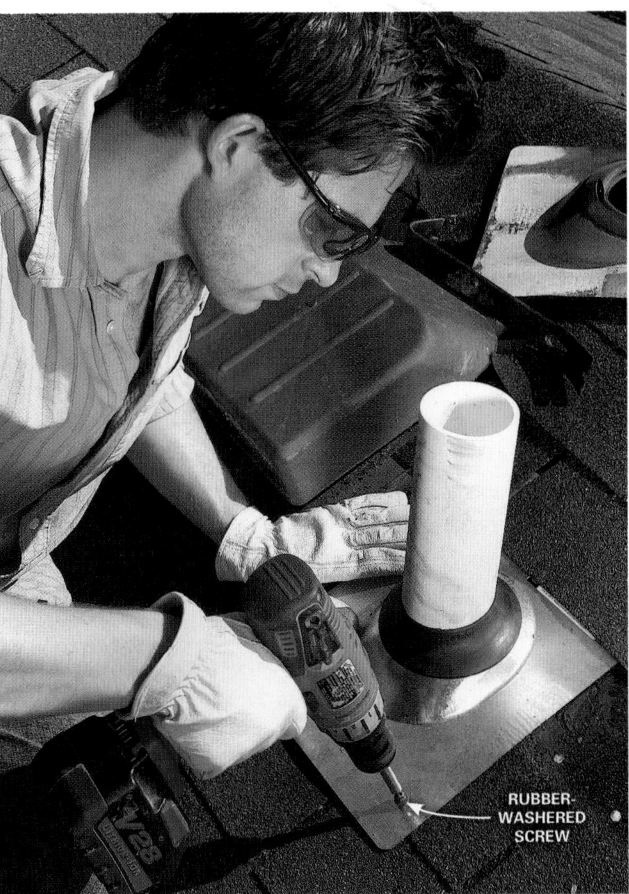

Solution: **Replace the old boot. Screw the base to the roof with rubber-washered screws. Don't use nails. They'll only work loose over time.**

2 Roof vents

Check for cracked housings on plastic roof vents and broken seams on metal ones. You might be tempted to throw caulk at the problem, but that solution won't last long. There's really no fix other than replacing the damaged vents. Also look for pulled or missing nails at the base's bottom edge. Replace them with rubber-washered screws.

In most cases, you can remove nails under the shingles on both sides of the vent to pull it free. There will be nails across the top of the vent too. Usually you can also work those loose without removing shingles. Screw the bottom in place with rubber-washered screws. Squeeze out a bead of caulk beneath the shingles on both sides of the vent to hold the shingles down and to add a water barrier. That's much easier than renailing the shingles.

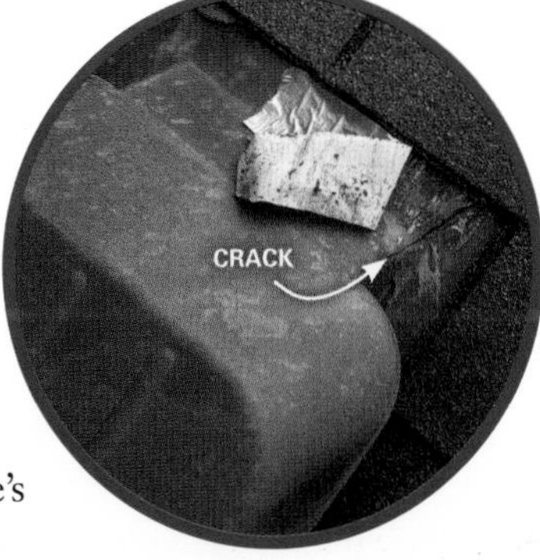

Problem: **Plastic roof vents can crack and leak. Duct tape is *not* the solution this time!**

Solution: **Replace the old vent. If you're careful, you won't have to remove any shingles to slip out the old one and slide the new one into place.**

3 Leaky walls and dormers

Water doesn't always come in at the shingled surface. Often, wind-driven rain comes in from above the roof, especially around windows, between corner boards and siding, and through cracks and knotholes in siding. Dormer walls provide lots of spots where water can dribble down and enter the roof. Caulk can be old, cracked or even missing between the corner boards and between window edges and siding. Water penetrates these cracks and works its way behind the flashing and into the house. Even caulk that looks intact may not be sealing against the adjoining surfaces. Dig around with a putty knife to see if the area is sealed. Dig out any suspect caulk and replace it with a siliconized latex caulk. Also check the siding above the step flashing. Replace any cracked, rotted or missing siding, making sure the new piece overlaps the step flashing by at least 2 in. If you still have a leak, pull the corner boards free and check the overlapping flashing at the corner. Often, there's old, hardened caulk where the two pieces overlap at the inside corner.

Problem: **Water that sneaks behind walls and dormers dribbles down into your house just like a roof leak.**

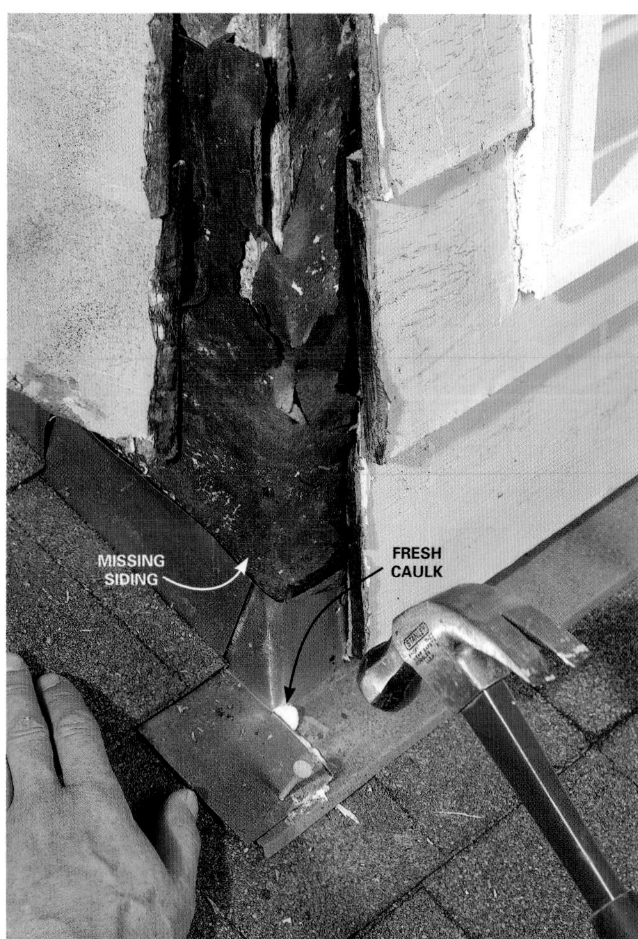

Solution: **Recaulk the corner flashing. Lift the overlapping section, clean it thoroughly and add a generous bead of fresh caulk underneath. Make sure the gap at the corner is filled with caulk.**

4 Step flashing

Step flashing is used along walls that intersect the roof. Each short section of flashing channels water over the shingle downhill from it.

But if the flashing rusts through, or a piece comes loose, water will run right behind it, and into the house it goes. Rusted flashing needs to be replaced. That means removing shingles, prying siding loose, and then removing and replacing the step flashing. It's that simple. But occasionally a roofer forgets to nail one in place and it eventually slips down to expose the wall.

Problem: **Unnailed step flashing can slip down and channel water into the wall.**

Solution: **Push a loose piece of step flashing right back in place and then secure it with caulk above and below.**

5 Small holes

Tiny holes in shingles are sneaky because they can cause rot and other damage for years before you notice the obvious signs of a leak. You might find holes left over from satellite dish or antenna mounting brackets or just about anything. And exposed, misplaced roofing nails should be pulled and the holes patched. Small holes are simple to fix, but the fix isn't to inject caulk in the hole. You'll fix this one with flashing.

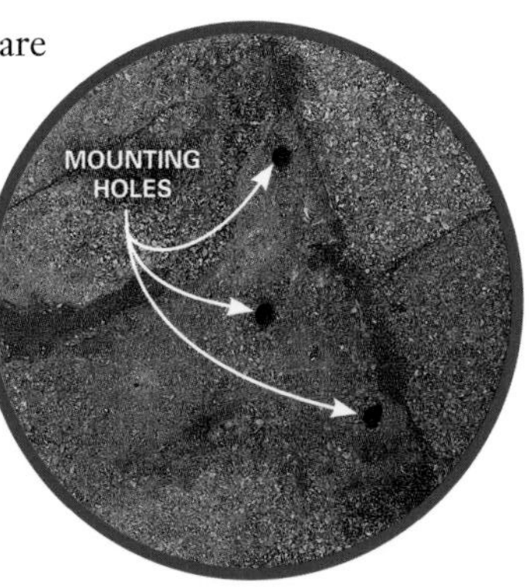

Problem: **Leftover mounting holes can let in vast amounts of water.**

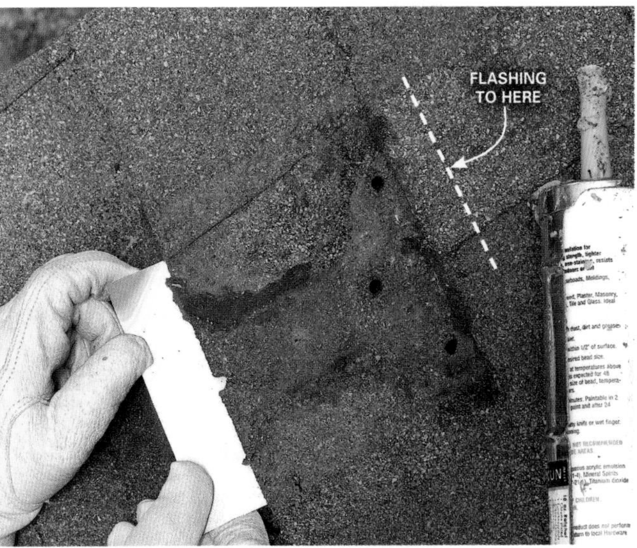

Solution: **Seal nail holes forever. Slip flashing under the shingle and add a bead of caulk under and over the flashing to hold it in place.**

Minor leaks can cause major damage

Have a roof leak? Well, you'd better fix it, even if it doesn't bother you much or you're getting a new roof next year. Over time, even small leaks can lead to big problems, such as mold, rotted framing and sheathing, destroyed insulation and damaged ceilings. The flashing leak that caused this $1,200 repair bill was obvious from the ceiling stains for over two years. If the homeowner had dealt with it right away, the damage and subsequent repairs would have been minimal.

pro tip

Don't count on caulk!

Rarely will caulk or roof cement cure a roof leak—at least for very long. You should always attempt a "mechanical" fix whenever possible. That means replacing or repairing existing flashing instead of using any type of sealant. Only use caulk for very small holes and when flashing isn't an option.

Repair gutter seams

For water to make it to the downspouts and drain properly, it has to stay in the gutter channel. When couplings or other fittings leak, the water drips instead right next to the foundation. A simple repair can stop the leak.

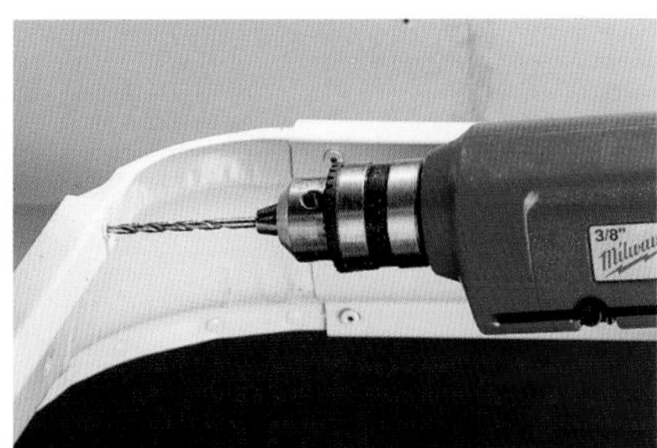

1 Separate the seam by drilling out the rivets. Use a drill bit slightly larger than the hole in the center of the rivet. Clean off any old sealant using a putty knife and sandpaper.

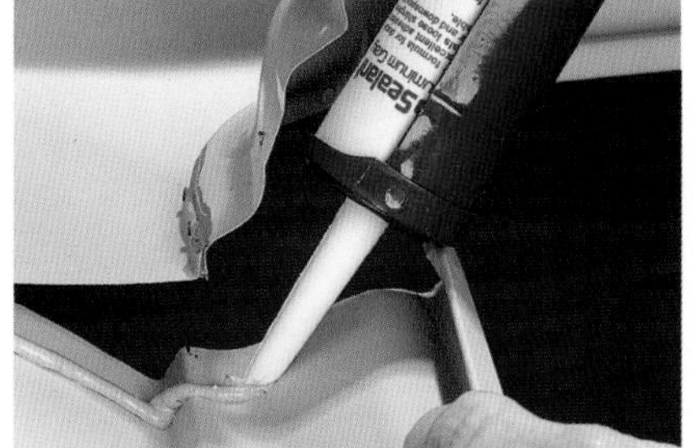

2 Apply a new bead of gutter sealant between the adjoining surfaces. Use a putty knife to work the sealer into corners and along edges. Reconnect the fittings and make sure they're tight.

3 In most cases, you can use new pop rivets that are the same size as the old ones. Check the diameter and depth range to make sure they'll fit the old holes and will cinch the joint tight.

Repair squirrel damage

Don't ignore the first signs of a bird or squirrel attack. Left unchecked, critters chewing through your exterior trim and into the soffits or roof can lead to major water and/or structural damage. You can install metal patches over the damaged areas. However, patches look ugly and are temporary fixes. If there are several areas of damage, consider this idea: Cover the perimeter of your roof trim, called fascia, with metal cladding (Photo 1).

For a last-forever job, use 24-gauge sheet steel, which comes in a variety of factory-applied colors. A sheet metal shop can bend most any size, shape or color cladding you need. Or purchase prebent aluminum fascia, in stock sizes, from a home center or lumberyard. Aluminum isn't as sturdy as steel, and you won't have as many color choices—but it will be cheaper and readily available.

If you have wooden crown molding around the edge of your roof, you have two choices. Either reinstall your wood crown over the metal fascia and expect squirrels may chew through it. Or leave the wood crown off and replace it with metal "D-style" drip edge (Photo 2).

Not only will this quick improvement keep wildlife away from your fascia trim, it'll retire you from the cycle of scraping and painting.

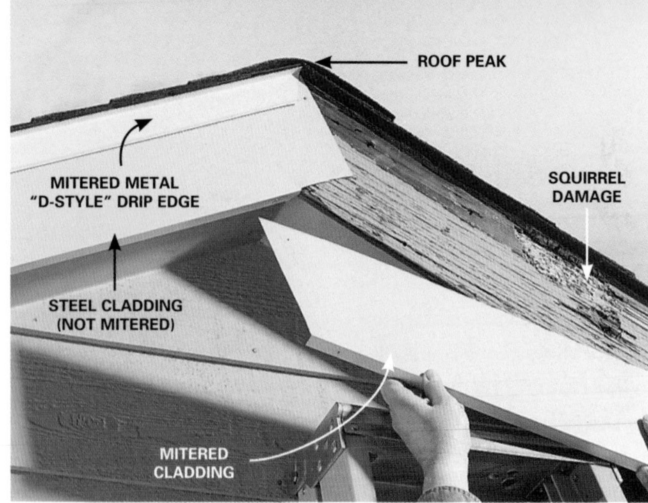

1 **Cover damaged fascia boards and roof sheathing edges with metal cladding. Sections of severely damaged wood should be cut out and replaced beforehand. Metal flashings and cladding should lap each other, as shown, to shed water. Use matching colored nails spaced approximately 3 ft. apart in a zigzag pattern. Nailing at closer intervals may cause buckling from the metal's expansion and contraction. Steel will buckle less than aluminum.**

2 **Install the metal drip edge. First, remove roofing nails, then slide the metal edging under the shingles. Use care in prying up old, brittle shingles. If you have difficulty nailing the drip edge from the top, use silicone adhesive to fasten it.**

pro tip

Think safety!

As with most home repairs or improvements, working on the roof involves a few specialized tools, but start with some common sense. First and foremost, leave the difficult situations—steep slopes and excessive heights—to professionals. It's just not worth the added risk to tackle those obstacles. Second, wait until conditions are right; wet or icy shingles, gusty winds or high temperatures increase the likelihood of a fall or damage to the roof. Keep away from overhead power lines. Wear soft-soled shoes that offer some grip, and sweep the roof to remove dirt, debris and loose shingle granules that might compromise your footing. Finally, stay off slate or tile roofs to avoid breakage.

Safe rooftop work involves a simple system. Wearing soft-soled shoes and a safety harness is the first step. Beyond that, you need a sturdy extension ladder, a few temporary slide guards and a broom to sweep the surface free of debris.

instant fix

Replace a damaged shingle

Asphalt shingles withstand years of abuse from wind, rain, sleet and snow, but they can tear like cardboard when struck by a falling tree limb or branch. Replacing the shingle will only take about 10 minutes— just be careful not to damage any other shingles.

If you don't have a few extra shingles stored in the garage or attic, take a scrap of the shingle to a home center or roofing supplier to find a match. You'll have to buy a full bundle.

It's best to work on the roof when the temperature is between 50 and 70 degrees F. Walking around on a hotter roof can damage the shingles.

The first step is to remove what's left of the damaged shingle. Each shingle has an adhesive tar sealant strip down the center that grips the shingle above it. The tabs from the damaged shingle and the tabs directly above it will all have to be freed from the sealant strip (Photo 1). Break this seal to get at the nails and get the damaged shingle out.

The next step is to pull out the nails and remove the damaged shingle. There will be eight or nine nails holding the shingle in place (four in the damaged shingle and four or five from the shingles directly above it). Remove the nails as shown in Photo 2.

Pull out the old shingle and slide a new one in its place. If the old nails are in good condition, reuse them, but if they're rusty or bent, replace them with new galvanized roofing nails of the same length. Align the new shingle with the rest of the row and nail it off (Photos 3 and 4).

1 **Push a stiff putty knife under the shingle tabs to break through the sealant strip. Rock the putty knife back and forth to help it slice through.**

2 **Slide a flat pry bar under the head of the nails (tap it with a hammer if necessary). Slip a scrap block of wood under the pry bar to help leverage the nail loose. Remove nails in the shingle itself and the nails in the row directly above it. Slide out the old shingle.**

3 **Slip the new shingle into place. Gently lift the tab of the shingle above, position the nails just above the sealant strip and nail the new shingle above the tab slots and at the ends. Move up one row and nail and repeat the process until you've replaced all the nails.**

4 **Seal the loose shingle tabs to the roof with roof cement and a caulking gun.**

Replace vent flashing

All-metal plumbing vents present two opportunities for leaks—first, where the flashing meets the roof, and second, where the vent pipe meets the flashing. When the latter situation occurs, caulking and similar fixes will prove to be only temporary cures. You'll have to replace the flashing, either with a rubber-sleeve version or the telescoping two-piece type shown below.

1 Carefully remove any shingles that lap over the top half of the flashing base. Pull the nails that secure the old flashing and remove it.

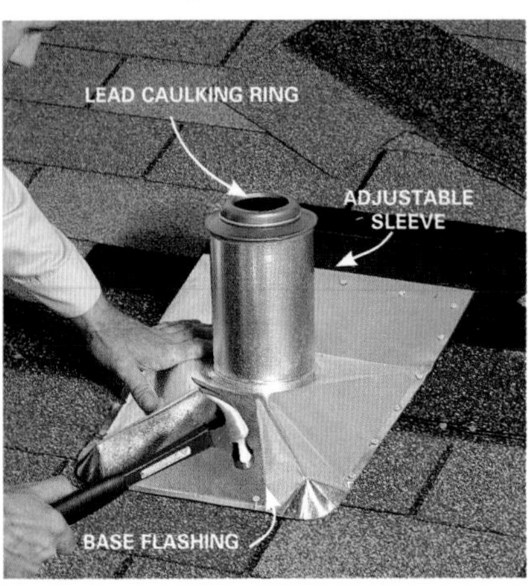

2 Fit the new base flashing over the pipe and nail along the edges. Slide the adjustable sleeve over the base flashing and vent pipe.

3 Notch and reinstall shingles to cover upper portion of base flashing. Apply roofing cement to overlapping tabs and exposed nail heads. Fold pliable ring over top of vent pipe.

instant fix

Seal a valley joint

Occasionally, a flashing that's still intact can allow water passage; this is especially true for valley flashing that doesn't have a raised fin or ridge in the center to help prevent fast-moving water from sloshing. If the roofer didn't cement the joint—and many don't—the shingles can curl up at the edge and eventually create a gap that water can easily penetrate.

1 Starting at the bottom edge, lift the shingle and apply a heavy, consistent bead of roofing cement along the flashing.

2 Drop and embed the first shingle into the cement. Lift the next shingle and lay another long bead of cement on the flashing and the top edge of the previous shingle.

3 Continue applying cement to both the flashing and the shingles as you work your way up. Press the shingles down to seat them.

instant fix

Straighten sagging gutters

If your metal gutters have developed a middle-age sag, it's time for a little tummy tuck! You'll find some version of a gutter support bracket that'll work on your gutters to lift the low spots. It'll help drain water better and help keep debris from accumulating. The style shown, is very easy to install. Another style of gutter hanger slides under the shingles and is nailed to the roof under the shingles. But test-bend your shingles first. Older shingles can be brittle and could break off when you lift them for the installation.

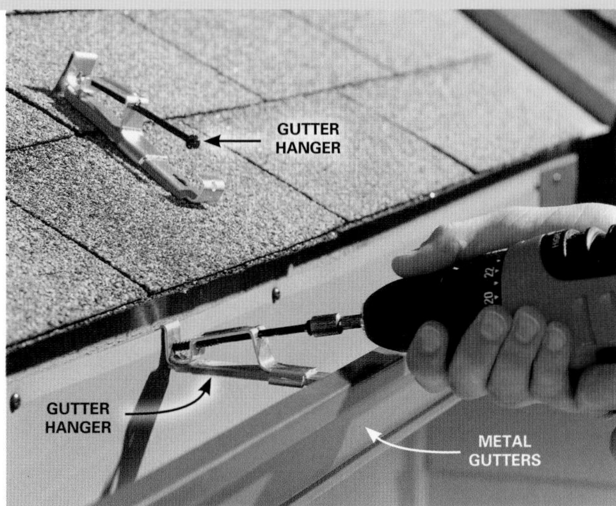

Hook the gutter hanger under the front edge of the gutter and over the back edge. Then drive the hex head screw through the wood trim behind the gutter. The hangers will be stronger if you screw them into a rafter. Look for nailheads, which indicate rafter locations. Add new gutter hangers about every 3 ft. along the entire length of the gutters if the old ones have let go.

instant fix

Stop overflowing gutters

If rainwater cascading down your roof valley causes a waterfall that washes out the petunias every time it storms, install a splash guard. It takes about 20 minutes to complete. You can find these precut splash guards in both brown and white aluminum at a home center, but you could easily make your own out of aluminum or sheet metal and spray-paint them to match your gutters. If you don't own a Pop riveter, attach the guards with 1/2-in. sheet metal screws instead.

1 Drill 1/8-in. holes through both the splash guard and the gutter to accommodate the Pop rivets used in the next step. Self-tapping 1/2-in. sheet metal screws will also work.

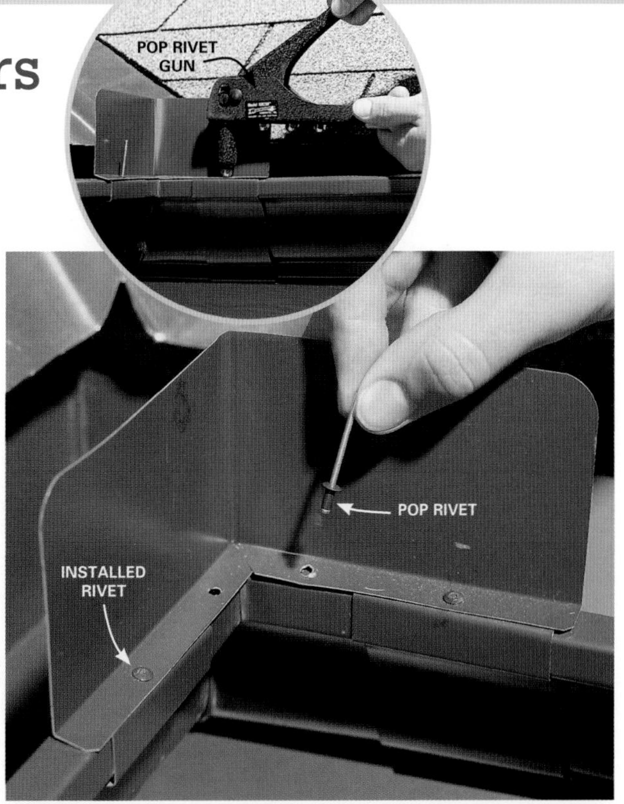

2 Press the head of a 1/8-in. rivet into each hole. Place the Pop rivet tool over the shaft of the rivet and squeeze the handle once or twice to compress the rivet and break off the stem.

Ice dams

Ice dams can be dramatic, sending streams of water into your home. But more often, the harm is so subtle you barely notice it. A little water trickles in, degrading insulation and supporting wood rot. But all you see is a small brown stain on the ceiling or drips from your soffits. Later, you may notice peeling paint or rusty nail heads. Don't ignore these signs; worse things are happening inside walls and ceilings. With help from our expert, find out how ice dams form, how to prevent them and what to do if you get them.

The trouble starts with a warm roof

Ice dams form on houses with poor insulation, inadequate ventilation or air leaks into the attic, all of which warm the roof. A warm roof melts the snow. As the meltwater trickles down to the colder areas of the roof, it freezes, forming an ice dam. More meltwater becomes trapped behind the ice dam, and having nowhere else to go, it runs underneath the shingles and into the house.

PHOTO: STEVE KUHL

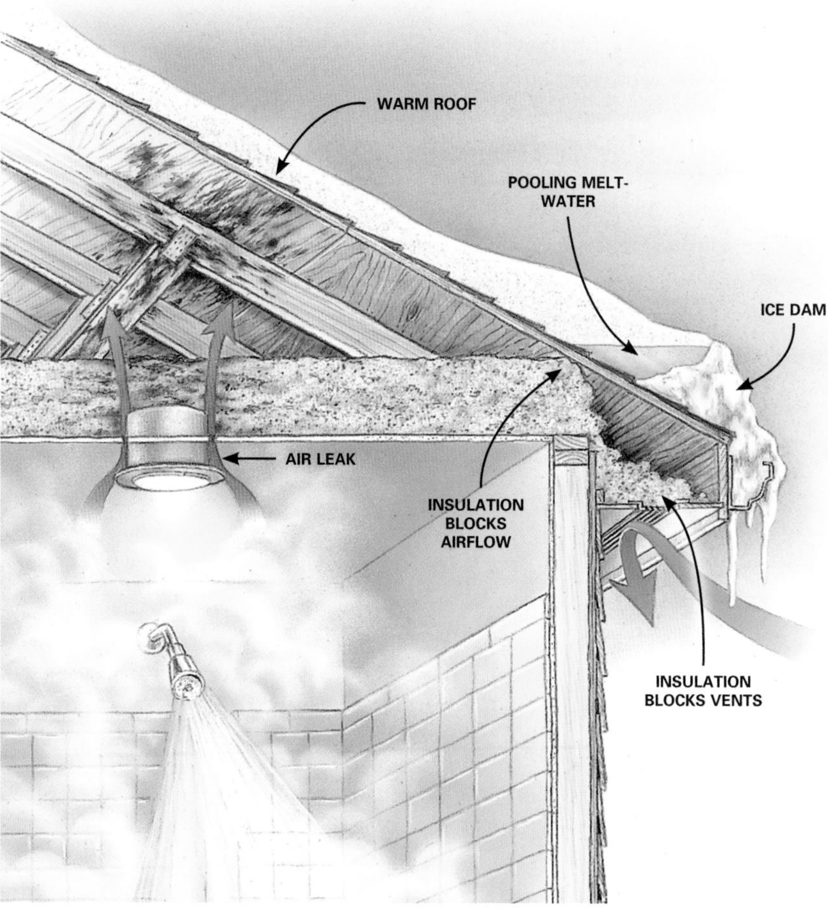

A low-pitch roof and a small eave add to the risk

The amount of time you have to stave off ice dam damage depends on your roof pitch and the size of your eave. Most ice dams form on a roof pitch of 9/12 or below. If your home has a steeper roof and a larger eave, a thick ice dam must form before water can leak into your home, giving you more time to react. With a low pitch and a smaller eave, you may only have hours to respond before water breaches your home. In this case, do what you can to prevent or safely remove the ice dam—or be ready to call an ice dam professional.

Hot homes promote ice dams

A warmer house often means a warmer roof and worse ice dams. If your home is prone to ice dams, lower the thermostat setting during peak ice dam season.

Water travels sideways

Once water from an ice dam leaks through the shingles, it often travels horizontally. Keep in mind that a water spot on your ceiling doesn't mean the roof leak is directly above. That leak may be several feet away.

Prevention is best

The smartest solution for ice dams is to prevent warm areas on your roof. Usually, that means sealing air leaks into the attic and adding insulation or roof ventilation. These solutions aren't always easy, but they eliminate the root cause.

For more on prevention, go to familyhandyman.com and search for "air leaks," "insulation" and "roof ventilation."

Wet insulation is worthless

When fiberglass or cellulose insulation becomes wet, it loses much of its R-value, allowing more heat to flow into the attic and making ice dams worse. Even after the insulation dries, the R-value may not be restored, creating a vicious cycle of more ice dams.

Insurance may not cover the damage

Insurance won't always cover ice dam damage. Some insurance companies will pay for repairs the first time, but after that, they may consider ice dams a known problem that you didn't correct—and deny your claim.

Gutters are irrelevant

A common myth is that gutters cause ice dams; they don't. Ice dams can extend over gutters (and damage gutters), but the real problem is warm areas on the roof.

Chopping is a risky solution

Think twice before hacking away at an ice dam with a hatchet or a chisel. Climbing a ladder and getting on your roof in icy conditions are truly dangerous; every year there are serious injuries and even deaths. Also keep in mind that cold asphalt shingles are brittle; chopping might damage them.

FASCIA

SOFFIT

PHOTO: STEVE KUHL

Read the icicles

Icicles that form in front of the fascia may indicate a looming ice dam problem—or not. But icicles or drips *behind* the fascia tell you that water has entered the house, then leaked out through the soffit or siding. Water inside the house is always bad even if you can't see it from inside.

Switch to LEDs

Recessed lights containing hot incandescent bulbs can create warm spots on your roof. This can happen in homes with attics and is even more common where there is no attic, as with the cathedral ceiling shown here. LED bulbs produce much less heat and sometimes solve that problem.

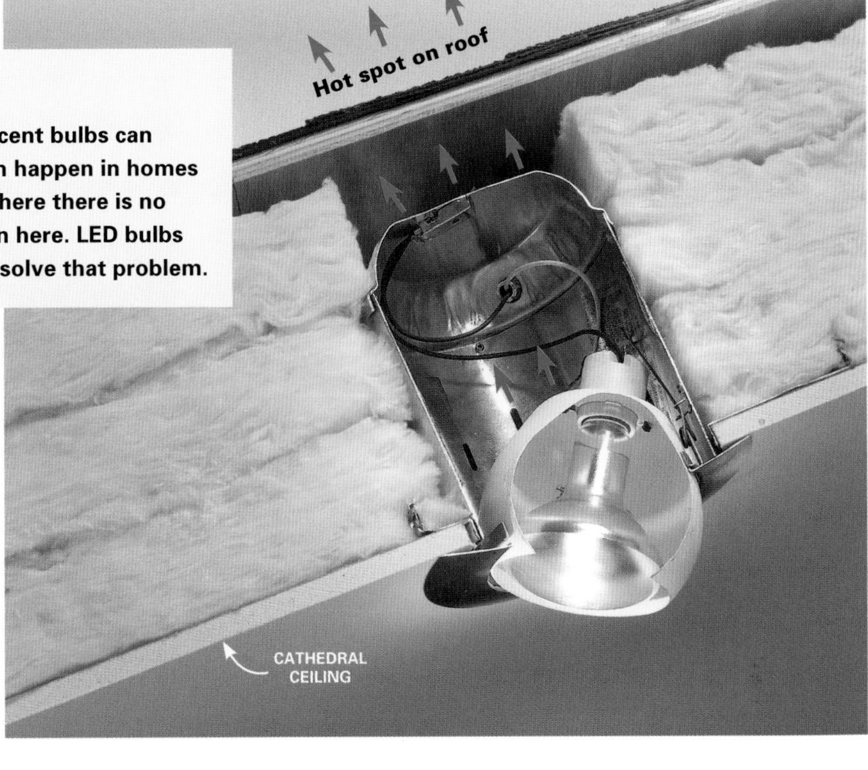

Minimize water damage

If water from an ice dam is coming through your ceiling, you can still minimize the damage. One way to do that is to control the water's path by punching a hole in the ceiling with a drill and letting water drain into a bucket.

Guide water that intrudes

Ice dams often cover a large area and cause a long chain of leaks along an exterior wall. Here's one way to minimize the damage: Use masking tape and painter's plastic to channel water into a bucket.

Do salt socks work?

To make salt socks, you fill socks with ice melter and toss them on the roof—on or just slightly above ice dams. The ice melter will cut channels through ice dams, allowing trapped water to escape. While nobody thinks they're the ultimate solution for ice dams, we've heard lots of real-world reports that they work as an emergency measure. Here are a few things to keep in mind:

- **The "socks" should be a sheer material so that the salt can contact the ice. Nylon stockings are the most common choice. Mesh paint strainers (sold at home centers) are another good option.**
- **For them to be effective, you need lots of salt socks, spaced every foot or two along the ice dam.**
- **They don't work immediately. It may take hours or all day before trapped water drains away.**
- **Ice melter is corrosive to metals and may harm plants, but those risks are mild compared with water damage inside your home.**

PHOTO: STEVE KUHL

caution

Climbing on an icy roof is treacherous. And although steamers are available for rent or purchase, they're expensive and difficult to use. We recommend hiring a contractor for this work.

PHOTO: STEVE KUH

Be careful whom you hire

You can hire a contractor to melt away your ice dams with a steam machine. Costs vary; some charge $500 per hour or more during busy periods. You can easily spend more than $1,000. If you do hire, make sure they use steam rather than a pressure washer. High-temperature pressure washers have a trigger and a colored tip on the wand and might blast the granules off asphalt shingles; steamers don't.

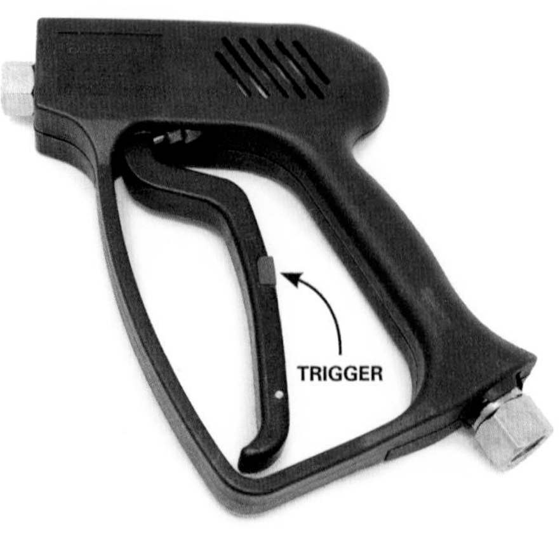

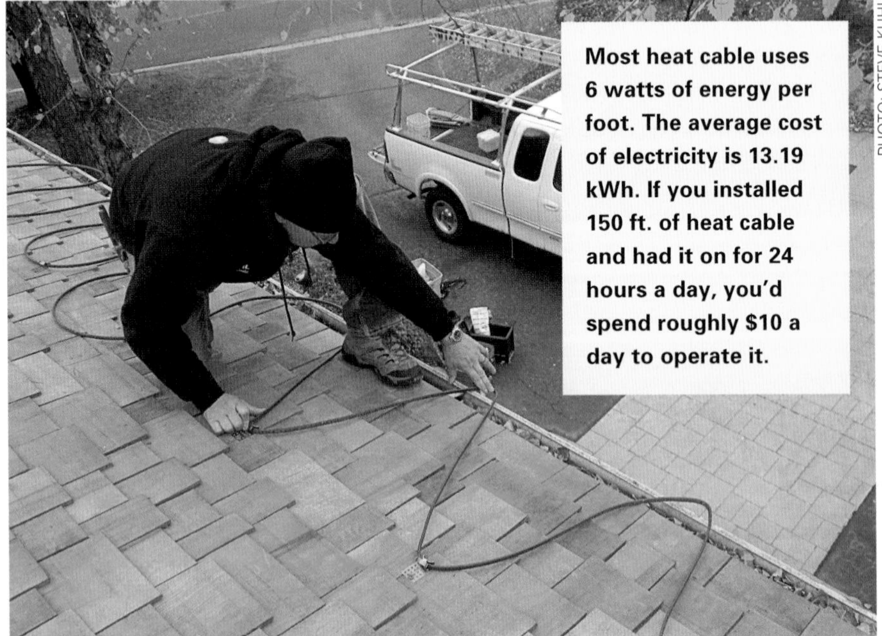

Most heat cable uses 6 watts of energy per foot. The average cost of electricity is 13.19 kWh. If you installed 150 ft. of heat cable and had it on for 24 hours a day, you'd spend roughly $10 a day to operate it.

PHOTO: STEVE KUHL

Plan ahead with heat cable

If preventing warm spots on your roof just isn't practical for you, heat cable can help. While it doesn't solve the underlying problem, it will provide pathways for water when ice dams occur, keeping water out of your home. If it's the middle of winter, laying heat cable on an ice dam won't work. So, plan ahead and install it in a serpentine pattern on your roof and leave it.

instant fix

Patch leaky gutters

1 **Clean the area around the leak with a stiff scraper and a wire brush, then rinse off all dust and wipe completely dry.**

Gutter leaks usually start at rusty spots or seams that have opened up because of expansion and contraction. If your gutter is still basically sound, the easiest way to stop the leak is by covering the damaged area with roof and gutter repair tape.

Prepare the gutter by scraping out as much old tar or caulk as possible. Wire-brush the metal thoroughly to get rid of rust and to give the tape a clean surface for bonding (Photo 1). If the gutter is badly rusted or has been heavily coated with tar that you can't scrape out, spray on a special adhesive primer before applying the tape.

Cut the tape with a scissors or a razor knife (Photo 2). Tear the paper backing off the tape and lightly adhere one edge of the tape to the top of the gutter. Roll the tape down the wall of the gutter, pushing it firmly into curves and corners (Photo 3). Work wrinkles and bubbles flat. Overlap long seams by at least 1 in. and end seams by 4 in.

2 **Cut the gutter repair tape long enough to overlap the leaky area by at least 6 in. in each direction.**

3 **Starting at the center, press tape firmly into place. Follow the contours of the gutter and smooth out all wrinkles.**

instant fix

Reattach a rain gutter end cap

For a long-lasting repair of those annoying gutter leaks, turn to silicone sealants. Silicone will act as an adhesive to keep the end cap securely in place, as well as a sealant to stop leaks and drips. Attach the end caps using the caulking and riveting techniques shown in Photos 1–3. Well-stocked home centers and hardware stores will have everything you need.

1 Pry off the end cap and chisel off all old gutter sealant from both the end cap and the lip of the gutter. Use a straight-slot screwdriver that's narrow enough to work down into the cap's groove. Wipe them clean. Restore any bent adjoining metal edges with a screwdriver and pliers. Dry-fit the parts to make sure they will join properly.

2 Fill the groove in the end cap with clear silicone caulk. Attach the end cap to the gutter by pressing the cap solidly against the lip, making sure the two are firmly seated together.

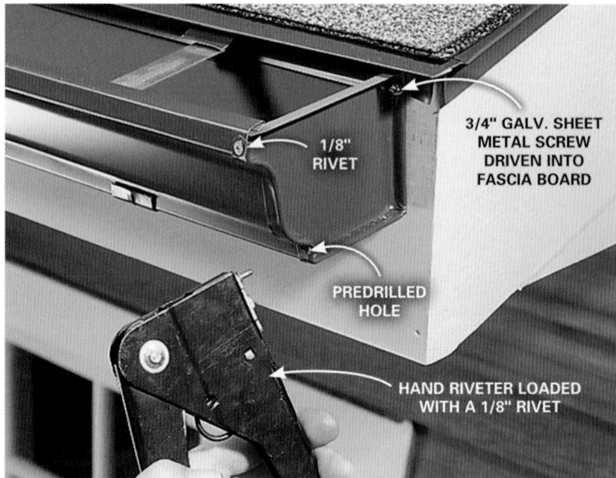

3 Maintain steady pressure on the end cap and drill three 1/8-in. holes as shown through the cap's flange. Then install the screw and two 1/8-in. dia. rivets. Wipe away excess silicone on the outside before it dries.

Easier gutter cleaning

An old plastic spatula makes a great tool for cleaning debris from gutters! It doesn't scratch up the gutter, and you can cut it to fit gutter contours with snips. Grime wipes right off the spatula too, making cleanup a breeze.

instant fix

Patch holes in aluminum and vinyl siding

All houses gradually accumulate holes in their siding from fasteners and from phone and cable lines. The only way to repair these holes perfectly in vinyl or aluminum is to replace the entire piece—a repair that ranges from challenging in vinyl to almost impossible in old aluminum.

For an easier, nearly-as-good fix that keeps water out and is almost invisible from several feet away, fill the hole with a color-matched caulk. Home centers don't usually stock it, but siding wholesalers that sell to contractors carry caulks specifically blended for dozens of different shades of siding. If you know the manufacturer and color name of your siding, you can get the exact blend developed for that shade. Otherwise, bring a sample piece or take a photo and ask a salesperson to help you match it.

COLOR-MATCHED CAULK

Before filling the hole, wipe the siding clean. Squirt enough caulk into the hole to fill the area behind the hole. Avoid smearing excess caulk all over the surrounding siding—the less you get on the siding, the less obvious the repair will be. Once the caulk is fully cured (which could be several days, depending on the type), trim it even with the siding with a razor blade.

Trim the hardened caulk flush with the siding using a straightedge razor blade.

instant fix

Stop soffit rattle

Aluminum soffits are "maintenance free," they come in a lot of colors and they're relatively inexpensive to install, but they can be noisy!

Most aluminum soffits fit into an aluminum channel mounted to the house. Sometimes, the channel is wider than the soffits and allows them to move. Add a blustery breeze, and the soffits outside your bedroom may have you longing for those restful nights when you had a colicky newborn's cradle parked next to your bed.

The solution may be as simple as a package of screen spline and a putty knife. The first step is to find the offending soffits. Set up a ladder near the area in question and tap on the soffits to see which ones rattle.

Next, take a plastic putty knife and insert a length of screen spline in between the soffit and the aluminum channel. The soffits may have been cut too short, so push the screen mold in far enough so it can't be seen from the ground but not so far that it slides past the end of the soffit. The final step: a good night's sleep.

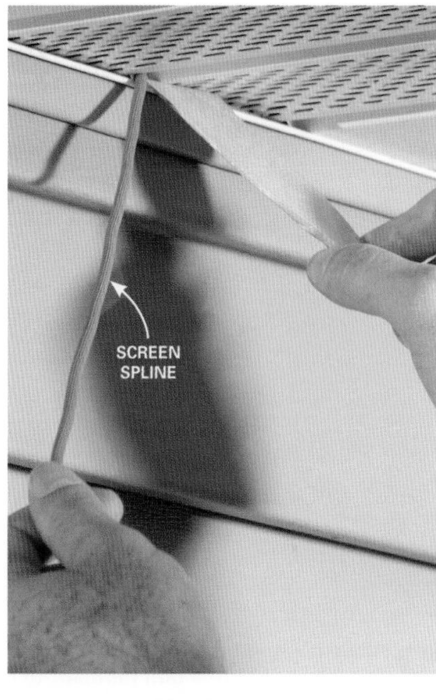

Patch stucco

Stucco is a composite of portland cement, sand, lime and water. It has its origins in hand-troweled adobe plaster and other traditional low-tech masonry finishes, but now it's often applied professionally with specialized materials, tools and skills. But patching and repairing smaller areas can easily be managed by a competent do-it-yourselfer. The trick is building it up in layers.

You can buy premixed dry stucco in bags, just like concrete or mortar, and add water until the mix is stiff but pliable. Wait for a dry, mild day so excess heat doesn't shorten the mix's working time. Break or chisel away the damaged area of old stucco and cut away the old metal lath underneath. Remove any loose debris and use a mist sprayer to keep the working area from drying out.

1 **Cut new metal lath for the repair, sizing it to overlap the old lath by 2 in. Fasten with roofing nails.**

2 **Trowel the first "scratch" coat on in layers that total 3/8 in. thick, working it vigorously into the metal lath.**

3 **While it's wet but starting to set, comb the scratch coat with a lath remnant to provide tooth for the next coat.**

4 **Trowel on the second "brown" coat until it's flush with the surrounding stucco. Use a straightedge to check its flatness.**

5 **Use a wet sponge float to feather the brown coat so it blends in with the edges of the surrounding area.**

6 **Knock down the bumps to create a matching texture, after using a dash brush to flick bits of stucco onto the surface.**

instant fix

Reattach loose vinyl siding

Vinyl siding is installed by interlocking the top and bottom edges of the panels. Properly installed, the panels should stay permanently locked together. If you have panels that have separated from poor installation, impact damage or severe weather, first check for clues that the siding was improperly installed. The installer may have tried to straighten unlevel courses by pulling the panels up taut, or pressing them down, then nailing them. Or perhaps the nails weren't driven straight and level, resulting in panels that later buckled.

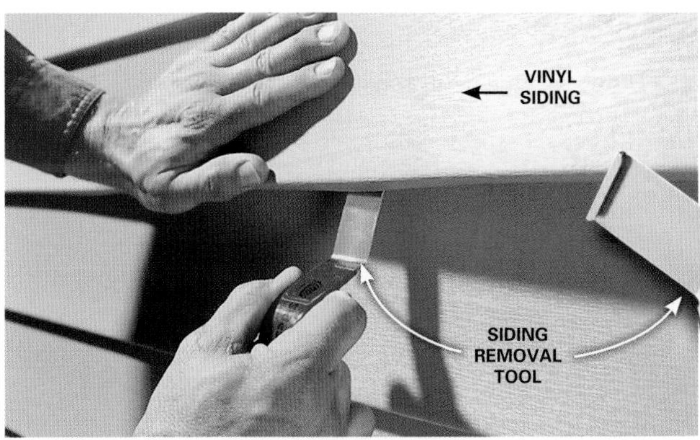

Hook the siding tool behind the locking face of the loose panel and pull down. Push the panel onto the locking face of the lower course to reattach it. If it doesn't reattach easily, check the nailing technique on the lower course. If the nails were driven too tight, the nailing flange may be dimpled. Its locking face won't be in a straight-line position to easily receive the next panel. Take a pry bar and carefully work it behind the nail-head. Back the nail out until the dimple is taken out of the nail-ing flange. The siding removal tool (shown) is a must for both removing siding panels and reconnecting them. When you're removing a locked panel, you'll have to wiggle the siding tool as you push it up to successfully grab the locking face's edge.

Vinyl siding panels may come undone because these problems—or repeated temperature changes—allow the panels to expand, contract and loosen.

Buy a siding removal tool at a home center or a siding retailer. This tool (left) can be used for vinyl, aluminum or steel siding. As shown, the hook on the tool grabs the locking face under the bottom edge of each panel.

To reattach a panel, first use the siding tool to grab the panel's locking edge, then pull down. At the same time, use the heel of your hand to push the panel edge to catch the locking face on the lower siding course. Work the siding tool and heel of your hand along the edge of the loosened panel in this manner until the two courses of vinyl have snapped back together.

Replace a sprinkler head

It's pretty easy to damage a sprinkler head with your mower if the head sits too high. And we're convinced that snowplow operators intentionally shear off sprinkler heads along the curb just for the entertainment value.

No matter how your sprinkler head got damaged or quit working, there's no need to call the irrigation company to do the repairs. This is a DIY job from start to finish. All you need is a new head, an assortment of different-length poly cutoff riser fittings and parts to build a homemade flushing tool. You can get all the parts for less than $15 at any home center. You'll also need a garden spade, poly sheeting, a wet/dry shop vacuum and a saw. Here's how to attack the job.

How to buy replacement sprinkler heads

A replacement sprinkler head doesn't have to be the same brand as the broken head. But it does have to be the same type: pop-up (stationary, rotor- or gear-driven rotor) or impact. And the new head must also match the inches-per-hour (iph) or gallons-per-minute (gpm) delivery rate of the old head. Plus, the spray pattern and throwing distance must also match. If you install the wrong head, it can over- or underwater that section of your lawn or garden and possibly cause other heads in that same zone to underperform. So you'll need all the specs from the broken head before you buy a replacement.

Locate that information on the nozzle, the top of the head (if it's still there) or on a label stuck to the body of the head (see "Remove the Broken Head" at right). If you can't find the specifications, at least find the brand and part number. Then look up the specs on the manufacturer's website. If you strike out on the specs and part number, take the old head to an irrigation service company and ask for a matching replacement head.

Buy a replacement head at a home center or online (sprinklerwarehouse.com is one source). The replacement head will most likely come with an assortment of snap-in nozzles, so you can adapt the head's delivery rate, spray pattern and throw rate to fit your needs.

Remove the broken head

Lay down plastic sheeting next to the broken sprinkler head. Then use a garden spade to cut an 8-in. circle around the old head. Pry out the sod and set it aside. Then dig down and around the old head, placing the dirt on the poly sheet (Photo 1). When you reach the water line, unscrew the broken head.

If the head is located at the low spot of a watering zone, chances are the hole will fill with water, and mud will get into the water line. Suck the mud out with your shop vacuum. (The water line gets flushed later.)

Set the new head height

If the old riser fitting came out with the old head, remove it and screw it onto the new head. Then test-fit the new head by screwing it into the water line. The top of the head should be flush with the ground, not sticking up into the grass. If it's not the right height, grab a new poly cutoff riser (about $1 each at home centers) with multiple threaded sections and cut it to the correct length (Photo 2). It may take a few tries (and a few risers) to get the height just right. Once you get the proper height, remove the head and flush the line using the steps shown here.

Build a flushing tool and flush the water line

No matter how careful you are, dirt is going to fall into the water line fitting. If you can't remove all the dirt with your shop vacuum, you'll have to flush it. Build a flushing tool with 3/4-in. PVC pipe and the fittings (about $5 in parts at home centers) shown in Figure A. Then flush the water line (Photo 3). Finish by sucking the water out of the flushing tool (Photo 4).

Install the head and backfill

Screw the new head into the flushed water line and begin backfilling the hole. Align the head so it sits straight in the hole as you tamp the dirt with your hand. Finish the job by replacing the grass. Water immediately to reestablish the grass roots.

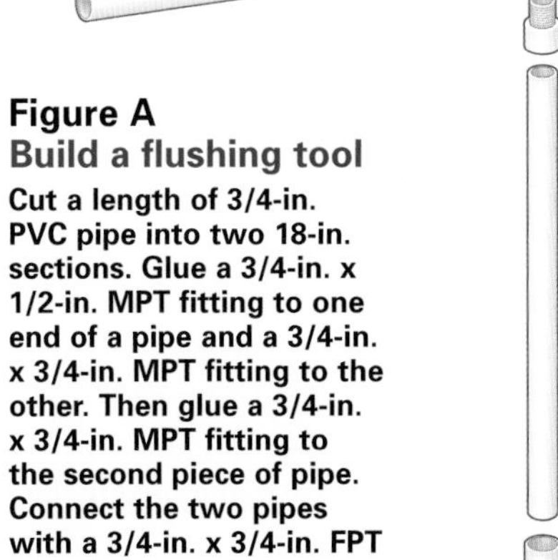

Figure A
Build a flushing tool
Cut a length of 3/4-in. PVC pipe into two 18-in. sections. Glue a 3/4-in. x 1/2-in. MPT fitting to one end of a pipe and a 3/4-in. x 3/4-in. MPT fitting to the other. Then glue a 3/4-in. x 3/4-in. MPT fitting to the second piece of pipe. Connect the two pipes with a 3/4-in. x 3/4-in. FPT elbow.

1 SCOOP OUT THE DIRT **Slice the garden spade straight down the sides of the hole to give you room to maneuver. Then lift the dirt up, out and onto the poly sheeting.**

2 CUT THE RISER TO LENGTH **Slice through the multiple-thread poly cutoff riser using a metal-cutting blade for a smooth cut. Deburr the cut edge with a knife. Then install the riser on the head, screw the head into the water line and check the height.**

3 FLUSH THE LINE **Screw the flushing tool into the water line and aim it into the street or away from your work area. Turn on the water for that zone and let it run for about 30 seconds.**

4 VACUUM OUT THE REMAINING WATER **Slide the vacuum hose nozzle over the vertical pipe and suck out all the remaining water.**

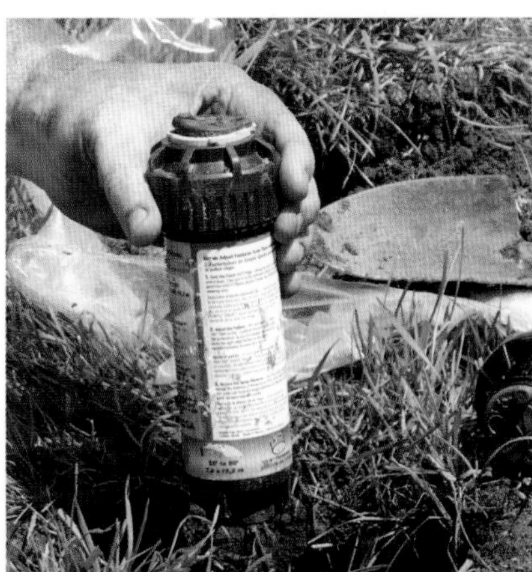

5 INSTALL THE HEAD AND BACKFILL **Screw the riser fitting into the irrigation tube, then the sprinkler head. Backfill with dirt and sod.**

7 fixes for a safer deck

A well-built deck will last for decades. But a deck that's rotting or missing fasteners, or that moves when you walk on it, may be dangerous. Decks built by inexperienced do-it-yourselfers, not inspected when they were built, or more than 15 years old (building codes were different back then!) are susceptible to serious problems. Every year, people are severely injured, even killed, when decks like these fall down. This has usually happened during parties when the deck was filled with guests.

Now for the good news. Most of the fixes are quick, inexpensive and easy. Home centers and lumberyards carry the tools and materials you'll need.

We'll show you the warning signs of a dangerous deck—and how to fix the problems. If you're still not sure whether your deck is safe, have it inspected by your local building inspector.

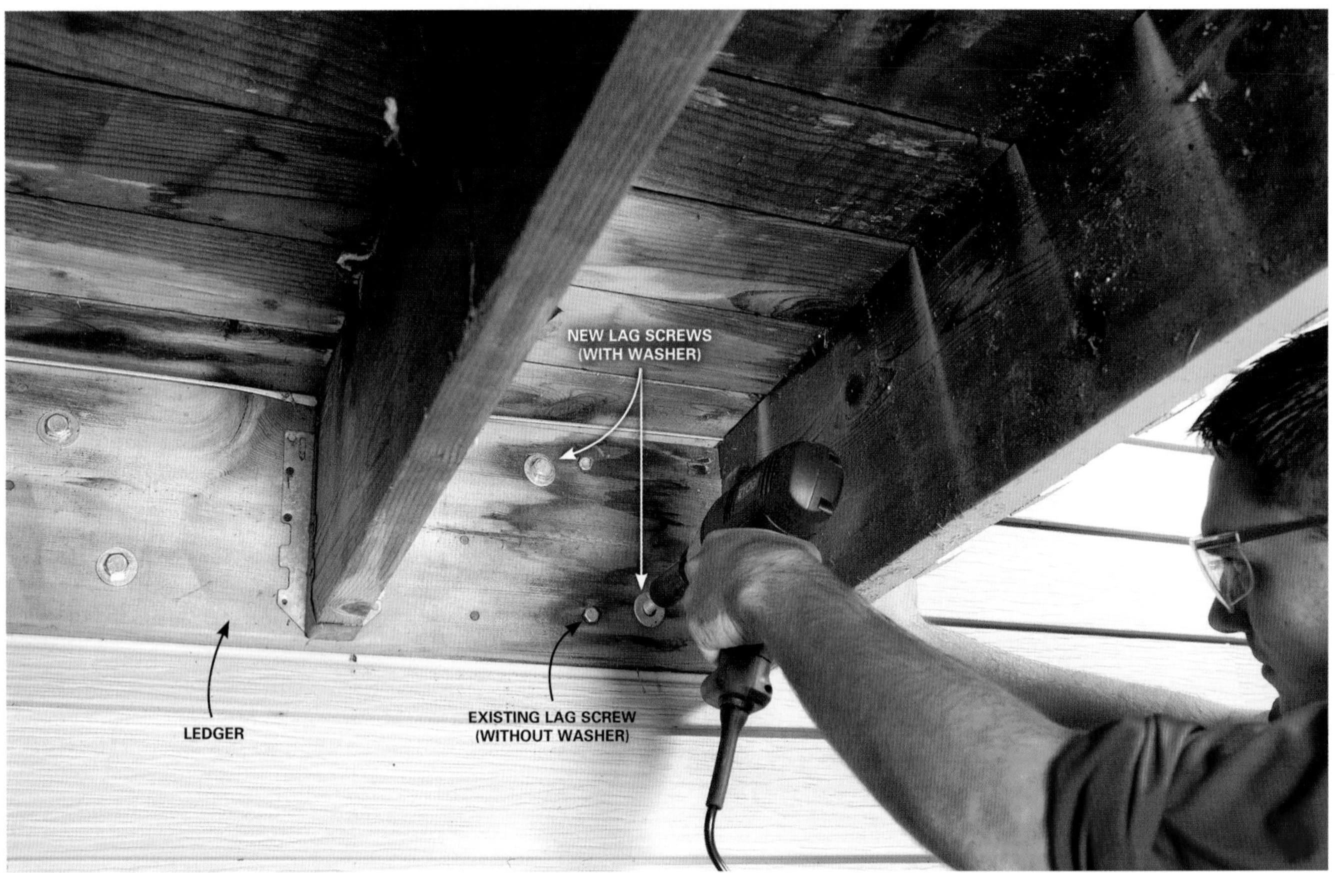

Fasten the ledger to the house with lag screws. Drive them fast with a corded drill and socket. Every lag screw must have a washer.

1 No lags in the ledger

SOCKET

The ledger board holds up the end of the deck that's against the house. If the ledger isn't well fastened, the deck can simply fall off the house. A building inspector we talked with said the most common problem with DIY decks is ledger boards not properly fastened to the house. For a strong connection, a ledger needs 1/2-in. x 3-in. lag screws (or lag bolts if you have access from the inside to fasten the washers and nuts) driven every 16 in. This ledger board was fastened mostly with nails instead of lag screws (and no washers).

Starting at one end of the ledger board, drill two 1/4-in. pilot holes. Offset the holes so the top isn't aligned with the bottom hole. Then drive the lag screws (with washers) using a drill and an impact socket (you'll need a socket adapter that fits in your drill). Don't countersink the screws—that only weakens the ledger board.

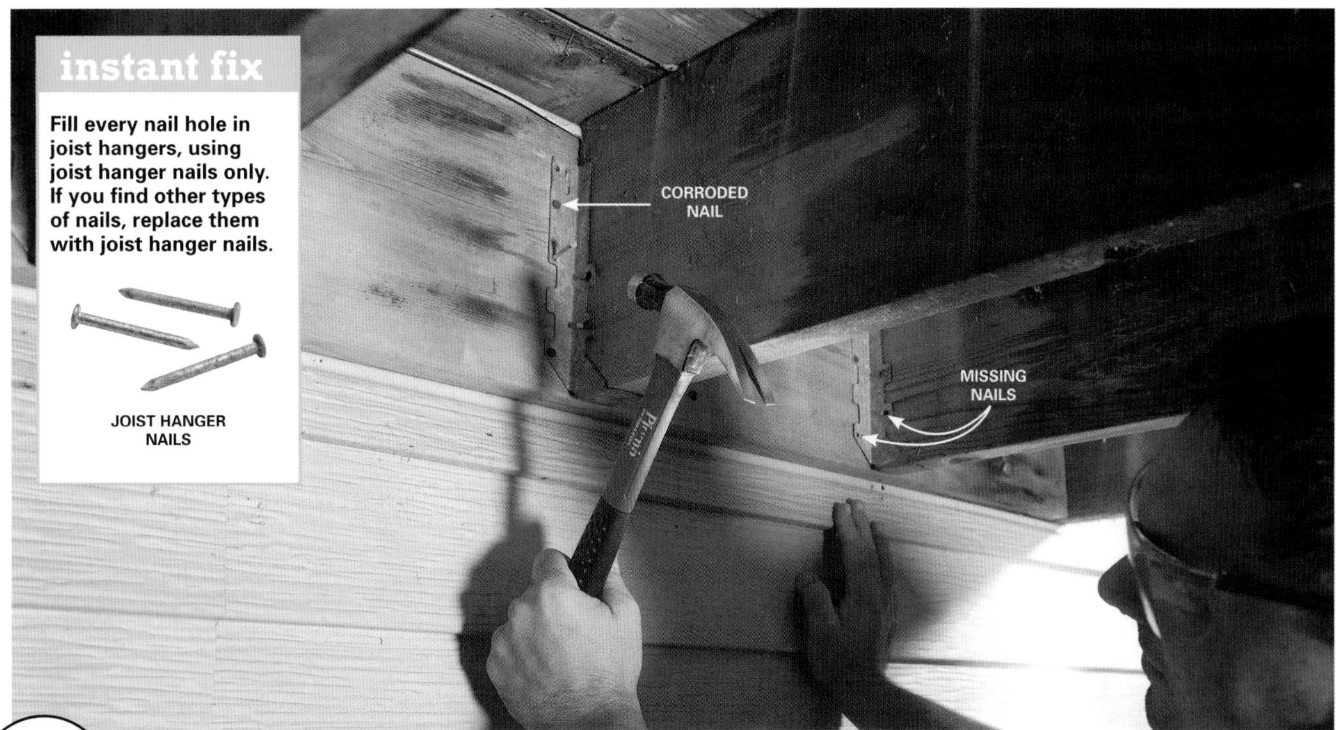

2 Missing nails in joist hangers

Granted, there are a lot of nail holes in a joist hanger—but they all need to be filled. Otherwise, the hangers can pull loose from the ledger board or rim joist. Deck builders sometimes drive a couple of nails into the hangers to hold them in place, then forget to add the rest later. This deck had only a single nail in some joist hangers. In other areas, it had the wrong nails. Joist hanger nails are the only nails acceptable. These short, fat, galvanized nails are specially designed to hold the hangers in place under heavy loads and resist corrosion from treated lumber.

3 Rickety railing posts

Loose railings won't lead to your deck falling down, but you could tumble off your deck. Railing posts attached only with nails are bound to come loose, and no matter how many new nails you drive into them, you won't solve the problem. Instead, add carriage bolts.

Measure the thickness of the post and rim joist, then buy 1/2-in.-diameter galvanized carriage bolts that length plus 1 in. Also get a nut and washer for each. Drill two 1/2-in. holes through the post and rim joist. Offset the holes, keeping one about 1-1/2 in. from the top of the joist and the other the same distance from the bottom (make sure to avoid drilling where a joist abuts the rim joist). Tap the carriage bolts through the holes, then tighten the nuts until the bolt heads are set flush with the post.

instant fix

Strengthen a loose railing post with carriage bolts. Drill a pair of holes through the post and framing. Angle the hole to avoid joist hangers.

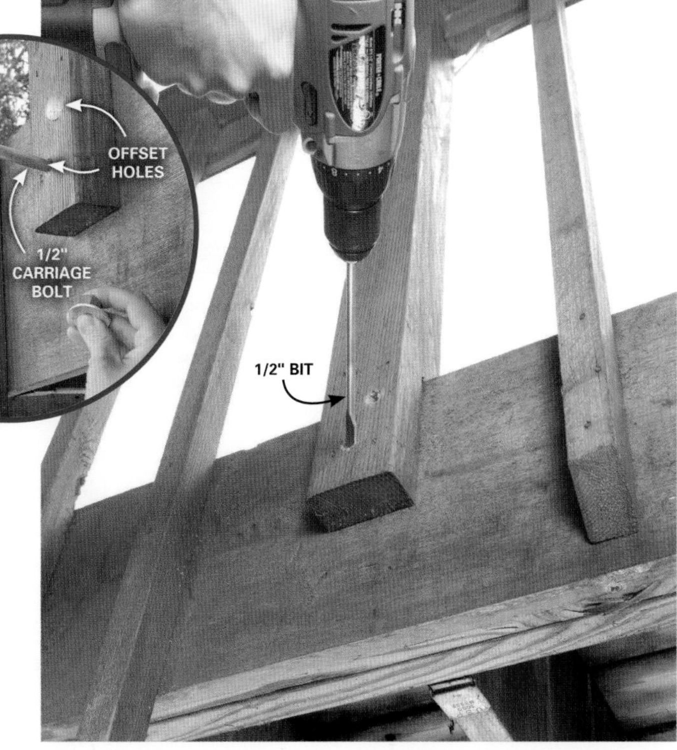

4 Rotted posts

Deck posts that rest directly on footings soak up water and then they rot, especially posts that aren't pressure treated (like this one, which is cedar). As the post rots, it loses its strength and can't support the deck's weight. Newer decks keep the concrete footings a few inches above ground and use a special base bracket to keep the posts dry. Replacing a rotted post is the best solution. Before removing the post, be sure you have everything you need for the replacement, including a wedge anchor.

Clear grass or stone away from the bottom of the deck post. Prod along the bottom of the post with a screwdriver or an awl. If the wood is spongy or pieces easily peel away, you'll need to replace the post. Start by nailing 2x4s or 2x6s together to use as temporary braces. Place scrap wood on the ground for a pad within 3 ft. of the post being replaced, then set a hydraulic jack over it. Cut the brace to size, set one end on the jack and place the other end under the rim joist. Slowly jack up the brace until it's wedged tight. Be careful not to overdo it. You're just bracing the deck, not raising it. If you hear the joist boards creak, then stop. Then place a second brace on the other side of the post (Photo 1). If you don't have jacks, you can rent them. Or you can set your temporary braces directly on the pads and drive shims between the posts and the rim joist.

Mark the post location on the footing, then remove the post by cutting through the fasteners that tie it to the rim joist. Use a metal blade in a reciprocating saw (or knock out the post with a hammer). If there's already a bolt sticking out of the footing, use it to install a new post base. If not, you'll need to add a 3/8- by 4-in. wedge anchor. Do this by placing the post base at the marks where the old post sat, and then mark the center. Remove the post base and drill the center mark with a 3/8-in. masonry bit. Drill down 3 in., then blow the dust out of the hole.

Tap the anchor into the hole with a hammer (Photo 2). Install the post base over the anchor. As you tighten the nut on the anchor, the clip expands and wedges tight against the hole walls to hold itself in place.

Cut a treated post to fit between the post base and the top of the rim joist. Set the post into place and tack it to the post base with 8d or 10d galvanized nails (Photo 3). Place a level alongside the post. When it's plumb (straight), tack it in place to the rim joist. Then install a connector and drive carriage bolts through the rim joist (see the next repair).

1 Prop up the deck with temporary braces so you can remove the rotted post. Stop jacking when you hear the deck begin to creak.

2 Tap a wedge anchor into a predrilled hole in the footing, then tighten the post base over it.

3 Set the new post into place and nail it to the base. Then plumb the post and fasten it to the rim joist or beam.

5 Wimpy post connections

Ideally, posts should sit directly under the beam or rim joist to support the deck. If the posts are fastened to the side of the beam or rim joist, like the one shown here, the weight is put on the fasteners that connect the post to the deck. This deck had only three nails in the post—a recipe for collapse. Nails alone aren't strong enough for this job, no matter how many you use. For a strong connection, you need 1/2-in.-diameter galvanized carriage bolts.

Add two of these bolts by drilling 1/2-in. holes through the rim joist and post. An 8-in.-long 1/2-in. drill bit costs $10. The length of the bolts depends on the size of your post and the thickness of the rim joist (add them and buy bolts at least 1 in. longer than your measurement). We used 8-in. bolts, which went through two 1-1/2-in. rim joists and a 3-1/2-in. post Tap the bolts through with a hammer, then add a washer and nut on the other side.

instant fix

Strengthen post connections with carriage bolts. Drill holes, knock the bolts through, then tighten a washer and nut on the other side.

instant fix

Stiffen a wobbly deck with a diagonal brace run from corner to corner. Drive two nails per joist.

6 Wobbly deck syndrome

If your deck gets a case of the shakes when you walk across it, there's probably no reason for concern. Still, in some cases, the deck movement puts extra stress on the fasteners and connectors. Over time, the joists can pull away from the rim joist or ledger board and twist out of their vertical position, which weakens them. Fastening angle bracing under the deck will stiffen it and take out the sway. The braces are mostly hidden from view and let you walk on your deck without feeling like it's going to fall down at any moment.

Run a treated 2x4 diagonally from corner to corner, under the deck. Drive two 16d galvanized nails through the brace into each joist. If a single board won't span the distance, use two, overlapping the braces by at least two joists. Cut the bracing flush with the outside edge of the deck.

7 Missing ledger flashing

The area around the ledger board should be watertight. Even small leaks can lead to mold inside the walls of the house and, even worse, the house rim joist (which supports the ledger) will rot and the ledger will fall off. Stand or crawl under the deck and look at the ledger board. If you don't see a metal or plastic lip over the top of the ledger board, add the flashing. Flashing was completely missing from this deck.

To add flashing, first remove the deck board that runs alongside the house. If the boards run diagonally, snap a chalk line 5-1/2 in. from the house, then set the blade in a circular saw to the depth of the decking boards and cut off the board ends. (Replace the cutouts at the end of the job with a 5-1/2-in.-wide board installed parallel to the house.)

For vinyl, wood or other lap siding, work a flat bar under the siding and gently pull out the nails (Photo 1). Insert the flashing behind the siding (Photo 2). If you have a brick or stucco house, you probably won't see any flashing because the ledgers are often installed directly over brick or stucco.

We used vinyl flashing, but you can also use galvanized metal or aluminum flashing. At each joist location, make a small cut in the flashing lip with a utility knife so it'll lie flat over the joists. The rest of the lip should fit over the top edge of the ledger board.

You should have flashing under the bottom edge of the ledger too. But since there's no way to add it without removing the ledger board, run a bead of acrylic caulk along the bottom of the ledger board to seal out water (Photo 3).

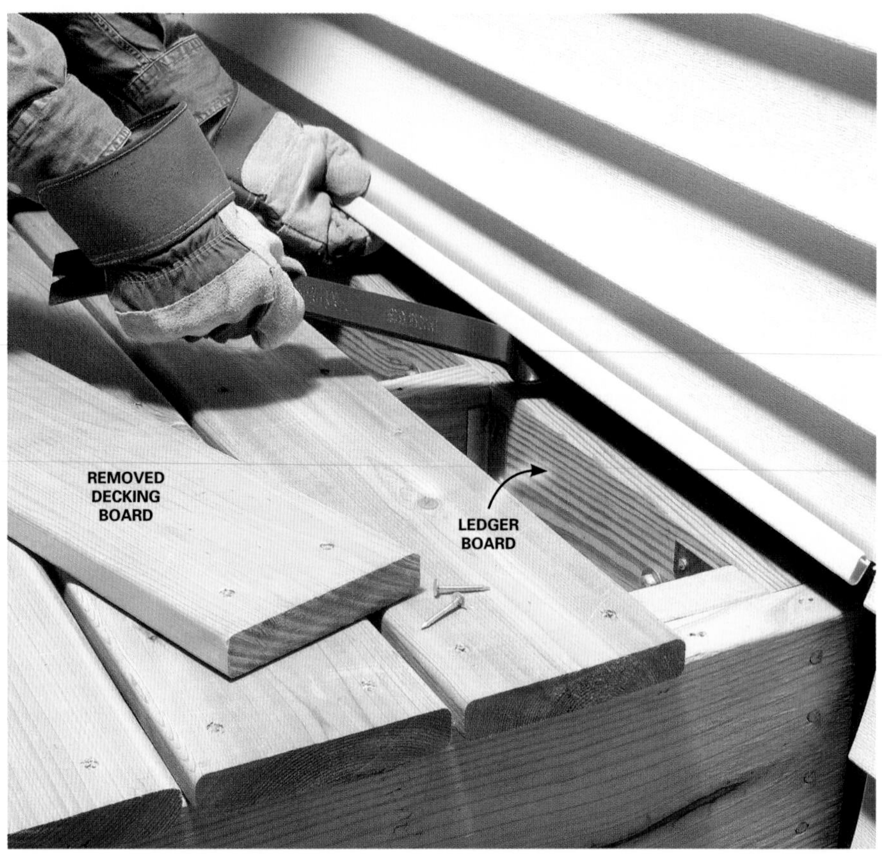

1 Pry the siding away from the house and remove the deck board that's over the ledger to clear the way for new flashing.

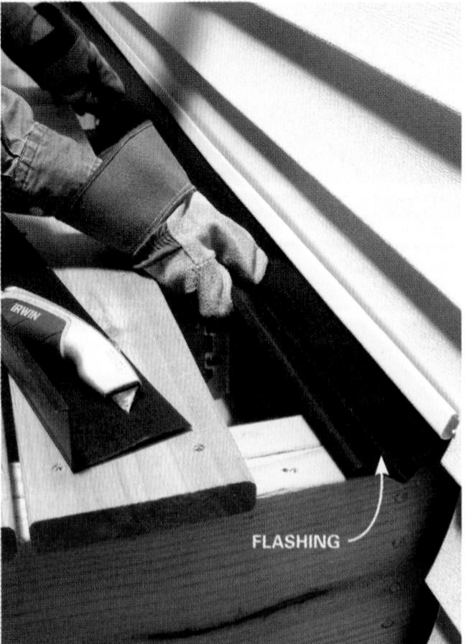

2 Slide the flashing behind the siding so the lip covers the top of the ledger. Reattach the siding.

3 Seal out water along the bottom edge of the ledger, if the bottom flashing is missing, by running a bead of caulk.

instant fix

Replace popped deck nails

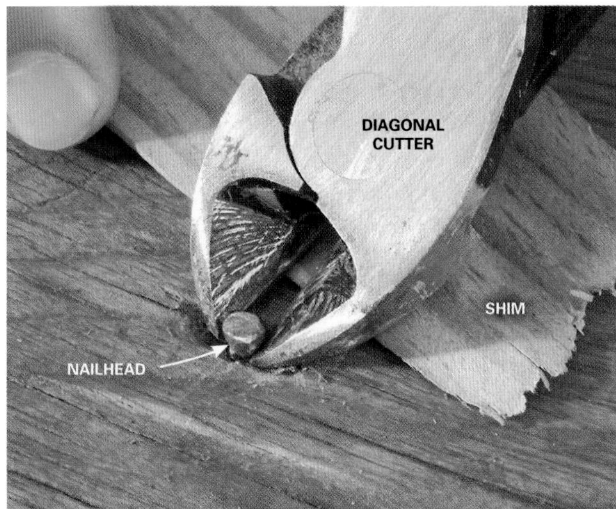

1 Grab slightly protruding nails directly under the head with a diagonal cutter. Roll the cutter back onto thin blocking to pry the nail up slightly.

2 Tap the claw of a cat's paw under the nailhead and lever the nail up. Finish pulling with a hammer or pry bar. Protect the deck board with a shim or thin block.

Decking swells and shrinks as it goes through repeated cycles of wet and dry seasons. This frequently causes nails to loosen and pop up above the deck boards. You can drive them down again, but chances are that's only a short-term solution. They'll probably pop up again after a few years. The long-term solution is to remove the popped nails and replace them with deck screws.

The trick is to pull the old nails without marring the decking. Always use a block or shim under your prying tool (Photos 1 and 2). And work on tough-to-get-out nails using several steps. A diagonal cutter works well for nails that only protrude slightly (Photo 1). The slim jaws can slip under the head. You'll only raise the nail a slight amount, so you may have to repeat this process two or three times. Once the nailhead is high enough, you can grip it with a cat's paw or hammer claw without marring the deck board (Photo 2). Be sure to use thin wood blocks to protect the decking. Minor dents will disappear when the wood swells after the next rain.

There's no need to drill a pilot hole if you send the screw down the old nail hole. However, one drawback of screws is that their heads are larger than nailheads and can be unsightly. We recommend that you buy deck screws in a color that most closely matches the aged decking.

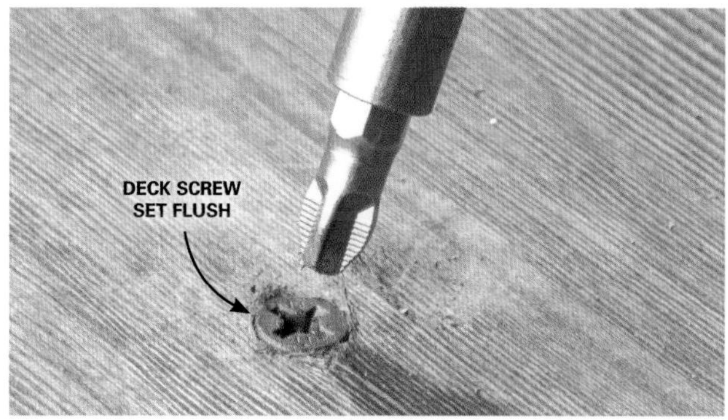

3 Stand on the deck board to hold it down. Then drive a 2-1/2 in. deck screw down into the old nail hole. Set the screwhead flush to the surface.

pro tip

Solutions for stubborn nails

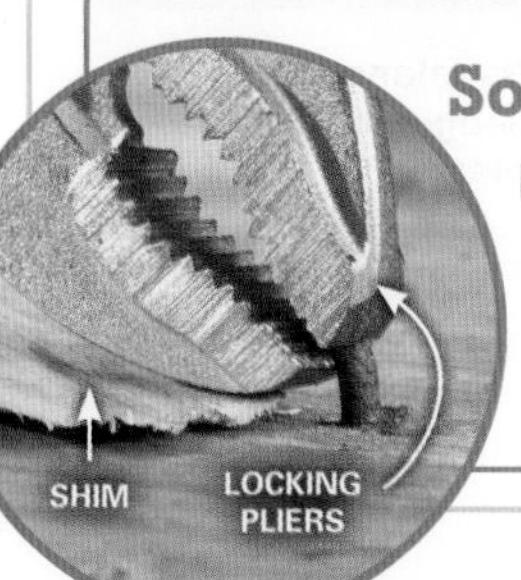

If the head breaks off a stubborn nail and you can't get it with a pry bar, try pulling it with locking pliers. Grip the nail tip and roll the pliers over to get it going (photo top left). If the nail shank breaks off, don't worry. Just drill a pilot hole beside the nail and drive in a screw. The screwhead will cover the nail (photo at right).

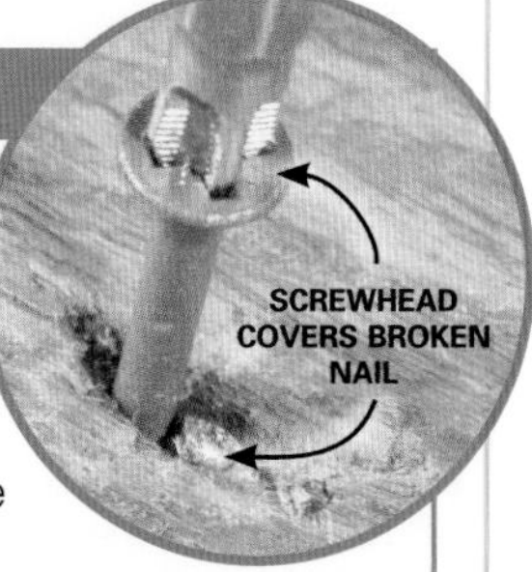

1 **Pressure-wash the railings with stripper. Keep the tip 6 to 10 in. from the wood and work from the top down. Spray balusters at the corners to scour two sides at once.**

Refinish your deck

If you've been putting off renewing your deck because you think it requires a lot of time, tools and know-how, take heart. Here's how to clean it up fast with the help of a pressure washer and special products that help remove dirt, mildew and old finishes. We'll also show you how to apply a fresh finish, using a foam applicator pad that glides along the wood and quickly applies a nice, even coat. No more messy rollers and brushes.

This process will work on any wood deck, including redwood, cedar and pressure-treated lumber (but not on composite decks). The only special tools you need are a pressure washer and a foam applicator pad. The project doesn't require any special skills. Just set aside at least four hours on one day to clean your deck, and another four hours several days later to stain it. You'll save several hundred dollars by doing the work yourself.

Rent a pressure washer

A pressure washer will scour away dirt and contaminants ingrained in the wood at the same time it sprays on a deck stripper to clean off previous finishes.

Rent a pressure washer from a home center or rental center. A pressure setting of 1,000 to 1,200 psi is ideal. Too much pressure will damage the wood and make the wand harder to control.

2 **Spray one deck board at a time, using a gentle sweeping motion. Avoid sudden stops. Work from the end of the deck toward the exit. Then rinse the entire deck with a garden hose.**

3 **Dig out trapped debris from between deck boards with a putty knife. Spray the deck lightly with a mixture of oxalic acid and water to brighten the wood.**

4 **Rinse the siding and windows with clean water at low pressure to remove chemical residue.**

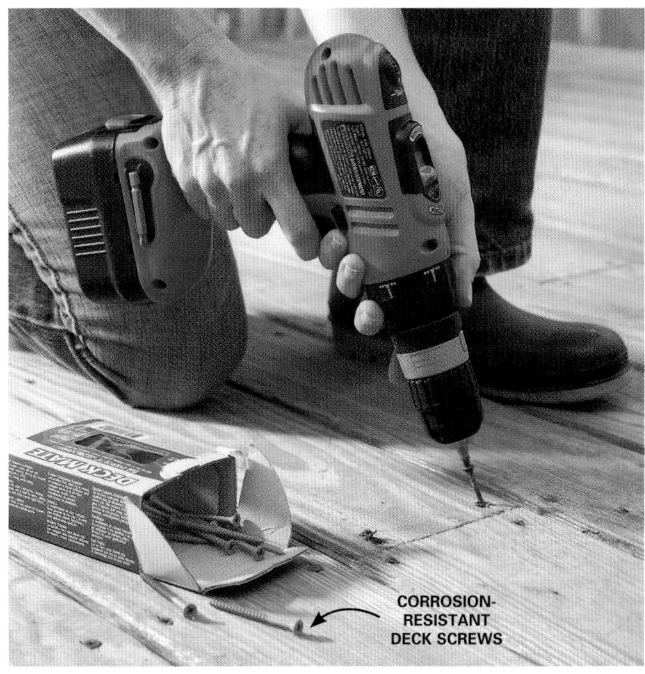

5 **Sink any raised nails and screws. Replace loose and missing fasteners with screws at least 1/2 in. longer than the original.**

6 **Remove mold, mildew or algae using non-chlorine bleach. Scrub the area with a nylon brush, then rinse with water. For tougher stains, repeat the process with a TSP substitute.**

7 **Drive the heads of stain-causing fasteners below the wood surface. Then sand out the stains using 80-grit sandpaper. Also sand rough or splintered areas.**

Rent a unit that allows for the intake of chemical cleaners (deck stripper and wood brightener) so you can spray them on through the wand. Most pressure washers have an intake hose that draws in cleaners from a separate bucket. (Use a plastic bucket. Chemicals in the cleaners can react to metal buckets.)

We used sodium hydroxide as the deck stripper. You probably won't be able to find straight sodium hydroxide, but you can find a deck stripping product with sodium hydroxide as the active ingredient in almost any home center or paint store.

We diluted our stripper to a 50/50 mix with water. Some sodium hydroxide–based strippers are premixed and don't require adding water. More commonly, you need to dilute the stripper with water. Read the label on the container to find out what's suggested for your stripper.

Protect your house and plants

Before you begin cleaning, make repairs to your deck, such as replacing cracked or split boards and broken balusters.

8 **Apply stain to the top rail, then the balusters and the posts. Work from the top down. Stain one section at a time, using a foam applicator pad. Brush out drips as you work.**

9 **Stain the deck boards using a foam applicator pad with an extension handle. Stain the full length of two or three boards at a time, working with the grain.**

Then heavily douse the plants or grass under and around your deck with water and cover them with plastic. Although most strippers aren't supposed to harm vegetation, it's still a good idea to protect plants and it only takes a few minutes. Once you've finished cleaning the deck, immediately remove the plastic.

Also spray down the siding with clean water to ensure that any stripper that splashes onto the house will easily wash off.

Scour away the old finish

With a 25- or 30-degree tip in the wand of the pressure washer and a psi of 1,000 to 1,200, apply the stripper to the deck, starting with the top rails and working down the balusters (Photo 1). Spray the rails with a continuous, controlled motion. Keep the wand moving so you don't gouge the wood.

Once you finish the railings, start on the deck boards. Wash along the length of the boards (Photo 2). You'll see the grime washing off the wood.

Go over stubborn mildew or other stains a few times rather than turning up the pressure or trying to heavily scour the wood. Later we'll tackle tough stains that won't come out with the stripper.

This stripping process washes away a small amount of the wood's lignin, which is the glue holding the wood fibers together. As the lignin washes away, the fibers stand up, giving the wood a fuzzy appearance. Don't bother sanding off the fuzzy fibers. They will gradually shear off and blow away.

After you've power-washed the entire deck, rinse all of the wood with plain water to dilute and neutralize the stripper. If there's still debris trapped between deck boards, such as leaves or twigs, remove it now (Photo 3).

Brighten the wood

A deck brightener will return the wood to its newly sawn color and make it more receptive to the stain. Use an oxalic acid–based brightener, which is available at home centers and paint stores. It works fast, won't harm the wood and is environmentally safe in the diluted solution that you'll use.

10 **Spray on the finish in hard-to-reach areas or surfaces that are difficult to cover with a paintbrush. Use a wide spray to avoid streaks. Work stain into crevices and narrow areas between balusters and posts with a paintbrush.**

pro tip

Choosing the best stain

You have two basic stain choices: oil-based and water-based. Oil stains are easier to apply, penetrate the wood grain and require less work when you reapply them. However, they only last two to four years.

Water-based (latex) stains last four to six years, but they'll eventually peel and require more prep work before recoating. Opaque latex stains generally last longer than semitransparent versions. When possible, test the stain on an inconspicuous section of the decking. We used a cedar color that worked well since the wood was pressure treated and somewhat dark in color. For a darker color, a redwood-colored stain is available, while a honey color is an option for a lighter, natural wood look.

Be careful not to choose a light-color stain if your deck was previously covered with a dark stain or is pressure treated (green). The light stain will not cover the dark wood or darker stain, and it will turn gray within a few weeks.

If you want a natural gray or silver deck, use a clear finish. It will protect the deck from mildew and algae, but not from the sun, allowing the deck to start graying in a month or two.

Like strippers, some deck brighteners come premixed and some need to be diluted with water. Read the label for the manufacturer's recommendations. We mixed our oxalic acid with an equal amount of water and ran it through the pressure washer's intake hose.

Change the tip in the wand of the pressure washer to a fan tip with a 40- or 45-degree angle. Then set the pressure to about 1,000 psi and spray the deck, once again starting with the top rails and working down to the deck boards. Apply just enough brightener to thoroughly wet the wood.

Oxalic acid will brighten the wood in a matter of minutes and does not require rinsing. But your siding does. Rinse off your siding with clean water at very low pressure (about 500 psi) to wash away any stripper or brightener overspray (Photo 4).

If your wood is cedar or redwood, you'll see a dramatic difference as the wood brightens to its fresh-sawn color. Our deck is pressure-treated pine, so the brightening of the wood is less noticeable.

Inspect the whole deck

With the deck clean, it's easy to spot any areas that need additional maintenance. Drive in any nail heads that are popping up until they're flush with the deck boards. Look for missing or loose screws, and replace them with corrosion-resistant screws that are slightly longer than the original (Photo 5). Replace missing nails with corrosion-resistant "trim head" screws, which are screws that have a small head and resemble a large finish nail.

If lag screws or bolts are loose in the ledger board, rails or posts, tighten them. Inspect the flashing between your deck and house to ensure it's still firmly in place.

Attack stubborn stains

Although the sodium hydroxide in the deck cleaner will remove most stains and mold, particularly stubborn ones require extra attention.

Use a non-chlorine laundry bleach to remove the stain. (This works especially well if the stain is from mold, mildew or algae.) Apply it to the affected area, then scrub with a nylon brush. Rinse the area with water.

For tougher stains, use trisodium phosphate substitute. Mix the TSP substitute with water and apply it to the stain. Let it sit for a minute or two, then scrub with a nylon brush and rinse with water (Photo 6).

To remove deep stains that don't come out with TSP substitute, let the deck dry. These "bleed" stains are often caused by fasteners. Sand the stains out, using 80-grit sandpaper and concentrating only on the affected areas. Some bleeds may be too deep to sand out. Rough or splintered areas may also need sanding. Spot-sand working in the direction of the wood grain until the surface is smooth (Photo 7).

Wear a dust mask, and sand only if the stain bothers you. You don't have to get every stain out. After all, imperfections are part of an outdoor deck.

Apply the finish—finally!

The deck will need a minimum of 48 hours to dry after the cleaning. If it rains, wait two more days for the wood to dry. Avoid staining in high heat, high humidity and in direct sunlight. Perfect conditions are an overcast day with the temperature in the 70s and no possibility of rain.

Start by staining the top rails and working down the balusters and posts (Photo 8). Run the applicator pad down the length of the wood, applying the stain in a steady, uniform manner. Don't go back over areas that are already stained. Unlike paint, stain gets darker with each coat.

If stain drips onto the deck, smooth it with the applicator pad to avoid spotting. Once the railings are complete, stain the deck boards. Load the pad with plenty of stain, yet not so much that it drips. Start by carefully "cutting in" stain along the house. If stain drips onto the siding, promptly wipe it off using a clean cloth and mineral spirits or paint thinner.

Attach a broom handle to the applicator pad. Glide the pad along the length of the deck boards, staining with the grain (Photo 9). Stop only at the end of a board. Otherwise, the overlap where you stopped and started could be noticeable.

Once the deck is finished, apply stain to the stair treads, working your way down the stairs.

Finally, use a paintbrush or spray bottle to work stain into tight areas that the applicator pad couldn't reach, such as lattice and crevices between balusters and the rim joist (Photo 10).

Allow the stain to dry at least 48 hours before walking on it. Feel the deck to make sure the stain is completely dry. Likewise, check the bottom of your shoes before walking back into the house.

pro tip

Pressure washer safety

To use the pressure washer:

- Wear appropriate safety gear and clothes. Rubber boots and gloves will protect your hands and feet. Safety goggles will keep the chemicals from splashing into your eyes, and a disposable respirator or dust mask will filter fumes.
- Keep the exhaust from the pressure washer at least 3 ft. away from any objects, including your house.
- Practice spraying the water until you find an appropriate power setting.
- Never point the wand at anything you don't want to spray.
- Cover electrical outlets.

Crack cleaner

Cleaning the expansion joints in a sidewalk or the spaces between deck boards doesn't have to be a tedious, on-your-knees job. Insert a "screw-in" hook into the end of a broom and drag the hook through the cracks. The hook will pull out debris, which can then be easily swept up.

Patch rotted wood

Do you have rotted wood? It's usually better to simply tear out the old board or molding and replace it than to repair it. But for windowsills and door jambs that are hard to remove and molding that would be tough to duplicate, patching with wood filler makes sense.

Fillers for repair of rotted wood generally fall into three categories. For small holes and cracks, there are fillers that harden as the water or solvent evaporates. Other fillers harden by a chemical reaction when water is mixed in. Finally, two-part fillers harden after you mix the two parts.

Two-part fillers are the most durable, and the best choice for long-lasting repairs. Although polyester and epoxy are both two-part fillers, they have unique characteristics that make them quite different to work with. We'll show you the differences and give you some tips for working with these two excellent wood repair fillers.

Epoxy and polyester fillers are two-part formulas that harden after you mix the parts. They're both excellent fillers, though with slightly different characteristics.

Use epoxy for a premium repair

Prepare for an epoxy repair by removing as much rotted wood as possible. Use an old screwdriver, chisel or 5-in-1 painter's tool to gouge out the damaged wood (Photo 1). If the wood is wet, cover it loosely with a poly tent and let it dry completely before starting the repair. Drill a

1 **Gouge out rotted wood with a chisel, screwdriver or other pointy tool.**

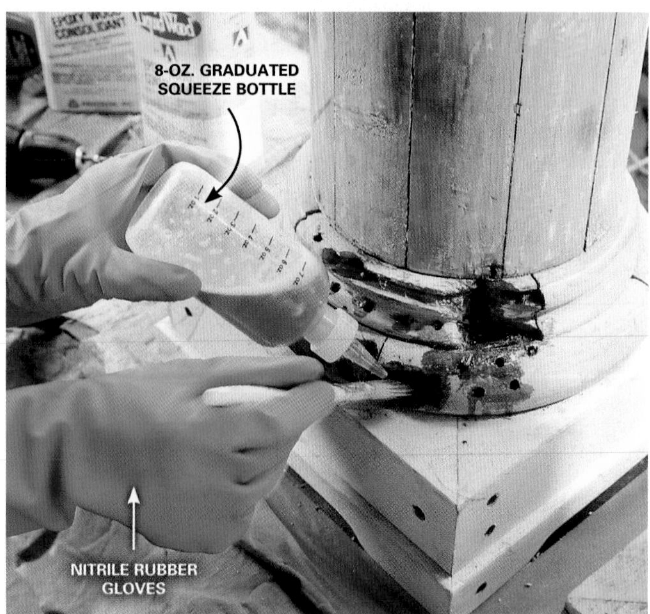

2 **Mix two-part epoxy consolidant in a squeeze bottle. Squirt it into the holes and repair area. Use a disposable brush to spread the consolidant and work it into the wood fibers.**

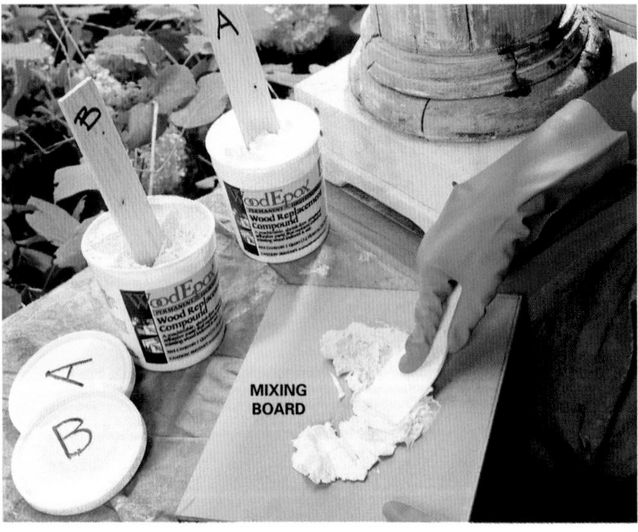

3 **Mix the two-part epoxy wood filler on a smooth board according to the manufacturer's directions.**

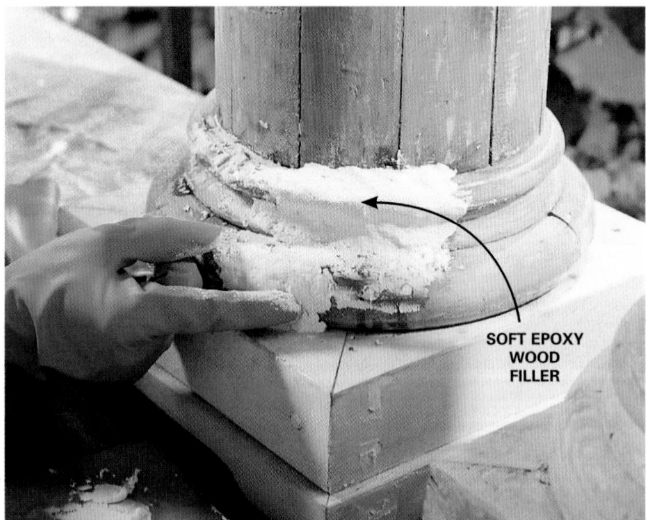

4 **Press the epoxy filler into the repair. Leave enough protruding so you can shape the repair after it starts to harden.**

pro tip

Working with epoxy

- Label the caps "A" and "B" and don't mix them up.
- Start with a clean container or mixing board each time you mix a new batch.
- Save epoxy by filling most of the cavity with a scrap of wood. Glue it in with epoxy filler.
- Carve the epoxy before it becomes rock-hard.

series of 1/4-in. holes around the rotted area if you suspect rotted wood below the surface, but don't drill all the way through. You'll fill these with consolidant to solidify the wood around the repair.

Start the repair by soaking the damaged area with epoxy consolidant (Photo 2). Mix the consolidant according to the directions. Wear rubber gloves and safety glasses when you're working with epoxy. You can mix the consolidant in a squirt bottle or a small plastic container. Use a disposable brush to work the epoxy consolidant into the wood fibers. Epoxy is difficult to remove after it hardens, so clean up drips and runs

5 **Rough out the shape with a rasp. Mix another batch of epoxy filler and add another layer if necessary. Fine-tune the repair with sandpaper, then prime and paint.**

right away with paper towels. You don't have to wait for the consolidant to harden before applying the epoxy filler.

pro tip

You can make a more spreadable filler by mixing a small batch of consolidant and a small batch of filler and then adding some of the consolidant to the filler to reach the desired consistency.

Next, mix the two-part epoxy filler on a mixing board (Photo 3). Then apply it with a putty knife or simply press it into place with your fingers (Photo 4). Roughly shape the epoxy, making sure it protrudes beyond the final profile. When the temperature is 70 degrees F, you'll have about 30 minutes before the epoxy starts to harden. Increase the working time by spreading the epoxy in a thin layer on your mixing board and keeping it cool. On a warm day, the epoxy will harden enough in three or four hours to start shaping it with a Surform plane, rasp and sandpaper (Photo 5). After rough-shaping with a plane or rasp, sand the filler with 80-grit and then 120-grit sandpaper. If you sand off too much (or didn't add enough epoxy to begin with), dust off the repair and add another layer.

Polyester is readily available and less expensive

If you've done any auto body repair, you've probably worked with two-part polyester filler.

The process for repairing wood is much the same whether you're using polyester filler or epoxy. Instead of epoxy consolidant, you'll use wood hardener to solidify and strengthen the wood fibers (Photo 1). Polyester begins hardening fast. Depending on the temperature, you'll have about 10 to 15 minutes to work before the filler starts to harden.

Also, unlike epoxy, polyester tends to sag when you're doing vertical repairs. One trick is to build a form and line it with plastic sheeting. Press the form against the filler and attach it with screws. Then pull it off after the filler hardens. Or you can wait until the sagging filler reaches the hardness of soap and carve it off with a putty knife or chisel or shape it with a plane or rasp (Photo 2). Most medium to large repairs will require at least two layers of filler. Complete the repair by sanding and priming the filled area and then painting.

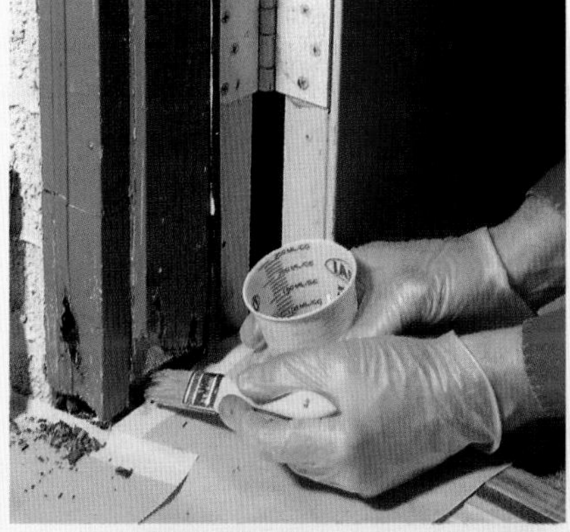

1 **Remove rotted wood with a 5-in-1 or other sharp tool. Then coat the area with wood hardener as shown. Mix polyester wood filler and press it into the recess with a putty knife.**

2 **Carve the partially hardened sagging wood filler with a putty knife or chisel. Add another layer of filler if necessary.**

1 Scrape away all the paint within 16 in. of the concrete. Scrapers with replaceable carbide blades work best. Also dig any old caulk out of joints.

3 ways to stop peeling paint

1 Wood close to the ground

If the lower ends of your garage door trim just won't hold paint, here's why: Concrete soaks up water, then releases moisture slowly. So any wood next to ground-level concrete stays damp, and that constant dampness breaks the wood/paint bond. The same goes for any wood that touches a deck, patio or other surface where water sits.

To correct the problem, create a gap between wood and horizontal surfaces. Then apply paintable water repellent to the bottom 16 in. of the wood. Properly applied repellents add several years to a paint job in areas highly vulnerable to moisture.

Begin by scraping away all the paint in the peeling area. Two or three coats of paint can usually be removed with a combination of paint scrapers and sandpaper (Photos 1 and 2). For heavier buildup, use a heat gun to soften the paint as you scrape. Be careful with a heat gun—it can melt nearby vinyl and weatherstripping. As you scrape, you may find that the wood has turned gray or black in some areas. Check for rot by probing these areas with a nail. Spots that are discolored but firm are simply weathered. Weathered wood doesn't hold paint very well, so sand away the gray surface. If you

2 Sand remaining paint off curves or in corners where scrapers don't reach. Coarse sandpaper, 60 or 80 grit, removes paint quickly and leaves a rough surface for better primer adhesion.

3 Undercut the trim to create a gap between the wood and concrete. Use a scrap of 1/4-in. plywood for a saw guide.

4 **Brush the bare wood with paintable water repellent. Keep repellent off existing paint. Wipe off any repellent that doesn't soak in.**

5 **Slip a folded paper towel underneath the trim, soak the towel with repellent and then squish the towel up with a putty knife to soak the underside. Let dry.**

6 **Coat the underside of the trim with primer using a bent putty knife. When the primer is dry, fill joints and nail craters with acrylic caulk.**

7 **Protect the trim with two coats of quality latex paint. Apply paint to the underside of the trim the same way you applied the primer.**

find soft areas, you've got rot. Small, shallow soft spots can be dug out and repaired with a two-part filler such as Minwax High Performance Wood Filler. But when rot is deep and widespread, it's best to replace the entire piece of wood.

Next, undercut the trim to create a gap (Photo 3). When you're done, scrape any dirt or gunk out of the gap with a putty knife and blow out the dust using a vacuum or air compressor. To avoid staining the concrete, run at least three layers of masking tape under the wood. Apply repellent to all bare wood (Photo 4) including the underside (Photo 5). Bend a putty knife in a vise to make a handy tool for reaching into tight areas. Remove the tape right after application.

The label on the repellent will tell you how long to wait before applying a primer. Many repellents require an oil-based primer, so be sure to read the label. When using paint and primer, don't ignore the temperature and humidity ranges listed on the label—weather conditions during application really do affect paint longevity.

pro tip

Apply *two* coats of paint. A single coat of paint may look fine, but two coats form a more durable film that resists moisture better and lasts longer.

caution

If your home was built before 1979, the paint might contain lead, which is extremely hazardous to children age 6 and younger. Call your local public health department for information on how to check for lead and handle lead paint safely.

1 Dig nails out of bad boards by driving a cat's paw under the nailhead and pulling. Then nudge the board above outward with a pry bar.

2 A board that won't hold paint

Sometimes a piece of wood siding or trim peels while neighboring boards don't, even though they all get the same sun and moisture exposure (Photo 1). In a case like this, the board itself is usually the problem.

Some boards won't hold paint because of "mill glaze," a glossy or waxy surface left when the board was planed at the mill. Cure this problem by sanding glazed areas. Grain pattern can cause a more common and difficult problem (photos below). Dark bands of grain (called "latewood") are less porous and stable than the lighter bands of wood, so paint doesn't stick to them very well. This isn't a problem when those dark bands are narrow and uniform. But when they're wide, paint soon loses its grip. In fact, you can sometimes see a board's grain pattern right through the paint as cracks and peeling develop along the latewood grain lines (Photo 1).

If you have a few bad boards on your house, you can delay peeling by sanding thoroughly with 60-grit paper before priming. That roughens the dark bands so they hold paint better. But the only long-term cure for a bad board is replacement. Before you get started, measure the width and thickness of your siding. Keep in mind that about an inch of

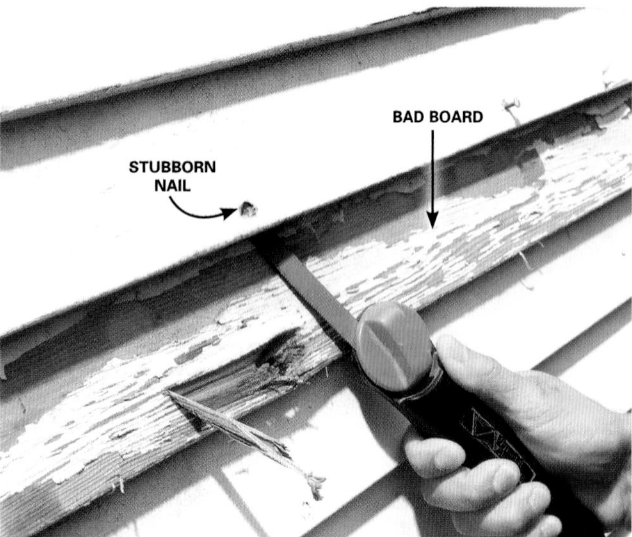

2 Pull the nails in the board above carefully. Slide a hacksaw blade under the siding and cut any stubborn nails. Remove the bad board.

3 Bend the remaining shank of cut nails down with side cutters or needle-nose pliers. Then grab it with nippers or locking pliers and pull it.

pro tip

Choosing wood

A board with tight, straight grain holds paint well. Wide bands of darker "latewood" lead to peeling. Regardless of grain, look out for "mill glaze," a wood surface that looks glossy and paint won't stick to.

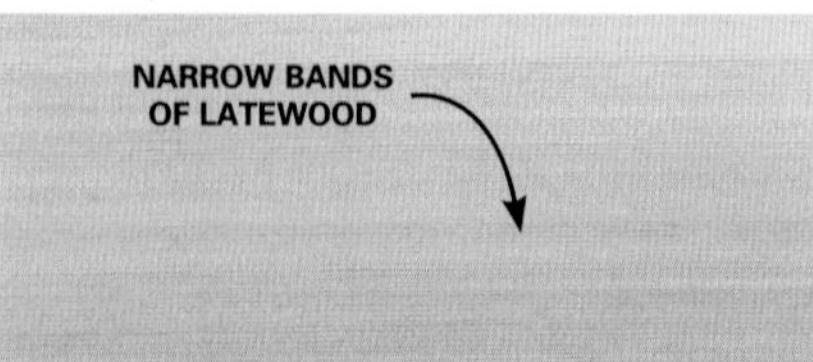

GOOD FOR PAINT

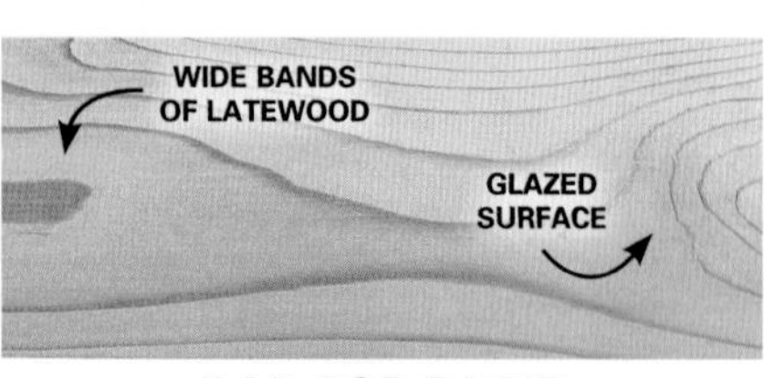

BAD FOR PAINT

4 **Prime the ends and backside of the new board before you install it. Also prime the exposed ends of adjoining siding.**

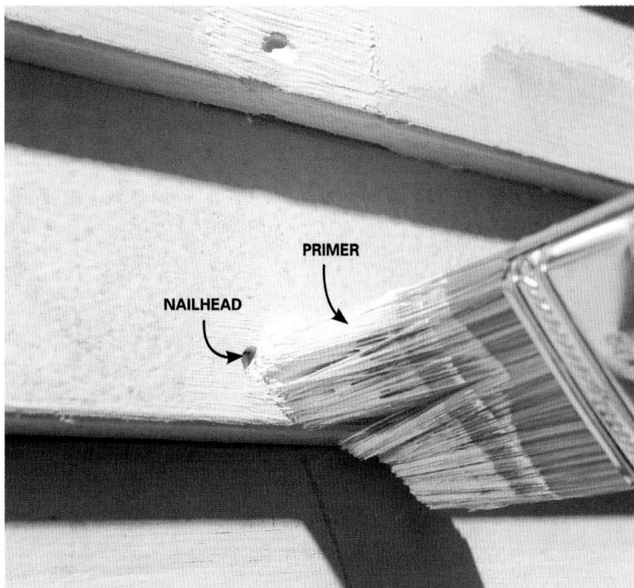

5 **Seal nailheads and craters with primer. Then fill the craters with caulk. You can apply acrylic paint right over acrylic latex caulk—no primer needed.**

the board's face is covered by the board above. Buy matching siding at a lumberyard; most home centers don't carry it.

To remove a bad piece of siding, you have to pull out two rows of nails: the ones in the bad board itself, and those in the board directly above. Siding is thin and splits easily, so the tricky part of this job is pulling nails without damaging surrounding boards. A cat's paw is the best tool for digging out nails if damage to the surrounding wood doesn't matter (Photo 1).

To get at the nails in the board above, shove a flat pry bar up under it and gently pry the board outward. In most cases, this will pop up the nailhead, so you can pull it with your hammer claw. If you run into a stubborn nail that won't move easily, don't use brute force and risk splitting the good board. Instead, slip a hacksaw blade behind the siding and cut the nail (Photo 2). You can't get the new board in unless you pull the remaining shank of the cut nail (Photo 3).

Before you install the new board, lightly sand it with 80-grit paper. If you come across shiny, glazed areas, sand them thoroughly. Then prime the backside and the ends (Photo 4). Also prime the ends of adjoining boards. This step pays off by slowing the moisture penetration that can lead to peeling at the joints. If the new siding is redwood or cedar, buy a special "stain-blocking" primer. Both of these woods contain natural chemicals (tannins) that can bleed through paint, causing brownish stains. A stain-blocking primer will seal in the tannins.

Nail the new board into place with 8d galvanized nails. Use a nail set to countersink the nailheads slightly below the wood's surface. Countersinking nails helps to keep the heads from protruding as the wood shrinks and swells. After you prime the sunken nailheads (Photo 5), keep an eye on them for a few minutes; primer may drip out of the craters and leave runs on your siding. When the primer is dry, fill the craters with caulk. Also caulk the ends of the board, where it meets trim or the next piece of siding. Finish the job with two coats of acrylic paint.

pro tip

Water repellents help paint last

Although seldom used, paintable water repellents have been proven to add years to the life of paint. Wood that stays dry holds paint longer. Repellents work by penetrating wood and sealing out moisture that works its way through the paint. Some repellents also contain preservatives that fight wood rot.

Most home centers and hardware and paint stores carry several water repellents, but check the labels carefully: *Most water repellents are not paintable.* If the label doesn't say how long the product needs to dry before priming, assume it isn't paintable. Wood that's exposed to sunlight for more than a couple of weeks starts to degrade and won't hold paint as well. So avoid repellents with drying times of more than two weeks.

SAFETY HARNESS

1 Scrape and sand to remove all paint from the area that's peeled. Keep a nail set handy so you can reset any protruding nails.

3 Siding close to the roof

Too often, builders install trim and siding right up against shingles and don't bother to seal the ends of the boards. It looks good at first, but trim and siding—whether they're wood or a manufactured material like hardboard—soak up moisture from the wet shingles and before long the paint peels.

The solution is to cut back the siding to leave about a 1-in. gap. This keeps the siding out of contact with the shingles and allows you to seal the ends so they won't absorb moisture. Keep in mind that if the intersection of your roof and siding has been covered with roof cement (a thick, tar-like compound), you may have to deal with roof leaks as well. Chances are you'll have to replace the metal flashing and some shingles after removing the cement.

Begin by removing all the paint in the badly peeling area (Photo 1). While scraping, you might discover cracked or rotten siding that needs replacing. There's no need to replace an entire board if only a section near the roof is damaged. Instead, cut off the damaged section with a hacksaw

2 Tear off any cracked or rotted siding, using a cat's paw and pry bar. Cut nails above bad boards using the technique shown in Photo 2, p. 204.

3 **Pry up cracked and rotted ends with shims and cut off the bad ends with a hacksaw. Make sure to stagger cuts on adjacent boards so the joints don't line up.**

4 **Cut the siding back from the shingles using a 3/4-in. thick board to guide your saw. Be careful not to cut into the metal flashing.**

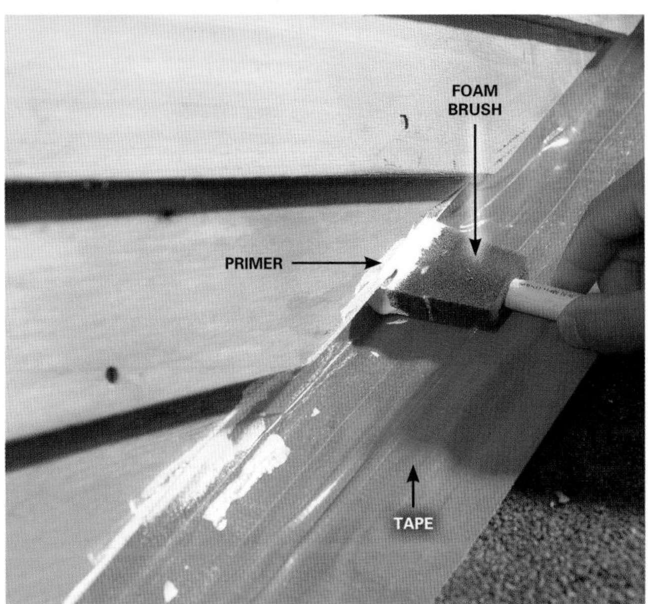

5 **Seal the cut ends with water repellent followed by primer so they can't soak up water. Treat the faces of the siding the same way. Protect the flashing and shingles with tape.**

6 **Finish the primed siding with two coats of paint. Duck down occasionally and check the undersides of the siding—it's easy to miss spots where the boards overlap.**

(Photo 3). Don't install any new boards until you've cut back the bottom edge of the siding.

Cutting back siding is slow, tedious work. A backsaw or a dovetail saw with an offset handle is the best tool for the job. The fine teeth cut slowly but neatly, and the offset handle prevents scraped knuckles (Photo 4). Don't cut all the way through the siding or you'll risk dulling the saw teeth and damaging the metal flashing behind the siding. Instead, stop your cut 1/8 in. or so from the flashing and then finish up by making several passes with a sharp utility knife. But be careful—it's possible to slice the flashing if you press too hard.

With the siding cut back, take the same steps covered in "Wood Close to the Ground": paintable water repellent followed by primer and two coats of paint on the faces and cut ends of the siding. At each step, use a disposable foam brush to coat the ends of the siding (Photo 5).

pro tip

Keep paint off your flashing and shingles with duct tape — masking tape may not stick to them very well.

10 Year
latex•ite
Driveway Treatment
• Ultra Flex Polymers = Flexibility
• UV Protection = Blackest Finish
• Texturized Formula
For Asphalt / Para Asfalto

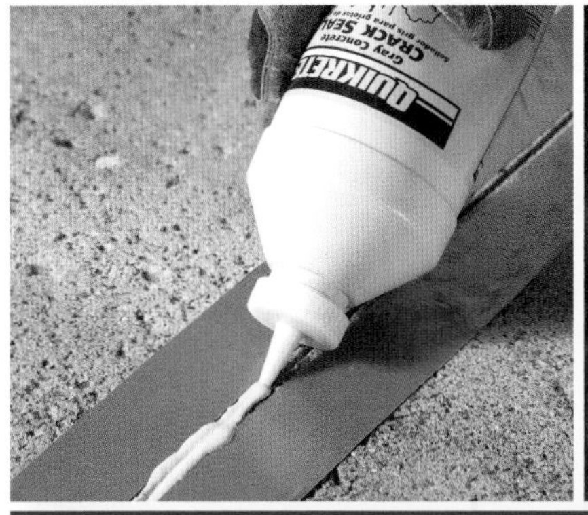

Chapter **two**

CONCRETE & ASPHALT

Renew a driveway

Most driveways are big and conspicuous. And a long stretch of gray, cracking asphalt can give a home a scruffy look, no matter how handsome the rest of the property is. So a fresh coat of shiny black sealer isn't just protection against expensive driveway damage—it's a face-lift for your home and yard.

Mother Nature is tough on asphalt. Sunlight breaks down the surface, creating pits and cracks. Then water seeps in, expands the cracks and erodes the gravel base below. Left alone, an asphalt driveway becomes a crumbling eyesore in about 15 years. But with a little maintenance, you can double the life of your driveway and save thousands in replacement costs.

You can keep your asphalt in tip-top shape by following the three steps we show here. Asphalt maintenance doesn't require special skills, and you'll only need a few inexpensive tools. You can get everything you need at home centers and hardware stores. However, as with exterior painting, high-quality results hinge on some sweat and careful prep work. Expect to spend about six to eight hours completing the job.

Fill cracks every year

Maintaining the asphalt skin is the best thing you can do to preserve your driveway. The asphalt layer serves primarily as a protective skin over the gravel base. The weight of your car is supported by the base, not the asphalt. If too much water gets through, the base erodes, causing additional cracking, potholes and total asphalt breakup.

1 **Clean out cracks, digging deep enough to completely remove roots. Clean the edges of the asphalt with a hand broom and blasts of air or water.**

2 **Stuff backer rod into wide or deep cracks, leaving about 1/2-in. depth to fill with crack filler. The foam rod conserves filler and makes the repair more flexible.**

3 **Pour in filler until it's even with the driveway surface. Smooth out overfilled areas with a putty knife. Check for voids in the filler the next day and refill them.**

The best way to keep the asphalt skin intact is to fill cracks, ideally every spring. Buy the high-quality pouring-type filler. Read the labels. Our experts recommend the ones containing rubber compounds. They typically handle cracks from 1/8 in. to 1/2 in. wide. For smaller cracks, small tubes of filler in a caulking gun are easier to use. For larger cracks, 1/2 to 3/4 in. wide, buy an extra-thick filler that you spread with a trowel, or tamp in asphalt patching material.

Fillers adhere to the sides of cracks, so your first task is to clean out the dirt and old, loose filler 1/2 in. to 1 in. deep. This is time-consuming. Use a screwdriver or a 5-in-1 tool (shown in Photo 2) for the packed areas. Go deeper if weeds have taken hold. If you don't get all their roots, they'll grow right up through the new filler. Clean the crack edges (Photo 1). You can use a pressure washer or a garden hose, but then let the driveway dry for at least a day before filling.

Fillers need at least 24 hours to dry, so don't fill cracks when rain is in the forecast. The filling technique varies with the product, so check the directions. With most products, you can simply pour the filler into cracks up to 1/4 in. wide. For wider cracks, stuff in backer rod first (Photo 2). Backer rod is available in several thicknesses at home centers.

Neatness counts when you're filling cracks (Photo 3). The jet-black filler contrasts with the gray asphalt and can look bad if you overfill or smear it.

Cracks that form a spider web pattern in a small area usually indicate that the base has softened. Water will settle in this spot and make the problem worse. Fillers will help for a while, but sooner or later you'll have to cut out and patch the cracked area. Cut the asphalt using a diamond blade in your circular saw (Photo 4). Then repack the gravel base by pounding it with a 6-ft. 4x4 or a hand tamper. Fill the cutout and pack with a 4x4 or hand tamper (Photo 5).

You can buy asphalt patching material at home centers and hardware stores, but it isn't nearly as durable as regular hot asphalt. For better performance, seal-coat the patch after about six months. And for areas larger than a few square feet, we recommend that you hire a pro.

pro tip

A week before you begin this project, apply a nonselective herbicide to kill roots.

4 Saw around heavily cracked areas using a circular saw and diamond blade. Chisel out all the loose asphalt down to the gravel base.

5 Fill the cutout with new asphalt. Be sure to repack the gravel base first. Then add asphalt in 1-in. layers, packing each layer with a hand tamper.

6 Cut back invading grass along the driveway. Left alone, grass roots will enlarge any cracks and gradually destroy the driveway from the edges inward.

7 Coat oil-stained spots with a primer before seal coating. Without thorough cleaning and primer, the seal coat won't stick to oily areas.

Clean up edges every two years

Asphalt edges are especially prone to cracking because the base erodes at edges more easily. Grass invades the cracks and increases erosion. So every other year, grab a shovel or lawn edger and cut back the grass (Photo 6). Then clean out and fill the cracks.

pro tip

For better performance, seal-coat the patch after about six months.

Seal-coat every four to five years

The purpose of a seal coat is to protect the asphalt against sun and water and to fill small cracks. It also dresses up the asphalt by covering fillers and patches. You don't need to do it every year. In fact, seal coat will peel if there are too many layers, and you'll permanently ruin the

8 **Apply the sealer around the perimeter of the driveway. Protect walls and the adjacent concrete with wide masking tape.**

9 **Spread the sealer by working back and forth across the driveway. Pull the broom or squeegee at an angie to plow the excess sealer onto the uncoated area.**

appearance of the driveway.

Home centers carry several sealers. Buy the best one (the most expensive!), especially if you're sealing your driveway for the first time. A better sealer means better long-term adhesion. Adhesion is vital, because you'll apply more coats in future years, and each fresh coat is only as good as the coat beneath it.

To ensure good sealer adhesion, the driveway must be clean and dry. Fill cracks and edge the driveway at least a week in advance. Scrub with a stiff broom. Then sweep or blow debris off with a leaf blower. You can use a garden hose or a pressure washer, but you'll have to wait for it to dry.

Sealer won't stick to oily spots left by a drippy car. First scrape off the oily gunk with a putty knife. Then apply a detergent (such as dishwashing liquid) or buy the sealer manufacturer's cleaner and scrub. After you rinse, examine the spot. If you see an oil film on the rinse water or if water beads up on the spot, scrub again. You can wash the entire driveway surface at this time, since you'll have to wait one or two days for the asphalt to dry anyway. When it's dry, apply primer (Photo 7) to the spots.

Before you apply sealer, check the weather forecast and the sealer's label to make sure you'll get good drying conditions. Seal coats are water-based, and a rainfall before they dry will ruin them. Drying times will slow in cooler and more humid conditions.

Coat the edges first using a stiff brush such as a masonry brush (Photo 8). Then coat the entire driveway using a seal-coating broom or squeegee (Photo 9).

pro tip

Although some sealers require only one coat, it's better to have two thin coats than one thick coat. And you're less likely to leave ridges or brush marks.

pro tip

Hiring an asphalt contractor

Before diving into an asphalt driveway repair project, call in a local pro for an estimate. That way, you can compare the estimate with the cost of doing it yourself. Keep in mind that a quality professional job will include hot-melt crack filler and hot asphalt patching material. These materials provide longer-lasting repairs than you can make yourself. And if your driveway has lots of heavily cracked areas or large potholes, the gravel base probably needs repair; that's a job best left to pros.

If you decide to hire a contractor, avoid those who give bids over the phone. Good contractors will examine your driveway and give you a detailed bid. They should also tell you the products they'll use and all the steps in their process. Seal-coating warranties are often for no more than a year. But patches should be guaranteed for the life of the driveway.

If large areas of your driveway look like this, call in the pros. A spider web of deep cracks usually calls for major base repair and lots of new asphalt.

For big repairs, pros cut out the bad section, add more base material, pack it with a plate compactor and then pack in new hot asphalt.

Stir the sealer before application even if the label claims it's a no-mix formula. Seal-coating isn't difficult, but it is messy. Wear old shoes and clothing you can toss. The worst mistake is stepping in drips, then tracking the seal coat across concrete or inside your home.

Be sure to read the manufacturer's directions and follow the recommended spread rate. Take care not to lay it on too thick. Puddles or thick areas will probably peel. Work the sealer into the surface. Although some sealers require only one coat, it's better to have two thin coats than one thick coat. And you're less likely to leave ridges or brush marks.

Finally, surround the driveway with stakes and string or tape. Keep everyone, including pets, off the finished surface until it dries. Otherwise you might find black, gooey paw prints on your kitchen floor!

pro tip

Work on a cooler, more humid day to slow drying so you have more time to spread the sealer smoothly.

Resurface a garage floor

A spalled (pitted) garage floor looks horrible. And patches will just pop out eventually. But you can resurface the concrete yourself, usually in less than a day. You'll need a pressure washer, concrete cleaner, a push broom and a floor squeegee. Buy enough concrete resurfacer material to coat the entire floor. Refer to the coverage specs on the bag to determine how many bags you need.

The resurfacing material won't bond to loose concrete, paint, grease, algae or mildew. So pressure-wash the entire floor with concrete cleaner and a clean-water rinse. Next, prefill any cracks and pits that are more than 1/4 in. deep (Photos 1 and 2).

1 **Find the deepest pits. Make a mark 1/4 in. from the tip of a pencil. Use it as a depth gauge to locate pits that need filling.**

2 **Apply resurfacer. Spread from the middle of the puddle and apply moderate squeegee pressure to force the resurfacer into the pores and pits. Then drag the squeegee backward to eliminate the edge ridges. Continue spreading until you get even coverage.**

3 **Fill cracks and joints. Apply tape to each side of the crack or joint and fill with crack sealer. Then level the sealer with a trowel and remove the tape.**

Saturate the concrete with water and then use a broom to push out any puddles from the pitted areas or low spots. Follow the mixing directions on the resurfacer bag. Then pour out a puddle and spread it (Photo 3). If the pits still show, let the material set up and apply a second coat later in the day. But you can stop with one coat if it provides good coverage. To apply a nonslip texture, lightly drag a clean push broom in one direction across the still-wet material (allow no more than five minutes of setting time before applying the broom finish).

Let the new floor dry for at least 24 hours before you drive on it. Follow the manufacturer's directions for additional hot-weather misting procedures or extra drying time for cool weather.

Renew concrete steps

Concrete steps break up, especially in northern climates. Water soaks into the concrete, freezes and breaks off the outside corners. Once that starts, the damage spreads along the front edge of the step, eventually turning the step into a ramp. That's not only ugly but mighty dangerous.

The best repair for severe corner and front edge breakage—short of completely replacing the steps—is to "recap" them. You break away the damaged areas, rebuild them with new concrete and then coat your entire steps to give them a uniform look. It takes about two days altogether.

Bust off the old surface

Start by rigging up your circular saw and grinder with water supply lines (Photo 1). All it takes is a few bucks' worth of sprinkler system parts from any home center to fabricate a water-cooling and dust-reduction system. Secure the assembly to the saw with hook-and-loop tape. Build another spray unit (with only one nozzle) for your angle grinder.

Set the circular saw blade to full depth and adjust the water flow. Then don your safety gear (goggles, hearing protection, knee pads and leather gloves) and connect your saw/grinder to a GFCI extension cord. Cut a grid pattern into the

caution

Plug your saw into an extension cord with built-in GFCI protection—or risk electrocution.

Tools and materials

Everything you need for this project is available at home centers.

- **Segmented diamond blades for a circular saw and grinder.**
- **Irrigation system tubing, valves, elbows, tee and hose adapter. Don't forget the GFCI extension cord!**
- **Concrete mixing tub, wood float, steel trowel and edger.**
- **Concrete bonding adhesive.**
- **Concrete mix; a "crack-resistant" mix is best.**
- **Resurfacer.**

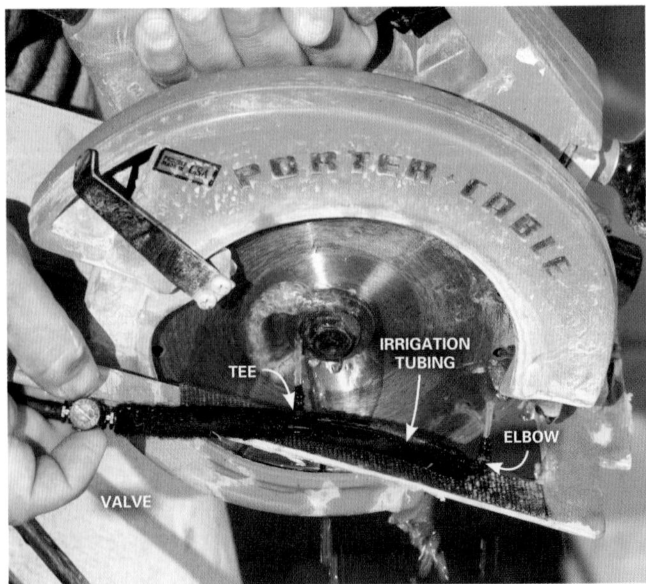

1 Turn your saw into a wet saw. Rig up a water line using irrigation system parts. Water keeps the blade cool and eliminates dust. In addition to the parts shown here, you'll need an adapter to connect the tubing to a garden hose.

2 Slice up the damaged area. Cut the stair tread into a 4- to 5-in. grid pattern. Sawing concrete is no fun, but the more cuts you make, the easier it will be to break off the step's surface.

3 Break out the blocks. Aim the chisel at the same depth as the saw cuts and whack away. The squares of concrete created by your saw cuts will pop off neatly (well, usually).

4 Cut into the corner. Your saw can't reach into the corner where the stair tread and riser meet. So cut with a grinder and chisel out the concrete. Add a spray system to your grinder similar to the one on your saw.

steps (Photo 2) and bust off the surface (Photo 3). You must remove at least 3/4 in. of concrete (3/4 in. is the minimum thickness for a cap). But a thicker cap is stronger, so try to remove 1-1/2 in. of concrete or more.

5 Fill the form. Work the concrete into the front of the form with your shovel or a stick. When the form is completely full, screed off the excess concrete.

Repair or replace?

The very best way to fix concrete steps is to demolish the old ones and pour new ones. No repair lasts forever. And replacement is the only real fix for steps that are sinking or have deep cracks. But if your steps are level and have only the usual damage that goes a few inches deep, you can save yourself a ton of money and/or labor by patching or recapping them.

Patching works well for small, shallow chips and cracks (less than 1/4 in. deep). Simply fill them with premixed concrete patching material. To patch cracked corners, chisel them out to a depth of at least 3/4 in. Then drill holes and drive in concrete screws as anchors, apply a bonding adhesive and fill with crack-resistant concrete. The patch won't match the color or texture of the steps, so you may want to recoat all the steps with concrete resurfacer for a uniform look.

If the cracks or voids extend over large areas of your steps, forget about patching. Go ahead and cap the steps following the procedure shown here.

Switch to the angle grinder to cut the remaining concrete where the stair tread meets the riser (Photo 4). Once you've removed the entire stair tread, run the circular saw lengthwise down the front and side edges of the step. Break off the faces with the maul and chisel.

Pour a new cap

Hose down the steps and let them dry. Then coat the chipped-out areas with concrete bonding adhesive.

Build a concrete form to match the original height of the step. Locate the front of the form about 1 in. out from the old face of the step. If that extra inch will cause the step to overhang the sidewalk, place a strip of 1/2-in.-thick foam under the form to create a gap between the step and the sidewalk. The gap will allow the sidewalk to rise during a freeze.

Next, mix the crack-resistant concrete and fill the form (Photo 5). Then finish the concrete (Photo 6). Remove the form after 24 hours.

Wait a week and then apply the resurfacer. Mix it in small batches. Then wet all the steps with a water spray bottle and apply the resurfacer (Photo 7).

6 Finish the concrete. Skim the surface with a wood float. When the mix hardens a little, round the edges with a concrete edger and smooth it with a steel trowel. Don't overwork the concrete or you'll weaken the surface.

7 Resurface the whole thing. Resurfacer hides the mismatch between old and new concrete and masks small imperfections. Pour it on and spread it with a masonry brush.

Fix a chipped step

The trickiest part of repairing a chipped step is getting the patch to stick. Begin by driving concrete screws into the damaged area (Photo 1). These screws, available at most hardware stores and home centers, will act like tiny pieces of rebar to secure the patch to the step. Screws that are 3/16 x 2-3/4 in. work well for most repairs. Use a 5/32-in. diameter masonry bit to predrill 1- to 2-in. deep holes. Apply bonding adhesive to further guarantee that the new patch will stick (Photo 2).

To make a form for your concrete patch, screw two short 1x4 boards together and wedge them against the step. Moisten this form with water before you fill it with concrete so it doesn't draw moisture from the mix and stick to your patch when you remove it. Ordinary concrete mix is fine for a large, 4-in. patch like ours. But use patching concrete without the large rocks for smaller or shallower repairs.

The concrete will firm up quickly. You can usually remove the form after 30 to 60 minutes. Then use a trowel to help blend the old and new surfaces and edges (Photo 4). Stay off the new concrete for two or three days; it'll be 30 days before it's fully cured and hardened.

pro tip

Protect your skin from the cement in the mix. Wear rubber gloves and goggles.

1 Drill 5/32-in. pilot holes 1 to 2 in. deep into the chipped area, then drive 3/16 x 2-3/4 in. concrete screws. Set the screwheads deep enough so the new concrete will cover them by at least 1/2 in.

2 Clean the chipped area thoroughly with a brush or shop vacuum. Apply bonding adhesive with a disposable brush.

3 Wedge 1x4 boards against the steps to hold the wet concrete while it stiffens. Anchor them with bricks or blocks. Fill the form with concrete and round over the edge with an edging tool or trowel to match the existing step.

4 Remove the forms when the concrete has stiffened long enough to hold its shape, then smooth the sides of the patch with a trowel. Texture it with a brush to match the existing step if necessary.

Repair cratered concrete

Concrete is durable, but it requires the right mix, finishing methods and weather conditions during placement and curing to create a lasting surface. If something goes awry during these early stages, or if a heavy impact creates damage, the surface can spall (separate) to expose the concrete to weather and even more damage. Patching a small problem area is fairly simple, but before you proceed, assess the condition of the entire slab. If the surface degradation is widespread rather than localized, it's likely the concrete wasn't properly finished and cured, so it makes more sense to replace the slab than attempt spot repairs.

To patch concrete, you first have to cut and break away the damaged surface and any loose or flaking material. This normally requires a circular saw fitted with a masonry or diamond blade, a maul, a cold chisel, and safety gear, including goggles, dust mask and hearing protection.

1 **Cut a shoulder around the spalled area with slow but steady pressure on the saw. Undercut the edges at a 5-degree angle to better lock in the patch.**

2 **Use a maul and a cold chisel to break out all the weak and loose concrete, especially near the edges. This generates flying chips and debris, so wear safety goggles.**

3 **Clean out all the debris and dust using a hand broom and a shop vacuum. Hose off the patch area with water, letting the excess evaporate.**

4 Remoisten the patch area, if necessary, with a wet sponge, then pack the patch mix into the cutout using a wood float. Build the mix up slightly above the slab.

5 Screed off the excess material by sliding a 2x4 side to side in a sawing motion. Refill any low spots and repeat until the surface is flat and uniform.

6 To match an existing rough or pitted texture of the surrounding concrete, rub the surface of the patch area with a sponge float, or use a broom to make the patch match.

7 Concrete ends up stronger when it can hold moisture and cure slowly. Keep the patch from drying too quickly by covering it with clear plastic sheeting for three days.

instant fix

Eliminate efflorescence

Efflorescence, the result of leaching mineral salts such as calcium carbonate, is the powdery white discoloration that can appear on brick, concrete and other masonry. Although it is unsightly it is not harmful to the brick. To remove it, mix a weak solution of muriatic acid and water, brush it on the wall, scrub and rinse with water. Wear goggles and rubber gloves.

Repair brickwork

Crumbling masonry joints start out ugly, and then things get uglier fast—bricks come loose, water seeps behind the wall and bees make their homes in the mortar holes. Let it go and the problem won't go away. In fact, the deterioration will accelerate and you'll have a much bigger fix on your hands. But you can mend the joints yourself with a process called tuckpointing.

Tuckpointing isn't difficult or expensive—the only real investment is your time. But you can pick away at it in your free time, area by area.

The steps we show here will work on any brick walls, chimneys and retaining walls. Tuckpointing won't fix cracking or crumbling bricks, or cracks in walls caused by a shifting foundation. Those problems call for more drastic fixes that we won't cover here.

Pick up tools and materials

First and foremost, you'll need an angle grinder with a 4- or 4-1/4-in. diamond blade.

You'll also need a few simple, inexpensive specialty tools that are available at masonry suppliers and some home centers. You'll need a brick trowel and a tuck pointer. If you have concave mortar joints, you'll need a masonry jointer that's the width of your joints. For flat joints, you'll need a joint raker. If you have just a few areas that need work, use a hammer and cold chisel to knock out the old mortar, but for more extensive work, plan on renting a rotary hammer drill fitted with a flat chisel to make the job go a heck of a lot quicker.

You'll also need mortar mix. If you need colored mortar, take a small piece of the old mortar to a masonry supplier and ask for help finding a mortar dye to match. But be aware of this—fresh tuckpointing always stands out against older mortar. However, it will eventually weather to match.

Start small

If you only have a few joints to tuckpoint, dive right in. But if you have a large wall to tackle, start in a small area to get a feel for the operation before you start hogging out entire walls. You'll hone your skills and get a good idea of

pro tip

Close your house windows to keep out the dust, and tell your neighbors who might be affected to do the same.

how much you can tuckpoint at one time. You'll have 30 to 60 minutes of working time once you mix the mortar.

Get ready for the dust

Tuckpointing is a dirty business. Grinding the joints creates a dust storm, with chunks of mortar covering the ground. Spread a drop cloth on the ground to catch the mortar so cleanup will take minutes instead of hours.

Grind out the joints

Before you can put new mortar in the joints, you have to cut out the damaged material. Start by grinding the top and bottom of the horizontal (bed) joints with an angle grinder (Photo 1). Hold the grinder with both hands to keep it steady and avoid grinding into the bricks. You only need to grind 3/4 in. into the mortar.

Start at outside corners and work inward. That keeps you from putting extra pressure on the corner bricks, which could knock them out of the wall. After you've finished the horizontal joints, do the vertical (head) joints (Photo 2).

Knock out the mortar

Use the rotary hammer drill to pound the mortar out of the joints. Set the drill on the rotating mode (it puts less pressure on the bricks). Again, work from the outside corners inward (Photo 3). Keep the chisel point in the mortar joint and keep moving the hammer. The drill makes quick work of removing mortar, but be careful. The powerful tool can also knock out bricks. If that happens, take them all the way out, chisel off all the mortar, then reset them when you fill the joints.

There's really no secret to knocking out the mortar. Just hold the drill at

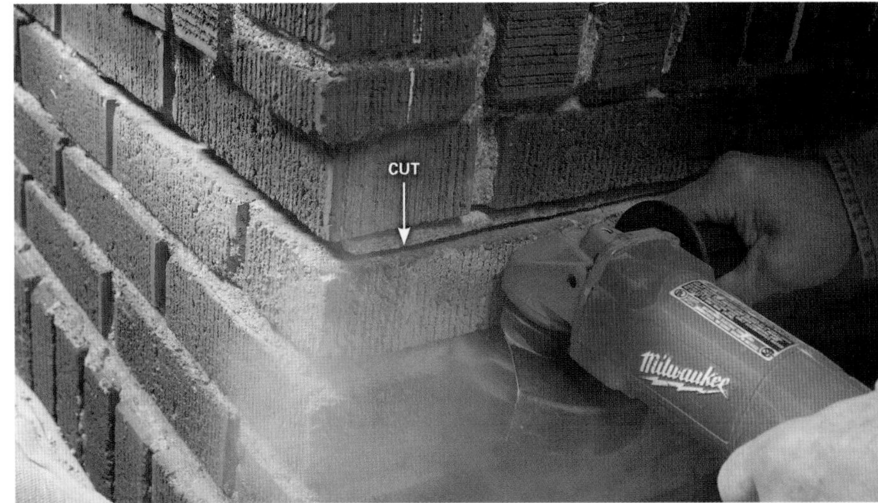

1 **Grind the horizontal joints first. Grind along the top and bottom of the horizontal joints. Get as close to the bricks as you can. If you accidentally grind against the bricks, the dust will turn the color of the brick.**

2 **Plunge-cut the vertical joints. Grind both sides of the vertical joints. Plunge the grinder into the joint and work it up and down to make the cuts. But be careful not to grind the bricks above and below the joints.**

3 **Hammer out the mortar. Keep moving the rotary hammer drill along the joints as you chisel out the mortar. Be sure to keep the chisel off the bricks so you don't knock them out of place.**

4 **Sweep out the joints. Use a small broom to sweep debris and dust out of the joints. Inspect the joints for any remaining stubborn mortar and knock it out with the drill.**

5 **Give the joints a bath. Stick a brush into a bucket of water and rinse out the joints. Your goal here isn't to make surfaces pristine, just to get rid of chunks and dust.**

6 **Whip up the mortar batch. Mix the mortar to the consistency of peanut butter with no dry spots or clumps. The mix is right when it sticks to your trowel when you hold it at a 45-degree angle. Let the mortar sit for 10 minutes before using it.**

about a 45-degree angle to the wall, squeeze the trigger and watch the mortar fall out. Caution: Wear eye protection—mortar pieces can go flying!

Clean out the joints

Once you've chipped out the damaged mortar, use a hand broom to sweep the joints. Sweep away mortar clumps and the dust (Photo 4). Use the rotary hammer drill to bust out stubborn chunks.

Then wash out the joints with water. But don't hose down the wall or you'll soak everything, including the ground where you'll be standing or kneeling. Instead, fill a bucket with water and brush the water into the joints (Photo 5). Don't worry about slopping water onto the bricks—you want them damp before you fill the joints anyway.

Mix the new mortar

If you're tinting the mortar, stir the dye and the mortar mix in a bucket before adding the water. Dye is typically sold in 1-1/2-lb. bags. Mix one-quarter of the dye with one-quarter of a 60-lb. bag of mortar mix. Stir in water until the mix is the consistency of peanut butter (Photo 6).

The mortar will last 30 to 60 minutes, but you may need to add water to keep it workable. After one hour, throw out what's left and mix a new batch.

Work the mortar into the joints

Use a brick trowel and a tuck pointer to pack the mortar into the joints. Most pros prefer this method to using a grout/mortar bag. Mortar that is hand-packed is more durable.

Scoop mortar onto the trowel. Hold the trowel next to the joint, then press the mortar into the joint with the tuck pointer (Photo 7). Pack the joint until it's flush with the front of the bricks.

Tool the joints

Let the mortar in the filled joints set for about 30 minutes. If you're

pro tip

The acid can slightly alter the bricks' appearance, so test it on a small area first. If it does alter the appearance, increase the ratio of water to acid.

tuckpointing a large area, continually check the first joints you filled to see if they're ready to tool (finish). Check by pressing the filled joint with your thumb. If your thumb leaves only a slight impression, it's ready to tool. If it goes in deeper, wait five minutes and try again. But don't let the mortar get too stiff—it can start to harden after just 30 minutes, making it difficult to tool the joints.

If you want rounded joints, press a masonry jointer into the top of vertical joints and pull the tool downward. The jointer will push out some of the mortar and leave a concave shape. For horizontal joints, start at a corner (Photo 8). Run the tool about halfway across the joint, then stop and finish tooling from the other side.

For flat joints, place a joint raker over an old joint to set the depth. Then run the raker along the new joints to make them flat.

Clean the bricks

Once the joints have set up (about 30 minutes after tooling), use a stiff-bristle brush to clean dried mortar off the bricks (Photo 9).

If the mortar refuses to come off, wait three days, then use muriatic acid. Use 10 parts water to 1 part acid (add the acid to the water, not the other way around).

caution

Be sure to wear eye protection and rubber gloves when working with acid. Brush the acid onto the bricks with a stiff-bristle brush, scrub the bricks and let the acid fizz. Then rinse the acid off with water. If there's still a little mortar residue left, treat it again.

7 Fill the joints. Load your brick trowel and hold it next to the joint. Work the mortar into the joint with your tuck pointer. Pack the joint full before moving on to the next one.

8 Strike the mortar joints. Drag the jointer along the vertical joints and the horizontal joints. Apply gentle pressure to tool out the ridges where the joints intersect. Finish one joint before moving on to the next.

9 Wipe down the bricks. Scrub the mortar off the bricks with a stiff brush. This also knocks down and smooths out any high spots along the joint edges.

Protect exterior stonework

Exterior stone, including manufactured stone, can be damaged when it absorbs water and freezes. Applying a waterproofing sealer to the stone and mortar extends their life and reduces stone chipping and mortar cracks.

A silane/siloxane product is best for this because it works without changing the color of your stone or mortar and allows the mortar to breathe. Buy a pump sprayer and silane/siloxane waterproofing product (about $30 to $65 per gallon at home centers and paint stores). To determine how much to buy, check the label for the product's coverage and measure the square footage of your stonework.

Mask off the surrounding area (Photo 1), then use the pump sprayer to apply a first coat followed by a "curtain" coat (Photo 2).

1 **PROTECT TRIM AND PLANTS** Mask off surfaces, such as trim boards, siding, house numbers and mailboxes. Cover plants and grass with tarps to prevent kill-off from the spray.

2 **APPLY IN TWO STEPS** Spray the stonework with the first coat of waterproofer. Then immediately apply a liberal, wet-on-wet "curtain coat" so that the solution drips down 6 to 8 in. over the entire surface.

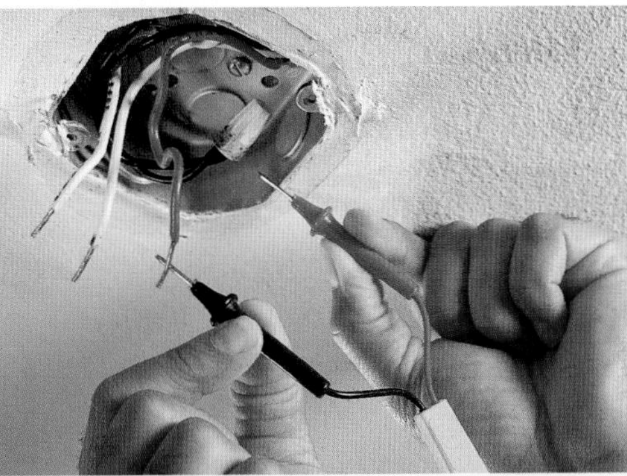

Chapter three

ELECTRICAL

Replace a ceiling fixture

Installing a new light fixture is a great way to instantly change a drab room into a dazzling one. Lighting showrooms and catalogs have a wide variety of fixtures to tempt you. And even though the bag of parts included with some fixtures may look daunting, the electrical connections are simple enough for even a beginner.

But poor installation techniques can result in a potentially lethal shock or fire. In this article, we'll help you choose a fixture that will mount safely on your electrical box and then show you the best techniques for testing a ground and connecting the wires.

Learn the temperature rating of your existing wires

It's hard to believe, but many of the light fixtures now sold at home centers and lighting showrooms can't be safely installed in most houses wired before 1985. These fixtures are clearly labeled with a warning that reads "For supply connections, use wire rated for at least 90 degrees C." The reason is simple: Fixtures with this label generate enough heat to damage the insulation on older wires and cause a fire hazard. Wires manufactured after 1985 are required to have coverings that can withstand the higher temperature.

If you know your wiring was installed before 1985, don't use fixtures requiring 90-degree–rated supply wires. To confirm that you have 90-degree–rated supply wire, look at the cable jacket or wire insulation. If you have plastic-sheathed cable (often referred to as Romex), look for the letters NM-B or UF-B printed on the plastic sheath. If your wiring is fed through conduit, look on the wire insulation for the letters THHN or THWN-2. If you're still unsure, either call an electrician or choose a fixture that isn't labeled with a supply wire temperature requirement

Heavy fixtures require strong boxes

If you choose a heavy light fixture (the one we bought weighed in at a hefty 25 lbs.), check your electrical box to make sure it will support the weight. The National Electrical Code (NEC) allows you to hang up to 50 lbs. from any electrical box that is threaded to accept No. 8-32 machine

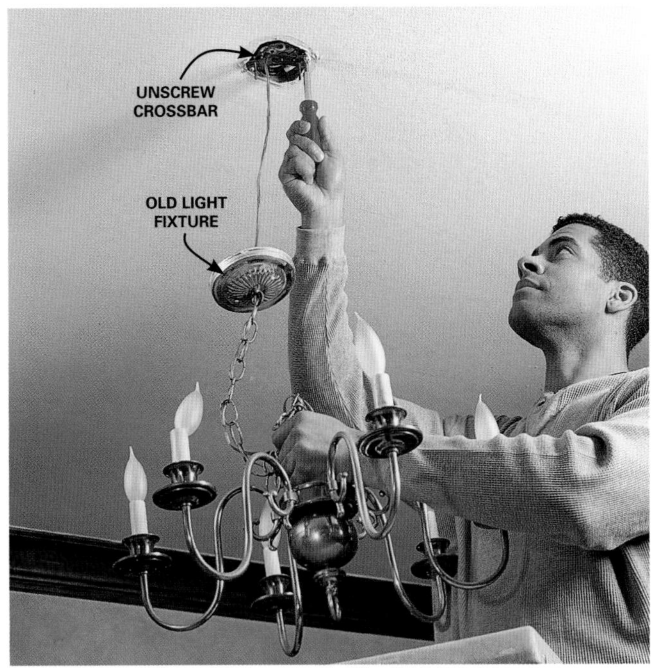

1 Turn off the power to the light fixture at the main circuit panel. Remove the nut or screws securing the dome-shaped canopy and lower it. Then remove the screws securing the crossbar to the electrical box and lower the fixture.

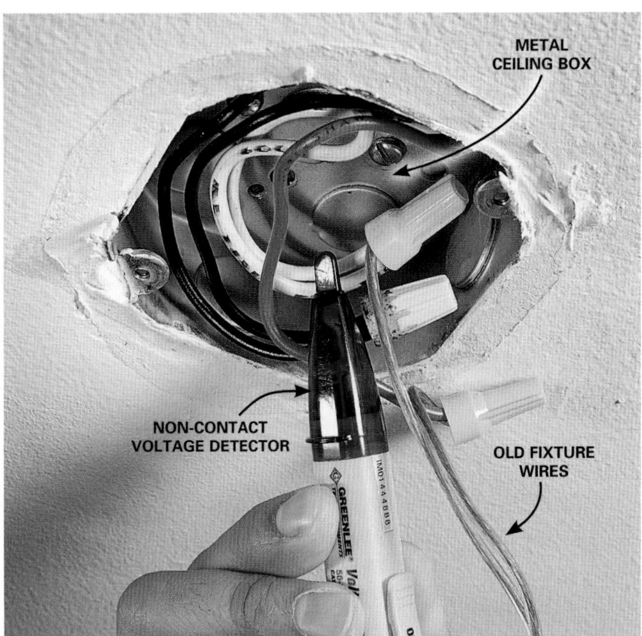

2 Test the wires to make sure the power is off. Move the tip of a non-contact voltage detector near each wire to make sure the power to all wires in the box is turned off (make sure the light switch is turned on). If the tester lights, switch off circuit breakers or loosen fuses one at a time until the tester light goes off. Disconnect the wires from the light fixture. Leave other wires connected and tucked into the electrical box.

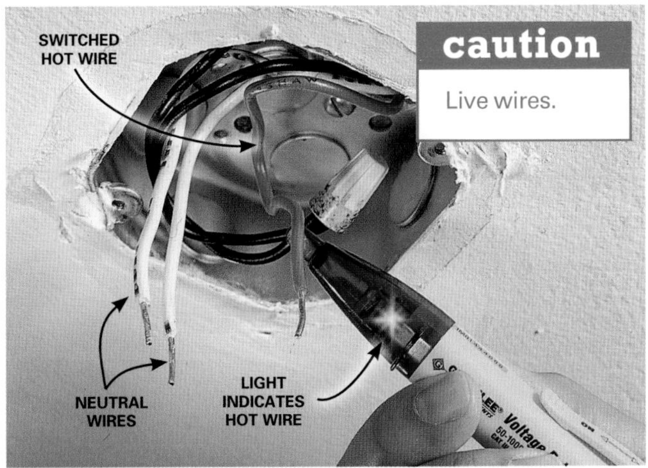

3 **TEST FOR GROUND: STEP 1**. Turn the power to the light back on at the main circuit panel (the light switch is still on). Use the non-contact tester again to make sure there is power to the colored (hot) wire.

Calculating box sizes

To figure the minimum box size required by the National Electrical Code, add: 1 for each hot and neutral wire entering the box, 1 for all the ground wires combined, 1 for all the clamps combined, and 2 for each device (switch or receptacle, but usually not light fixtures) installed in the box. Multiply this figure by 2 for 14-gauge wire and 2.25 for 12-gauge wire to get the minimum box volume in cubic inches. Plastic boxes have the volume stamped inside.

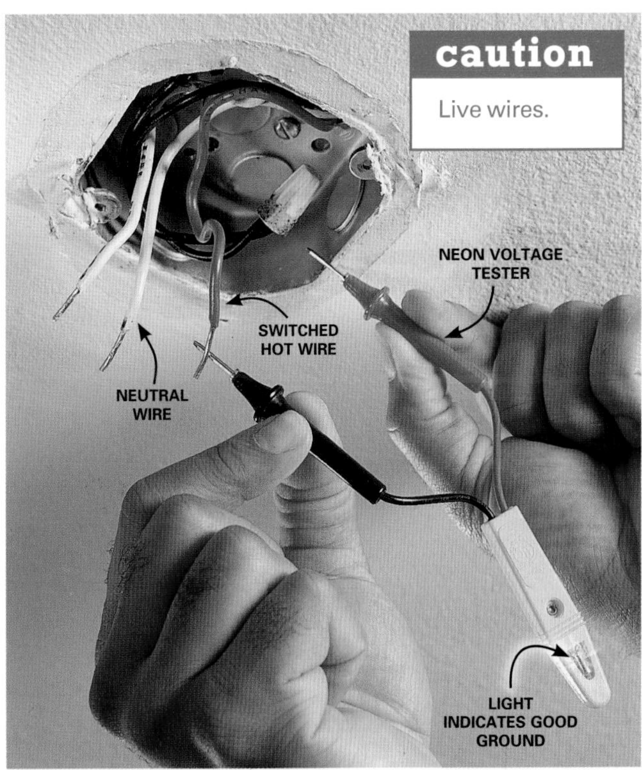

4 **TEST FOR GROUND: STEP 2.** Touch the leads of a neon voltage tester between the hot wire and the metal box (or between the hot wire and bare copper ground wire if you have one). If the tester lights, the metal box or bare copper wire is grounded and you can proceed. If the tester doesn't light, indicating there is no ground, call in a licensed electrician to supply one. (It's often difficult.) Turn off the power at the main circuit panel before continuing.

Figure A

Whether your light fixture is held to the box with screws or a threaded pipe, the two mounting systems shown here, the key to an easy installation is assembling and adjusting the parts before you crawl up on the ladder. To do this, first thread the screws or pipe through the crossbar. Then, while the fixture is still on the ground, line up the crossbar with the top of the canopy and adjust the screws or pipe in or out until about 1/4 to 1/2 in. is protruding through the canopy. Mount the crossbar to the electrical box, then connect the wires and finally the fixture.

Mounting with screws and cap nuts

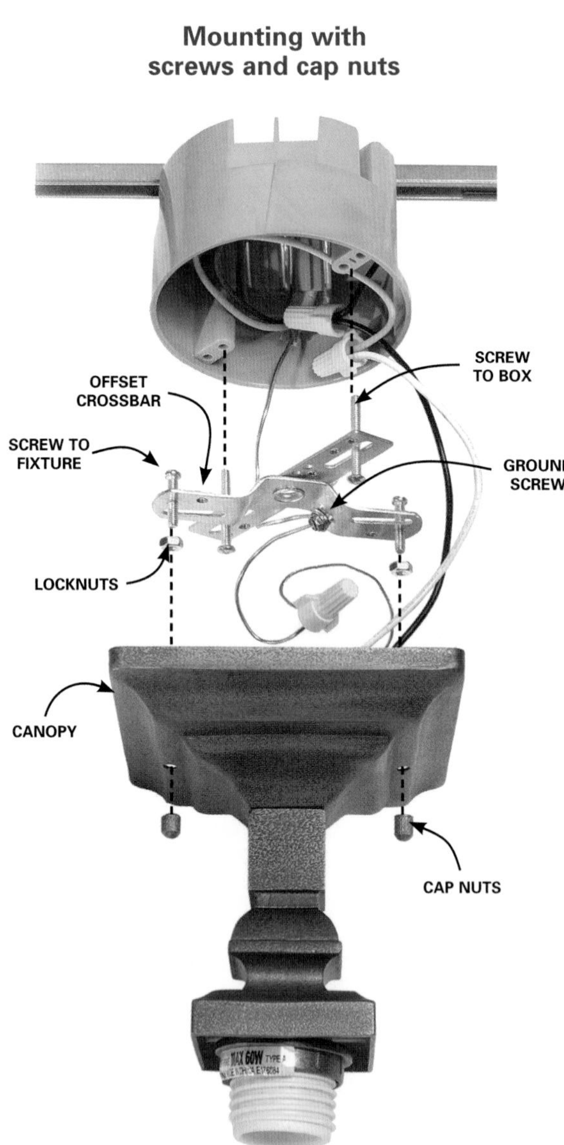

Mounting with a threaded pipe

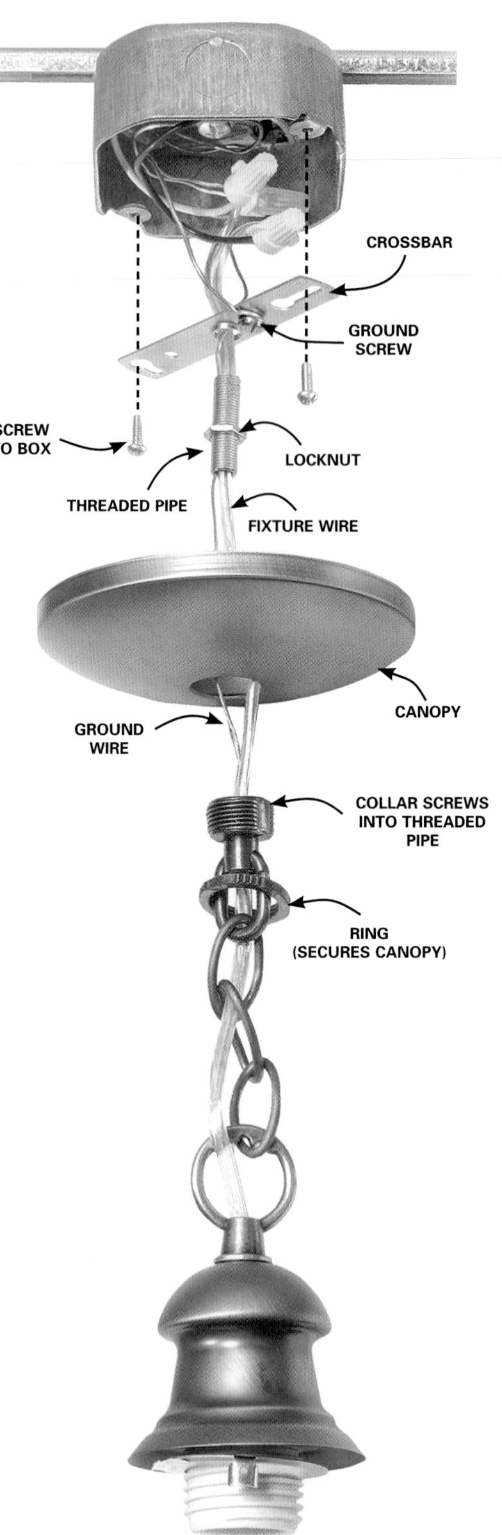

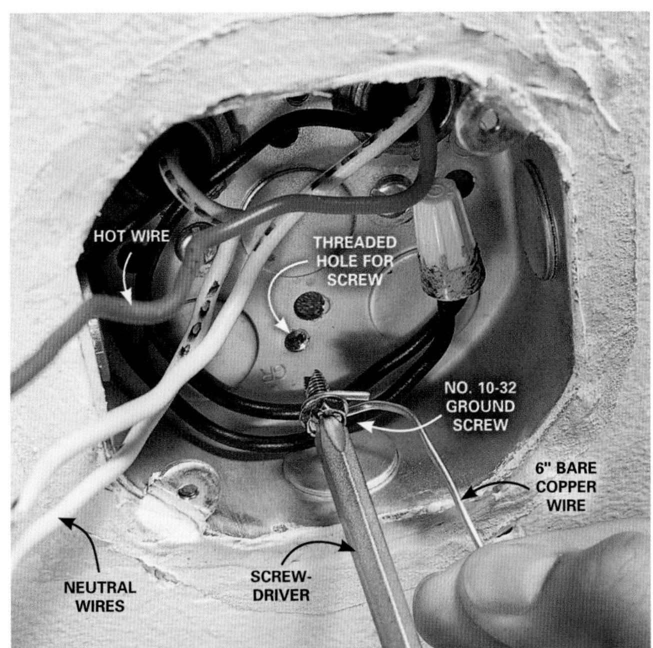

5 Attach a ground wire to the metal box if it's not already present. Wrap the end of a 6-in. length of bare copper wire around a No. 10-32 ground screw and drive it into the threaded hole in the bottom of the box. Wrap the wire at least three-quarters of the way around the screw in a clockwise direction. Tighten the screw to secure the ground wire.

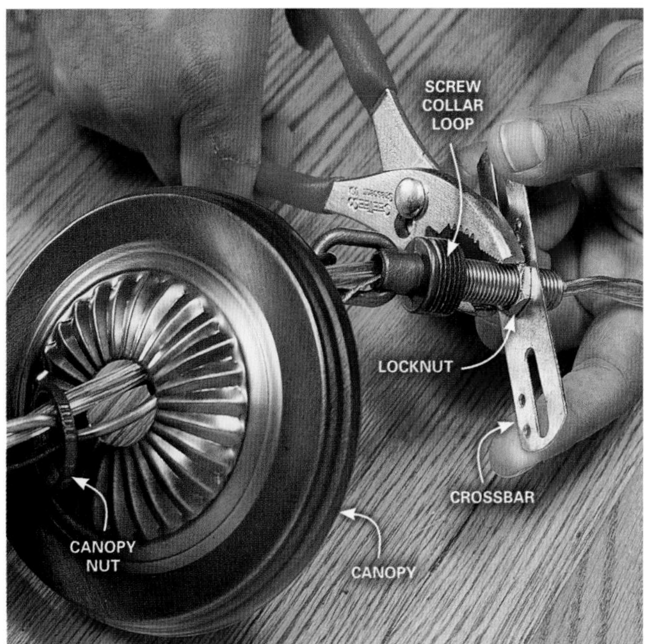

6 Preassemble the mounting strap assembly. Align the back of the canopy (the side that fits against the ceiling) with the crossbar and adjust the length of the pipe until about 3/8 in. of the threads on the screw collar loop extend through the canopy. Lock the threaded pipe in this position by tightening the locknut against the crossbar.

caution

If you have aluminum wiring, don't work on it yourself. The connections require special techniques. Call in a licensed pro who's certified to work with it. For more information, go to cpsc.gov and search for "aluminum wiring."

screws for attaching the crossbar (**Figure A**). This includes almost every type of ceiling box. For practical purposes, make sure your electrical box is securely fastened to solid framing before you hang a new light fixture from it. If your light fixture weighs more than 50 lbs., it has to be supported independent of the electrical box. An easy solution is to install a fan brace box that's designed to be installed without cutting any additional holes in your ceiling. Check the label to make sure the box is designed to support more than 35 lbs.

Most ceiling boxes are large enough

The NEC dictates how many wires and clamps you can safely put in an electrical box. Typical 1-1/2 to 2-in. deep octagonal or round ceiling boxes are quite large and overcrowding is rarely a problem. Even so, you should run through the calculations to be sure. See "Calculating Box Sizes," p. 73. But if you encounter a round box that's only 1/2 in. deep, replace it. Once again, the easiest way to install a new electrical box in an existing ceiling is to use a special fan brace and box made for retrofitting.

Ground the light fixture to avoid dangerous electrical shocks

Because most light fixtures are metal or have exposed metal parts, they need to have an equipment ground to be safe. First you have to make sure a grounding means is available (Photos 3 and 4). If your house is wired with plastic-sheathed cable with a bare copper ground wire, you're probably covered, but test it to be sure, using the same procedure we're using to test the metal box. Once you've determined that a ground exists, it's simply a matter of making sure that all the metal parts—electrical box, fixture-mounting strap and light fixture—are securely connected to the ground (Photos 5 and 8). If your crossbar doesn't have a threaded hole for a ground screw, connect a ground wire to it with a special grounding clip.

Make sure you get the polarity right

The two lamp cord wires on many hanging light fixtures are hard to tell apart. However, it's critical to correctly identify the neutral wire and connect it to the neutral wire(s) in the box. Connecting it to the hot wire will energize the threaded bulb socket and create a potential shock hazard.

Reduce overhead work by preassembling parts on the ground

You'll save time and aching arms by assembling and adjusting the mounting hardware before you climb the ladder. The photos on Figure A show the two most common mounting systems. In either case, the trick is to thread the machine

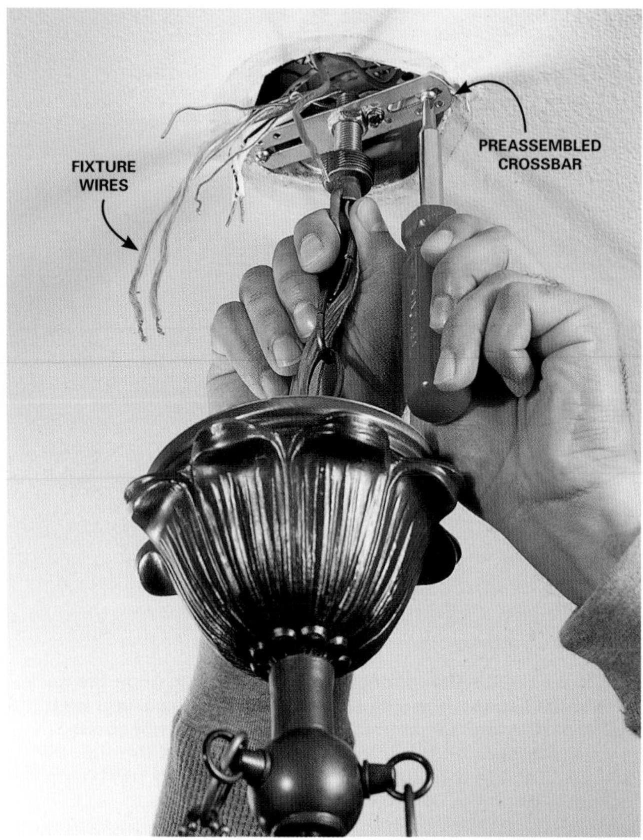

7 Position all the wires to one side of the crossbar. Then screw the crossbar to the electrical box with the screws. You'll need a helper to support the fixture while you do this.

screws or threaded rod into the crossbar first. Then slide the canopy over the screws or rod. Align the crossbar with the back of the canopy and adjust the length of the screws or rod to protrude about 1/4 to 3/8 in. through the canopy. Tighten the locknut(s) to hold the screws or rod in this position. For hanging fixtures, adjust the length of the chain by removing lengths, but don't cut the wires shorter until you've hung the fixture and confirmed that it's the right height.

Reconnect the same wires

After testing to make sure none of the wires in the box are hot (Photo 2), disconnect the hot, neutral and ground (if your old fixture has one) from your old fixture and leave other wires bundled in the box. Reconnect the new fixture to these same wires (Photo 8). If the old wires have twisted or damaged ends, cut them off and remove 1/2 in. of the insulated covering with a wire-stripping tool. Connect the wires from the new fixture with appropriately sized wire connectors. Read the packaging to determine the correct size. When you connect stranded fixture wire to solid wire, extend the stranded end about 1/8 in. beyond the solid wire before you twist on the wire connector. Stranded wire occasionally clogs the threads in a connector, preventing a tight grip. Discard the connector and use a new one if it spins freely without tightening.

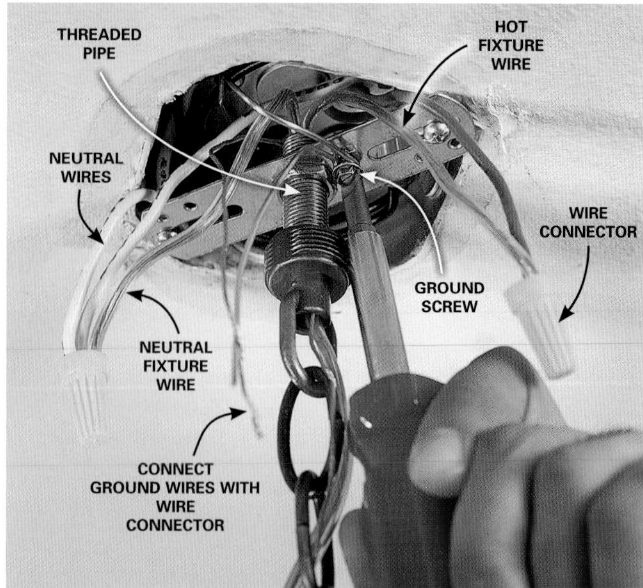

8 Connect the neutral wire from the light fixture to the neutral white wire(s) in the box. If your fixture is wired with lamp-style cord rather than white (neutral) and black (hot) wires, identify the neutral wire by looking for silver conductors, printing, squared corners, or ribs or indentations on the insulation. The unmarked wire is the hot wire. Connect it to the colored (usually black or red) hot wire in the box. Complete the hook-up by looping the ground wire clockwise around the ground screw on the crossbar, tightening the screw, and connecting the end of the wire to the ground wire from the light fixture.

9 Fold the conductors into the ceiling box and slide the canopy over the protruding threaded support. Secure it with the decorative nut to complete the installation.

Complete the installation by installing the canopy (Photo 9). If it doesn't fit tight to the ceiling, readjust the screws or threaded rod. Add light bulbs, switch on the power and turn on the switch to check out your work.

How to reset a circuit breaker

You probably know how to reset a circuit breaker, but what about your kids or the baby-sitter? Use this tutorial to show them how.

The electrical panel

You'll usually find the main circuit breaker panel—a gray, metal box—in a utility room, garage or basement. Don't worry about opening the panel's door. All the dangerous stuff is behind another steel cover. Behind the door is the main breaker for the entire house (usually at the top of the panel) and two rows of other breakers below it, each controlling individual circuits.

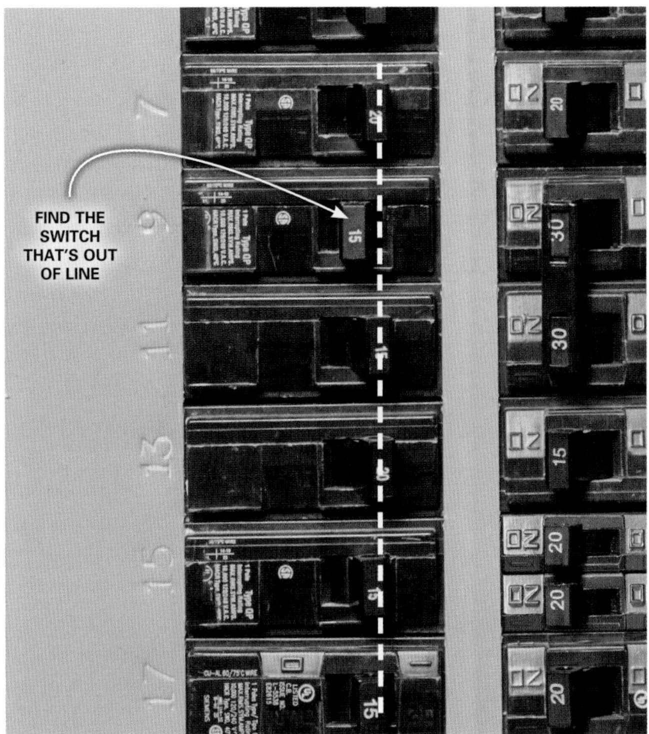

1 FIND THE TRIPPED BREAKER When a breaker trips (shuts off), it's usually because too many things were running on one circuit at the same time and it got overloaded. So if you're running one or more high-amperage appliances like hair dryers, toasters or space heaters, and the breaker trips, just shut off the devices and reset the breaker.

But if the breaker trips for no apparent reason, there may be a short circuit—a much bigger problem, usually best left to an electrician to figure out. A tripped breaker isn't always easy to spot. If you're lucky, there will be a list of circuits on the back of the panel's door and you'll be able to find the tripped one quickly (sometimes those lists are labeled wrong, however). If not, you'll have to find it by eye. Look for a partially tripped breaker that's about halfway between the "off" and "on" positions (see photo above). Avoid the temptation to switch off and on all the breakers, or you'll find yourself resetting electronic devices like clocks around the house or losing work underway on computers. You could even damage delicate electronics.

2 RESET THE BREAKER To reset a breaker, move the switch all the way to its "off" position, then back to "on" (see photos). You might hear a few beeps from smoke detectors and appliances when you turn the power back on, but that's normal. You're good to go!

3 types of breakers

You're likely to see switches for three different types of circuit breakers in a panel—single pole, double pole and "tandem." Single-pole breakers feed 120-volt circuits for ceiling lights and most wall outlets, while double-pole breakers feed 240-volt circuits for appliances like electric ranges and central air conditioning systems. "Tandem" breakers also have two switches. They take a single slot inside the circuit breaker panel and turn it into two 120-volt circuits to save space.

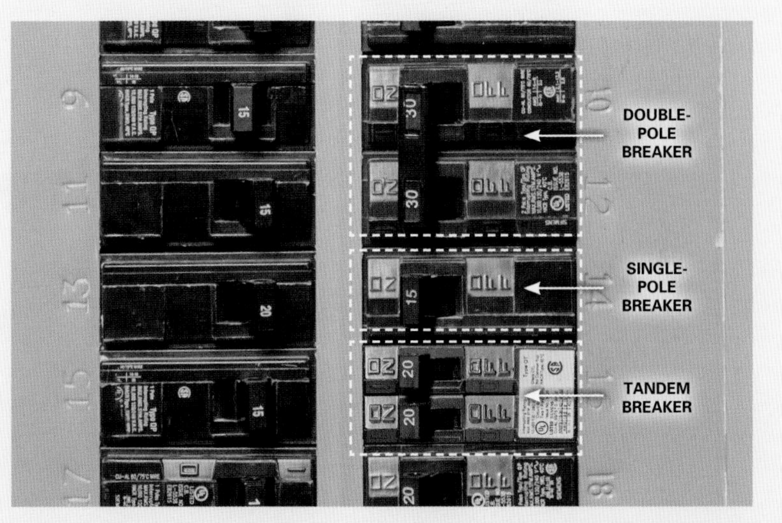

Super easy USB outlet

Besides the tangled mess they create, bulky chargers devour outlet space. For a clean solution, add a USB wall outlet at a more convenient height than a typical wall outlet. Doing this is fast and easy if you place the new USB outlet in the same cavity as an existing outlet. Then you won't have to cut into walls to run cable through studs.

What you'll need

This a great project for electrical beginners, and everything you need is available at a home center. If you don't own any electrical tools, expect to spend about $15 on the basics.

Before you shop, determine whether your cable is 12- or 14- gauge; you'll need the same size cable for your new outlet. For reference, 12-gauge wire is about the thickness of a nickel, and 14-gauge is about the thickness of a dime.

The new junction box you'll use is called an "old work" box. It mounts on drywall and doesn't need to be fastened to a stud. We chose a "two-gang" box that allows for a second outlet. It also requires a larger hole in the wall, which makes feeding cable into the existing box much easier.

Outlets with USB ports come in various configurations and cost $15 to $30 at home centers. For a wider selection, shop online.

To comply with electrical code changes, you may have to buy an AFCI outlet ($30) to replace the existing outlet. Ours is protected by an AFCI circuit breaker.

Getting started

USB ports don't draw much power, so you can add a USB outlet to any

You may need a larger junction box

Electrical codes contain strict rules about how many wires, connectors, switches and outlets can go in a junction box. Since you're adding wires, your existing box may not be large enough according to code. To see the formula, go to familyhandyman.com and search for "adding a receptacle." For help installing a larger box, search for "crowded electrical box."

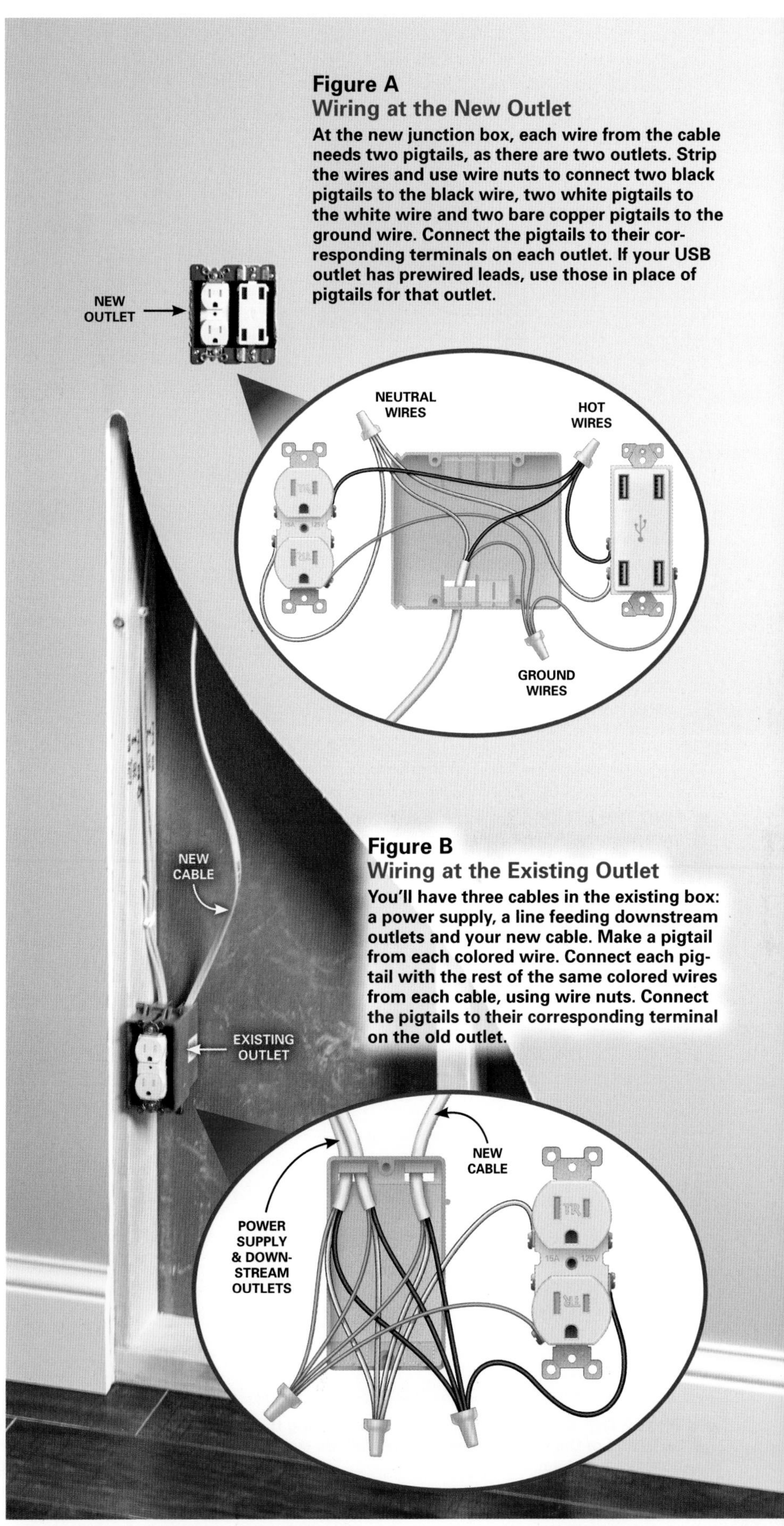

Figure A
Wiring at the New Outlet

At the new junction box, each wire from the cable needs two pigtails, as there are two outlets. Strip the wires and use wire nuts to connect two black pigtails to the black wire, two white pigtails to the white wire and two bare copper pigtails to the ground wire. Connect the pigtails to their corresponding terminals on each outlet. If your USB outlet has prewired leads, use those in place of pigtails for that outlet.

Figure B
Wiring at the Existing Outlet

You'll have three cables in the existing box: a power supply, a line feeding downstream outlets and your new cable. Make a pigtail from each colored wire. Connect each pigtail with the rest of the same colored wires from each cable, using wire nuts. Connect the pigtails to their corresponding terminal on the old outlet.

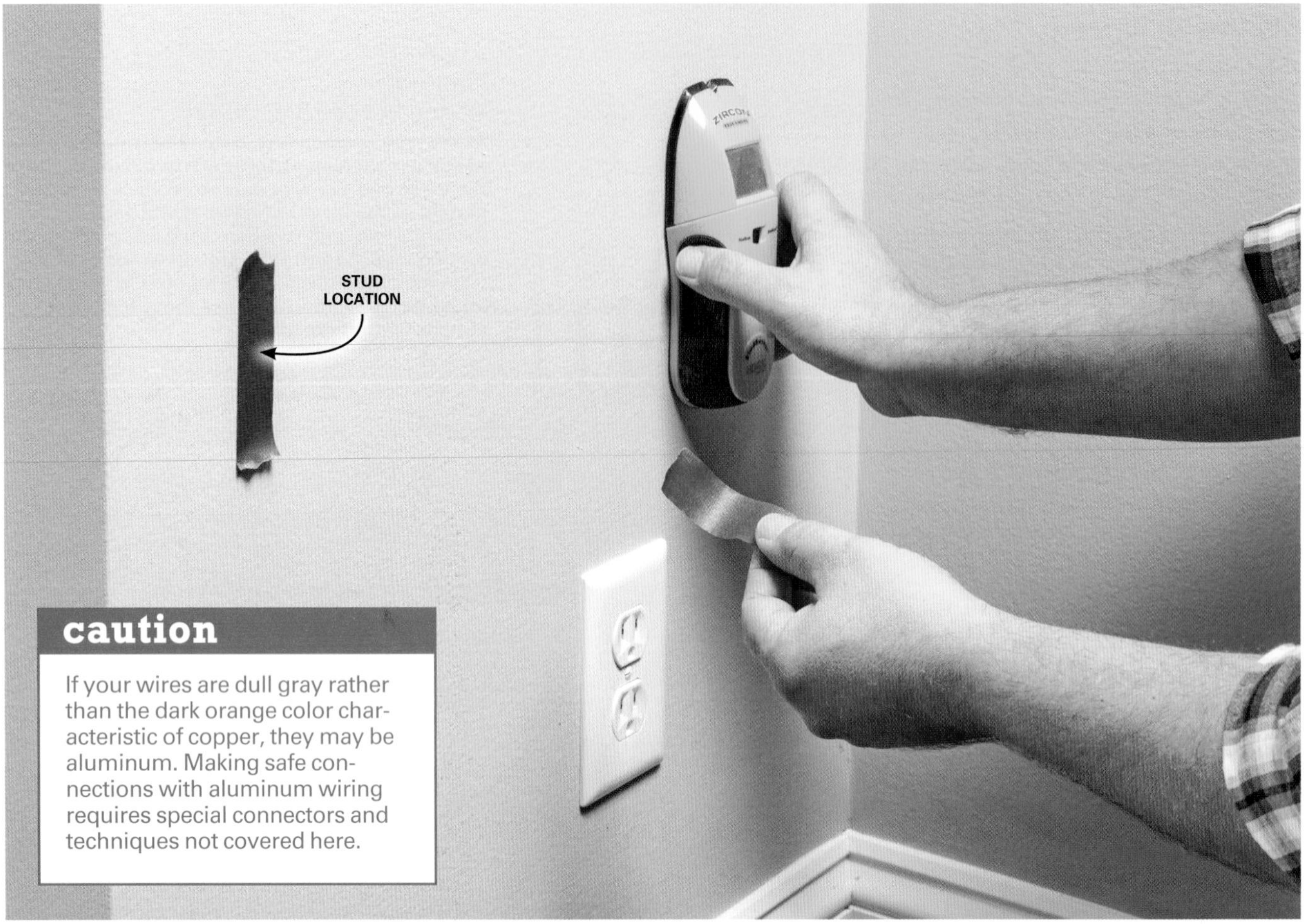

STUD LOCATION

caution

If your wires are dull gray rather than the dark orange color characteristic of copper, they may be aluminum. Making safe connections with aluminum wiring requires special connectors and techniques not covered here.

1 FIND THE STUDS Locate the studs with a stud finder and mark them with tape. You can place the new outlet anywhere between the studs.

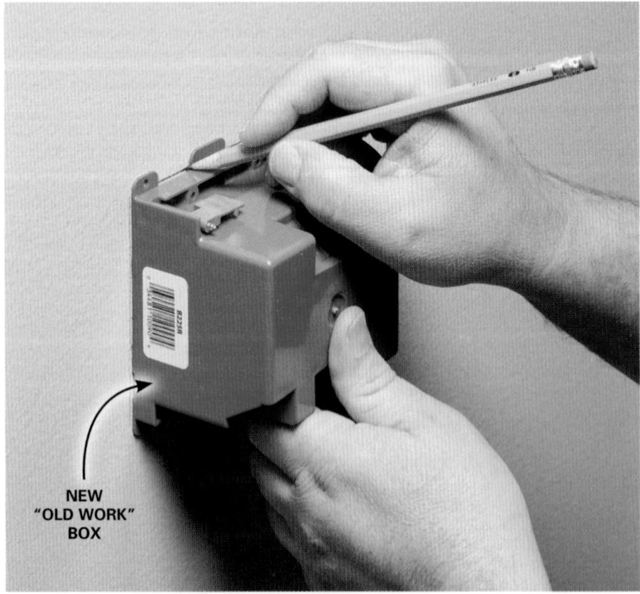

2 TRACE THE BOX Mark the cutout while holding the open end of the new box against the wall. Be sure to hold the box level.

3 CUT THE HOLE Stab a drywall saw into the wall and cut along your marks. Test-fit the box and enlarge the hole slightly if needed.

existing outlet except a switched outlet or a dedicated outlet for an appliance, such as a stove or refrigerator.

Once you've chosen your power source outlet, switch off the breaker for that circuit. Then use a noncontact voltage tester to verify that the power is off.

Install the box and cable

Locate the two studs that flank the existing outlet (Photo 1) and find a good position in the wall cavity for the new outlet. Hold the new "old work" box in place against the wall, making sure it's plumb and level, and then trace around it (Photo 2).

Cut the hole as accurately as possible (Photo 3). An "old work" box relies on a snug fit in the cutout for stability, as it's not attached to a stud. If your new outlet is on an exterior wall, use a box that maintains the vapor seal to keep out drafts.

Disconnect the old outlet and then feed the new cable to the existing box. Don't skimp on cable; a little extra inside the wall is good, and you'll trim the ends when you're ready to make the connections. Run cable into the new box, and then mount the box to the wall (Photo 4).

Connect the wires and receptacles in both boxes (Photo 5 and Figures A and B). Mount the outlets, reinstall the faceplates, turn the power back on and test the outlets.

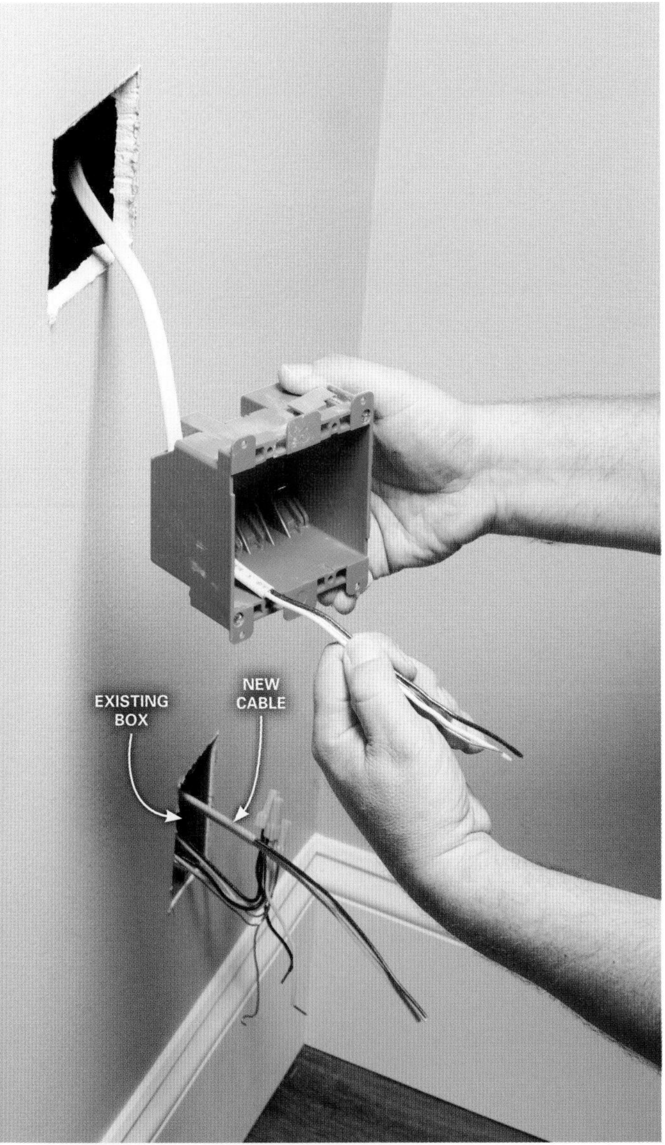

4 RUN THE CABLE **Reach inside the wall and feed the cable into the existing box. Then feed the cable into the new box and install it.**

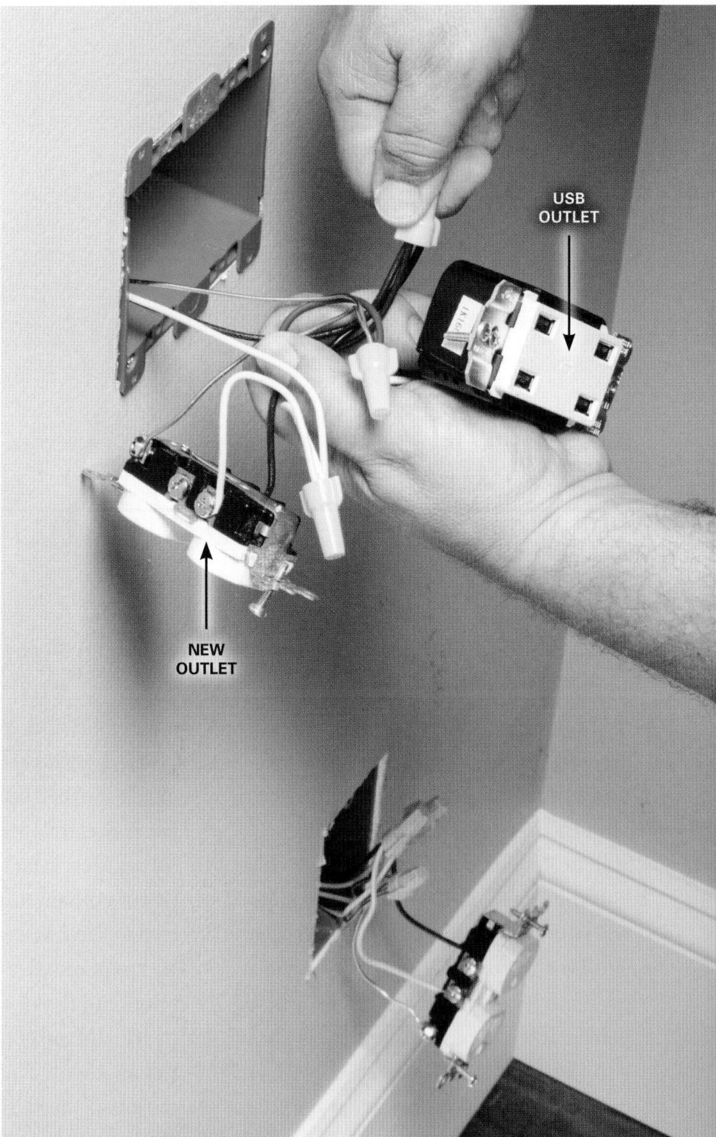

5 MAKE THE CONNECTIONS **Reconnect the outlet at the power source and connect the new outlets. Our USB outlet came with lead wires. Yours may have terminal screws like those on standard outlets.**

Pro tips for troubleshooting a dead outlet

When an outlet goes dead, it's easy to jump to conclusions and assume the worst. But more often than not, the problem is something simple, and you can save the cost of a service call just by taking a few steps to trace the cause. Don't worry if you're not comfortable doing electrical work. Better than half the time you'll solve the problem without even lifting a tool. We'll show you how to start your search for the problem by checking in the most likely places. If that doesn't work, we'll show you where to look for loose connections that may be to blame, and how to fix them. Of course, there will always be problems that are best left to an electrician. But if you take these steps first, there's a good chance you'll find the solution.

1 First, see if other outlets are dead

Before you head for the circuit breakers, take a few minutes to check if other outlets, lights or appliances are affected. Switch lights on and off and test nearby outlets for power (use a voltage tester or plug in a lamp to test the outlets). Unplug lamps and appliances from dead outlets to eliminate the possibility that a short or overload from one of them is causing the problem. Note the location of dead outlets or mark them with a piece of masking tape so you'll be able to find them again after you've turned off the power.

Replace burned-out fuses

Look inside the fuse for charred glass or a broken filament—evidence of a blown fuse. Unscrew the suspect fuse and replace it with one of the same type and amperage.

2 Check the circuit breakers

After you unplug all the devices from the dead outlets, the next step is to check for a tripped circuit breaker or blown fuse. You'll find the circuit breakers or fuses in the main electrical panel, which is usually located near where the electrical wires enter the house. Garages, basements and laundry rooms are common locations. Locate the panel and open the metal door to reveal the fuses or circuit breakers. Photos 1 – 4 show a typical main panel and the process for resetting a tripped circuit breaker. Remember to turn off your computer before you switch the circuit breakers on and off.

Tripped circuit breakers aren't always apparent. If you don't see a tripped breaker, firmly press every breaker to the "off" position (Photo 3).Then switch them back on. If the tripped breaker won't reset without tripping again, there could be a potentially dangerous short circuit or ground fault condition. Switch the circuit breaker off until you've located the problem. In most cases, a tripped circuit breaker is caused by a temporary overload on the circuit or a short circuit in some device plugged into the circuit. But in rare cases, a loose wire in an electrical box could be causing the problem. Follow the photos in Step 4 to look for and repair loose connections.

pro tip

A radio is a great tool for checking circuits. Crank up the volume and plug it in. At the circuit breaker box, you'll be able to hear whether the circuit is on or off.

1 Locate the circuit breaker box (or fuse box) and open the door to search for tripped circuit breakers.

2 Locate tripped breakers by looking for breaker handles that aren't lined up with the rest. Last, push the breaker handles toward the "on" position. Tripped breakers will "give" a little rather than feel solid.

3 The first step in resetting a tripped breaker is to switch it off. Don't just flick the handle; press the handle firmly to the "off" position. You should hear a click.

4 Finally, reset the breaker by pushing the handle firmly to "on." It should line up with all the rest. If it "pops" back to the tripped position, there's a problem in the wiring or in something that's plugged into the circuit.

3 Check the GFCIs

GFCI (short for "ground fault circuit interrupter") outlets, those unusual outlets with the test and reset buttons, are required in areas of the house where shock hazards are greatest. They protect against deadly electrical shocks by sensing leaks in the electrical current and immediately tripping to shut off the power. But it's easy to overlook a tripped GFCI as the source of a dead outlet problem. That's because in areas where GFCI-protected outlets are required, electricians often save money by connecting additional standard outlets to one GFCI outlet. A current leak at any one of the outlets will trip the GFCI and cause all of the outlets connected to it to go dead. These GFCI-protected outlets are supposed to be labeled (Photo 1), but the label often falls off.

Look for GFCIs in bathrooms, kitchens, basements, garages and on the home's exterior. Test and reset every GFCI you find (Photo 2). If the GFCI "reset" button doesn't pop out when you press the "test" button, there may be no power to the GFCI or you may have a bad GFCI. On the other hand, if the "reset" button trips again every time you press it, there may be a dangerous current leak somewhere on the circuit. In either case, solving the problem requires additional electrical testing that we won't cover here. Refer to other electrical repair manuals or call an electrician for help. If resetting all of the GFCIs didn't power up your dead outlet, then the last resort is to look for loose connections.

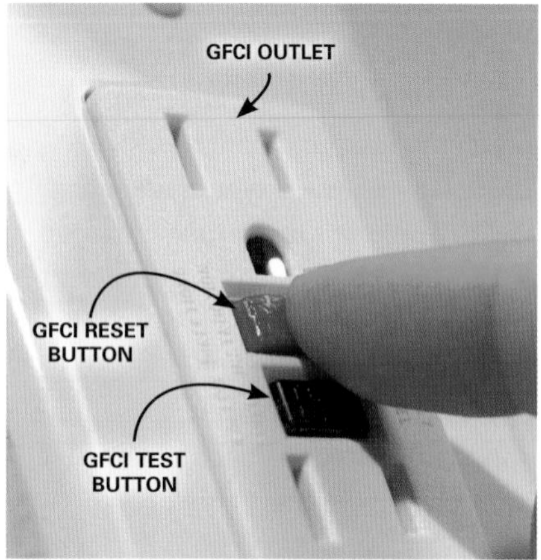

4 Still no power? Look for a bad connection

If checking the breakers and resetting the GFCIs haven't restored power to the outlet, the next step, without getting into circuit testing, is to remove the outlet from the box and look for loose connections.

We'll show you three common types of loose connections: loose terminal screws, loose stab-in connections, and loose wires at wire connectors. You may find one or more of these when you remove your outlet and look in the electrical box.

Loose or broken wires

The first problem we show is a loose connection under the outlet's terminal screw. In Photo 2, you can see the charred outlet and melted wire insulation that are a result of heat generated by the loose connection. These telltale signs aren't always present, though, which is why you should double-check the connections by gently bending each wire to see if it moves under the screw.

1 **First make sure all computers are turned off and everyone in the house knows you'll be turning off the power. Then switch off the main circuit breaker. Keep a flashlight handy because all the lights will go out.**

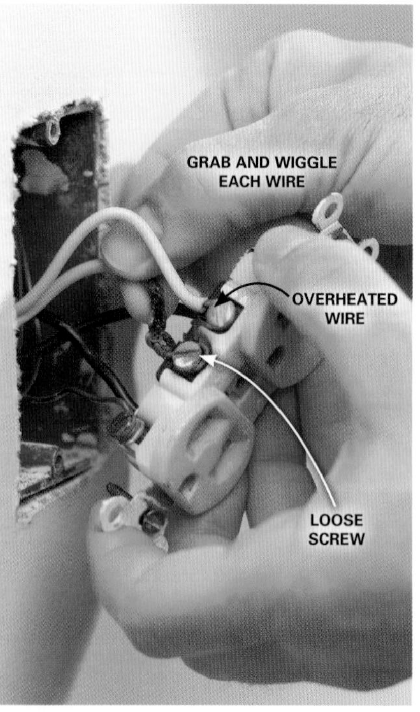

2 **Inspect the screw terminals for broken or loose wires. Carefully bend the wire at each screw terminal to see if it's loose (it will turn under the screw or the screw will move). Also look for broken, burned or corroded wires or screws.**

If you do discover a loose connection at an outlet, whether it's at the screw terminal or a stab-in connection, we recommend replacing the outlet with a new one. That's because loose connections almost always create excess heat that could damage the outlet and lead to future problems. Photo 3 shows how to install a new outlet.

If the outlet you're replacing is wired like the one shown in Photo 2, with pairs of hot and neutral wires (wires under all four screws), connect the pairs of like-colored wires along with a third 6-in. length of wire, called a pigtail, under one wire connector (Photo 2). Then connect the loose end of each pigtail to the appropriate outlet screw.

This method reduces the chance that a loose connection under a screw will cause a problem with other outlets on the circuit.

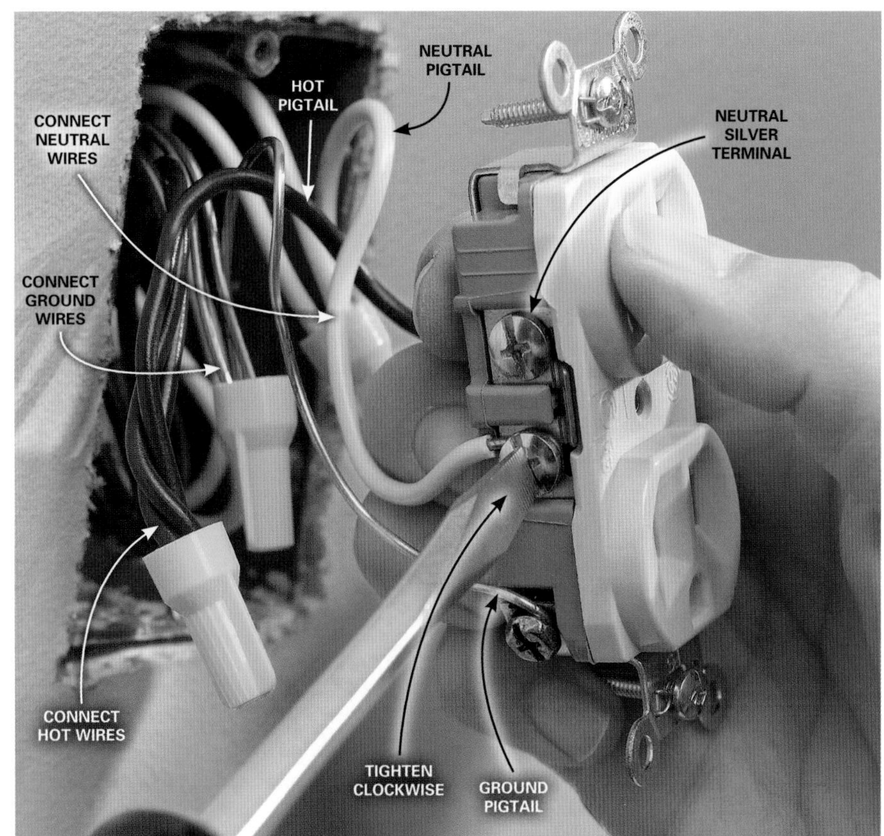

3 **Install a new outlet by bending a loop in the ends of the hot, neutral and ground wires. Connect the hot (black) wire to the brass screw, the neutral white wire to the silver screw and the ground wire to the green ground screw. Loop the wires clockwise around the screws and tighten.**

caution

If you have aluminum wiring, don't mess with it! Call in a licensed pro who's certified to work with it. This wiring is dull gray, not the dull orange that's characteristic of copper.

Loose wires at the stab-in connections

As a timesaver for electricians, some outlets can be wired by pressing stripped wires into holes on the back of the outlet. This wiring method is allowed by the electrical code, but it isn't good practice since these stab-in connections can loosen over time and cause problems. Look for these stab-in connections as you troubleshoot your dead outlet. Tug each wire to check for loose connections. If you find loose stab-in connections, don't just reinsert the wire. Instead, cut and strip the end of the wire and connect it to the screw terminal on the side of the outlet. Or better yet, cut and strip all of the wires and connect them to a new outlet (Photo 3).

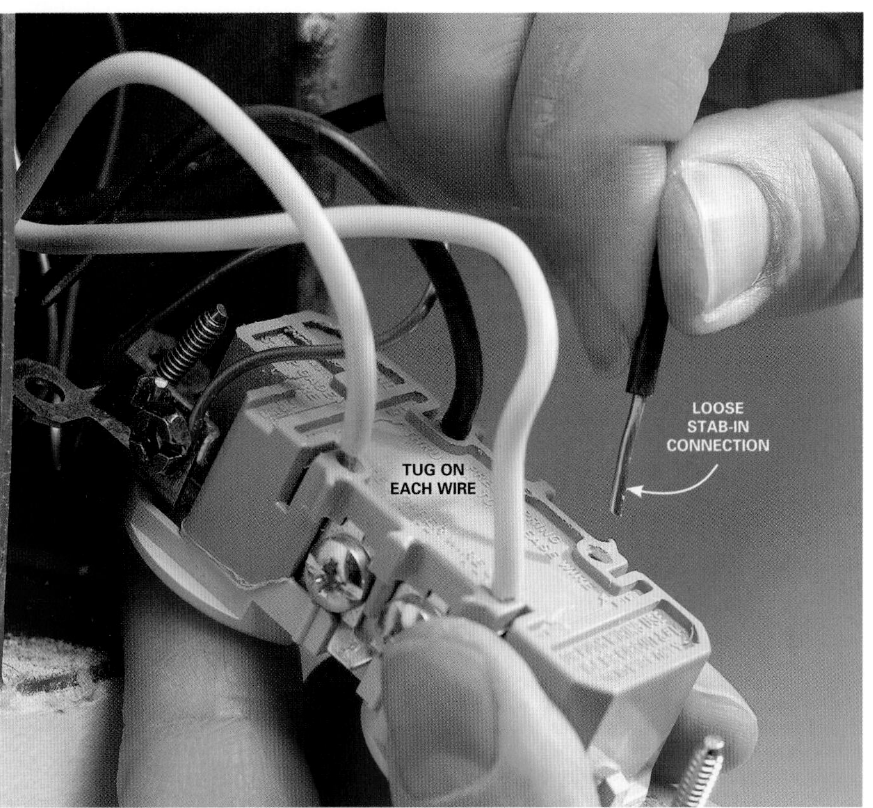

Check wire connections for loose wires

A wire that's come loose from a wire connector is another problem that can cause a dead outlet. Follow the steps in Photos 1 and 2 to find and fix this type of loose connection. If you don't find any loose connections in this box and are still anxious to pursue the problem, expand your search to other outlets in the vicinity (start with the ones you marked earlier with masking tape). Make sure to turn off the main circuit breaker (Photo 1, p. 84) when you're checking for loose connections.

When you're done looking for loose connections, reinstall the outlets and switch the main circuit breaker back on. Now test the outlets again to see if you've solved the problem. If you still have dead outlets, it's time to call an electrician.

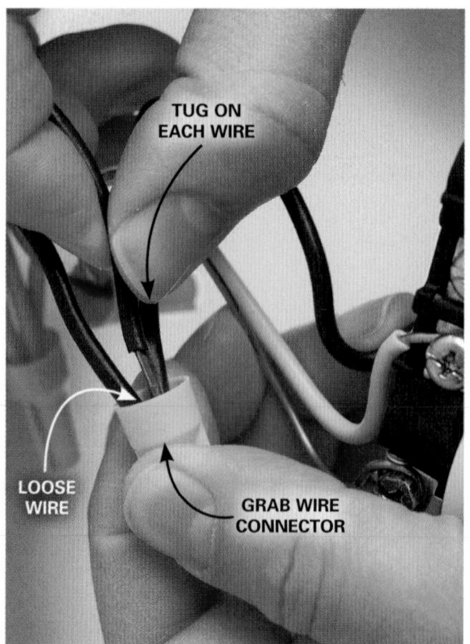

1 Grab the wire connector. Tug on each wire in the bundle to see if any are loose. If you discover a loose wire, remove the wire connector. Cut and strip all the wires in the bundle to expose 1/2 in. to 3/4 in. of fresh copper wire (check the instructions on the wire connector container for the exact stripping length).

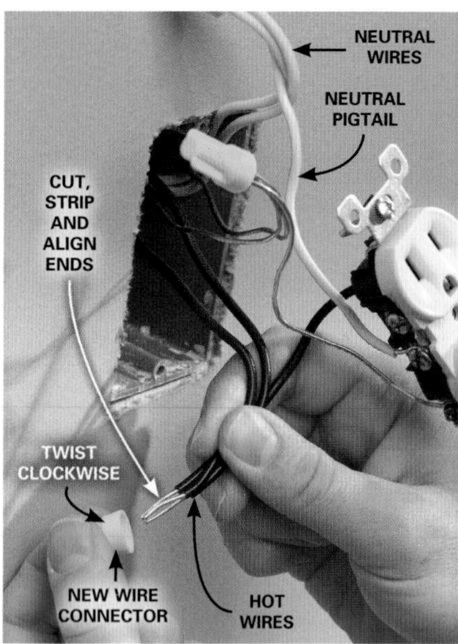

2 Gather the wires, making sure their ends are lined up, and twist on a new wire connector. Twist clockwise. Match the connector to the number of wires by reading the label on the wire connector packaging.

Replace smoke alarms

If the smoke alarms in your house are 10 years old or more, it's time to replace them. To get started, remove each alarm from its mounting plate. Most alarms have arrows that tell you which way to rotate the alarm for removal. You may have to use both hands and twist hard.

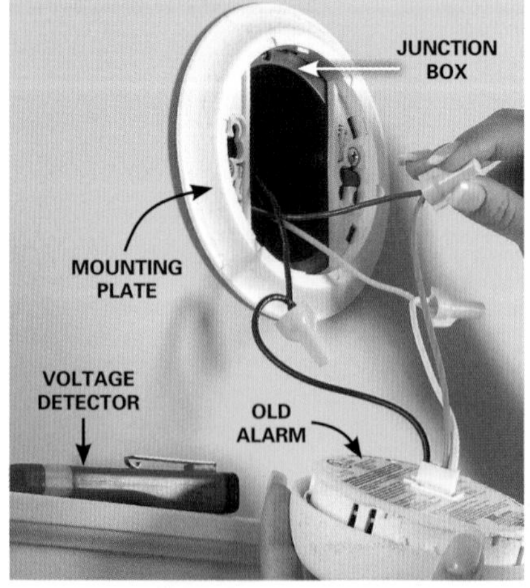

1 Turn the power off. Remove the alarm and use a non-contact voltage detector to check the wires to make sure the power is off. Disconnect the wires and unscrew the mounting plate from the junction box.

If you find that your alarms are connected to wires, don't be intimidated. Replacing a "hard-wired" alarm is easy. If your old alarms are connected to three wires as shown here, that means the alarms are interconnected—when one alarm detects smoke, they all howl. To ensure that your new alarms will work together, buy alarms of a single brand and model and replace them all. You'll also need a non-contact voltage detector (Photo 1) and a wire strippers.

Turn off the power at the main electrical panel and disconnect the old alarm (Photo 1). Check to make sure the power is off with your voltage tester. If the wires aren't connected as shown here (with each wire connected to another of the same color), make a simple sketch so you can connect the new alarm the same way. Your old alarm may be connected to two wires instead of three. Your new alarm will have a third "interconnect" wire (usually red or orange), but leave it unconnected if the old alarm had just two connections. Check the manufacturer's instructions for other details. Write a replacement date (when it's 10 years old) on the alarm's back or mounting plate. Turn the power back on and push the alarm's test button. If you connected three wires to each alarm, they should all sound at the same time.

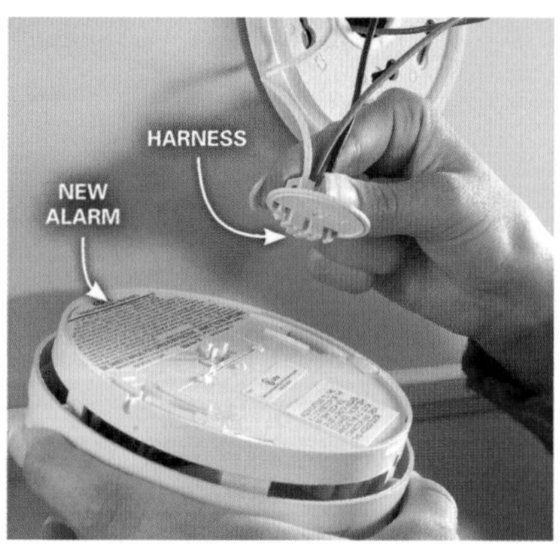

2 Screw the new mounting plate to the junction box and connect the wires. Plug the harness into the new alarm, stuff the wires into the box and mount the alarm on the plate.

Replace a pull-chain light fixture

Pull-chain light fixtures are handy for basements and storage areas—until they quit working. The internal switch mechanism can wear out, or pulling too hard on the cord can snap the chain or completely pull it out of the fixture. Replacing the broken fixture is simple and inexpensive. Pull-chain fixtures are made from either plastic or porcelain, but we recommend the porcelain because it withstands heat better and lasts longer.

Before starting, flip the circuit breaker or pull the fuse to disconnect the power to the light, then test to make sure the power is off (Photo 1). Replace the broken fixture as shown in Photos 2 and 3. There may be an unused bare ground wire inside the electrical box. If it falls down while you're replacing the fixture, wrap it in a circle and push it up as far into the electrical box as possible.

caution

Turn off power at the main panel.

1 Turn off the power, remove the light bulb and unscrew the fixture from the electrical box. Pull the fixture down, but keep your hands away from the wires. Touch one voltage tester probe to the black wire, and the other to the white wire. If the voltage indicator doesn't light up, the power is off.

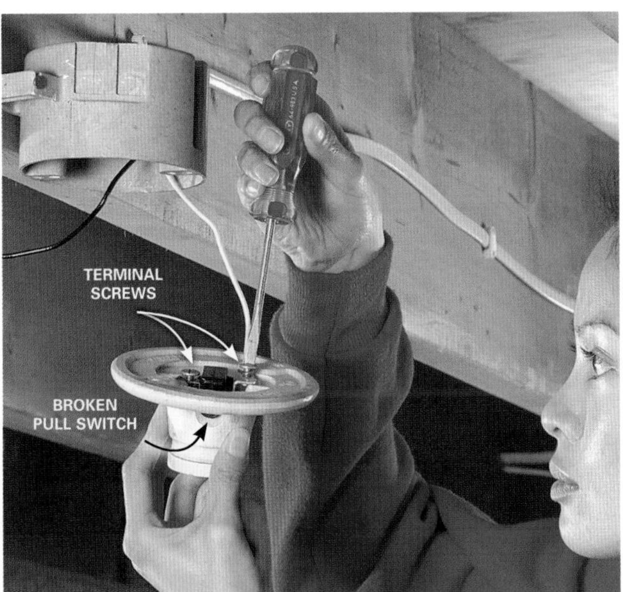

2 Loosen the terminal screws and unhook the wiring from the old fixture. If the wire ends are broken or corroded, strip off 3/4 in. of sheathing, and bend the bare wire end into a hook.

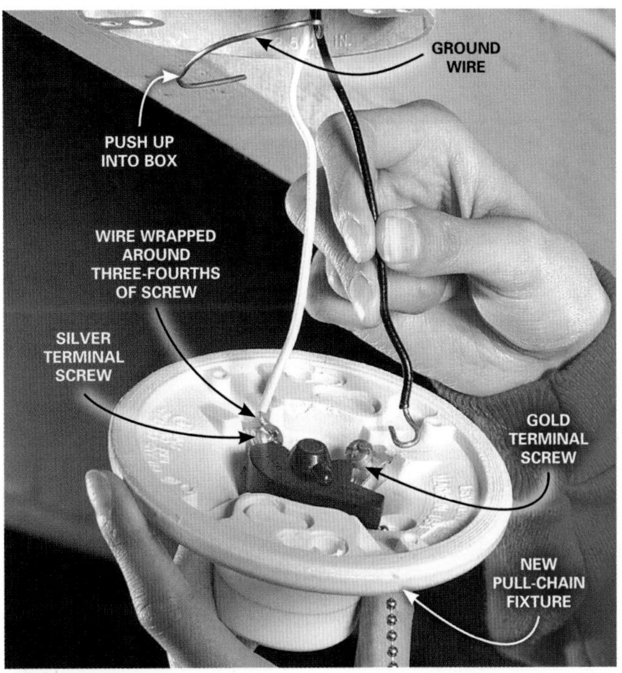

3 Attach the black wire to the gold terminal screw on the new fixture and the white wire to the silver terminal screw. Wrap the wires clockwise so they cover at least three-quarters of the terminal screws. Firmly tighten the screws so the copper wire compresses slightly. Twist the fixture to spiral the wires into the electrical box. Screw the new fixture to the box snugly, but don't overtighten it or the porcelain might crack.

caution

If you have aluminum wiring, don't work on it yourself. The connections require special techniques. Call in a licensed pro who's certified to work with it. For more information, go to cpsc.gov and search for "aluminum wiring."

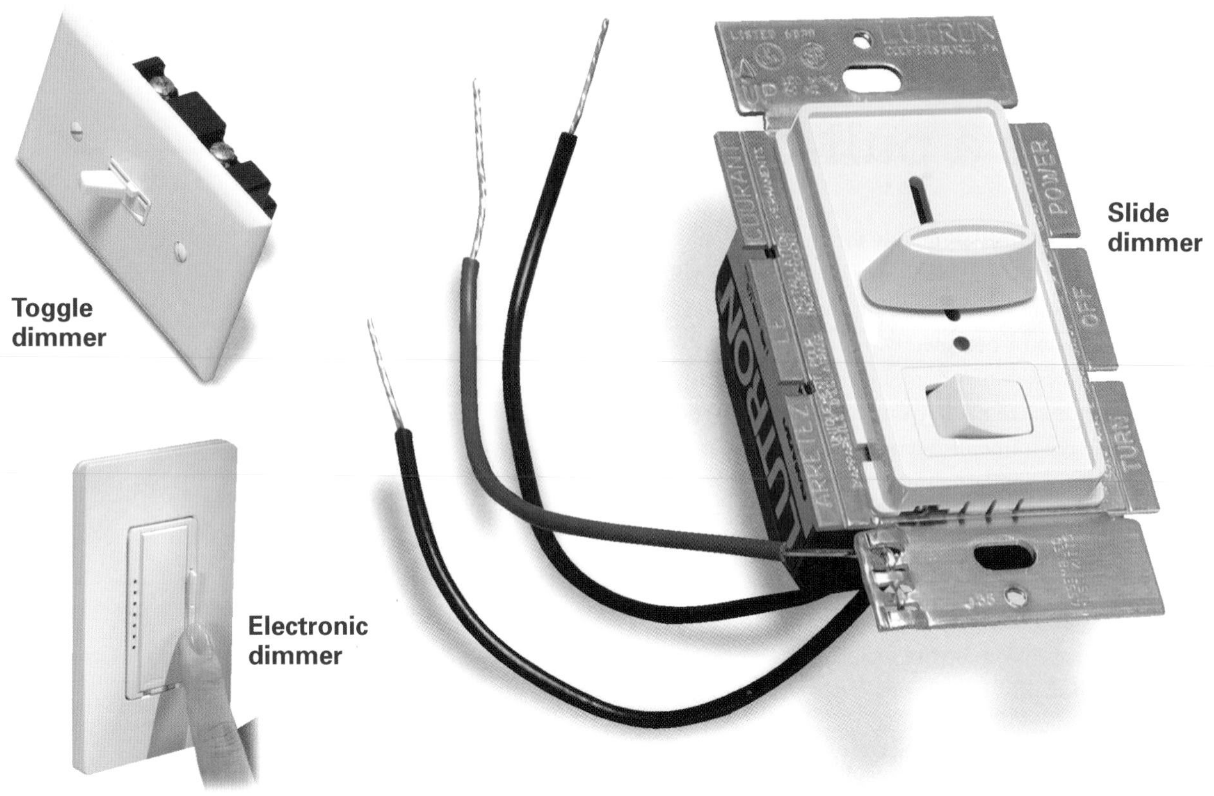

Install a dimmer switch

It doesn't take long to replace an ordinary light switch with a full-feature dimmer. But while you're at it, to make your home safer, you should upgrade the wiring to meet the latest requirements of the National Electrical Code. Our step-by-step instructions will show you how to install the dimmer, concentrating on details that will guarantee a safe installation.

The tools you'll need are inexpensive and will come in handy for all your electrical projects. You'll need a screwdriver, wire stripper, inexpensive voltage detector and needle-nose pliers to install a dimmer.

Double-check for hot wires in the box

Turn on the light and have a helper watch as you switch off the circuit breakers, or unscrew the fuses one at a time until the light goes out. Leave this circuit turned off while you work.

In Photo 1, we're using a non-contact voltage detector to double-check for voltage before removing the switch. These detectors are available at hardware stores and home centers. This type of tester will detect voltage without direct contact with the metal conductor. That's huge—it means you can check potentially hot wires before you handle them. After you unscrew the switch and pull it away from the box, probe around inside the box with the detector to make sure there are no other hot wires from another circuit.

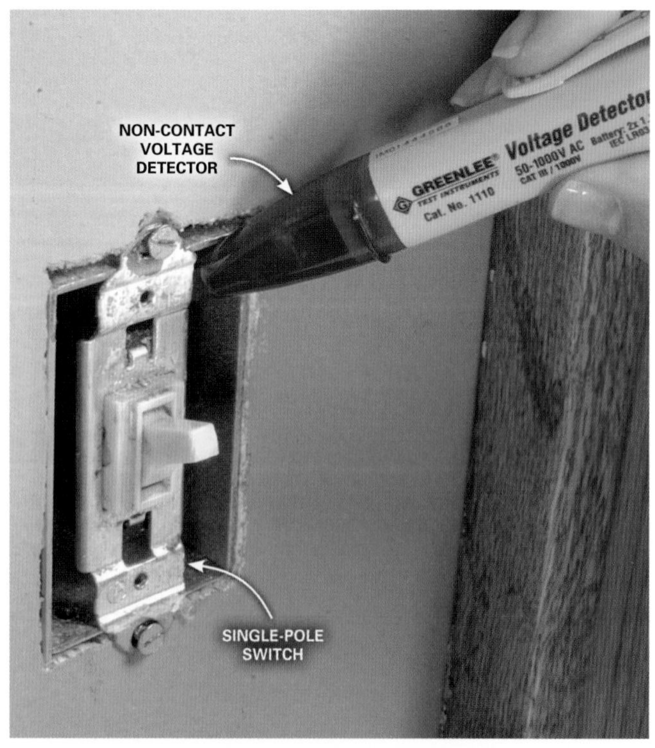

1 **Turn off the power at the main circuit panel. Hold the tip of a non-contact voltage detector near each screw terminal to be sure the power is off. Then unscrew the switch and pull it from the box.**

Make sure the box is large enough

Too many wires and devices stuffed into a box can cause dangerous overheating, short-circuiting and fires. The National Electrical Code specifies minimum box sizes to reduce this risk.

To figure the minimum box size required by the electrical code, add: 1 for each hot and neutral wire entering the box, 1 for all the ground wires combined, 1 for all the clamps combined, and 2 for each device (switch or receptacle) installed in the box. Multiply this figure by 2 for 14-gauge wire and 2.25 for 12-gauge wire to get the minimum box volume in cubic inches.

pro tip

If the circuit breaker is labeled "15 amp," the wires are probably 14-gauge, or 12-gauge for 20-amp circuit breakers.

To help determine the gauge of the wire in your switch box, look at the amperage of the circuit breaker or fuse in the main electrical panel. Fifteen-amp circuits are usually wired with 14-gauge wire and 20-amp circuits require 12-gauge or heavier wire.

Compare the figure you get with the volume of your existing box. Plastic boxes have the volume stamped inside, usually on the back. Steel box capacities are listed in the electrical code.

Figure A
Common metal box sizes

Height/width/depth (inches)	Volume (cubic inches)
3 x 2 x 2-1/4	10.5
3 x 2 x 2-1/2	12.5
3 x 2 x 2-3/4	14.0

2 **Measure the height, width and depth of metal boxes and refer to Figure A above to determine the box volume. Plastic boxes have their volume stamped inside.**

We've listed the volume of the most common steel boxes in Figure A. If you have a steel box, measure it (Photo 2) and consult the chart to see if it's large enough. If your box is too small, replace it with a larger one. It's possible to replace a box without cutting away the wall, but it's a tricky job. It's easier to remove about a 16-in. square of drywall or plaster and patch it after the new large box is installed.

Test your ground before you connect it

New dimmers have either a green grounding wire or a green ground screw that you'll have to connect to a grounding source if one is available. Houses wired with plastic-sheathed cable almost always have bare copper ground wires that you'll connect to the dimmer. But test first using the procedure shown in Photo 3 to verify that the wire is connected to a ground.

Some wiring systems, like ours, rely on metal conduit for the ground. If you have one of these systems, Photo 3 shows how to test the metal box to verify that it's grounded. If it is, attach a short ground wire to the metal box with either a metal grounding clip as shown in Photos 4 and 5 or a green ground-

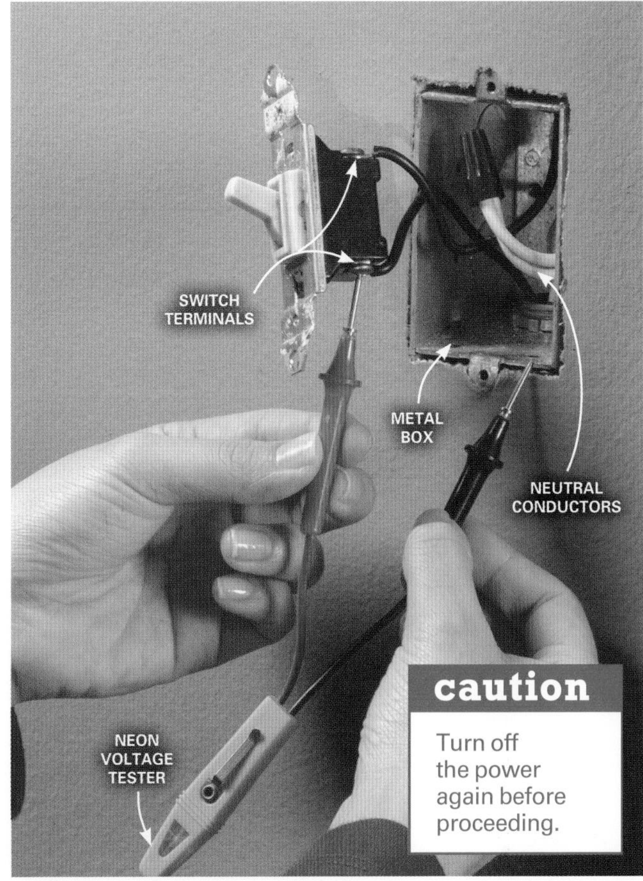

3 **Test for a ground. Turn the power back on. Then place the leads of a voltage tester between each screw terminal and the metal box. If the tester lights, the box is grounded.**

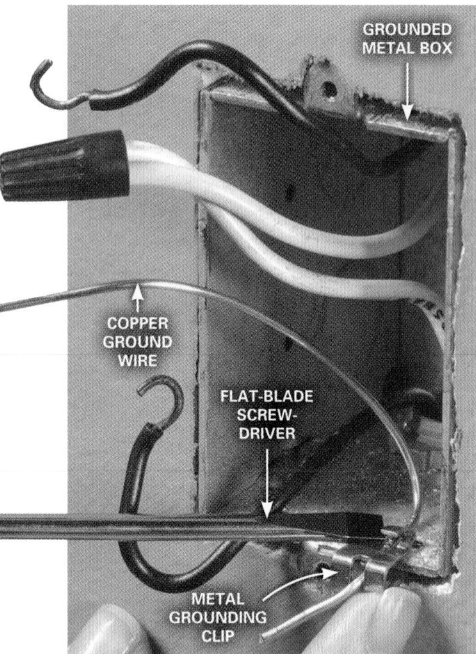

4 **Press a grounding clip and 6-in. length of bare copper wire onto the metal box with a screwdriver. Cut away a little bit of drywall under the box to provide clearance for the clip.**

5 **Bend the ground wire back onto the clip and squeeze it down tight so it won't interfere with the dimmer switch.**

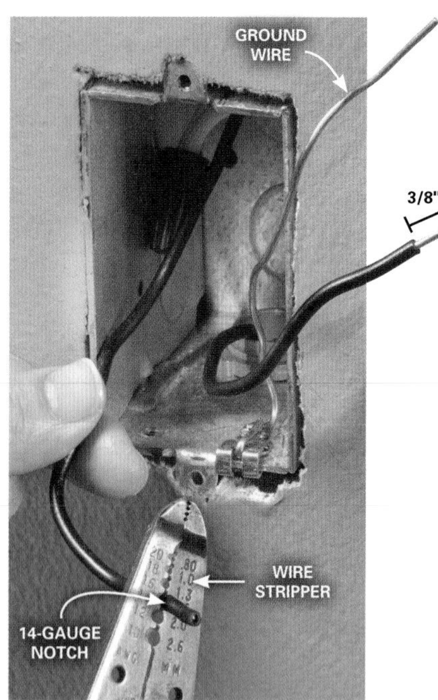

6 **Clip off the bent end of each wire with the wire cutter. Strip 3/8 in. of insulation from the end of the wires.**

caution

If you have aluminum wiring, don't work on it yourself. The connections require special techniques. Call in a licensed pro who's certified to work with it. For more information, go to cpsc.gov and search for "aluminum wiring."

7 **Hold the wires together with the stranded wire protruding about 1/8 in. beyond the solid wire. Match the size of the wire connector you're using to the size and number of wires being connected. Check the manufacturer's specifications on the package to be sure. Twist a plastic wire connector clockwise onto the wires to connect them. Stop twisting when the connector is snug.**

caution

Call an electrician if the original switch is connected to two white wires. This may indicate a dangerous switched neutral.

8 **Fold the wires neatly into the box. Screw the dimmer to the box with the screws provided. Finish the job by installing the cover plate and turning on the power to test the new dimmer.**

ing screw screwed into the threaded hole in the back of the box. Then connect it to the dimmer.

If testing reveals your box isn't grounded, you can still install the dimmer, but you must use a plastic cover plate and make sure no bare metal parts are exposed.

The easy part is installing the dimmer

Some dimmers, like the one we're installing, have stranded wires attached. Photos 7 and 8 show how to install this type of dimmer. Others have screw terminals instead. For these, strip 3/4 in. of the insulated covering from the wires in the box and bend a loop in each with a needle-nose pliers. Place the loop clockwise around the screw terminals and close the loop around the screws with the needle-nose pliers. Then tighten the screws.

It doesn't matter if you reverse the two switch wires to a single-pole dimmer. But if you're replacing a three-way switch with a three-way dimmer, label the "common" wire (it'll be labeled on the old switch) when you remove the old switch so you can connect it to the "common" terminal on the dimmer.

In most cases, the two switch wires will be some color other than green or white, usually black. But one of the wires may be white if your house is wired with plastic-sheathed cable (like Romex). Put a wrap of black tape around the white conductor to label it as a hot wire.

pro tip

Buying dimmers

If the switch you're replacing is the only switch controlling the light, buy a standard single-pole dimmer. If the light can be switched on and off from two or more switches, buy a three-way dimmer switch. But you won't be able to dim the lights from every switch location unless you buy a set of special dimmers with advanced electronics and install one at each switch location.

Most dimmers are designed to handle 600 watts. Add up the wattage of all the light bulbs you'll be dimming. Then read the dimmer package to make sure it can handle the load. Heavy-duty 1,000- and 1,500-watt dimmers are also readily available. Read the package if you'll be installing dimmers side by side in the same electrical box because the wattage rating is reduced to compensate for extra heat buildup.

Finally, you have to use a special device, not a dimmer, to control the speed of ceiling fans and motors. Most fluorescent lights can't be dimmed without altering the fixture.

Repair an extension cord

The price of heavy-duty extension cords has jumped in recent years because of rising copper prices, so rebuilding old, damaged ones with new plugs or receptacle ends is a smart move.

Cut off the old plug, then cut back the insulation jacket with a sharp razor knife (Photo 1). Don't push the blade in—just score the rubber jacket gently until you can tear the rubber off, so you don't accidentally cut into one of the wires.

Strip the wires (look for a stripping gauge on the plug or in the instructions), then separate the wires and screw them into place. This step can be fussy, especially with stiff 12-gauge wire, but resist the temptation to cut the insulation jacket back—the more of the jacket you can leave inside the plug, the less likely it is to tear or pull out of the plug clamp when the cord is yanked out of an outlet.

Close the plug and screw it together tightly so the cord is locked in. Our replacement plug had a reversible gasket with a curved side for heavy cords. Other types use screws to hold the cord in place.

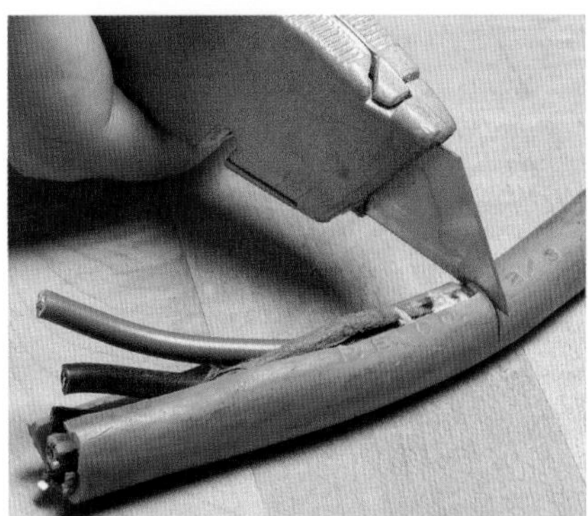

1 Make a shallow cut lengthwise through the outer jacket, then lightly score around the cord until you can break the jacket off.

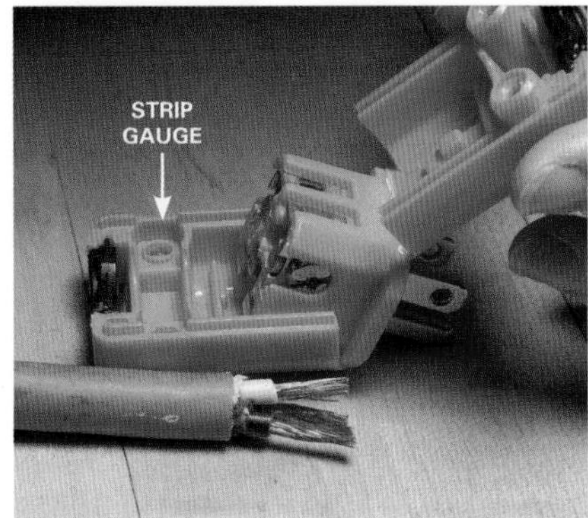

2 Cut and strip the wires to the length indicated in the strip gauge, leaving as much of the outer jacket as possible.

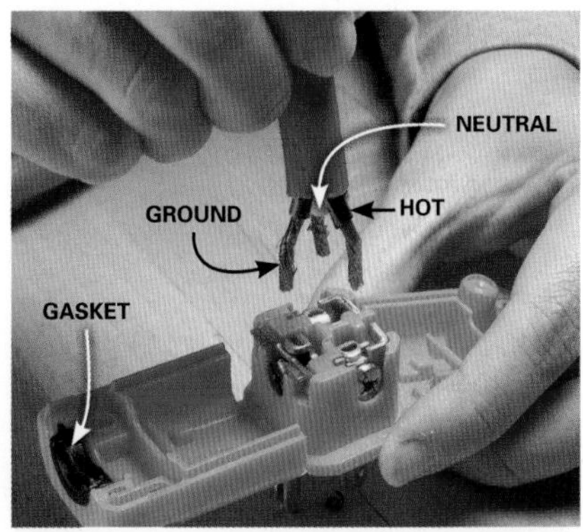

3 Twist the wires tight, then screw them into the plug—black to the gold screw, white to silver, green to green.

Repair a dead doorbell

If your doorbell doesn't ring, there are four possible culprits: the button, the chime, the transformer and the wiring that connects them all. The repairs are simple and the whole system is low voltage, so you don't have to worry about dangerous shocks (unless you have to replace the transformer). Here's how to determine which part is at fault.

Inspect the wiring

A complete inspection of doorbell wiring is usually impossible, since most of the wire is hidden inside walls. But some wire is visible in every home, and that's usually the stuff that gets jolted loose or broken. Inspection takes only a minute. You may find a few inches of wire exposed near the transformer (described below) or several yards running through an unfinished basement. Doorbell cable consists of three or more thin wires inside a plastic sheath (Photo 1). Look for areas where the sheath is damaged and also for pinched or badly kinked sections. Sometimes the only way to tell for certain whether wires inside the sheath are damaged is to carefully slice open the sheath with a utility knife. If you find broken wire, strip the broken ends and rejoin them with wire connectors. Often there's not enough slack in the wire to allow for new connections. In that case, add a short section of wire between the broken ends (Photo 1). A spool of 18-gauge wire is available at hardware stores and home centers. The color of the wire doesn't matter.

pro tip

If you have doorbell buttons at the front and back of your house and one of them works, you can be sure that the non-working button or the wiring connected to it is bad.

Bypass the button

If you don't find a broken wire, remove the doorbell button by unscrewing it or prying it out of its hole with a putty knife. If the bell rings when you bypass the button (Photo 2), replace the button. Buttons are available at home centers and hardware stores. If the bell doesn't ring, reconnect and reinstall the button.

Check the chime

When a doorbell works properly, small armature rods inside the chime strike metal bars or tubes to create sound. Sometimes the armature sticks or you have a loose wire. To find out, remove the chime cover. Many covers simply lift off. Others are fastened with latches or screws. With the cover off, make sure the wires are firmly connected to the screw terminals.

You'll need a test light to check the chime itself. Be sure to get a low-voltage tester. Standard voltage testers look just like the one shown here, but they won't detect low voltage. Touch the common terminal (labeled "com" or "trans") with one of the tester probes.

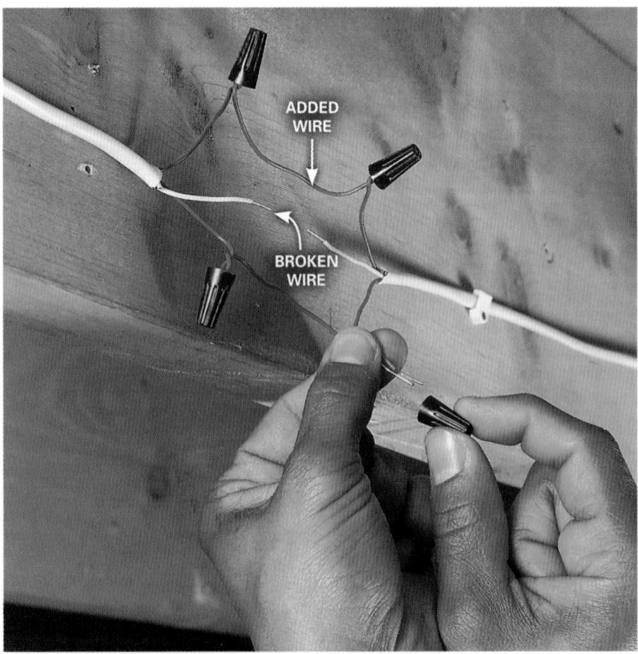

1 **Inspect the wires for damage. Repair breaks with twist-on connectors. Splice in new wire to add length and allow for connections.**

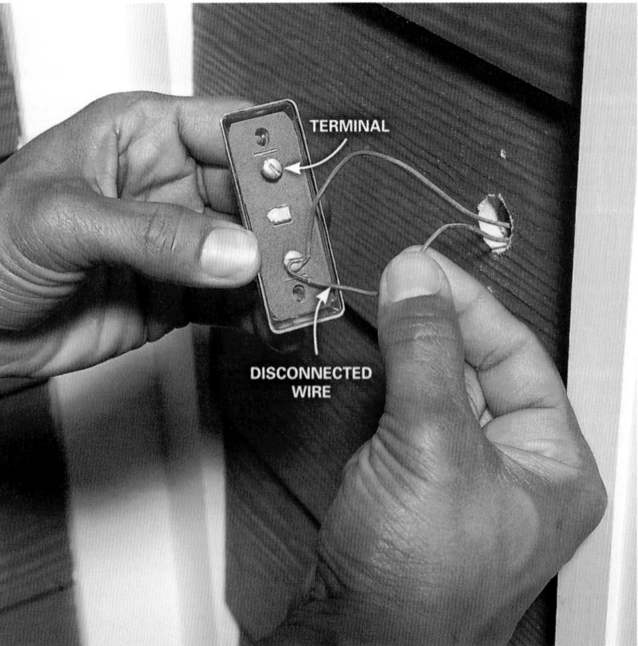

2 **Remove the doorbell button and disconnect one wire from its terminal and touch it to the other terminal. if the chime rings, it's the button that's bad.**

With the other probe, touch the front or back door terminal while a helper pushes the button (Photo 3). If the tester lights up, you know the chime is receiving power and there's something wrong with the chime itself. Sometimes the armatures are too grimy to move. Clean them with rubbing alcohol and move them with your finger (Photo 3 inset). Then try the button again. If the chime still doesn't ring, replace it. Label the wires as you remove the old chime and connect them identically to the new chime. If the tester doesn't light up when your helper pushes the button, the chime isn't receiving power because of a broken switch, transformer or wiring.

Test the transformer

The transformer, which converts standard household voltage to low voltage, is the least likely component to cause doorbell trouble. It can be located anywhere in your home, but you're most likely to find it on a metal junction box near your heating/cooling system or mounted on the outside of your main electrical panel. First, make sure the bell wires are securely connected to the transformer terminals. Then test the transformer (Photo 4). If the transformer is mounted on a junction box, you can replace it yourself. Be sure to turn off the power to the circuit at the main panel and then make sure it's off by using a non-contact voltage detector before disconnecting wires. If the transformer is mounted on the main panel, we recommend that you hire a licensed electrician to open the panel and replace it.

When all else fails, go wireless

If none these tests exposes the problem, you can bet that a wire is broken somewhere inside a wall. You might be able to locate and repair the break without tearing into walls, but the odds are against you. So the best solution is a wireless system. With a wireless doorbell, the button sends a radio signal that triggers the chime. On the downside, an electronic chime may not create the harmonious ring of metal, and both of its components require new batteries periodically.

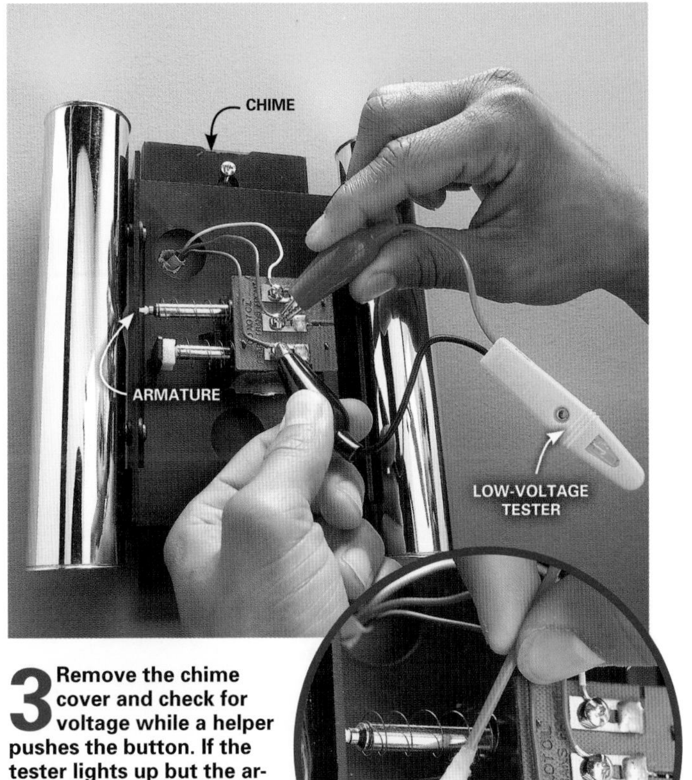

3 Remove the chime cover and check for voltage while a helper pushes the button. If the tester lights up but the armatures don't move, clean them with rubbing alcohol.

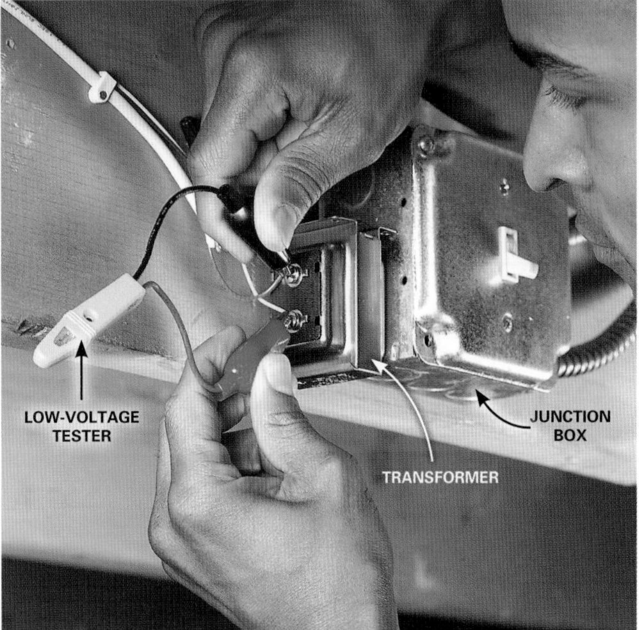

4 Test the transformer by touching the screw terminals with a low-voltage test light. If the tester doesn't light up, replace the transformer.

Fix a broken fluorescent light socket

Fluorescent light fixtures are durable and virtually maintenance free, but occasionally, service and repair are required. If you've got a fluorescent fixture that doesn't light up, flickers on and off, or won't hold a bulb, we'll show you how to troubleshoot the problem. Replacement parts are easy to install and can be found at home centers and hardware stores.

If the fixture won't light up at all, it may not be getting power. Check the circuit breaker or fuse box, and reset or replace the necessary equipment.

Fluorescent light bulbs typically last many years, but when one flickers on and off, or the end turns light gray to black in color, it needs to be replaced. Photo 1 shows a bad bulb and how to replace it. Replace the bulb with the same size bulb.

Another common problem is cracked sockets, caused by bumps from other objects or stress from removing a bulb. Shut down power to the light, remove the bulbs and then open up the fixture to gain access to the broken socket (Photo 2). There will be two or four wires coming into the socket. Keep the wiring straight by swapping wires from one side of the socket at a time as shown in Photo 3.

If the fixture still doesn't work, then the ballast is probably shot. The ballast boosts the incoming voltage to start the tubes, and then regulates the current to provide continuous light. Ballast replacement can cost as much as a new fixture, so buying a new fixture may be a better investment.

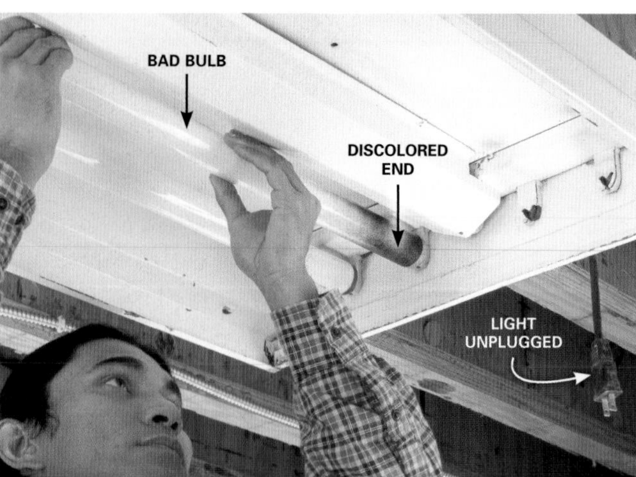

1 **Unplug the light and twist the bulb 90 degrees with both hands. Pull one end straight down to free it from the socket and then lower the entire bulb.**

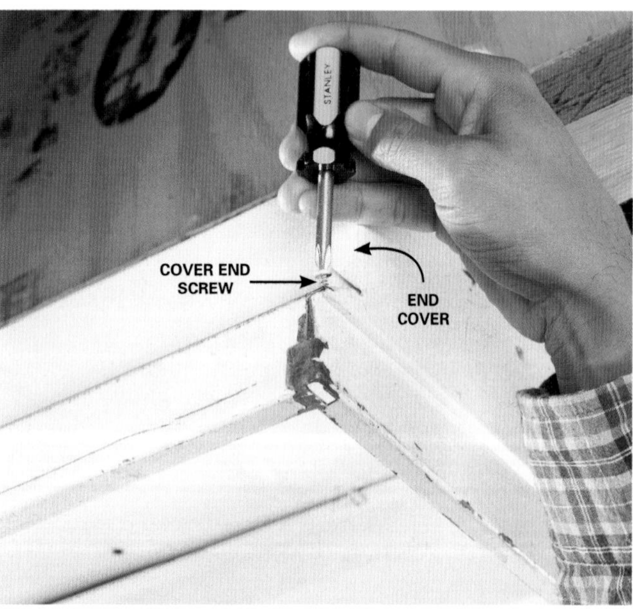

2 **Unscrew the fixture end cover. Screw locations will vary, but double-bulb units typically have a screw on each side, and four-bulb units typically have an additional screw on the top center edge. Remove all screws and pull off the cover.**

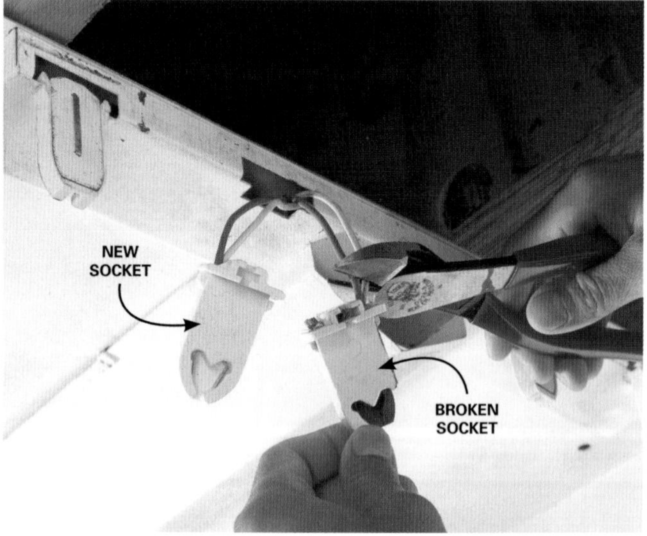

3 **Slide out the socket to expose the wiring. It's very important to keep the wiring order straight, so cut one side of the old socket wiring loose at a time. Strip the wiring back 1/2 in., then press the bare wire ends into the terminal slots on the new socket. The terminal slot works like a barbed fishhook; once a wire is pushed in, it cannot be pulled out. Repeat the process for the remaining wires and then replace the socket.**

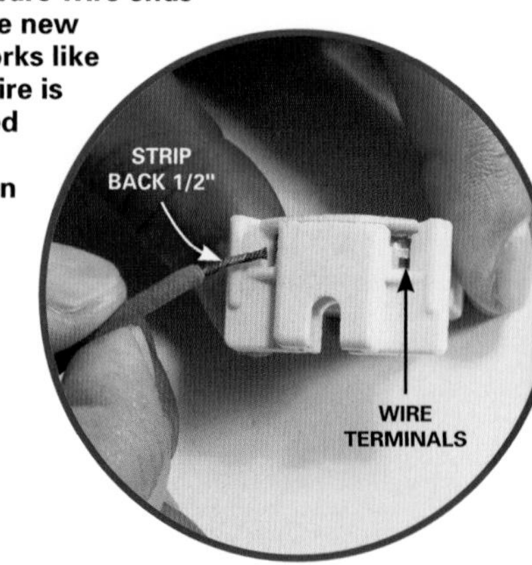

caution

Unplug the light before making repairs, or turn off the circuit at the main panel.

Tighten a loose outlet

A loose outlet pushes in every time you insert a plug. Often it happens because the cutout around the outlet box is too big. When the drywall is taped, gaps around the electrical boxes are filled with mud, which supports the outlet ears. In a heavily used outlet, this mud breaks loose, leaving the outlet ears unsupported. Eventually the cover plate cracks. A scrap of 12- or 14-gauge electrical wire and a few common tools are all you'll need to lock that outlet down tight.

Start by shutting off the power to the outlet (Photo 1). Photos 2 and 3 show how to convert scrap electrical wire into a coiled spacer, which will bridge the gap between the outlet and the electrical box. Once the spacer is completed, install it between the outlet and electrical box as shown in Photo 4. Note: If the face of the box isn't flush with a wood or combustible-material wall, or the box is more than 1/4 in. behind a drywall wall, you must add a box extender.

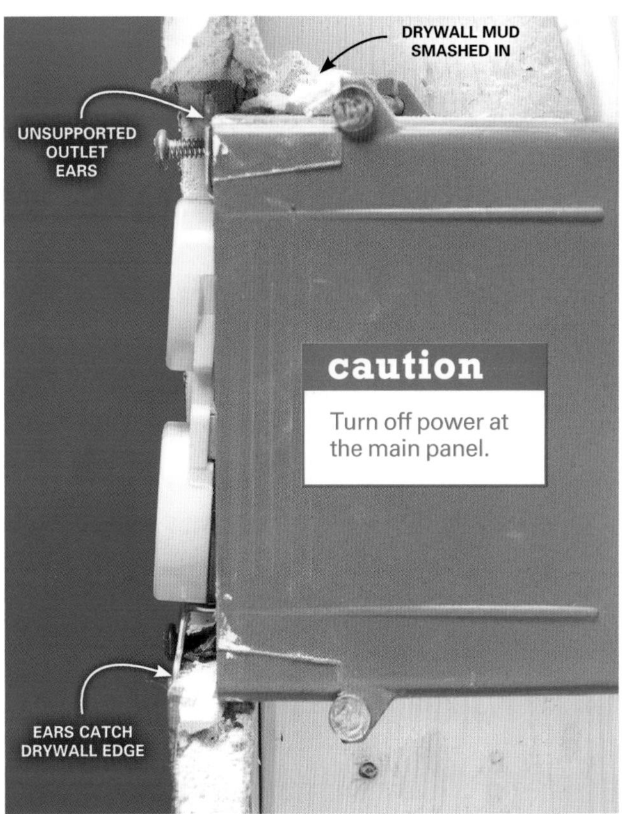

caution

Turn off power at the main panel.

1 **Turn off the power at the main panel and remove the broken cover plate. The drywall is often broken behind the outlet ears, leaving them unsupported.**

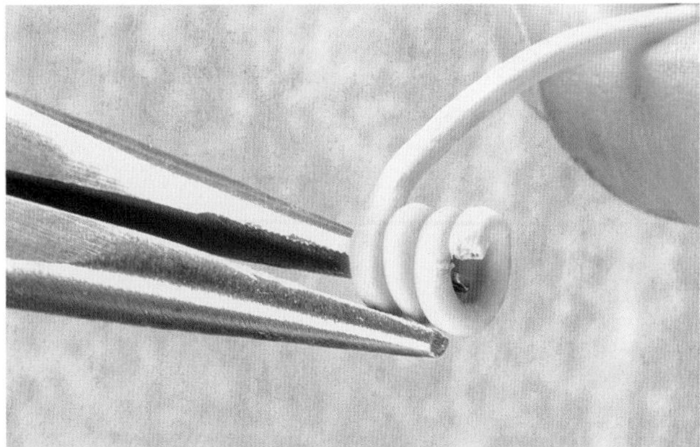

2 **Strip the exterior sheathing off a 12-in. scrap of 12- or 14-gauge electrical cable and remove one of the individual wires. Twist the wire into a tight coil with needle-nose pliers.**

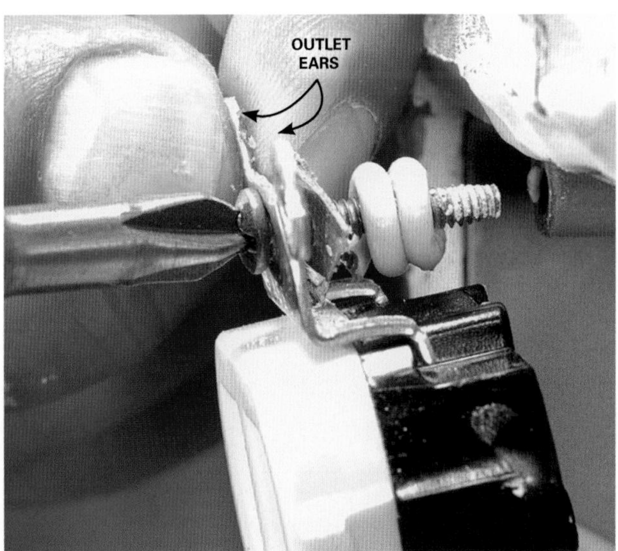

4 **Slide the coil spacer over the outlet-mounting screw. Screw the outlet down until the outlet ears are flush to the wall.**

3 **Press the coiled end tight to the outlet-mounting screw hole. Snip the coil so it extends just past the wall; the insulation will compress slightly when tightened.**

Chapter **four**

PLUMBING

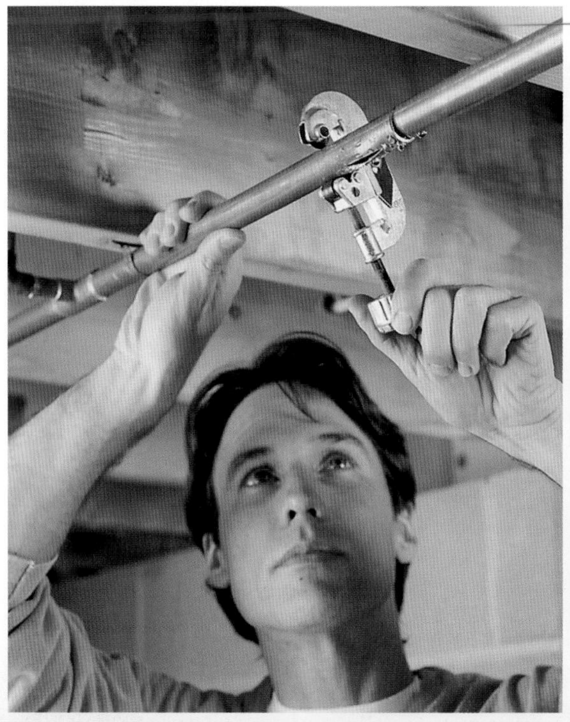
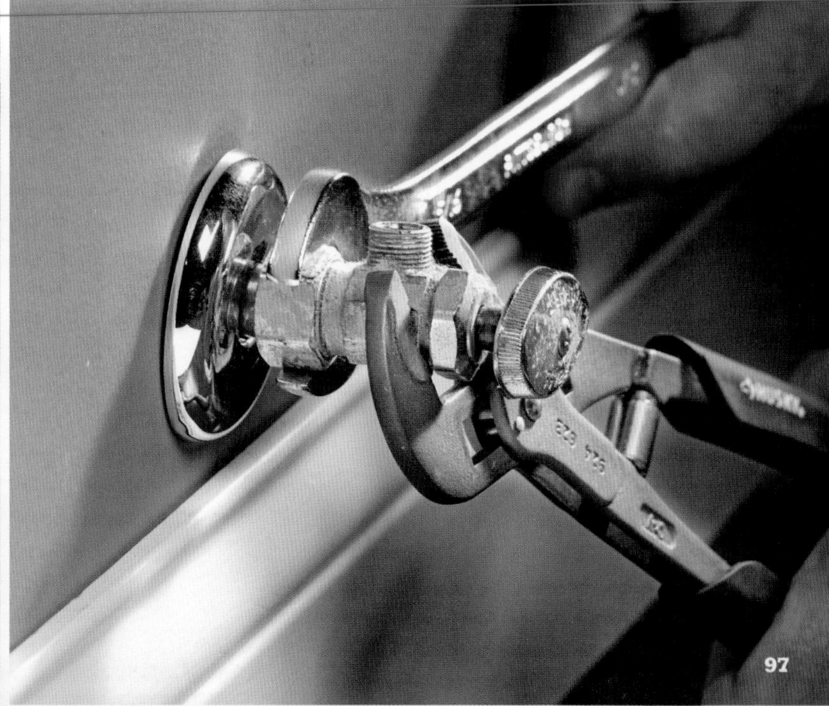

Repair a rotary ball faucet

Water flow and temperature in a rotary ball faucet are controlled by a hollow ball that rotates in a socket. Delta and Peerless are two of the major brands. Your faucet may have a brass or plastic ball. Both work well, although the long-lasting stainless steel ball comes with most repair kits. We recommend that you buy a repair kit that includes the ball, springs, seats and O-rings for the spout, as well as a small repair tool. With this kit, you'll be prepared for almost any repair.

If water is leaking out around the base of the handle, you may be able to fix the leak by removing the handle (Photo 1) and simply tightening the adjusting ring slightly. Turn it clockwise with the spanner tool included in the repair kit. If the faucet drips from the end of the spout, replace the seats and springs (Photo 4).

Reassembly is straightforward. Drop the springs in the recesses and press the rubber seats over the top with your fingertip. Then align the groove in the ball with the pin in the socket and drop in the ball. Align the lug on the plastic cam with the notch in the valve body and set it over the ball. Thread on the cap with the adjusting ring and tighten it with the slip-joint pliers. Now you can turn on the water to check for leaks. If water leaks from around the ball stem, use the spanner tool to tighten the adjusting ring until the leak stops. Replace the handle and you're done.

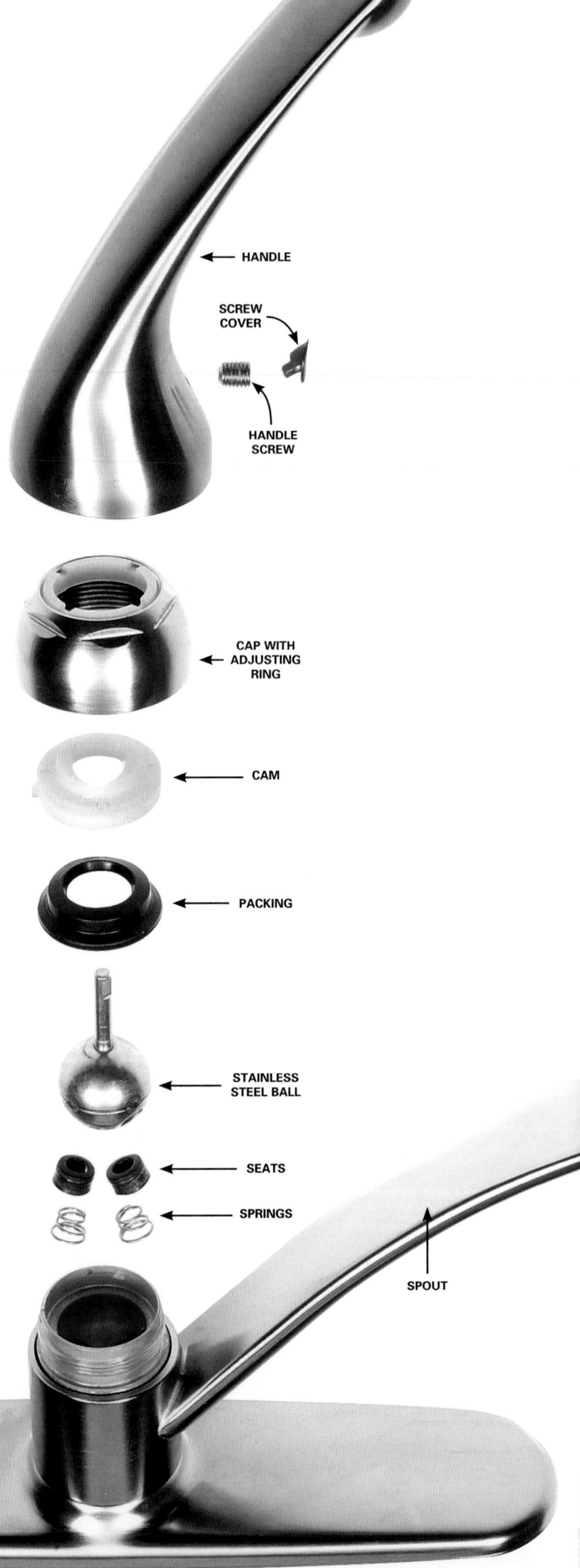

1 Lift the handle and pry off the decorative cover to expose the Allen screw. Turn the screw counterclockwise until it's loose enough to lift the handle up from the stem.

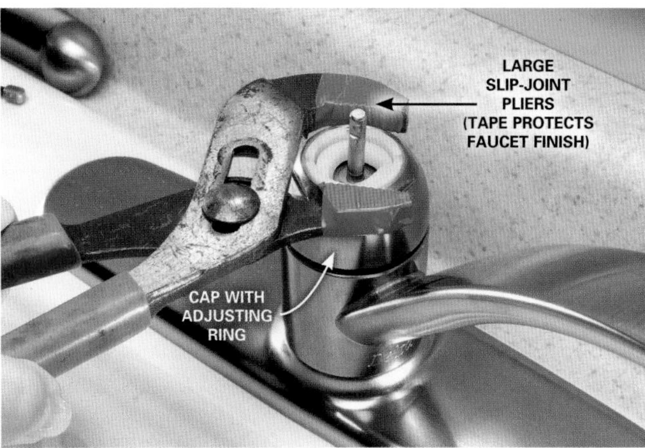

2 Unscrew the cap by turning it counterclockwise with slip-joint pliers.

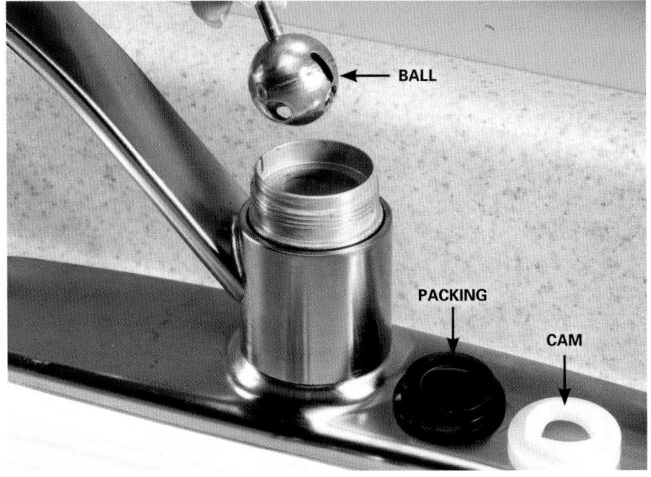

3 Lift off the plastic cam and packing. Lift out the ball and inspect it. Replace the ball if it's scratched, cracked or visibly worn.

4 Lift out the two rubber seats and springs with a screwdriver. Make note of the orientation of the tapered spring and install the new springs and seats the same way. Reassemble the faucet.

Follow these basics for all faucet repairs

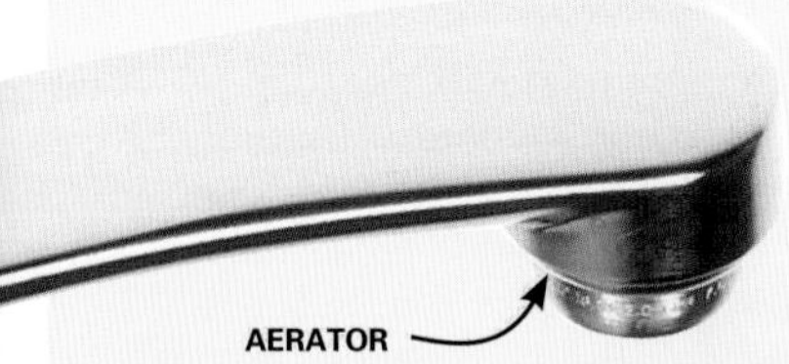

Before you start, examine the faucet closely to determine where the water is coming from. Leaks around the base of the spout require a different repair than a drip from the end of the spout. Then turn off the water supply to the faucet. You'll probably find shutoff valves under the sink. If those valves don't work or if you don't have any, you'll have to close the main water valve to your entire home. After you turn off the water, open the faucet in the center position to relieve water pressure and make sure the water is shut off. Finally, cover the sink drain holes with strainer baskets or rags to avoid losing small parts down the drain.

Pay close attention to the order and orientation of parts as you remove them. Your smartphone camera is handy for recording each step. For easier reassembly, set the parts aside in the order they were removed. When all the parts are out, inspect the interior of the valve for bits of deteriorated gaskets or mineral deposits. Loosen mineral deposits by soaking them in vinegar. Slow water flow can be caused by plugged holes in the faucet body. Use a small screwdriver or penknife to clean them out. Before you replace worn parts and reassemble the faucet, hold a rag over the faucet and open the water shutoff valve slightly to flush out debris that may have been loosened during the cleaning and inspection.

After the faucet is reassembled, open the faucet to the middle position and gradually open the shutoff valves to turn on the water. Leave the faucet open until water flows freely and all the air is out of the pipes. If the water flow through the faucet is slow, the aerator may be plugged. Unscrew the aerator and clean it out.

Repair a cartridge-style faucet

Many faucet brands use a cartridge of some type. We show how to replace a Moen cartridge, but the process is similar for other brands. To stop drips at the spout or correct problems with hot and cold mixing, remove the cartridge and either replace the O-rings on the cartridge if they're worn or replace the entire cartridge. Take the cartridge to the home center or hardware store to find a replacement.

Photos 1 – 6 show how to remove the cartridge. Replacement cartridges for Moen faucets include a plastic spanner cap that allows you to twist and loosen the cartridge to make it easier to pull out (Photo 5). Don't be surprised if the cartridge seems stuck.

It may take considerable force to pull it out. Really stubborn cartridges may require the use of a special cartridge-pulling tool.

Reassemble the faucet in the reverse order. Pull the stem up before inserting the cartridge. You may have to twist the cartridge slightly to line it up for the brass retainer clip. Use the plastic spanner cap or the tips of needle-nose pliers to rotate the cartridge. Slide the brass clip into the slots in the valve body to hold the cartridge in place. Look for the small notch on top of the stem and rotate the stem until the notch faces you (Photo 4). Install the remaining parts and reattach the handle. The directions that come with the stem will help orient you here. Then test the faucet. If the hot and cold water are reversed, simply remove the handle, dome assembly and handle adapter and rotate the stem 180 degrees.

pro tip

Find the right replacement parts

You'll often find the brand name stamped on the faucet. And this information will help when it comes time to find repair parts. But in most cases, the safest bet is to take the worn parts to the store with you.

If you have a Delta or other rotary ball faucet, you're in luck because you'll find repair kits in most hardware stores and home centers. Cartridges and repair kits for Moen "cartridge-type" faucets are also readily available. But if you have another brand or a disc-type faucet, you may have to order parts, since there are too many variations for most stores to keep in stock. It helps to know the faucet's model name or number when searching for a replacement cartridge. Otherwise, take the cartridge with you to the store so you can match it to a photo in the parts catalog. Plumbing supply specialists are also a good source of repair parts.

1 Pry off the handle cap (gently) with a knife. Turn the Allen screw counterclockwise to remove it and lift off the handle.

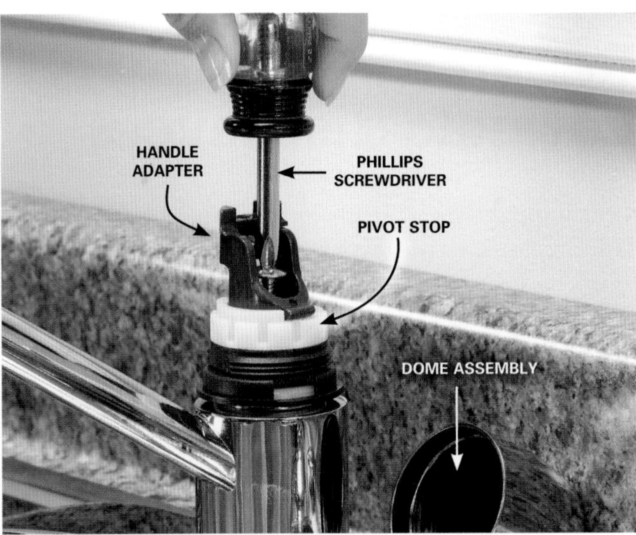

2 Unscrew the dome assembly under the handle. Then unscrew the metal handle adapter and lift it off. Lift off the plastic pivot stop.

3 Remove the retainer nut by turning it counterclockwise with large slip-joint pliers.

4 Pry out the brass retainer clip with the tip of a screwdriver. Grab the clip with pliers and pull it the rest of the way out to avoid losing it.

5 Loosen the cartridge by slipping the plastic spanner cap (included with the new cartridge) over the cartridge and twisting it back and forth.

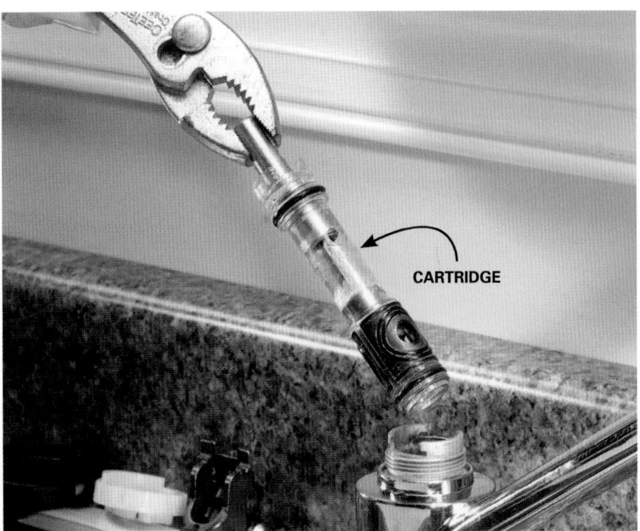

6 Grab the cartridge stem with a pliers and pull it straight up and out. Replace worn parts and reassemble the faucet in the reverse order.

Repair a ceramic disc faucet

Ceramic disc valves are simply another type of cartridge. Discs inside the cartridge control the water flow. This type of valve is sturdy and reliable and rarely needs fixing. In fact, many manufacturers offer a lifetime guarantee on the cartridge. If yours is damaged, check with the manufacturer to see if it's covered by a warranty. Leaks can result from faulty rubber seals or a cracked disc inside the cartridge. Since it's difficult to spot a cracked disc, and disc cartridge replacements are very expensive, it's best to start by replacing the seals and reassembling the faucet. Then if the faucet still leaks, remove the disc cartridge and take it to the store to order a replacement.

Early versions of ceramic disc faucets may be more fragile and can crack if subjected to a blast of pressurized air. That's why it's important to leave the faucet open as you turn the water back on. This allows air trapped in the lines to escape. When the water runs smoothly, it's safe to turn the faucet off. Manufacturers have improved the strength of ceramic discs on newer faucets to withstand air blasts, as well as abrasive debris that may get dislodged from the inside of pipes.

pro tip

If you're buying a new faucet, choose a ceramic disc type. Ceramic valves are by far the most reliable.

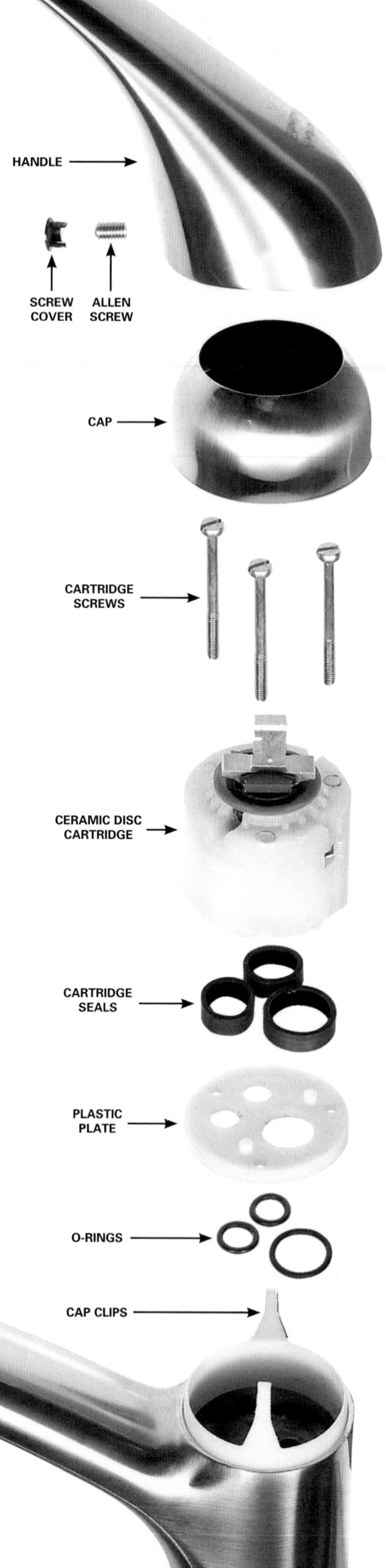

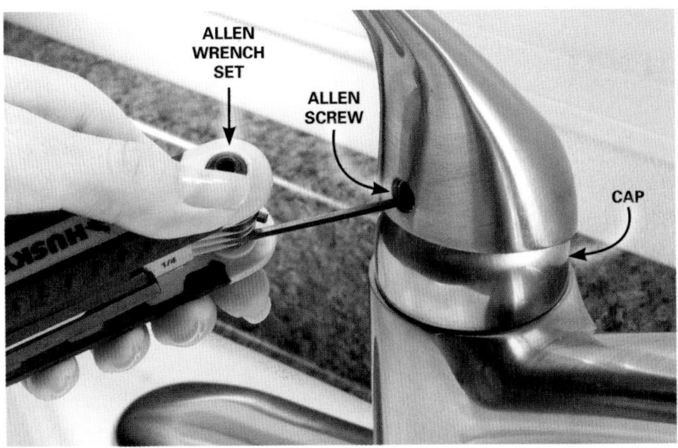

1 Pry off the decorative screw cover with your fingernail or the tip of a knife. Unscrew the handle screw by turning it counterclockwise with an Allen wrench. Lift off the handle. Unscrew or unclip the cap.

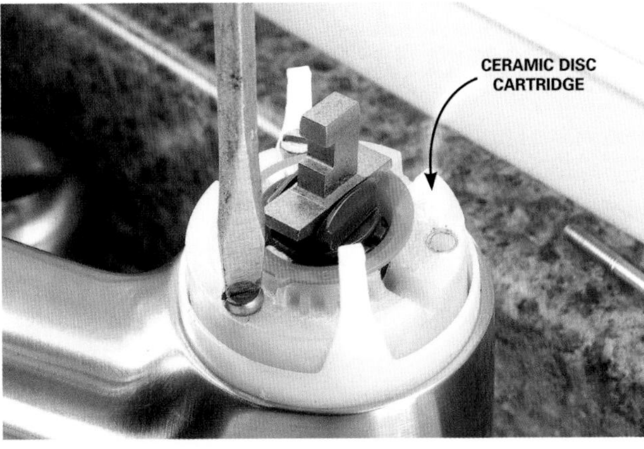

2 Remove the screws that hold the disc cartridge to the faucet body and lift out the cartridge.

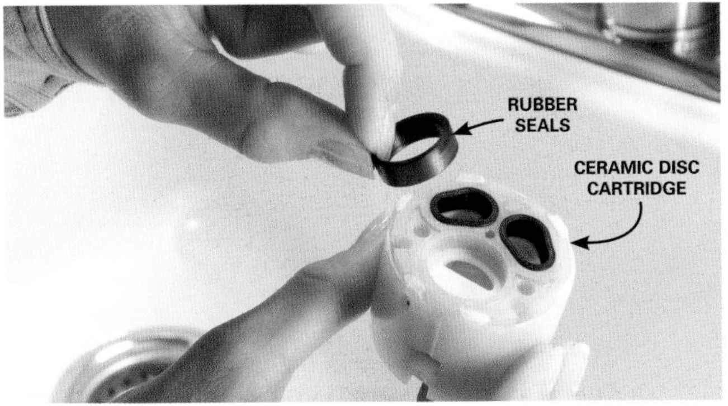

3 Inspect the cartridge for mineral buildup and carefully clean it out. Then replace the rubber seals on the underside.

4 Lift out the plastic plate (on some faucets) and replace the O-rings under it. Inspect the holes in the faucet body and clean them out if they're clogged.

instant fix

Repair a leaky spout

Leaks around the base of the spout are caused by worn O-rings located under the spout. All that's usually required to access these O-rings for replacement is to wiggle and pull up on the spout to remove it (Photo 1). Depending on your faucet, you'll also have to remove the handle and other parts to access the spout. Be persistent. The spout may be a little stubborn. Spout O-ring kits are available for many faucets, or you can take the old O-rings to the hardware store or plumbing supply store and match them up with new ones. Remember to pick up a small toothpaste-type tube of plumber's grease while you're there.

In Photo 1, you can see the diverter valve, which controls water to the sprayer. Their appearance varies considerably among brands, but you'll usually find them under the spout. If your sprayer isn't working properly, first clean it in vinegar or simply replace it. If this doesn't work, the diverter valve may be clogged. If it doesn't simply pull out, contact the manufacturer or ask a knowledgeable salesperson for help with cleaning it.

1 Remove the handle and cartridge. Twist and pull up on the spout to remove it and expose the O-ring seals.

2 Slip the tip of a screwdriver under the O-rings to slide them out of the groove. Install the new O-rings, lubricate them with plumber's grease and reinstall the spout.

Repair a washer-type faucet

A leaky faucet has a torturous way of wearing on nerves and water resources. Even a slow drip can waste hundreds of gallons per month. Luckily, most dripping washer-type faucets can be cured in 30 minutes for less than a dollar.

To repair a washer-type faucet, you'll need to replace the washer on the bottom of the valve stem and sometimes replace the valve seat as well. Replace washers for both the hot and cold water while you're at it, not just the one that's leaking. Before you begin, turn off the water-supply valves and close the sink stopper so small parts won't disappear down the drain.

pro tip

As you reassemble the faucet, dab a little grease on the screws and seat threads. They'll screw in more smoothly and come apart easier for future repairs.

Most faucet handles are secured by a screw, which is sometimes covered by a snap-on cap or button. You may need to tap, wiggle or pry the handle a bit to remove it. The washer on the end of the valve stem may be flat or beveled. The new washer should be the same profile and fit snugly inside the circular lip without having to be forced.

With your finger, feel down inside the area where the stem assembly enters the faucet to determine whether the valve seat is rough or grooved. If it is, replace it with a new valve seat that exactly matches the old in diameter, height and threads.

1 Remove the screw that holds the handle, then loosen and remove packing nut. Remove stem assembly.

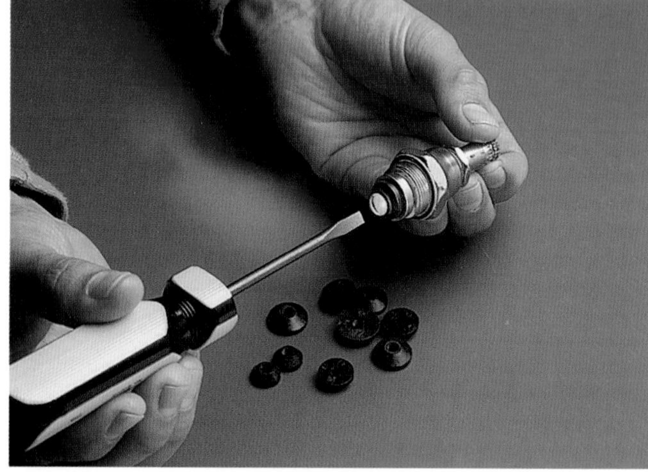

2 Remove worn washer and replace it with correct type: flat or beveled. New washer should fit snugly without being forced.

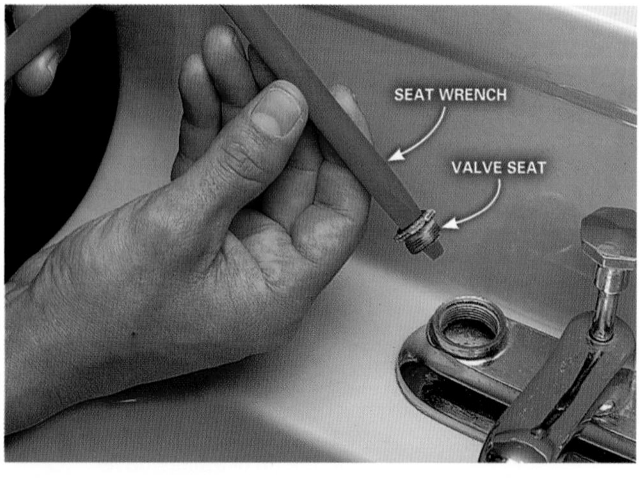

3 Use seat wrench to remove worn valve seat. New seat must match old one exactly in diameter, height and number of threads.

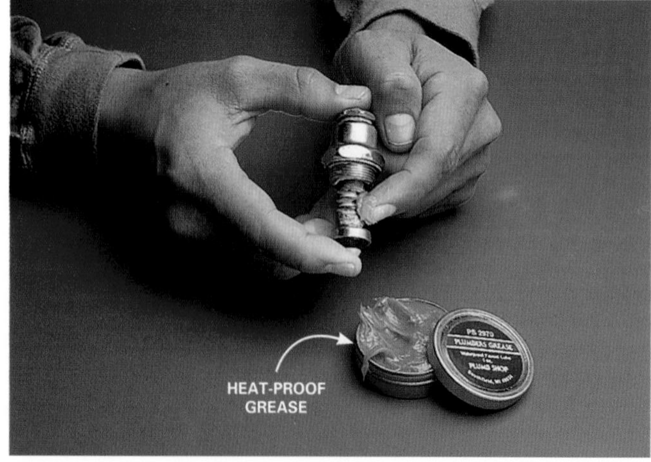

4 Lubricate working parts of stem assembly with heat-proof faucet grease. Reassemble faucet.

instant fix

Restore free flow to a clogged faucet

If the flow from your kitchen or bathroom faucet isn't what it used to be, the aerator is probably plugged. An aerator can clog slowly as mineral deposits build up, or quickly after plumbing work loosens debris inside pipes. Usually, a quick cleaning solves the problem. Remove the aerator (Photo 1) and disassemble it. You may need a small screwdriver or knife to pry the components apart. Scrub away any tough buildup with an old toothbrush (Photo 2) and rinse each part thoroughly. Gunk can also build up inside the faucet neck, so ream it out with your finger and flush out the loosened debris.

If the mineral buildup resists scrubbing and you have a standard cylinder-shaped aerator, you can replace it. Take your old aerator along to the home center or hardware store to find a match. If your aerator has a fancy shape (like the one shown here), finding a match won't be as simple. So try this first: Soak the aerator parts in vinegar overnight to soften mineral buildup. If that doesn't work, search online for the brand of your faucet followed by "faucet parts." With a little searching, you can find diagrams of your faucet and order a new aerator.

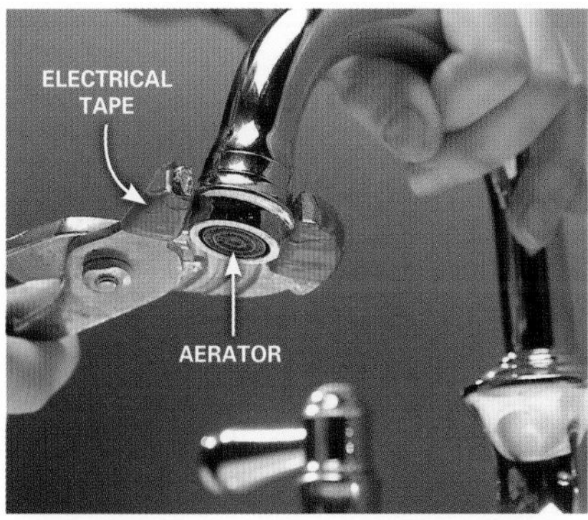

1 Wrap the jaws of pliers with electrical tape and unscrew the aerator. Close the stopper so the small parts can't fall down the drain.

2 Disassemble the aerator and lay out the parts in the order you remove them to make reassembly foolproof. Scrub the parts and reassemble them.

instant fix

Replace a sink sprayer and hose

Over time, sink sprayers often break or become clogged with mineral deposits. Or the sprayer hose can harden and crack or wear through from rubbing against something under the sink. The best solution in these cases is replacement.

You can pick up just the sprayer head or a head and hose kit at a home center or hardware store.

Photo 1 shows how to remove the entire sprayer head and hose assembly. You may be able to get a small open-end wrench up to the sprayer hose nipple, but space is very tight. If there isn't enough room to turn the wrench, you'll have to purchase a basin wrench at a home center or hardware store. If your sprayer hose is in good condition, simply unscrew the head and replace it (Photo 2).

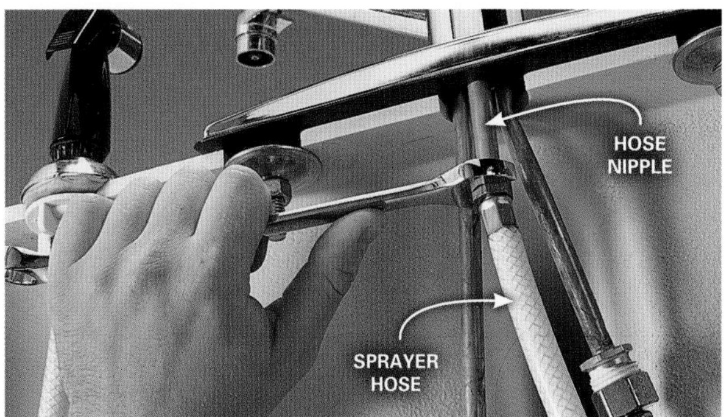

1 Use an open-end or basin wrench to unscrew the sprayer hose from the hose nipple. Pull the old sprayer and hose out of the sink grommet. Slide the new hose through the grommet on top of the sink and reconnect it to the faucet.

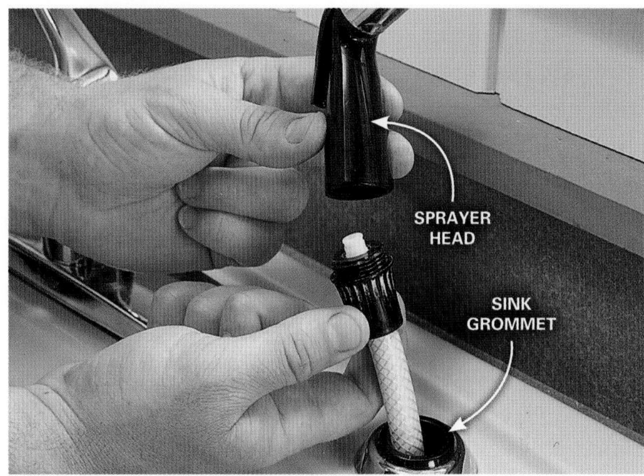

2 Hold the base of the sprayer in your hand and twist off the sprayer head. Screw on the new head.

Replacing shutoff valves

If you're servicing or replacing a toilet or sink faucet, the first step is to shut off the water supply valve that feeds the fixture. But the simple task of shutting off the valve can be the start of a whole set of unexpected headaches.

Unless your house is fairly new, chances are you have multi-turn shutoff valves at every toilet and faucet. Shutoff valves perform flawlessly for years. But when they aren't opened or closed for a long time, you may find that the valve handle either won't turn or will turn but won't stop the water flow completely. And even if the valve does shut off the water, it may leak when you reopen it—the last thing you need after a plumbing repair!

You can spend time rebuilding the old valve, but the problems will just reappear years from now. The best way to deal with bad valves is to replace them with modern quarter-turn ball valves. They rarely lock up, leak or wear out and cost only $10. Best of all, they'll take just an hour or so to install. Here's how to put them in.

Identify the valve connection style

Shutoff valves connect to copper plumbing pipes in one of two ways: compression fitting or sweat fitting. Identify the connection type used in your home by referring to the photos on p. 109. If you have an older home with galvanized pipes, we suggest hiring a plumber to do the switch-out. Unscrewing the old valve and screwing on a new one may seem easy enough. But if the pipe is rusted internally or the threads are rotted, this "simple" plumbing job can turn into a plumbing nightmare. If your home is plumbed with PEX or plastic pipe, these instructions don't apply.

Once you identify the connection type, buy a quarter-turn shutoff ball valve to match the size of the incoming copper pipe and the size of the supply tube connection. If you're replacing a sweat valve, you'll need a torch, flux, solder, emery cloth, wire brushes and a flame protection cloth to shield the wall. This is also a good time to replace an old supply tube and a corroded escutcheon (wall trim plate).

Prepare for valve replacement

Shut off the water at the main shutoff valve. If you have a gas water heater, turn the knob to the "pilot" position. Shut off the circuit breakers to an electric water heater. Then open a faucet on the lowest level of your house and another faucet on an upper level to drain the pipes. Then disconnect the supply tube from the shutoff valve. Replace the valve.

After replacement

Close the new valve. Then open the water-main shutoff valve and let the water run until all the air is out of the pipes. Then shut off the upper and lower faucets. Check the new valves for leaks. Turn the water heater gas valve back to "on" or flip on the circuit breakers to the electric water heater.

Replace a sweat valve

Hold the valve with pliers, loosen the packing nut and unscrew the entire valve stem. Peek inside and remove the old washer if it's stuck on the seat. Removing the valve stem allows any remaining water to drain out, making the unsweating process easier. Before you do any torch work, make sure there's a fire extinguisher nearby and safeguard the wall with a flame protection cloth. Then remove the old valve (Photo 1) and the remaining solder (Photo 2).

Clean the tubing with emery cloth. If you're replacing a sweat valve with a compression valve, sand off all traces of solder before adding the new escutcheon, nut and sleeve. Otherwise, remove enough old solder to allow the new sweat valve to slide onto the tubing. Remove the stem and wire-brush the opening in the new quarter-turn valve and apply flux to the valve and the copper tubing. With the flame protection cloth in place, heat the valve just enough to draw in the solder.

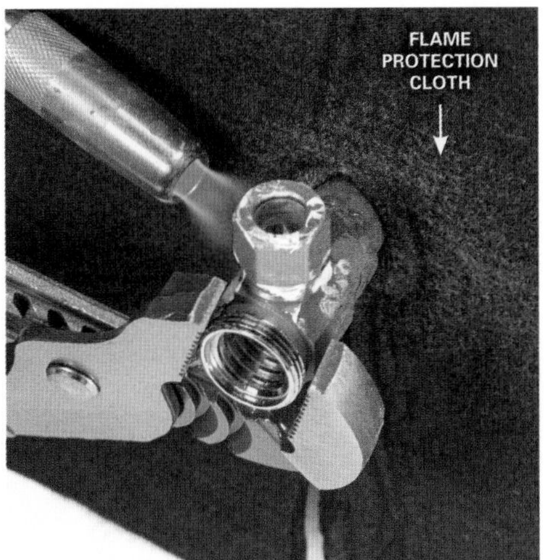

1 REMOVE THE OLD SWEAT VALVE Drape the flame protection cloth over the copper tubing and tape it to the wall. Adjust the torch to a small flame and aim it toward the body of the valve. As soon as the solder melts, twist and pull the valve off the copper tubing with pliers.

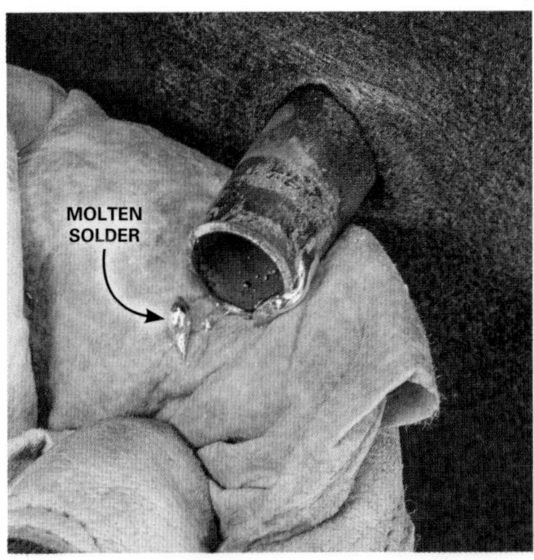

2 CLEAN EXCESS SOLDER Put on a leather glove and grab a damp cotton rag (microfiber cloth will melt). Heat the remaining solder with the torch until it's molten. As soon as the solder melts, wipe away the excess solder with a damp rag. Be sure to wear leather gloves to prevent steam burns.

Valve types

SWEAT VALVE: A sweat shutoff valve doesn't have any hex flats where the copper tubing enters from the wall. Replace a sweat valve with another sweat valve or a compression valve.

COMPRESSION VALVE: Examine the portion of the valve closest to the wall. Look for a hexagonal compression nut and matching hex flats on the body of the valve next to the compression nut. If the valve has a compression nut but no hex flats, look for two flats on the sides of the valve body.

THREADED VALVE: Look for threads and hex flats where the steel pipe enters the valve.

Remove and replace a compression shutoff valve

To remove a compression-style valve, hold the valve body with an adjustable or open-end wrench, or slip-joint pliers. Grab the compression nut with another wrench and turn it clockwise to loosen it. Then pull the valve off the copper tubing.

Next, remove the old compression sleeve and nut. Grab the old sleeve with pliers, using minimal pressure to avoid distorting the copper tubing. Then rotate and pull it off the tubing. If the sleeve is stuck, saw it (Photo 1) and break it (Photo 2).

Slide the new escutcheon and compression nut onto the copper tubing. Then add the new compression sleeve (Photo 3). Insert the new valve and apply a very light coating of pipe dope to the compression sleeve. Next, screw the compression nut onto the valve until snug. Hold the valve with a wrench or pliers and tighten the nut a one-half to three-quarters turn (follow the manufacturer's tightening instructions). Connect the supply tube and test for leaks.

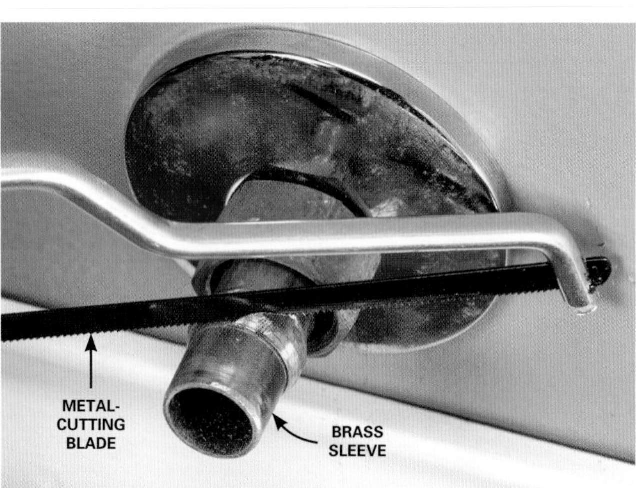

1 SAW PARTIALLY THROUGH THE SLEEVE Use a hacksaw to cut partially through the sleeve at an angle. Use short strokes to avoid cutting into the copper tubing. Check your progress and stop cutting before you reach the copper.

2 TWIST AND BREAK THE SLEEVE Insert a flat-blade screwdriver into the cut and twist the screwdriver to break the sleeve. Slide off the old sleeve, old compression nut and the escutcheon (if you're going to replace it).

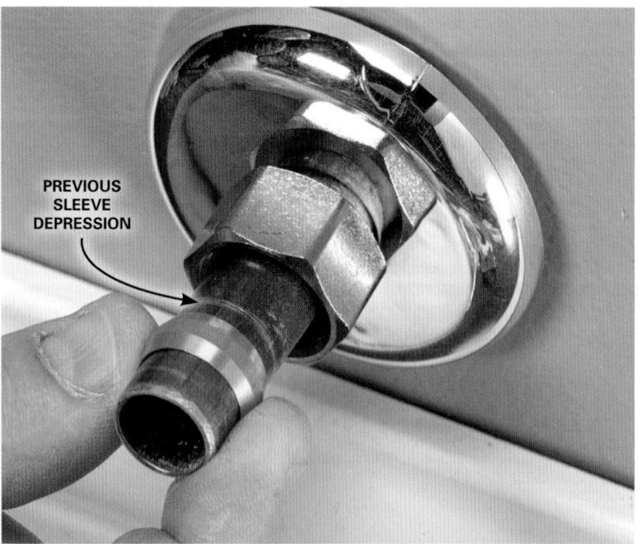

3 POSITION THE NEW COMPRESSION SLEEVE Slide the new compression sleeve onto the copper tubing. If the old sleeve left depression marks, locate the new sleeve slightly forward of the marks.

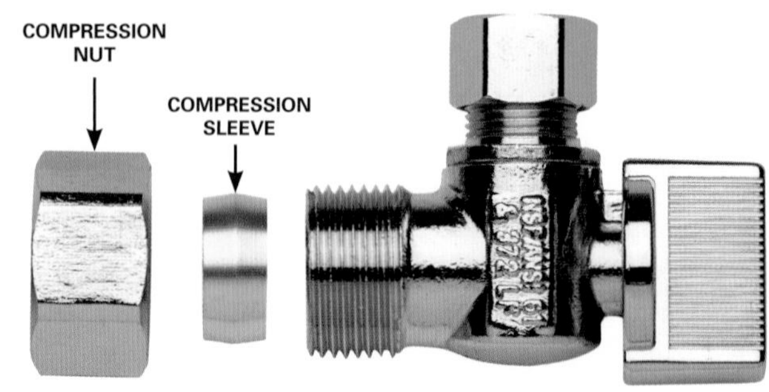

pro tip

Tip for replacing a shutoff valve

When you replace a compression-style shutoff valve, it's always best to use a new compression sleeve. But sawing through the sleeve without cutting into the copper tubing can be tricky, and sometimes you just don't have enough room to use a saw. That's where a compression sleeve puller earns its keep (one choice is the Pasco No. 4661; $50 at toolup.com). Crank out the screw and slide the jaw behind the compression nut. Then turn the screw until the pilot fits into the copper tubing. Continue turning until the sleeve slides off. That's it. Just slide on the new compression nut, sleeve and valve and then tighten.

Can you use a push-fit valve?

Several companies make quarter-turn push-fit ball-style shutoff valves that install without tools. They're a good alternative to sweat and compression fittings if you have enough tubing projecting out from the wall and if that tubing is in good shape. They make the job even simpler. If your stub-out tubing is perfectly symmetrical, long enough and has a square-cut end, you might be able to use a push-fit valve to replace your old compression or sweat valve.

Most push-fit valves require at least 1 in. of stub-out tubing. So measure the length of the stub-out and refer to the valve manufacturer's length requirements before buying. If your tubing will work, shop for a valve that meets your configuration needs (straight or angled). Push-fit valves are available with and without a permanently mounted supply tube. We don't recommend the permanently installed supply tube version because you have to shut off the water and replace the entire unit if the supply tube ever needs replacement.

Before installing a push-fit valve, remove any burrs from the open end. If you're replacing a sweat valve, remove all traces of solder and ensure the tubing is perfectly round. Then mark the installed length on the tubing and push the valve onto the tubing until it reaches the mark.

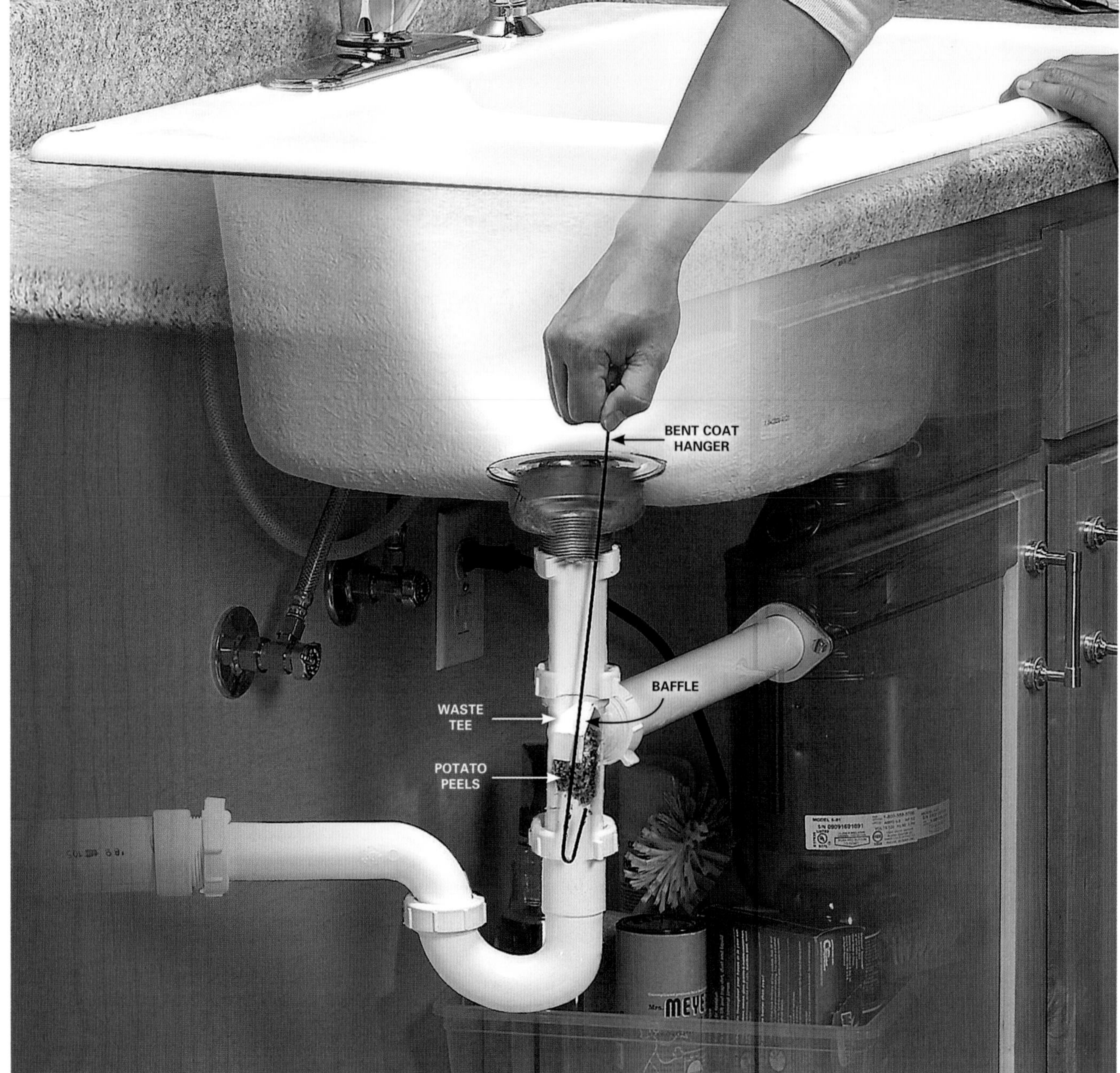

Unclog a kitchen sink

When the water in your kitchen sink won't drain or drains slowly, don't reach for the chemical drain cleaner. Instead, try this three-step method recommended by one of our favorite plumbers. The first two steps we'll show you don't even require you to remove the trap or take anything apart. If you're lucky, all you'll need is a bent coat hanger. But if the clog is in the trap or farther down the drain, you'll need a 1/4-in. drain snake. You can buy an inexpensive snake that's simply a cable running through a bent pipe that allows you to twist the cable, but we recommend spending a little more money for a cable that's enclosed in a drum. This type is much easier to use.

Before you get started on any of our solutions, suck all the water out of the sink with a wet-dry shop vacuum or sponge it into a bucket. You'll be able to see what you're doing, and if you do have to disassemble plumbing, it'll be less messy.

1 The coat-hanger trick

If you have a two-bowl sink and only one side is clogged, there's a good chance this fix will work. First look under the sink to locate the waste tee. If your drain setup looks something like the one shown here and the water is backing up on the side without the waste tee, you may be able to remove the clog with a bent coat hanger (opening photo). There's a baffle inside the waste tee that is meant to direct water down the drain, but since the baffled area is narrower than the rest of the drain, food often gets stuck there. Garbage disposers are notorious for causing clogs, especially at the baffle. The trick is to bend a hook on the end of a coat hanger wire and use it to dislodge the clog. Use pliers to bend a hook that will fit through the slots in the basket strainer. Peek under the sink to get a rough idea how far down the waste tee is from the basket strainer. Push the bent hanger down the drain. Then twist and pull until you feel it hook onto the baffle. Now wiggle it up and down while twisting it to remove the clog. Run water in the clogged sink to tell if you've removed the obstruction. If the sink still doesn't drain, there's a clog farther down. Move on to Step 2.

2 Run a snake through the basket stainer

There are several advantages to this approach. You don't have to remove all the stuff from under the sink, struggle to take apart and reassemble drains, or worry about spilling dirty drain water when you remove the trap. Also, pushing the cable down through the basket strainer allows you to clean the slime-covered cable as you withdraw it by running clean water down the drain. (Believe us, this is a nice bonus!) And finally, since the drain is still fully assembled, you'll be able to tell, by running water in the sink, whether you've unclogged the drain.

You have to modify the end of the cable on your drain snake to use this method, however (photo below). Then you snake out the drain by pushing the cable down through one of the slots or holes in the basket strainer.

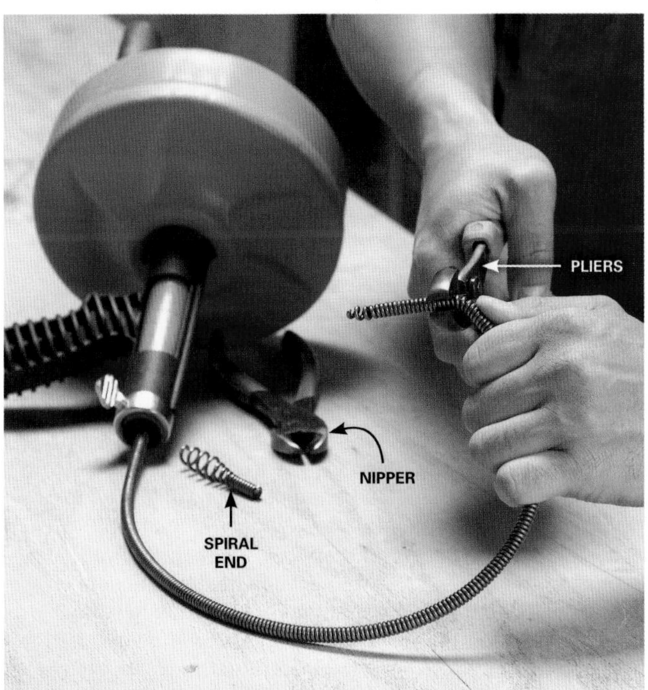

1 Modify your drain snake to fit through the slot in the basket strainer. First clip off the spiral end. Then bend the last few inches at about a 30-degree angle with pliers. Finally, unwind the tip slightly to form a small hook.

pro tip

Never have another clog!

Garbage disposers and grease are the two biggest contributors to clogged sink drains. Here's the first rule for avoiding clogs: Don't use your garbage disposer like a trash can. If your family sends vast amounts of food down the disposer, you'll have a clogged sink someday. Disposing of turkey carcasses, gummy foods like pasta and fibrous items like banana peels in the sink is asking for trouble. The same goes for heaping plates of leftovers. Scrape the big stuff into the garbage can and use the disposer for the small stuff.

The second rule: Never pour grease down the drain. And running hot water along with it won't help. The grease will just congeal farther down the drainpipe where it'll be even harder to clear.

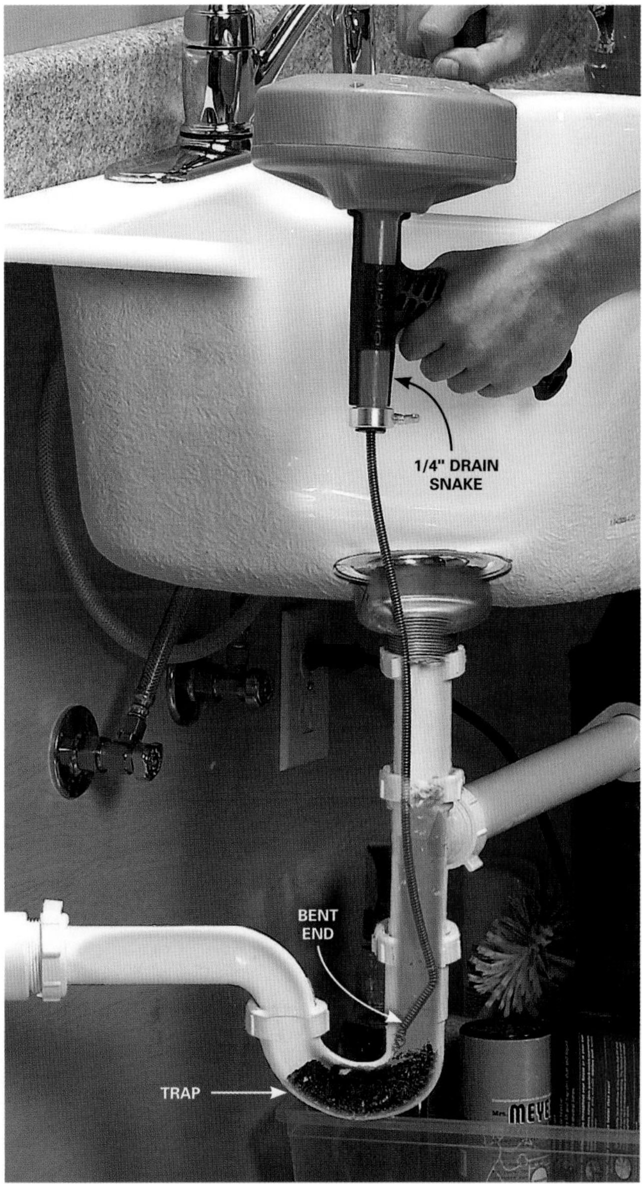

3 If you can't unclog the drain using one of the steps above, then it's time to take off the trap and waste arm and feed the drain snake directly into the drainpipe. Remember to remove as much water from the sink as possible before you remove the trap. Then place a bucket under the trap to catch any remaining water. Use large slip-joint pliers to loosen the slip-joint nuts on both ends of the trap. Unscrew the nuts and remove the trap. Do the same with the nut that secures the waste arm to the drain and remove the waste arm.

Before you reach for the drain snake, look up into the baffle tee to make sure the baffle area is clear. Then look into the trap to make sure there's no clog in the bottom. If both spots are clear, then the clog is farther down in the drainpipe and you'll need a drain snake.

With this method, the only way you'll know if you've unclogged the drain is to reassemble the trap and run water down the drain. If you've got a metal trap and drain arm, we recommend replacing them and the other metal drain parts with plastic. Plastic parts are easy to cut and assemble. They're also easier to take apart if you have a problem in the future, and they don't corrode.

1 If the previous two approaches didn't work, remove the trap and waste arm to get to the clog. You'll have two fewer bends to get around with the snake and have an easier time reaching deep clogs.

pro tip

The art of running a snake

There's an art to using a drain snake, and the more experience you have, the better you'll be at it. Here's how you do it. Loosen the setscrew or chuck to allow the cable to come out of the drum freely. Now feed the cable into the drain until you can't push it any more. It may be stuck on the clog or simply meeting resistance where the drainpipe bends.

Position the end of the drum so there's about 8 in. of cable showing between the drain and the drum, and tighten the setscrew or chuck onto the cable. Withdraw the cable about an inch so that it's free of the obstruction, and start turning the drum while you push it toward the drain. Continue until you've pushed the exposed cable down the drain. Then repeat the process by loosening the setscrew and withdrawing another 8 in. of cable. If the end of the cable gets stuck and you keep turning the drum, the cable will start to spiral inside the drain. You want to avoid this, so stop turning the drum if you feel that the cable isn't turning freely anymore. Withdraw the cable about 6 in. and try again.

Several things can happen at this point. You might bore through the clog, allowing water to run through and dissolve the remaining clog. You might push the clog to a point where the diameter of the pipes is larger and it can wash down the drain. Or you might hook the clog with the end of the snake and pull it out. This is where your intuition comes into play. When you think you've unclogged the drain, withdraw the snake. If you've pushed the cable down through the basket strainer, you can rinse it off as you retrieve it by running water. Otherwise, put on some gloves and wipe the cable off with a rag as you push it back into the drum.

When you're done cleaning the drain, pull the cable out of the drum, rinse it off, and wipe it down with an oil-soaked rag to keep it from rusting.

Unclog a bathroom sink

Clogged or slow-draining sinks and tubs are more than a nuisance; they can put your entire bathroom or kitchen out of action and disrupt your family's busy schedule. But as frustrating as they make life, most drain clogs can be quickly cleared, even by a novice, in 10 to 15 minutes.

The first step in clearing a clog is locating it. This task often takes some trial and error, but here are some clues. If only one fixture is clogged, the problem is either in the stopper mechanism, the P-trap or the drain leading away from the fixture. If a group of fixtures is affected, look for the clog downstream from where their drains join.

1 Plunge the sink drain. Fill the sink with 2 in. of water. Completely cover the drain hole with the plunger bell. Cover overflow hole with a wet sponge to maintain pressure. Make the first plunge slowly to expel air from bell; then plunge in and out vigorously 15 to 20 times. Add water as needed to keep the bell covered and air out.

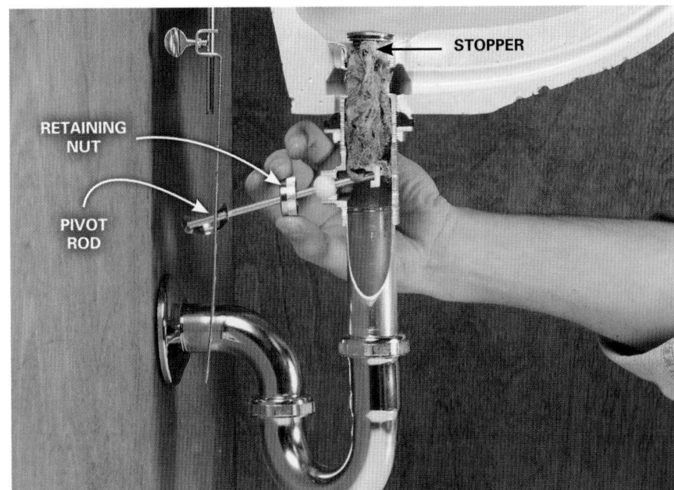

2 Clear stoppers of hair and debris. For sinks with stoppers locked in place by a pivot rod, first remove all standing water from the sink. Unscrew the retaining nut on the back of the sink drain and remove the pivot rod from the stopper. Remove stopper and clear away clog. Reinstall stopper assembly and test drain to make sure retaining nut doesn't leak.

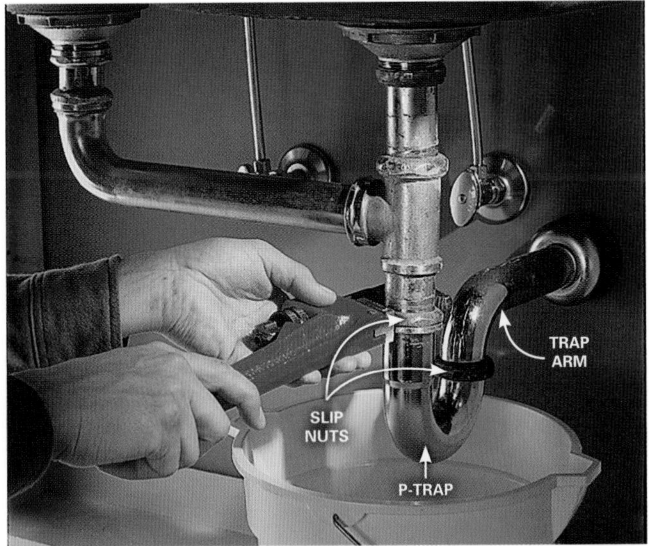

3 Clear the P-trap. Place a bucket under the trap, loosen slip nuts using pipe wrench if necessary, remove the trap and clear the debris. Reassemble the trap.

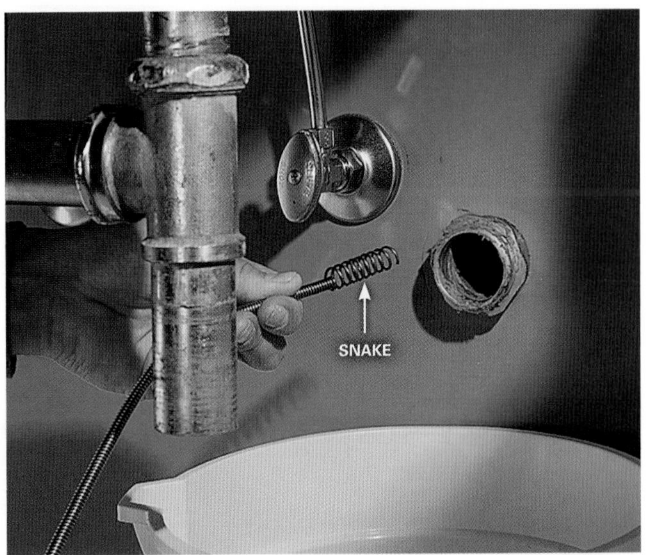

4 Snake the drain. Remove the trap arm, slide the spiral end of the snake into the drain and feed it all the way to the clog if possible. Don't mistake an elbow in the drain pipe for the clog. Lock the snake's offset handle in place and crank the snake clockwise while pushing it forward. Slide the handle back and relock as necessary. The spiral end helps work the snake around bends and break up clogs.

Clear a clogged toilet

For about 90 percent of toilet clogs, you need only one special tool—a plunger with a flange-type cup. Toilet clogs are relatively easy to clear because after the clog passes the wax ring, the drain pipe becomes significantly larger, allowing the clog to float away.

Understanding how toilets work will help you diagnose your toilet troubles. Toilets require two things to flush well—a smooth, unobstructed drain and good siphoning action. As the flapper valve lifts, water flows into the rim chamber. Some of the water will exit through the rinse holes to clean the bowl and create the swirling action at the bottom; the rest passes through the siphon-jet chamber, where it picks up speed as it exits the siphon-jet hole. Together, these two water sources create the force necessary to carry waste over the back part of the drain and leave behind a clean bowl. When any part of the water path is limited, troubles begin.

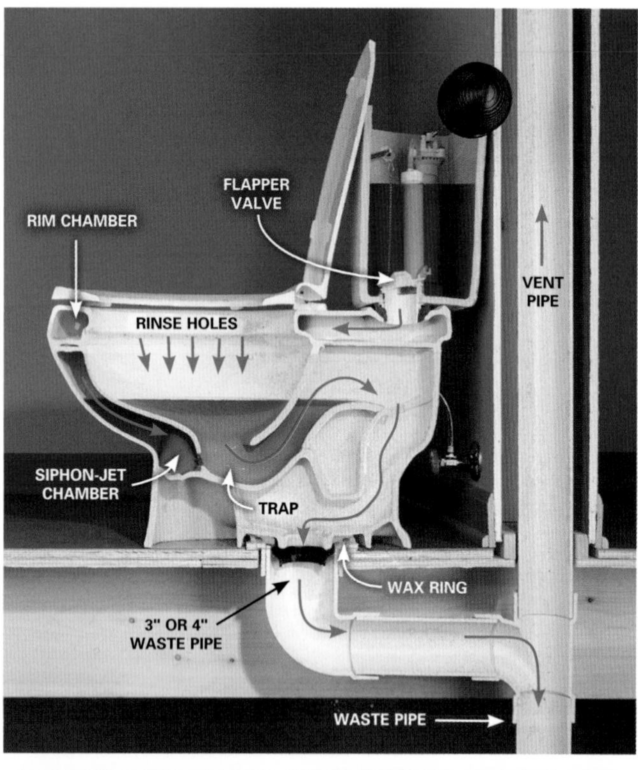

1 **Don't flush the toilet if you suspect a clog. Make a first plunge gently to expel air from the plunger bell; then plunge vigorously in and out. Keep the plunger covered with water. If the plunger fails to clear a clog, use a closet auger, as shown in Photo 3.**

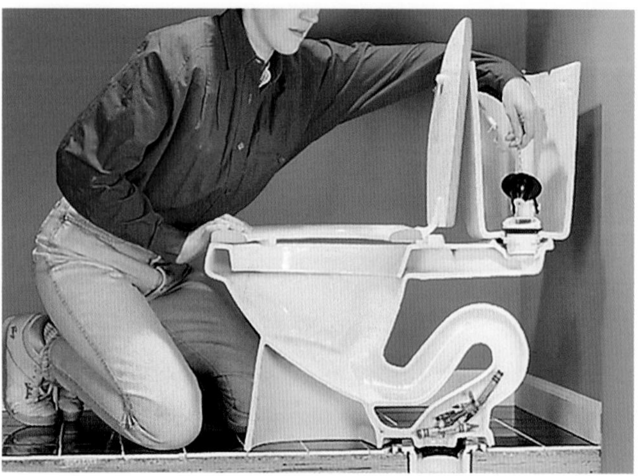

2 **Test the drain by letting in small amounts of water—don't use the flush handle. Instead, remove the tank lid and manually open and close the flapper to see whether water goes down easily. If it's still plugged, you'll have to push the flapper down to restore the seal quickly.**

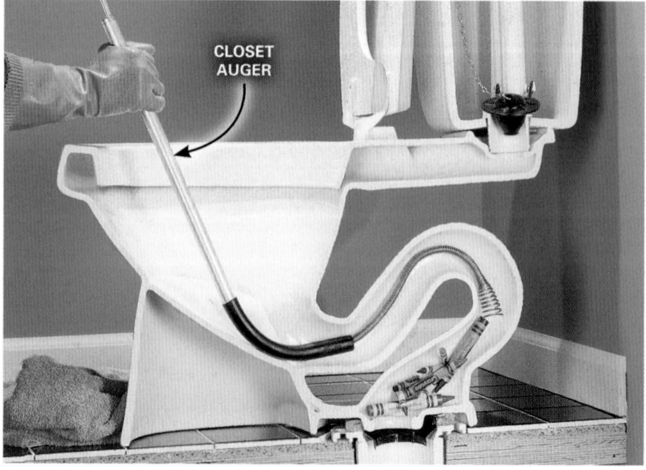

3 **For stubborn clogs, spin a closet auger or regular snake through the drain. The hooked spring end should break through the clog or grab the obstruction (such as a rag) so you can pull it out. Once a clog passes the wax ring into the wider drain, it should move easily**

Unclog a bathtub drain

In bathrooms, by far the most common source of clogs is a wad of hair and soap scum wrapped around the stopper mechanism or, in a shower, lying just underneath the drain cover. Always check for this problem before resorting to taking drains apart for snaking.

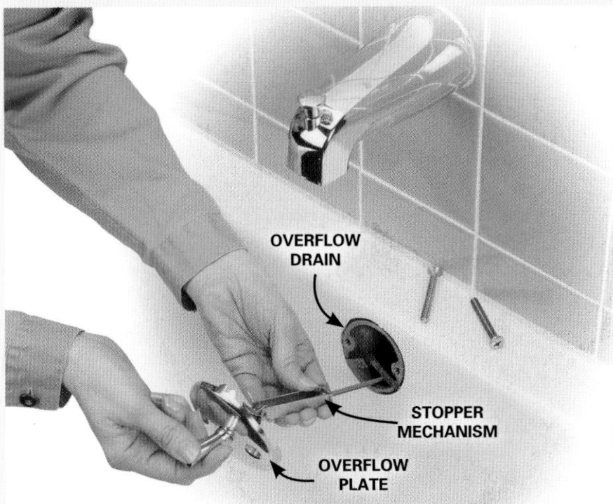

1 **Unscrew overflow plate and remove it and the stopper mechanism from the bathtub drain. Some tub stoppers have two main parts—a spring or weight in the vertical overflow drain and an arm attached to the stopper plug in the horizontal tub drain. Clean stopper parts, cover overflow hole and plunge drain. Reassemble stopper.**

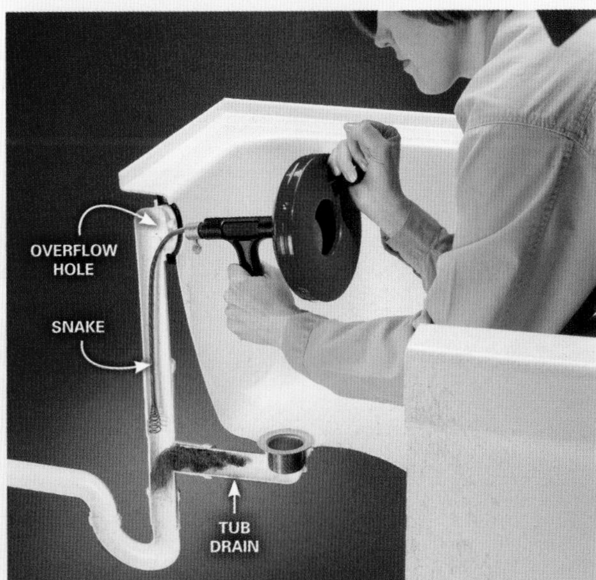

2 **If clog remains, run the snake down the overflow hole to clear obstructions. If still unsuccessful, replace overflow plate and stopper mechanism, and remove P-trap through access hole or from below. Then run snake down the drain as you would a sink drain.**

instant fix

Unclog a showerhead

Over time, hard-water minerals in tap water build up and clog the spray holes in showerheads. Fix this problem by removing the showerhead and cleaning it. Buy a lime-removing product to loosen the scale, or soak the head overnight in vinegar (either white or apple cider). Check the owner's manual or manufacturer's Web site to confirm that vinegar won't harm the finish.

Carefully remove the showerhead and open the holes using the steps shown in Photos 1 and 2. If the showerhead is too stuck to remove, try filling a plastic bag with vinegar, tying the top of the bag around the top of the showerhead and submerging it overnight in the vinegar.

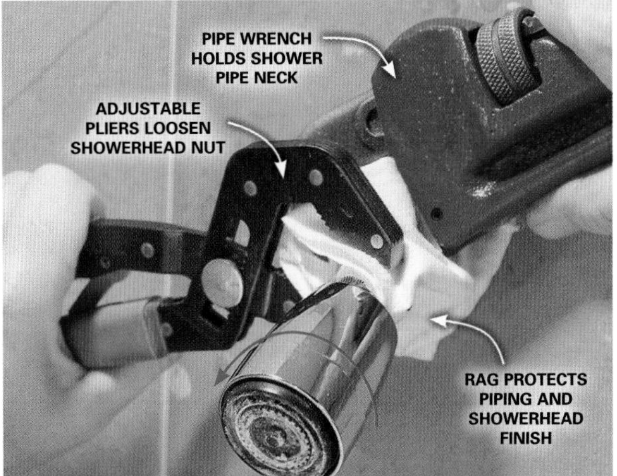

1 **Unscrew the showerhead by gripping the shower neck with a pipe wrench (as shown), grabbing the nut on the showerhead with adjustable pliers and turning the pliers counterclockwise until the nut loosens. Protect the finishes on the showerhead and wall pipe by wrapping them with a cloth.**

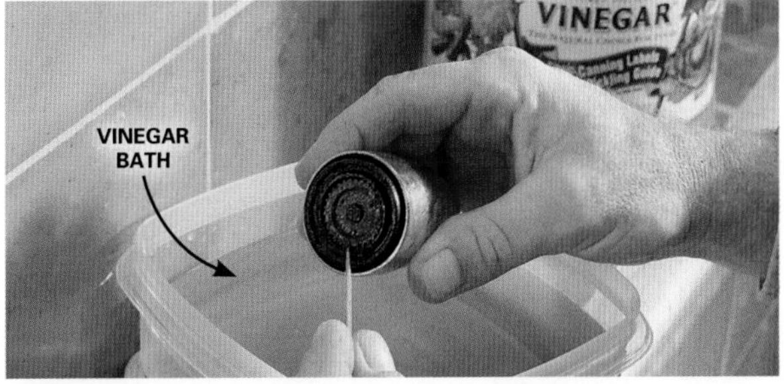

2 **Open the showerhead holes by soaking the head overnight in a vinegar bath and poking the loosened mineral scale free with a toothpick. Rinse the showerhead in tap water, then reinstall it by applying Teflon tape to the wall pipe threads, screwing it on and tightening it by reversing the technique in Photo 1. Complete the repair by turning on the cold water in the shower and blasting out any remaining mineral gunk.**

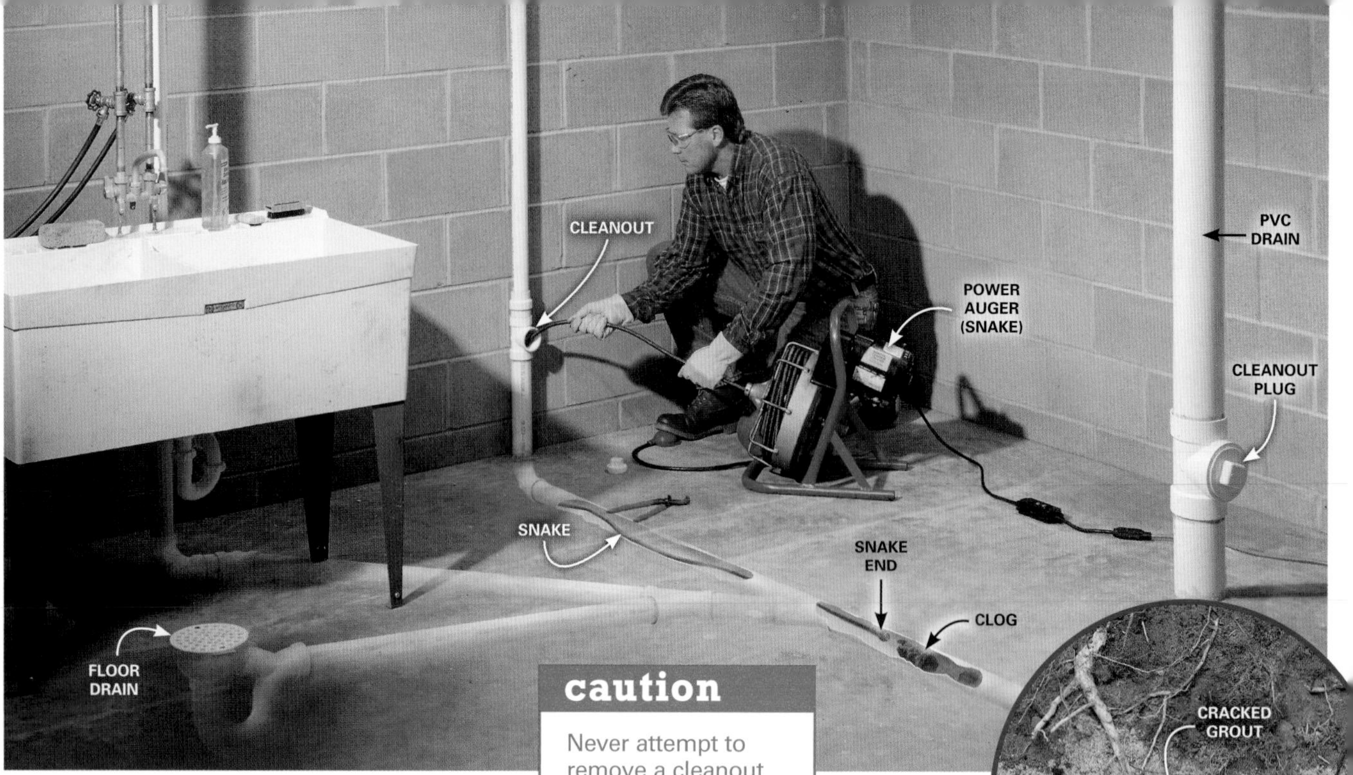

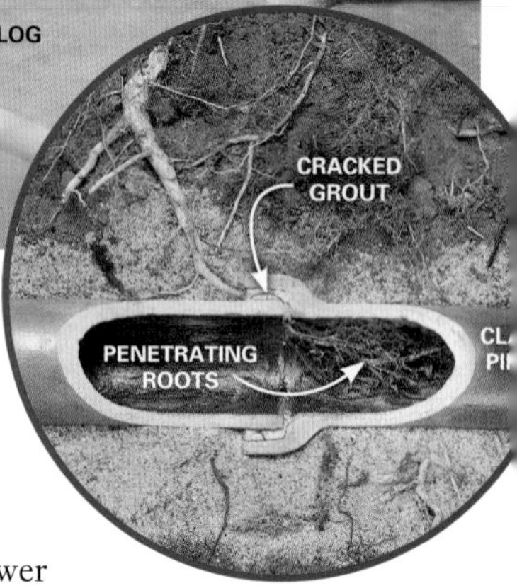

Unclog a main drain

caution

Never attempt to remove a cleanout plug from, or run a cable into, a drain that contains chemical drain cleaner.

If a group of fixtures, or a floor drain, is backed up, you have a clog in one of the main drain lines. These clogs often require that you remove cleanout plugs and open the drain using heavy-duty power-driven augers. Frequently these clogs form when tree roots penetrate the main drain or when certain foreign objects are sent down the drain.

To clear the drain, you can call a professional or rent a drain-cleaning machine. Be careful removing the cleanout plug—it may release a flood of backed up wastewater, so be prepared with buckets and rags.

Tree roots work their way through cracks or joints in older sewer lines made of clay tile, cast iron or other piping. Newer sewer lines, made of plastic, don't suffer from this problem. When a drain becomes root-bound, it needs to be reamed out using a root saw, but the problem will soon recur unless one of the following extra measures is taken:

- Dig up the old line and replace it with plastic.
- To slow root growth, treat the drain with poison formulated to kill nearby roots.
- Seal the line by having the existing pipe lined with an internal plastic fabric and epoxy.

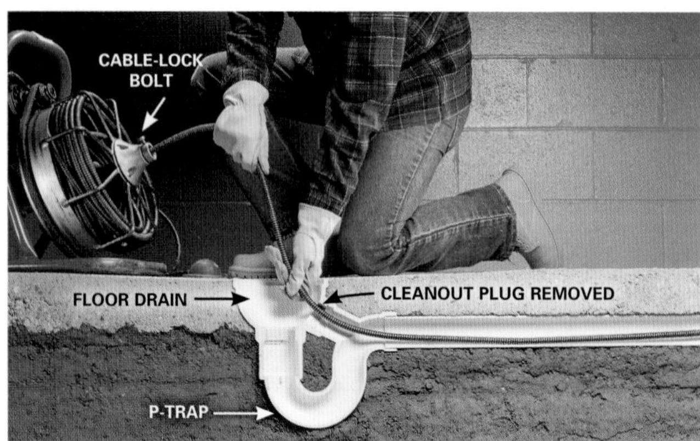

1 Remove the cleanout plug from the floor drain or cleanout. Feed cable into the drain with the motor off until you can't push any farther. Start and stop the motor using the foot switch as you feed cable. Proceed slowly. Do not allow tension to build up if the cable head stops and the cage continues to rotate. To chew through the clog, tighten the cable-lock bolt and loosen and feed cable as needed.

2 Attack the clog through the main drain cleanout, if necessary. Correctly installed systems will ensure the snake follows the correct path. Stubborn or stripped cleanout plugs can be replaced with special friction-fit plugs.

Stop a running toilet

A toilet that won't stop running can drive you crazy, especially if it happens when you're trying to fall asleep. But there is good news: You can put an end to this water torture yourself, even if you have no plumbing know-how. You may be able to solve the problem in just a few minutes without spending a dime. At worst, this fix will cost a few hours and $25 in toilet parts.

Finding the problem is usually simple

A toilet runs constantly because the fill valve that lets water into the tank isn't closing completely. A toilet runs intermittently because the valve opens slightly for a few minutes. In either case, you have to figure out why that valve isn't stopping the incoming water flow.

First, look for leaks. A leak in the tank can make a toilet run constantly or intermittently. If your toilet is leaking, you've probably noticed it already. But take a look just to be sure. If you find leaks coming from the tank bolts or flush valve, you'll most likely have to remove the tank from the bowl so you can replace the tank bolts, the rubber washers and the gaskets on the flush valve. If there are leaks around the fill valve, tighten the locknut (see Photo 6, p. 121). Leaks can come from cracks in the tank, too. In that case, the only reliable solution is a new toilet.

If you don't find any leaks, lift off the tank cover. At first glance, the array of submerged thingamajigs inside may look intimidating. But don't let them scare you. There are really only two main parts: the flush valve, which lets water gush into the bowl during the flush; and the fill valve, which lets water refill the tank after the flush. When a toilet runs constantly or intermittently, one of these valves is usually at fault.

To determine which valve is causing the trouble, look at the overflow tube. If water is overflowing into the tube, there's a problem with the fill valve. If the water level is below the top of the tube, the flush valve is leaking, allowing water to trickle into the bowl. That slow, constant outflow of water prevents the fill valve from closing completely.

We cut away the fronts and backs of new toilets to show you how to replace these parts. Your toilet won't look so pristine inside. You'll find scummy surfaces, water stains and corrosion. But don't be squeamish—the water is as clean as the stuff that comes out of your faucets.

Figure A
Toilet cutaway

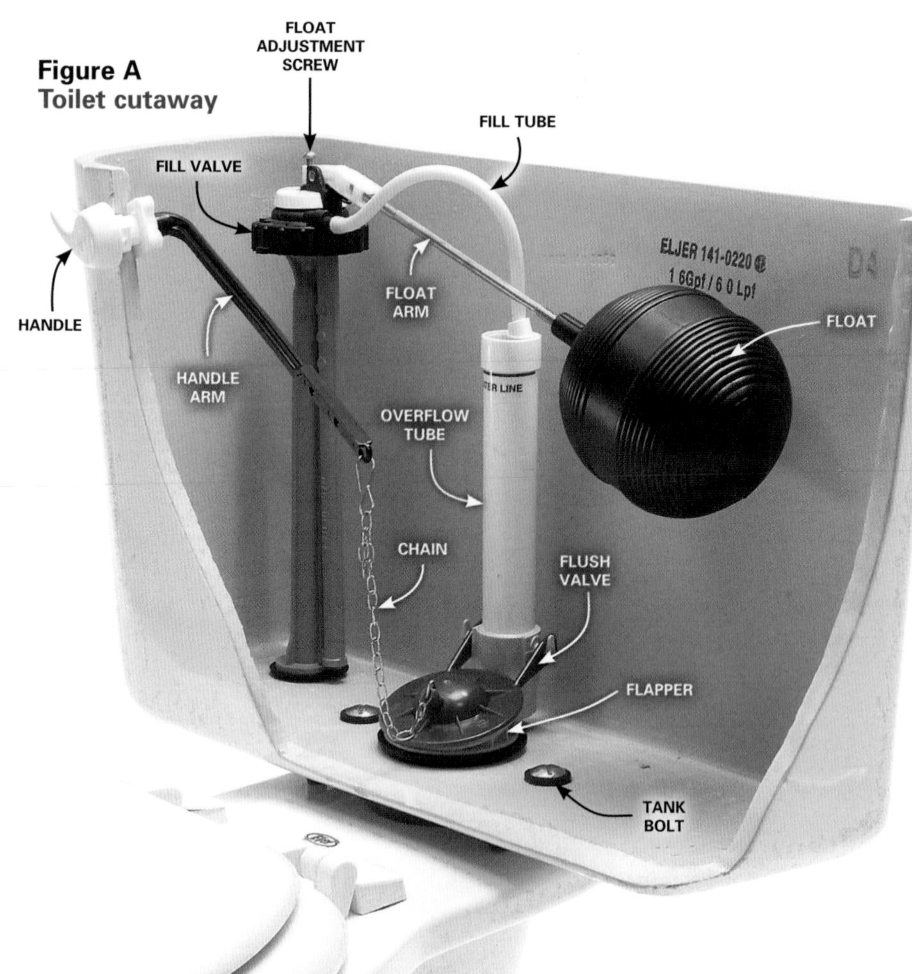

Repair the fill valve

You may have to replace the fill valve, but these three fixes are worth a try first:

Fix 1: Adjust the float

If your valve has a ball that floats at the end of a rod, gently lift the rod and listen. If the water shuts off, you may be able to stop the running by adjusting the float. Some fill valves have a float adjustment screw on top (see Figure A). If there is no adjustment screw, bend the float arm (photo right). If you have a Fluidmaster-style fill valve, make sure it's adjusted properly (Photo 8.) You don't have to empty the tank to make these adjustments.

pro tip

After you bend the float arm, make sure that it doesn't interfere with the movement of the handle arm or chain.

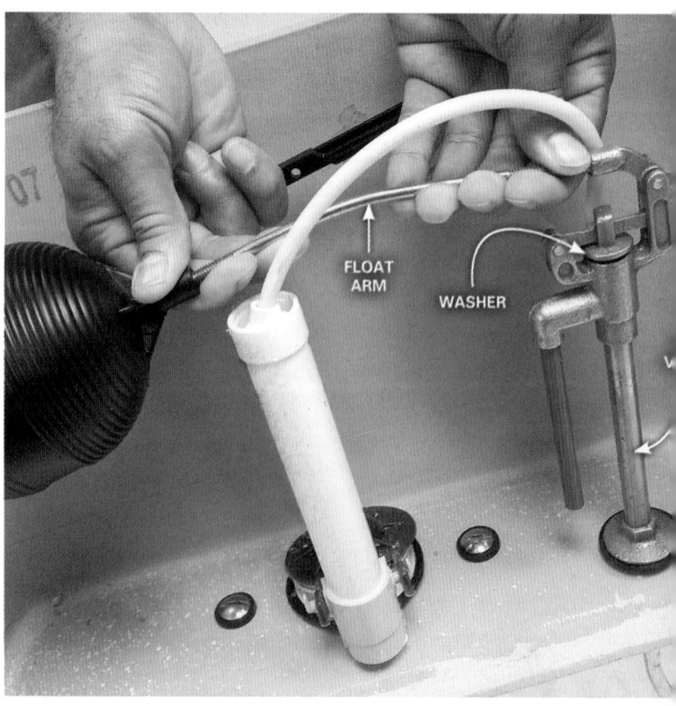

1 **Gently bend the float arm down to put extra pressure on the valve. (To adjust a float that doesn't have an arm, see Photo 8.) Then flush the toilet to see if it works.**

Fix 2: Flush the valve

Hard water, debris from old pipes or particles from a break in a city water line can prevent a flush valve from closing completely. Running water through it from the supply line will clear the debris. Photos 1 and 2 show you how to do this on one common type of valve. Even though other valves will look different, the clearing process is similar. However, you may have to remove a few screws on top of the fill valve to remove the cap.

1 Remove the fill valve cap. On this type of valve, press down and turn counterclockwise. Remove screws on other types of valves.

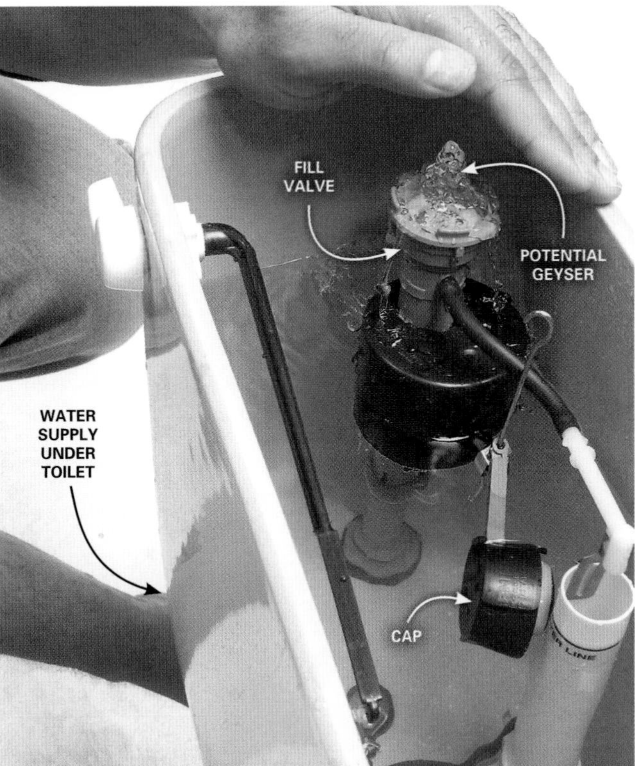

2 Cover the valve with your hand. Turn on the water (cautiously, so you don't get a cold shower!) and let it flush out the valve for a few seconds.

Fix 3: Replace the washer

When you remove the cap to flush out the valve, inspect the washer for wear or cracks. Replacing a bad washer is cheap and easy (Photo 3). But finding the right washer may not be. The most common washers are often available at home centers and hardware stores. Other styles can be hard to find. If you decide to hunt for a washer, remove it and take it to the store to find a match. Plumbers usually replace the whole fill valve rather than hunt for a replacement washer.

pro tip

Sometimes you don't have to replace a leaking washer. Just gently clean it to remove mineral buildup.

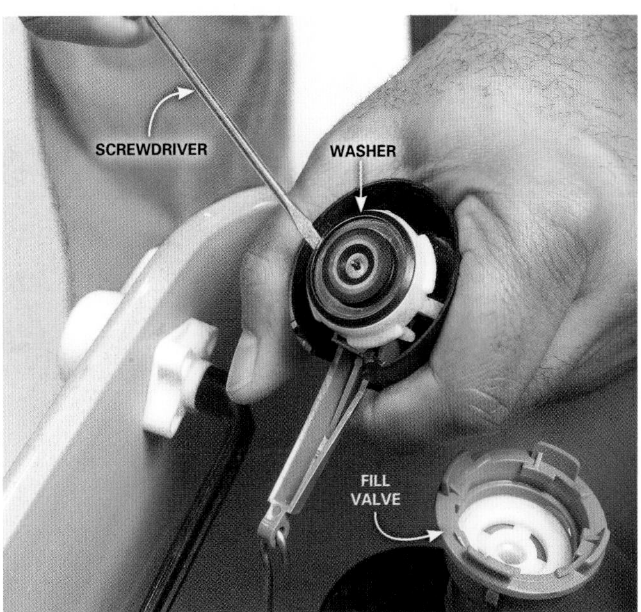

3 Replace a worn, cracked valve washer by prying the old washer out of the cap with a small screwdriver. Press the new one into place.

Fix 4: If you can't fix the fill valve, replace it

Replacing a fill valve requires only a few basic tools (an adjustable 'pliers and a pair of scissors) and an hour of your time. A kit containing the type of valve we show here and everything else you need available at home centers and hardware stores.

Your first step is to shut off the water. In most cases, you'll have a shutoff valve right next to the toilet coming either through the floor or out of the wall. If you don't have a shutoff, turn off the water supply at the main shutoff valve, where water enters your home. This is a good time to add a shutoff valve next to the toilet or replace one that leaks. This is also a good time to replace the supply line that feeds your toilet

1 Replace the fill valve. Turn off the water at the shutoff valve. Flush the toilet and hold the flush valve open to drain the tank. Sponge out the remaining water or vacuum it up with a wet/dry vacuum.

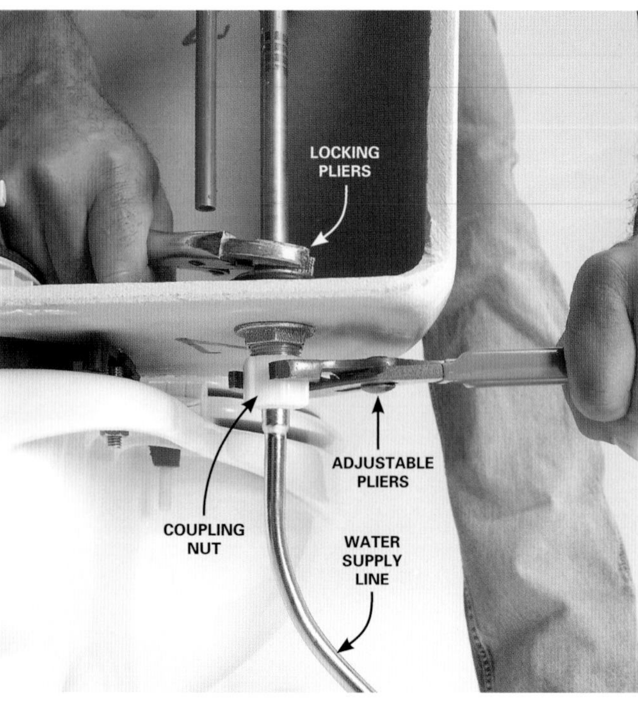

2 Unscrew the coupling nut that connects the supply line. If the valve turns inside the tank, hold its base with locking pliers. Tip: Throw a towel on the floor underneath to catch water that will drain from the line.

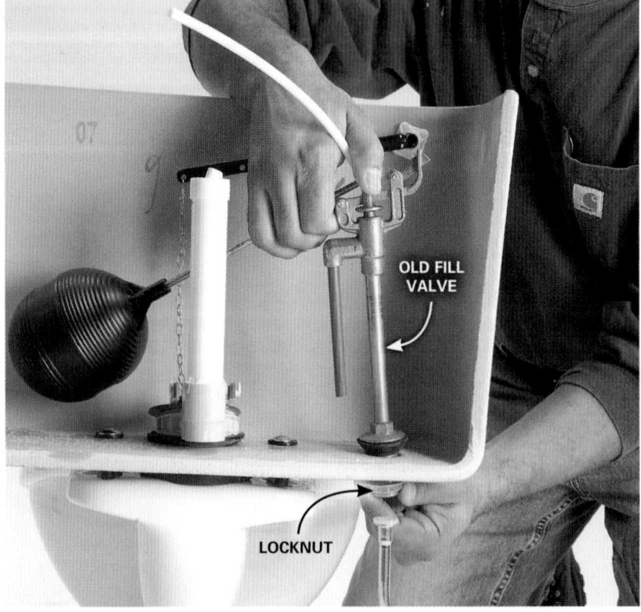

3 Remove the locknut that holds the valve to the tank. Push down gently on the valve as you unscrew the nut. Pull out the old valve.

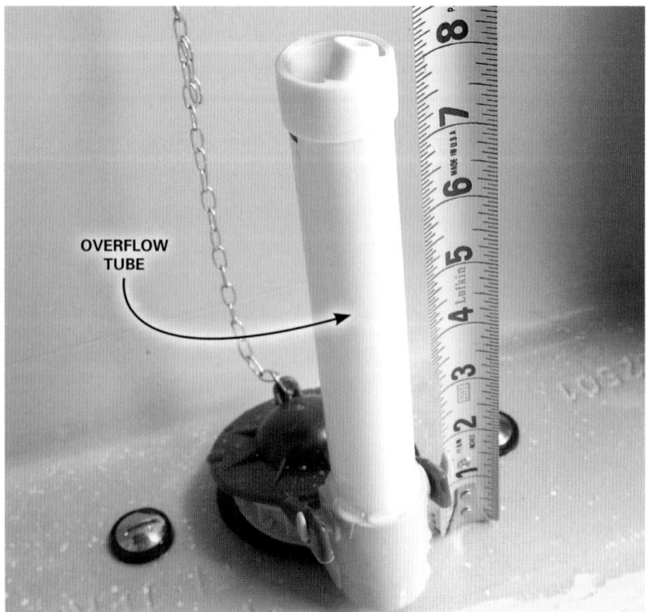

4 Measure the desired water level. If there isn't a label on the overflow tube, just measure the height of the overflow tube.

(Photo 6). Photos 1 – 8 show how to replace the valve. If the height of your valve is adjustable, set the height before you install the valve (Photo 5). If your valve is a different style from the one we show, check the directions. After mounting the valve (Photo 6), connect the fill tube (Photo 7). The fill tube squirts water into the overflow tube to refill the toilet bowl. The water that refills the tank gushes from the bottom of the fill valve. When you install the valve and supply lines, turn the nuts finger-tight. Then give each another one-eighth turn with a pliers. When you turn the water supply back on, immediately check for leaks and tighten the nuts a bit more if necessary.

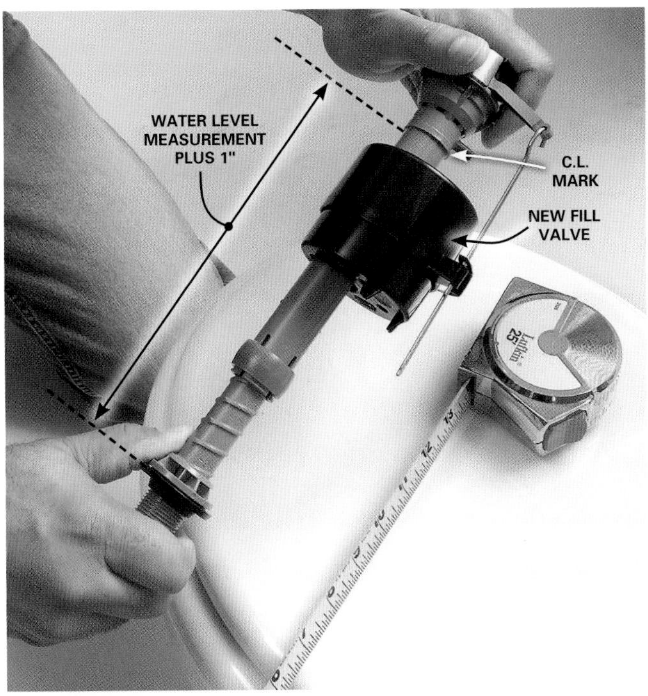

5 **Adjust the height of the new fill valve by holding the base and twisting the top. The height from the base to the CL (critical level) mark should be your water level measurement plus 1 in.**

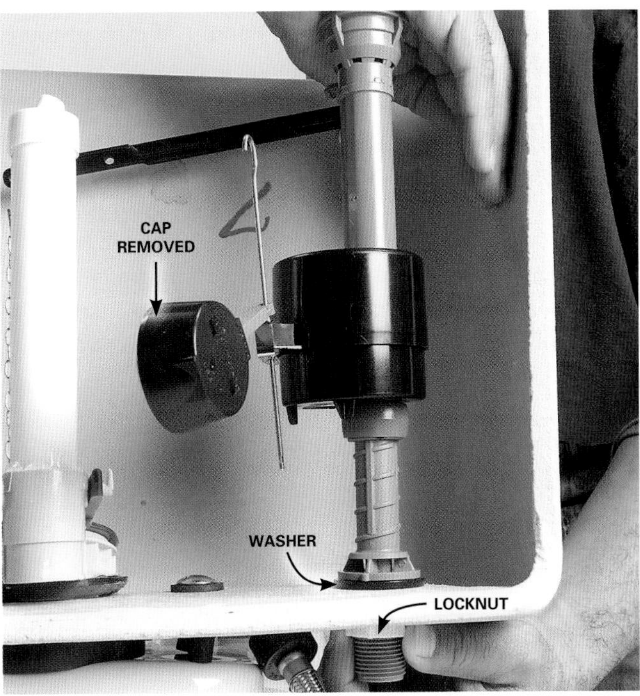

6 **Remove the cap, press down to compress the washer and turn the locknut finger-tight. Connect the supply line and flush the valve as shown in Photo 2. Reset the cap, turn on the water and check for leaks.**

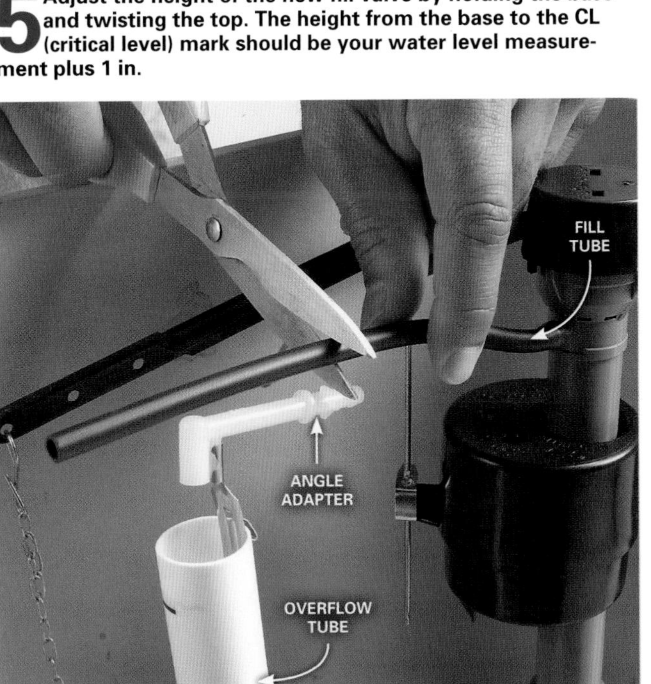

7 **Slip the fill tube onto the fill valve. Clip the angle adapter onto the overflow tube. Then cut the tube to fit and slip it onto the angle adapter.**

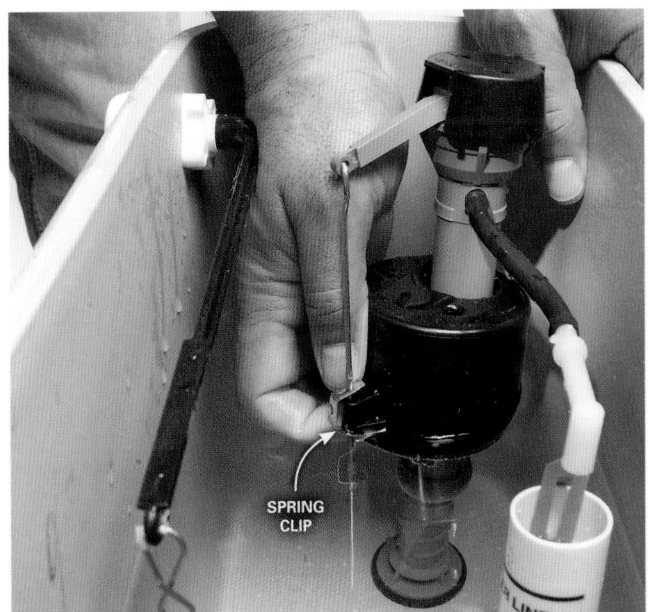

8 **Turn on water to fill the tank. Pinch spring clip and slide float up or down to set water level 1 in. below the top of the overflow tube or to the water line marked on the tank.**

2 Fix the flush valve

When a flush valve causes a toilet to run, a worn flapper is usually the culprit. But not always. First, look at the chain that raises the flapper. If there's too much slack in the chain, it can tangle up and prevent the flapper from closing firmly. A chain with too little slack can cause trouble too. Photo 3 shows how to set the slack just right.

Next, test the flapper as shown in Photo 1. If extra pressure on the flapper doesn't stop the running noise, water is likely escaping through a cracked or corroded overflow tube. In that case, you have to detach the tank from the bowl and replace the whole flush valve. Since the overflow tube is rarely the cause of a running toilet, we won't cover that repair here.

If pressing down on the flapper stops the noise, the flapper isn't sealing under normal pressure. Turn off the water, flush the toilet to empty the tank and then run your finger around the rim of the flush valve seat. If you feel mineral deposits, clean the flush valve seat with an abrasive sponge or Scotch-Brite pad. Don't use anything that might roughen it. If cleaning the flush valve seat doesn't solve the problem, you need to replace the flapper.

Replacing your flapper may require slightly different steps than we show (Photos 2 and 3). Your flapper may screw onto a threaded rod or have a ring that slips over the overflow tube. If you have an unusual flush valve, finding a replacement flapper may be the hardest part of the job. To find a suitable replacement, turn off the water, take the old one with you to the home center or hardware store. (Turn off the water before removing the flapper.) You may not find an identical match, but chances are you'll locate one of the same shape and diameter. If not, try a plumbing supply store or search online. It helps to know the brand and model of your toilet. The brand name is usually on the bowl behind the seat. In some cases, the model or number will be on the underside of the lid or inside the tank. Matching an unusual flapper can become a trial-and-error process. Even professional plumbers sometimes try two or three flappers before they find one that works well.

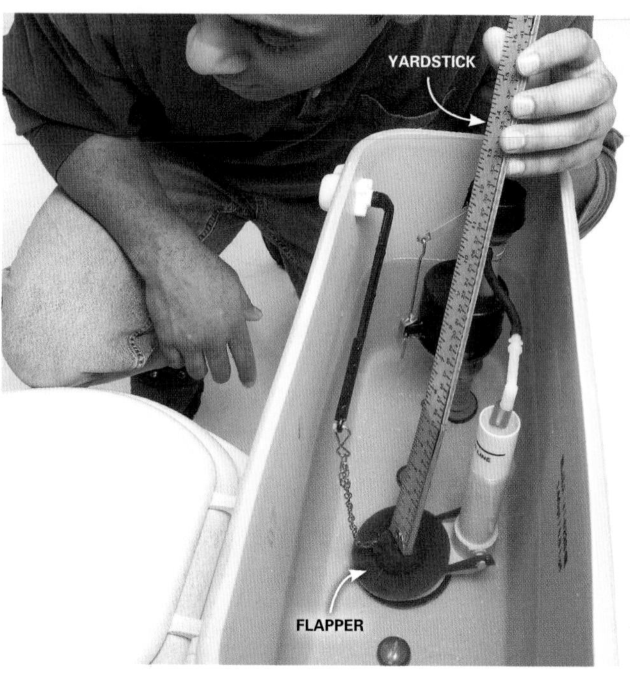

1 Push down on the flapper with a yardstick and listen. If the sound of running water stops, the flapper needs replacing.

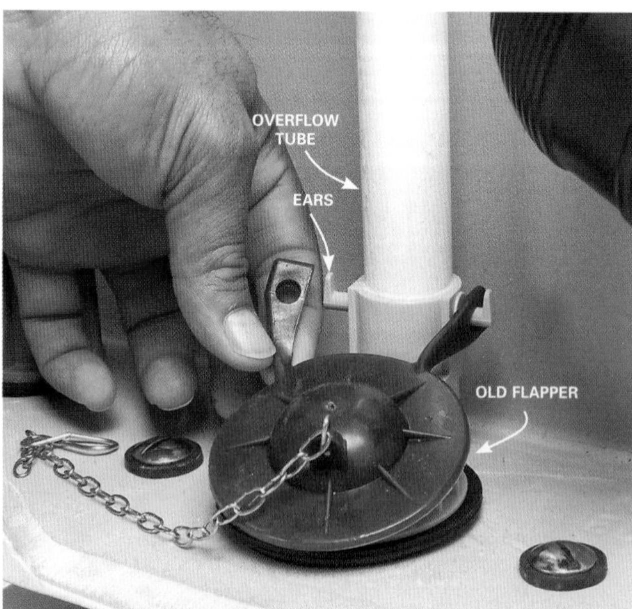

2 Remove the old flapper from the ears of the overflow tube and detach the chain from the handle arm.

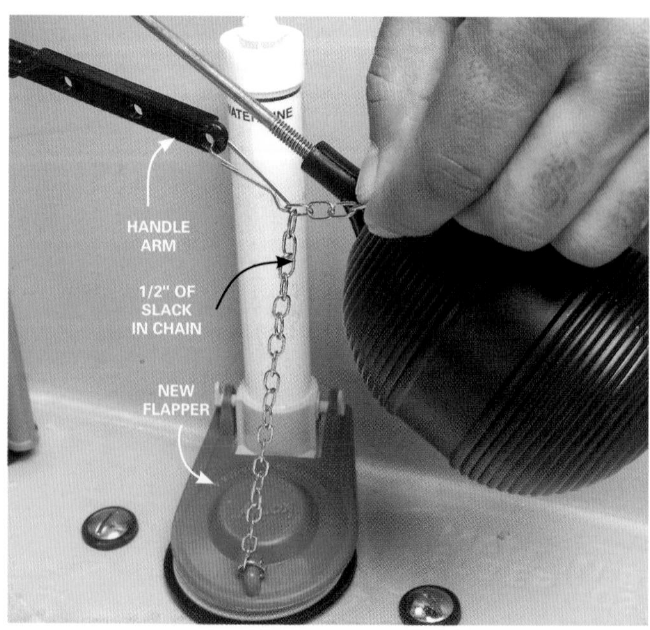

3 Attach the new flapper to the overflow tube and hook the chain to the handle arm. Leave 1/2 in. of slack in the chain. Turn the water back on and test-flush the toilet.

Troubleshoot toilet tank problems

When you flush a toilet, a carefully balanced series of events takes place in the tank. As you push the flush handle, the tank-stopper ball is lifted from its valve seat, allowing water to flow from the tank into the bowl. When the tank is nearly empty, the tank ball falls back into the valve seat, cutting off the flow.

As the tank's water level falls, so does the float, opening up the supply, or ballcock, valve just as the tank ball seals the tank. The tank then refills through the tank fill tube, and the bowl and trap refill from the bowl fill tube directing water down the overflow tube. As the float rises, it shuts off the ballcock valve and the toilet is ready for action once again. When any part of this balancing act is out of whack, you'll need to make one of the repairs shown in the chart below.

If your toilet tank or bowl develops a leak, check all pipes and connections. If a pipe or tube is corroded or the tank or bowl is cracked, replace it. If the leak appears near a joint, clean away any corrosion, replace any gaskets or washers and tighten the connection. Be careful when tightening bolts and nuts mounted to porcelain—the porcelain may crack and ruin the toilet.

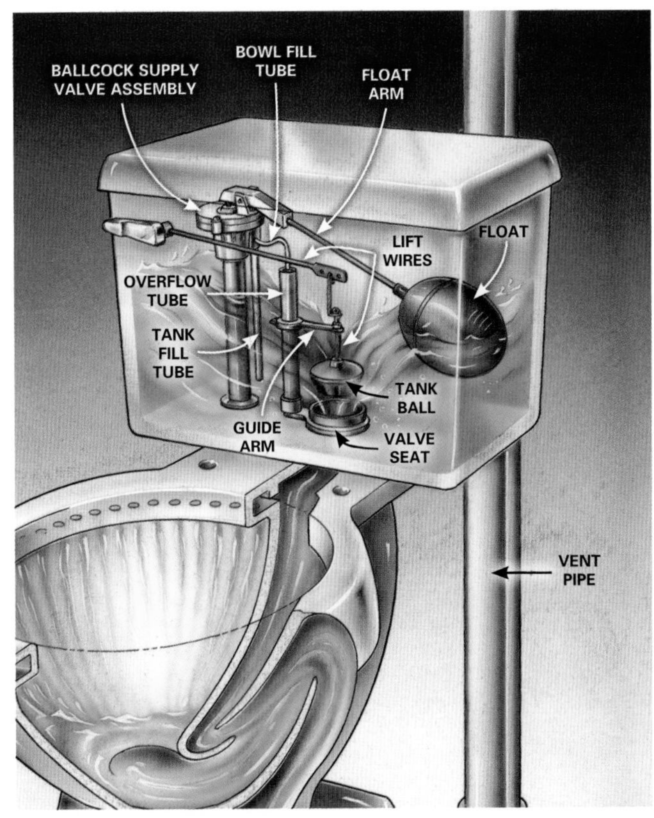

Problem	Solution
Water runs continuously.	**Adjust lift wires or chain to align tank ball. Clean valve seat.**
Water spills into overflow tube.	**Bend the float arm down.**
Water runs after flushing.	**Bend the float arm. Clean the valve seat. If the float is waterlogged, replace it. Replace tank ball or flapper.**
Whistling sounds occur.	**Put new washers in the ballcock-valve plunger. Replace ballcock assembly.**
Splashing sounds are heard.	**Reposition the refill tube to eject directly into overflow tube. Put new washers in the ballcock-valve assembly.**
Tank flushes partially.	**Shorten the lift wires or chain to make the tank ball rise higher. Bend the float arm upward to raise the water level.**
Tank sweats.	**Insulate the tank by lining it with sheets of polystyrene or foam rubber. Have plumber install tempering valve to warm the water in the tank.**
Tank leaks.	**Tighten connections to the water-supply line. Check gaskets and washers around discharge pipe and mounting bolts to the bowl.**
Toilet leaks at base.	**Tighten bolts at base of bowl. Disconnect the toilet from the floor and replace the wax seal under the bowl.**

instant fix

Hush a rattling lid

If the lid to your toilet tank rattles or wobbles, remove it and add a dab of silicone caulk to the four corners of the tank lip. After it dries, replace the lid; the noises should disappear.

Replace the drain assembly for a kitchen sink

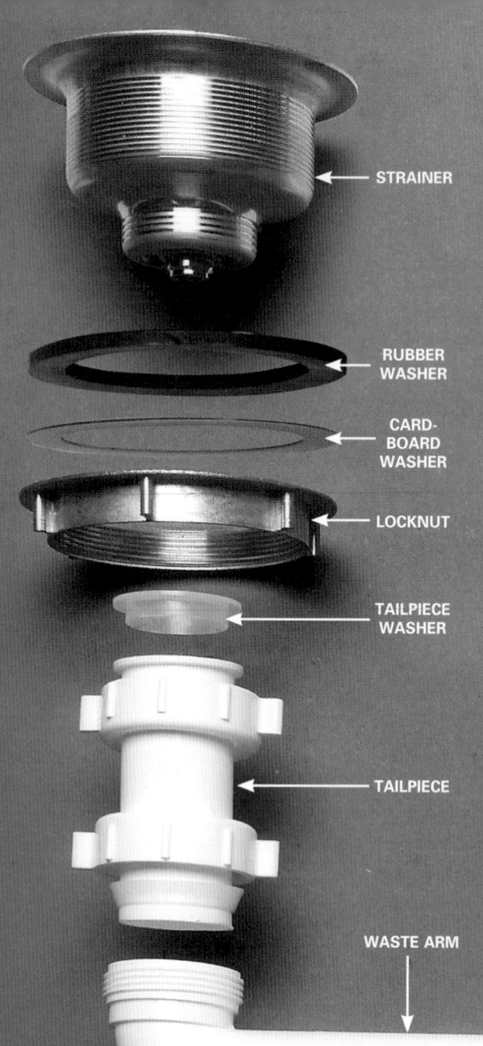

Some leaks can't be stopped with straightening or tightening. Stripped nuts won't tighten and old washers won't seal because they're stiff and distorted. You could get new nuts, washers or drain parts. Since plastic pipe is so inexpensive and easy to install, the smart, reliable fix is a whole new drain assembly. You can buy everything you need at home centers. Kits for side outlet assemblies (like the one shown here) or center outlet assemblies (where the trap is beneath the center of the sink) contain most of the essential parts. But you might also need:

- Long tailpieces (Photo 1). The tailpieces that come with kits are often only a couple of inches long.
- A trap arm extender (Photo 2). The arm that comes with the kit may not reach the drainpipe that protrudes from the wall.
- A dishwasher wye that has a connection for your dishwasher hose.
- A disposer kit that allows the waste arm to connect to a garbage disposer.

Photos 1–5 detail the whole replacement process. Here are some pointers for a smooth project:

- You'll have to cut a few pipes: both tailpieces, the waste arm and maybe the trap arm. A fine-tooth hacksaw works best.
- When in doubt, mark and cut pipes a bit long. Better to cut twice than cut too short and make an extra trip to the hardware store.

1 Attach the tailpiece to the basket strainer, but don't fully tighten it yet; you'll have to remove and cut it later.

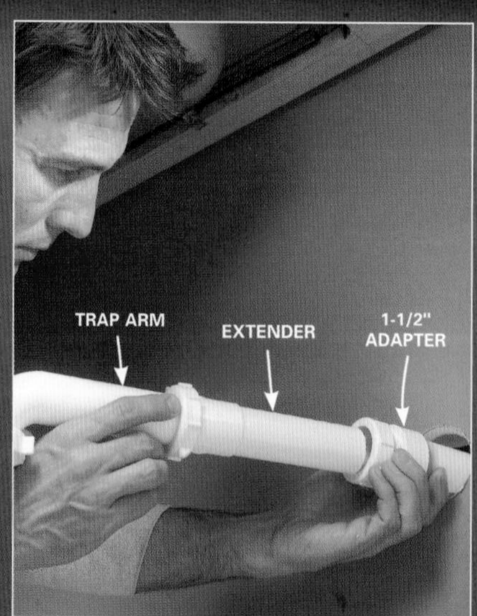

2 Slide the trap arm into the adapter. Then attach the trap and slide the arm in or out to position the trap directly under the tailpiece. You may need to cut the arm or add an extender.

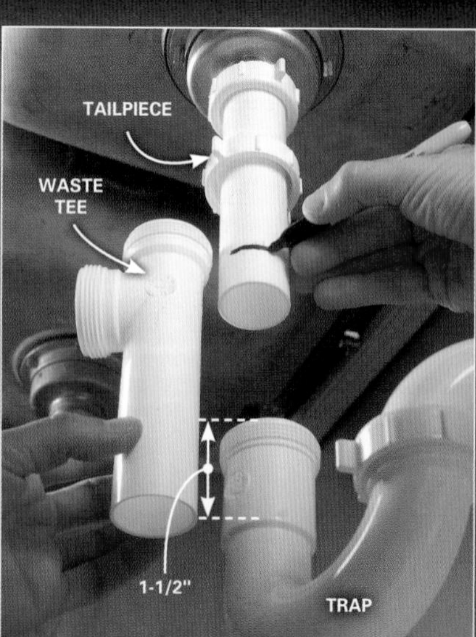

3 Hold the waste tee alongside the tailpiece about 1-1/2 in. below the top of the trap. Mark the tailpiece 1/2 in. below the top of the tee. Cut both tailpieces to the same length and install them.

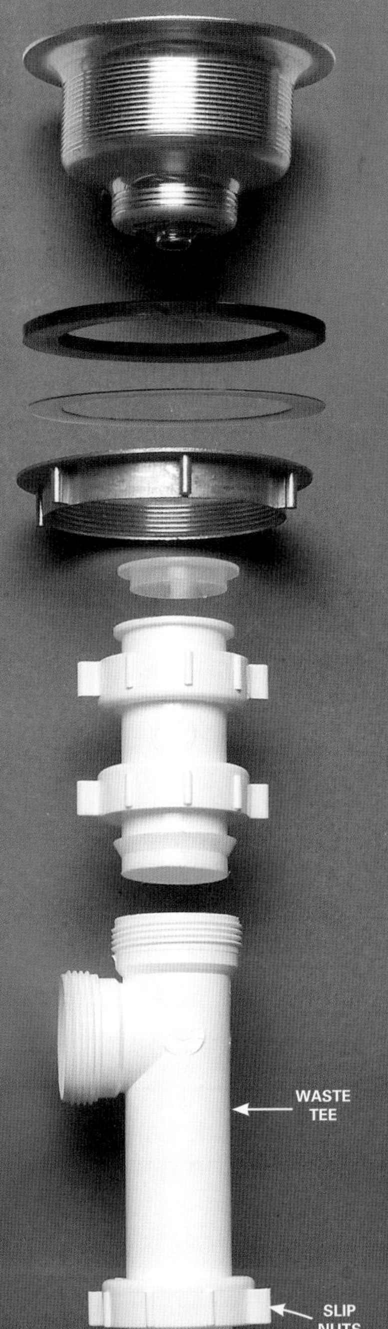

■ Don't forget to insert tailpiece washers (Photo 1). Other joints require cone washers. The only joint without a washer is the ground joint at the trap.

■ Assemble everything loosely until the whole assembly is complete. Then tighten all the slip nuts.

■ Hand-tighten the slip nuts. If any joints leak when you test the new assembly, tighten them slightly with slip-joint pliers.

■ When you're all done, test the assembly for leaks.

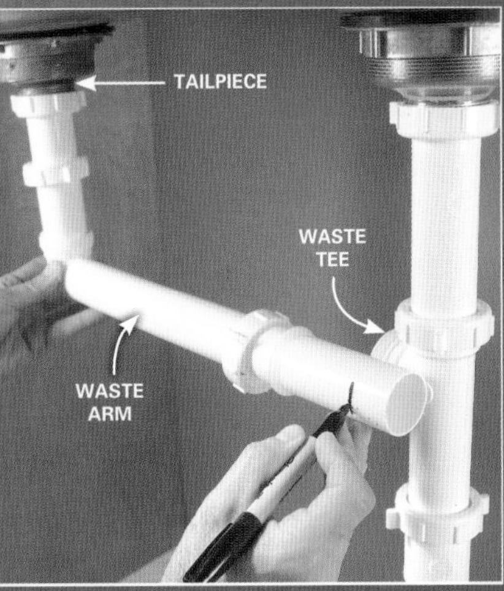

4 Slip the waste arm onto the second tailpiece, make it extend about 3/4 in. into the tee and mark it. Cut and install it.

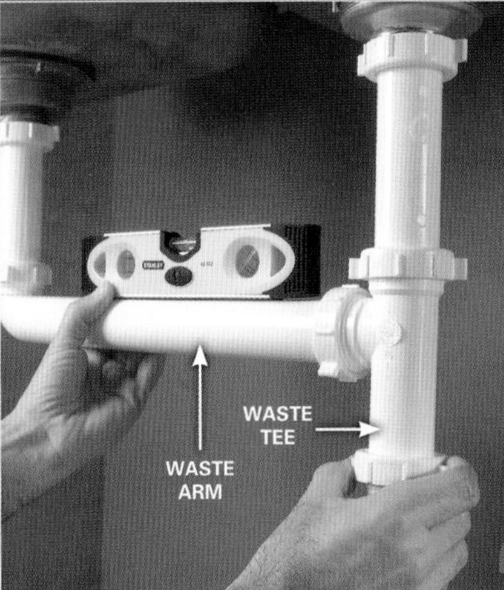

5 Loosen the slip nuts and slide the tee up or down so the waste arm slopes slightly down toward the tee. Tighten all the nuts.

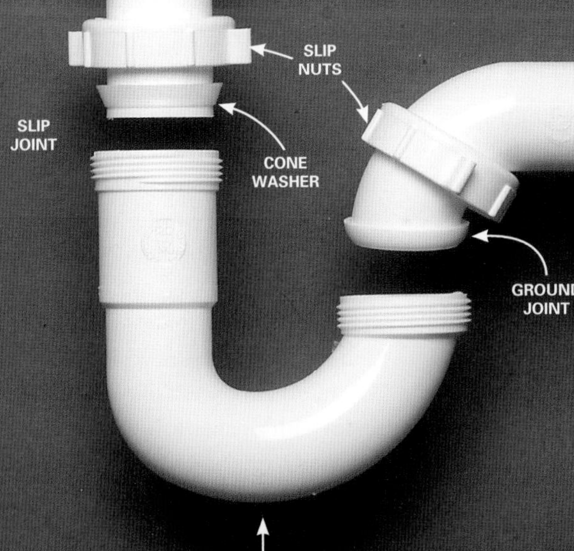

pro tip

Brush a little Teflon pipe thread sealant on male threads. It lubricates the threads and makes slip nuts much easier to tighten. Check the label to make sure the sealant is safe for plastic.

Replace a sink strainer

Kitchen sink basket strainers/drain assemblies work great when they're new. But with daily use and cleaning, the chrome or painted finish starts to wear off. The basket strainer stopper may also start leaking. Once that happens, you can forget about soaking pots and pans overnight. You might think that the solution is to buy a new basket strainer. Good luck finding one that fits and seals. You can buy a "universal" replacement that'll work as a strainer. But it usually doesn't seal well because it's not an exact fit. So your best option is to replace the entire drain assembly.

You can replace the drain assembly yourself, but it's much easier with two people. You'll save about $100 in labor. The hardest part of the job involves removing the old drain locknut. If your locknut comes off easily, you can finish the entire job in less than an hour. However, a drain locknut that's corroded is tougher to deal with. We'll show you two quick ways to conquer stubborn locknuts. And we'll offer some tips on shopping for a new, longer-lasting basket strainer/drain assembly. Let's get started.

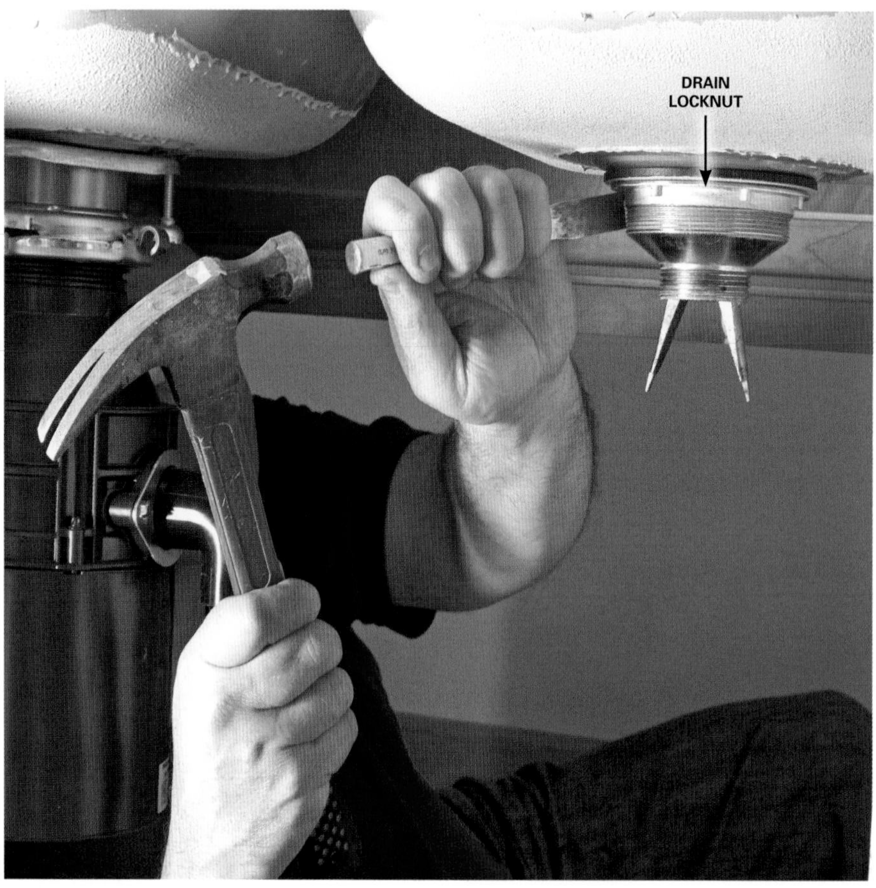

Remove the drainpipes

Place a bowl under the P-trap. Then use slip-joint pliers to loosen the compression nuts at the drain tailpiece and both nuts on the trap. Completely unscrew the tailpiece nut and swing the P-trap out slightly. Then unscrew the trap nuts completely and remove and drain the entire trap and tailpiece assembly to give yourself more working space.

Loosen and remove the drain locknut

Crawl under the sink and check for corrosion on the large drain locknut. If it's corroded, spray all around the nut with rust penetrating oil and allow it to soak for at least 15 minutes. Then have a friend hold the drain so you can loosen the locknut (Photo 1). Loosen the locknut with a hammer and chisel (Photo 2). If the locknut won't loosen or the entire drain spins and your helper can't hold it, cut it off (Photo 3).

If you don't have either a helper or a rotary cutoff tool and you've tried but can't loosen the locknut yourself, there's still another option to try. Head to the home center or hardware store and fork over about $25 for a sink drain wrench to loosen the nut and a plug wrench to help hold the drain (Photo 4). Once you get the locknut off, pull the entire drain up and out of the sink.

Clean the sink flange and install the new drain

Scrape off the plumber's putty or silicone from around the drain flange in the basin and under the sink. If the old drain was caulked with silicone, use silicone remover to clean it. Then apply a fresh bead of silicone around the flange in the basin and insert the new drain. Next, install the new O-ring and locknut in the order shown here (Photo 5). Tighten the locknut until the rubber O-ring compresses slightly. Then reassemble the trap and tailpiece and attach it to the new sink drain. Clean off any excess silicone in the basin with a paper towel. Then clean off the O-ring and locknut.

Test for leaks by filling the sink with water and releasing it while you check the pipes under the sink.

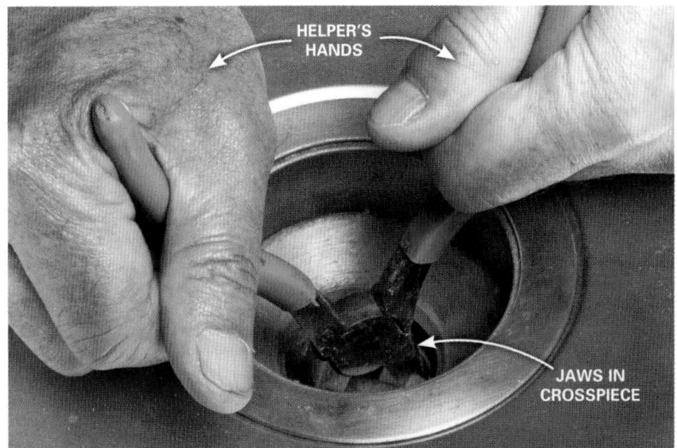

1 HOLD THE DRAIN TO LOOSEN THE LOCKNUT Jam needle-nose pliers into the crosspiece section at the bottom of the drain. Have your friend spread the pliers and hold it tightly in the drain to prevent it from turning while you loosen the locknut.

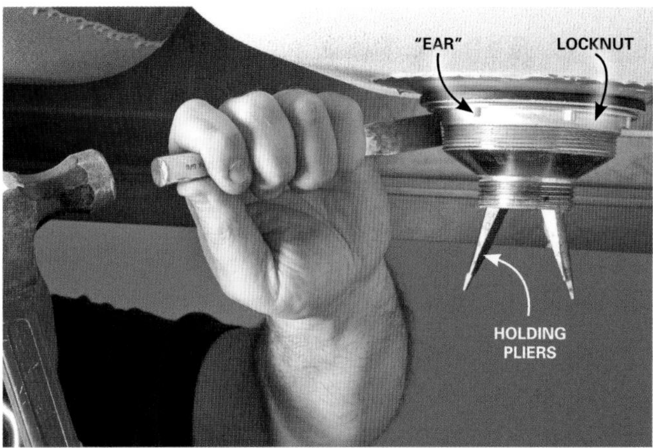

2 LOOSEN THE LOCKNUT Place the chisel tip against a locknut "ear." Then smack the chisel with a hammer. Move the chisel to the next ear and repeat until the nut spins by hand.

3 DRASTIC MEASURES FOR STUCK NUTS If all else fails, chuck a metal cutoff wheel into a rotary tool and cut the locknut. Cut until you reach the cardboard ring above the nut. Don't cut into the sink. If the nut still doesn't spin, fit your chisel into the cut area and smack it with a hammer to crack it open. Wear eye protection.

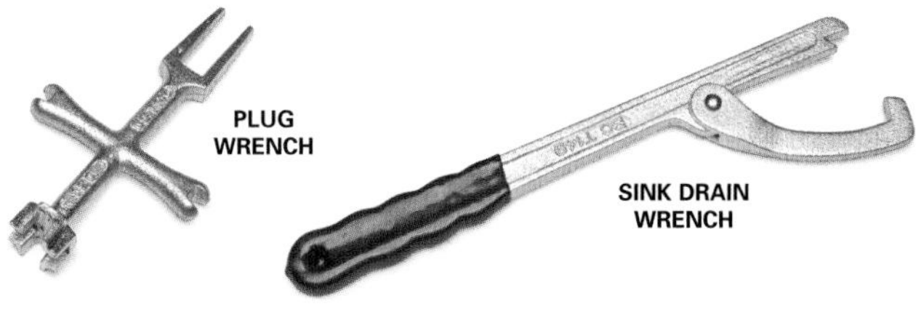

4 NO HELPER? NO PROBLEM! You can buy these tools for $25 at any home center. Loosen the locknut with the sink drain wrench while you hold the drain with pliers and the plug wrench.

5 INSTALL THE NEW STRAINER Slide the rubber O-ring on first. Then add the cardboard O-ring and the locknut. Tighten the nut until it starts compressing the rubber O-ring.

Buying tips

You have to spend at least $50 to get a high-quality strainer/drain assembly with a durable finish and a reliable stopper mechanism. The best strainers have either a spin-lock or a twist-and-drop style stopper. The spin-lock stopper doesn't have any parts that can wear, but screwing it in and out can be annoying. The twist-and-drop style is much easier to use but requires occasional O-ring replacement.

Avoid push-in style strainers that have a nonreplaceable neoprene stopper or a plastic knob. The plastic parts break and can lose their sealing ability if exposed to boiling water.

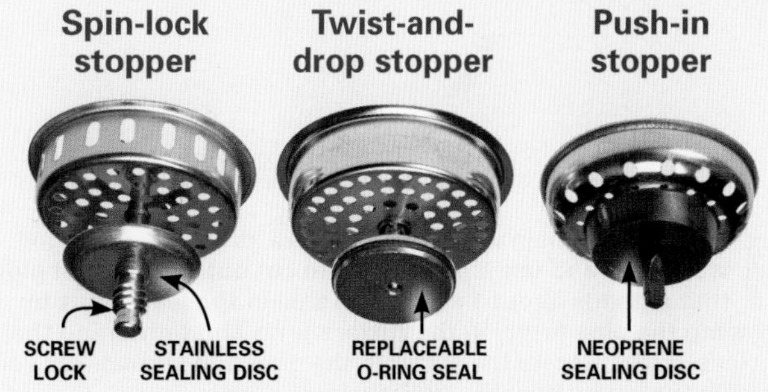

Repair a leaking copper pipe

When a copper water pipe corrodes and leaks, or bursts from freezing, you have to fix it fast. If the leak is pinhole-sized and less than 1/2 in. of pipe must be removed, you can make the repair by cutting the pipe and soldering ("sweating") on an ordinary pipe coupling.

But to repair longer sections, use a long "repair" coupling, which you can find at home centers and well-stocked hardware stores. You can buy a sweat coupling sized to repair 1/2-in. or 3/4-in. copper pipe.

Mark the leak, shut off the main water valve and drain (or thaw and drain) the affected pipe. Cut out the damaged section (Photo 1), then measure the gap and, from the sweat coupling, cut a repair piece that's 1 in. longer than the damaged section.

The key to a good solder joint is to keep the inside of the pipes dry, so keep a cotton rag stuffed in each pipe end to absorb dribbles of water until just before you solder. Open a faucet above that level to keep pressure from building up and dribbling more water into your repair. Then complete the steps shown in Photos 2–4 for a leak-proof repair.

Once finished, turn the main supply valve on and check for leaks.

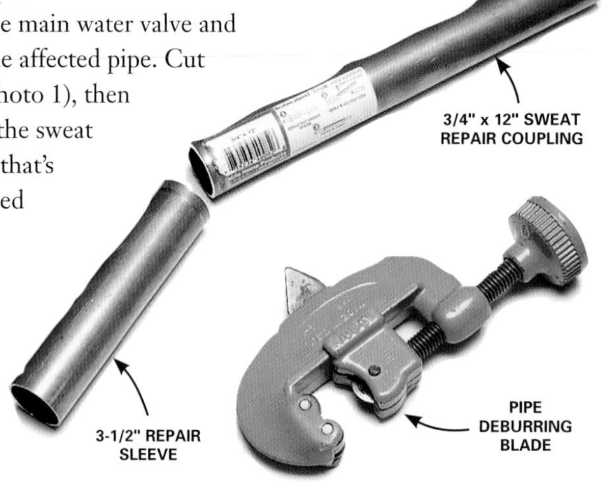

Cut the repair sleeve from the 12-in. repair coupling stock. Smooth the rough-cut inside edges of the sleeve by inserting the blade of the pipe cutter into the cut ends and turning the cutter until the sleeve will slide over the pipe ends without snagging. Clean the sleeve's inside edges for soldering with a 3/4-in.-dia. wire fitting brush.

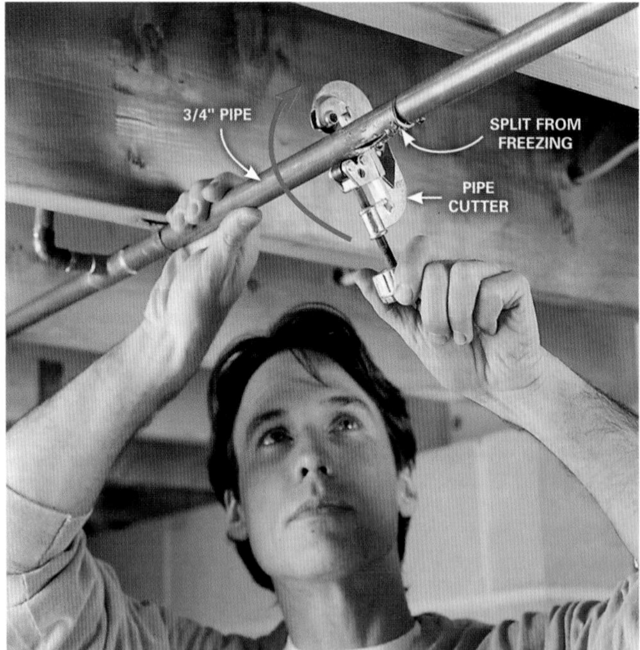

1 Shut off the main water supply valve, drain the damaged water line and use a pipe cutter to cut out a section of pipe that extends about 1 in. to each side of the leak. Start by gripping the pipe firmly in the cutter's jaws and tightening the cutter's screw. Rotate the cutter in the direction shown—as you tighten the screw handle—until the pipe snaps.

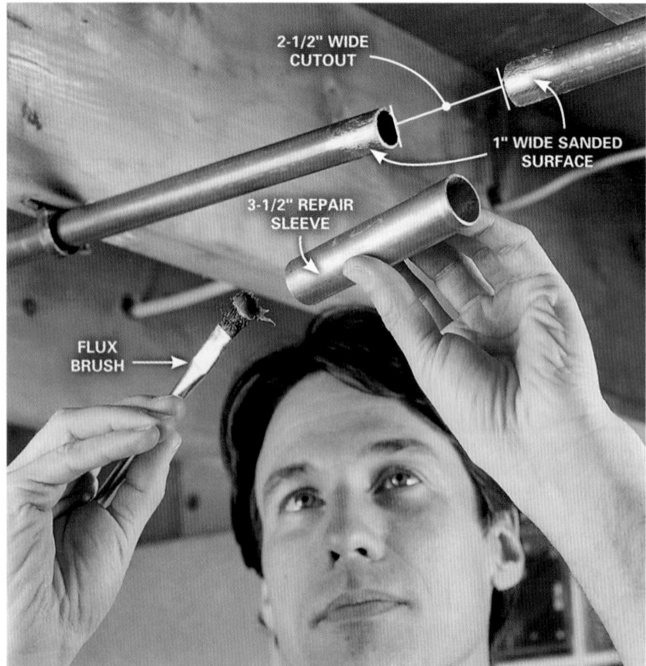

2 Clean corrosion from the inside of the repair sleeve using a wire fitting brush. Clean the outside of the pipe with plumber's sandcloth or emery paper. Brush flux onto all four cleaned surfaces.

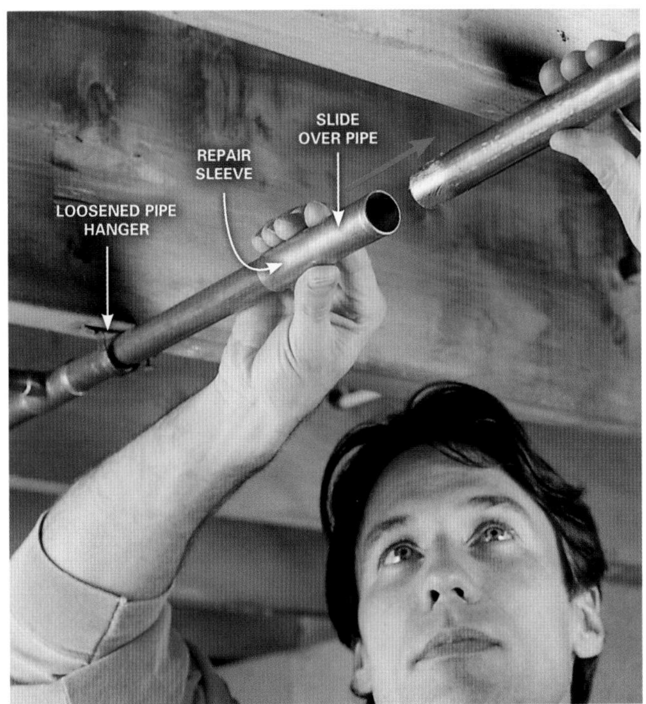

3 Slide an end of the sleeve first over one pipe and then slip it back over onto the other. You may have to loosen nearby pipe hangers. Center the sleeve over the pipe ends so that about 1/2 in. of each pipe is inside the sleeve.

4 Hold the tip of the torch flame to one side of the joint and hold the tip of the solder wire to the opposite side. Pull the solder away when enough of it melts to completely fill the joint.

Emergency shutoff valves

Shutoff valves allow you to control water flow to all or parts of the water-supply system to reduce damage from a supply leak or to make repairs or replace fixtures. The main shutoff, whether indoors or outdoors, is generally near where the service line enters the house, usually next to the meter. On a private system, it will be near where the line leaves the pressure tank. You'll also find shutoff valves at the water heater, boiler, individual fixtures and outdoor water lines.

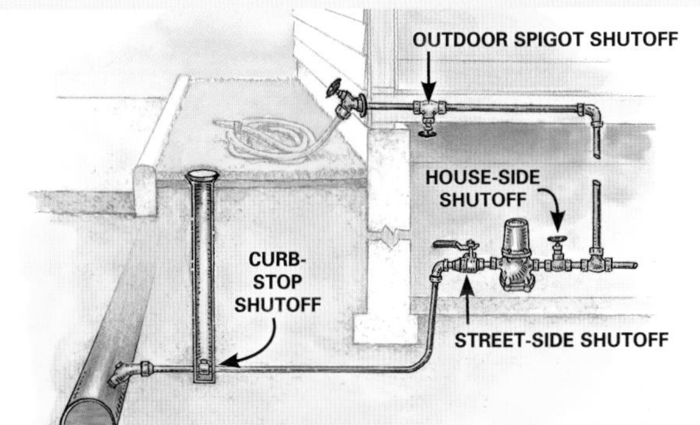

MAIN SHUTOFF. This valve controls the flow of all water entering the water-supply system.

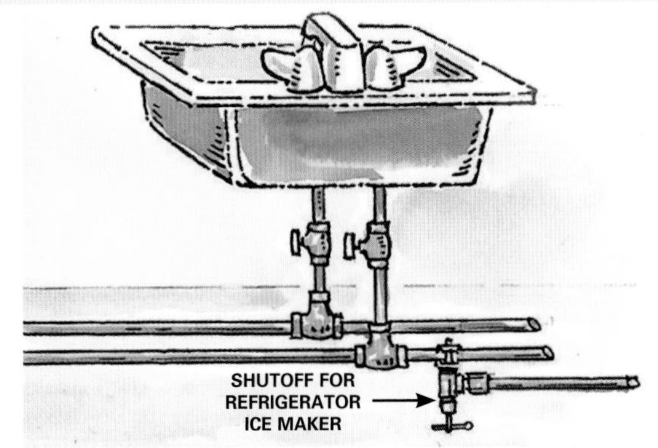

FAUCET SHUTOFF. Separate valves control the hot and cold water.

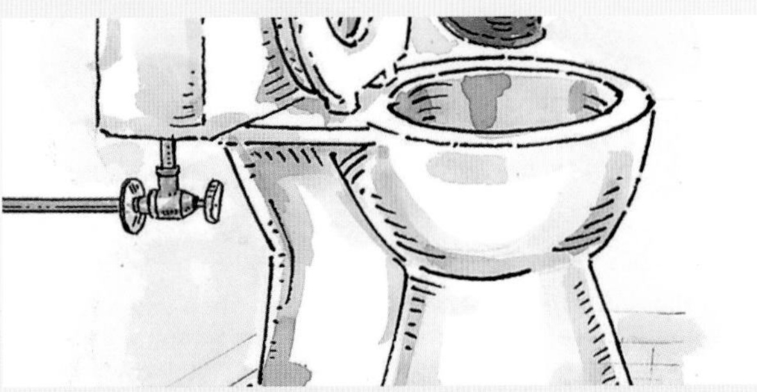

TOILET SHUTOFF. This valve is usually on the cold-water supply located underneath the tank.

Reset and fix a rocking toilet

Frequently a toilet leaks simply because the wax ring has lost its seal. By far the most common reason for a broken seal is a toilet that rocks when you sit on it. A toilet that rocks even slightly will eventually compromise the wax ring. If you find no evidence of other problems after you pull the toilet, simply replacing the wax ring and resetting the toilet should fix the problem. Usually toilets rock because of an uneven floor—especially tiled floors. After you set the toilet, shim gaps between the toilet and the floor before caulking around the toilet (Photo 3). That'll prevent the toilet from rocking and ruining another seal later.

Before you mount the toilet, push and wiggle the wax ring to help it stick to the porcelain around the horn. That'll keep it from falling off as you lower the bowl. When you reset the toilet, it's important to drop it directly into place. If it's not aligned directly over the bolts when the wax ring meets the toilet flange, you risk distorting the wax ring and ruining the seal. Marking bolt locations with masking tape will help you see their position (Photo 2) as you lower the bowl.

1 Push the new wax ring onto the toilet horn with the rounded side toward the toilet. Mark the water closet bolt positions on the floor with masking tape.

2 Align the bolt holes with the masking tape and lower the toilet bowl straight over the bolts. Push down on the rim of the toilet to seat the wax ring, then close the lid and sit on the toilet for a few minutes to force the toilet all the way to the floor. Stop when the porcelain surface rests on the finished floor.

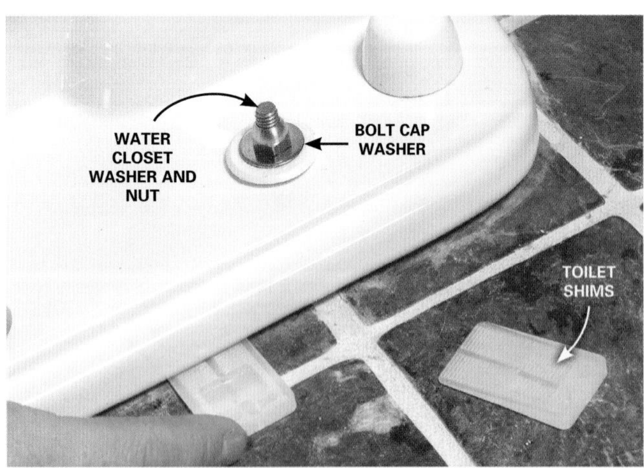

3 Slip the bolt cap washers over the bolts, then snug down the water closet washers and nuts with a wrench. Be careful not to overtighten the nuts, especially over gaps between the toilet and the floor. Slip toilet shims under any toilet edge gaps and cut off the excess length. Some shims are pretty tough. If a utility knife won't cut through the plastic, you may have to chop them off with a sharp wood chisel.

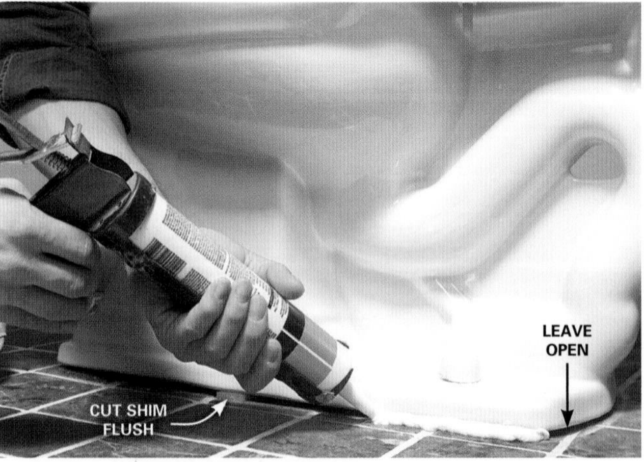

4 Caulk around the toilet base with silicone caulk, leaving the back end of the base uncaulked. The gap leaves a space for moisture under the toilet to escape. (Some local codes require caulk around the entire base.)

instant fix

Clean the rinse holes of a poorly flushing toilet

If your poorly flushing toilet worked well in the past and you live in an area with hard water, chances are the rinse holes around the bottom of the rim have become clogged with lime deposits. Clear rinse and siphon holes are crucial for complete flushing action. Even though the water from the tank will eventually find its way into the bowl, high water volume on the first surge is important for good flushing. There has to be a "critical mass" of water for solids to be flushed.

As a first step, ream out the rinse holes with a bent coat hanger (Photo 1). To do a thorough job, dry the bottom of the rim, then roll up paper towel "ropes" and seal them against the bottom of the rinse holes with plumber's putty pushed against the bottom of the rim (Photo 2). Then seal the siphon jet hole with another glob of putty and pour a bottle of lime remover into the overflow pipe (Photo 3). Let it sit for at least eight hours to allow the lime remover to dissolve deposits. Remove everything and flush the toilet several times.

1 Clean the rinse holes.

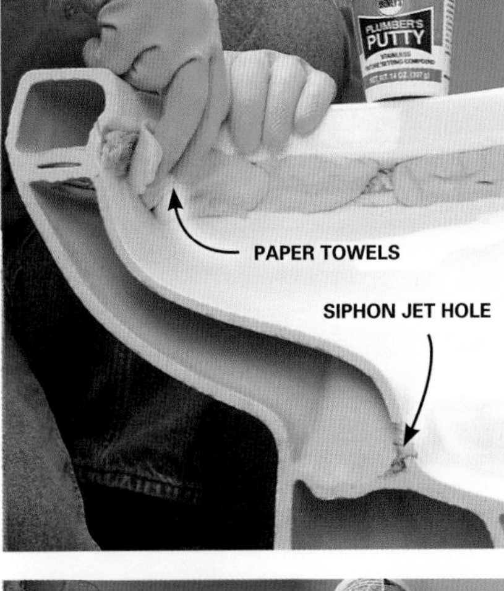

2 Seal the rinse holes.

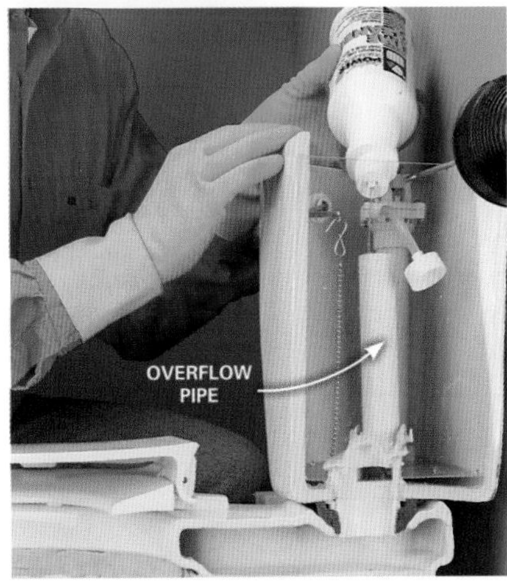

3 Remove lime deposits.

Replace a leaking wax ring

When water leaks out from under a toilet, the wax ring must be replaced immediately to avoid water damage. Shut off and drain the water, and loosen one end of the supply tube. Remove the two flange nuts holding the toilet in place—be prepared to use a hacksaw to cut them if they're frozen in place. Plug the drain temporarily with a rag, then scrape the old wax from the toilet base and flange. Install a new wax ring with a rubber or plastic collar. Remove the rag and lower the toilet straight onto the bolts. Sit on the toilet to compress the wax; it will reseal the connection between flange and toilet bowl. Reinstall the nuts, washers and supply tube.

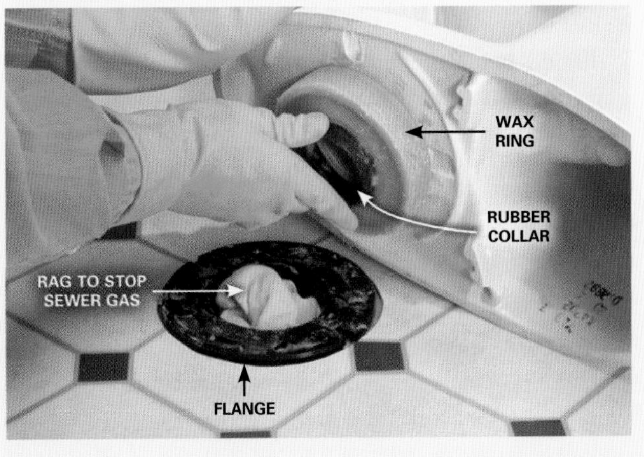

Tighten connections and straighten crooked pipes

The washers that seal pipe joints won't hold water unless one section runs straight into the other. The "ground" joint on the trap has no washer, but it too will leak if it's misaligned. Eyeball the leaking joint to check its alignment. If it's crooked, simply loosen the nut, straighten the pipe and retighten. Since the whole assembly is interconnected, you might misalign one joint while straightening another. Don't be surprised if you end up loosening and tightening several joints to straighten just one.

If a joint is aligned but leaks anyway, tighten the slip nut. Use two slip-joint pliers on metal pipes: one to hold the pipe, the other to tighten the nut. If you have old metal pipe, you might find that it has worn thin and collapses when you put pliers on it. With plastic pipe, hand-tighten first. If that doesn't stop the leak, use pliers. But be gentle; plastic threads are easy to strip.

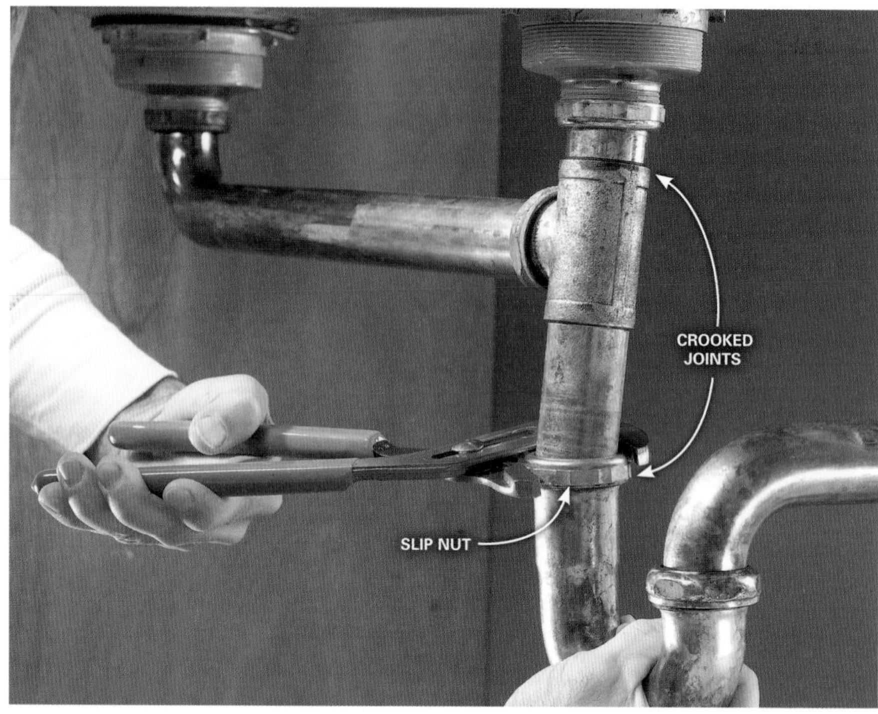

Loosen slip nuts, then straighten crooked pipes. Retighten metal nuts with slip-joint pliers. With plastic nuts, hand-tighten first. If that doesn't stop the leak, gently snug up the nut with pliers.

instant fix

Stop leaks

Silicone tape is different from other kinds of tape because it's self-fusing—it sticks to itself, not the surface it's being applied to. So it doesn't matter if a drainpipe you're taping is wet or greasy. Another advantage of this tape is that when it's removed, there's no sticky residue.

Besides being a temporary solution to a leaky trap, the tape can be used for a litany of projects: weatherproofing, sealing leaking drain lines, wrapping sport and tool grip handles, harnessing cables, keeping rope ends from fraying, hose repair, corrosion protection and more. It really is a versatile product.

The tape is relatively expensive and may not completely replace your duct or electrical tape, but it's worth adding to your workshop arsenal. Having a roll in your glove box may not be a bad idea either. If your local hardware store doesn't stock silicone tape, find it online.

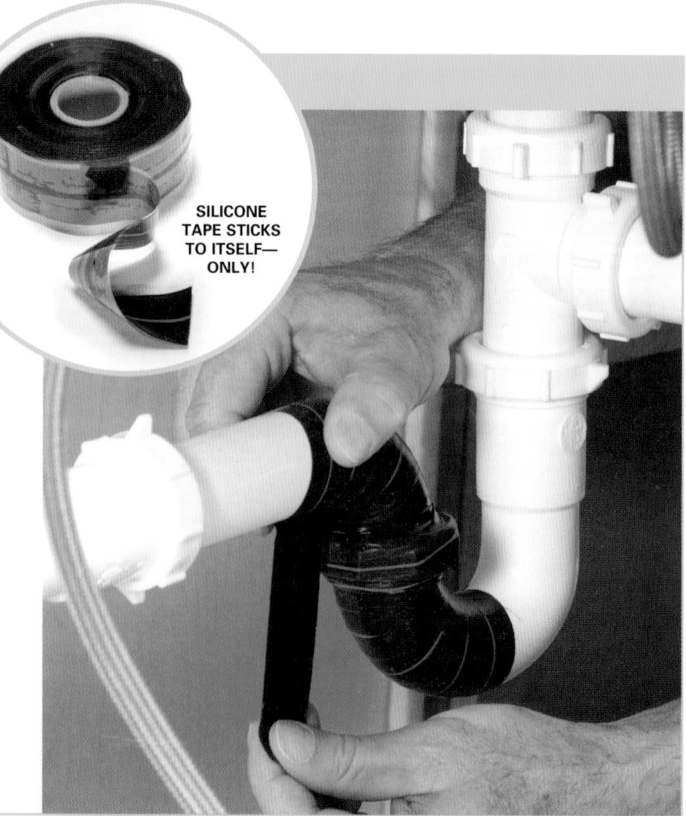

instant fix

Shutoff valve leaking?

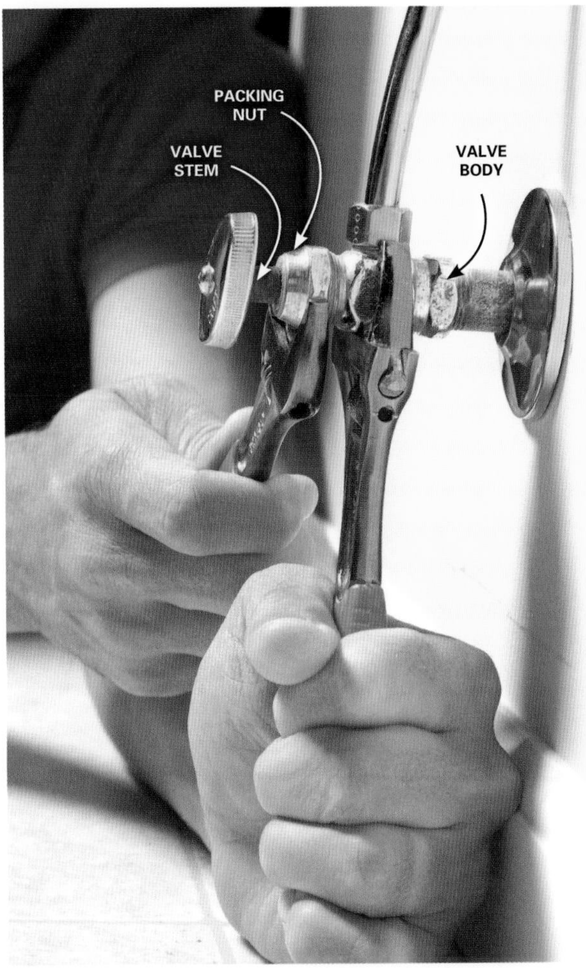

Tighten the packing nut to stop the leak. Place one wrench on the valve body and a second wrench on the packing nut. Then turn the packing nut clockwise to tighten while holding the valve in place with the second wrench.

Don't panic. Here's a simple fix that works more than half the time and doesn't cost a dime to try. Many shutoff valves have a packing nut or packing material that surrounds the valve stem. The packing can shrink or get worn over time, causing water to leak out around the valve stem. This usually happens after someone has closed and opened the valve for a repair or for some other reason. The good news is that in most cases simply tightening the packing nut will fix the problem. Go easy, though. If you tighten it too much, the valve won't turn. Quarter-turn shutoff valves don't have a packing nut. If this type leaks around the stem, you'll have to replace it.

Install a new adapter on old steel pipe

The drainpipe coming out of the wall has an adapter on the end. This adapter has a washer and slip nut and works just like the other joints in your drain assembly. If your drainpipe is plastic you shouldn't have any problems. But if your drainpipe is old galvanized steel, you might run into corrosion that makes the slip nut almost impossible to loosen or retighten.

Here's how to bypass those rusty old threads: Unscrew the old slip nut. Cut it off with a hacksaw if you have to, but try not to cut deep into the drainpipe's threads. Buy a plastic trap adapter, a rubber transition coupler, a section of plastic pipe and cement. The pipe and adapter can be PVC (white) or ABS (black); just be sure to get the right cement for the type of plastic (PVC also requires purple primer). Cement the adapter to a 4-in. piece of pipe and join the plastic pipe to the old metal pipe using the rubber coupler.

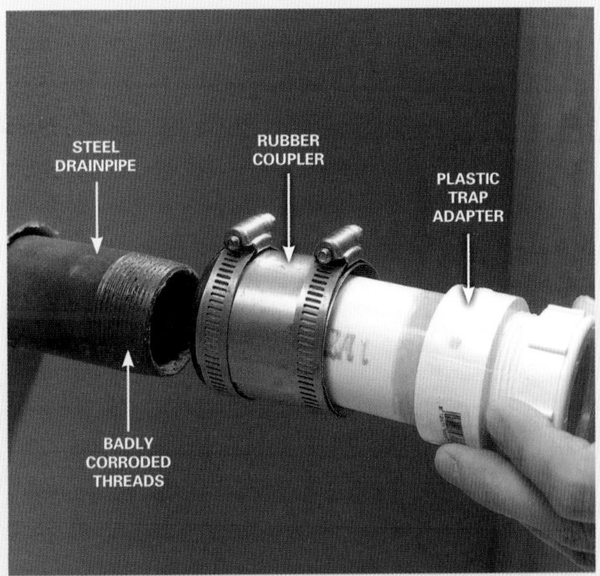

ENERGYGUIDE
FPS
RIDGID
PROFESSIONAL
6.5
16

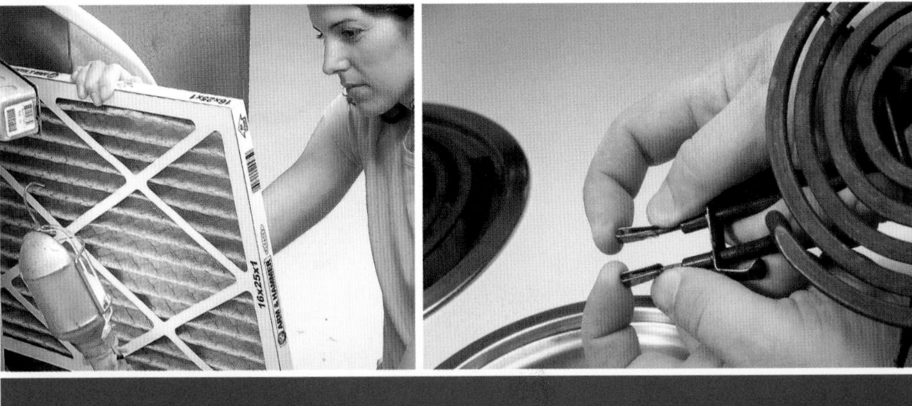

Chapter **five**

APPLIANCES

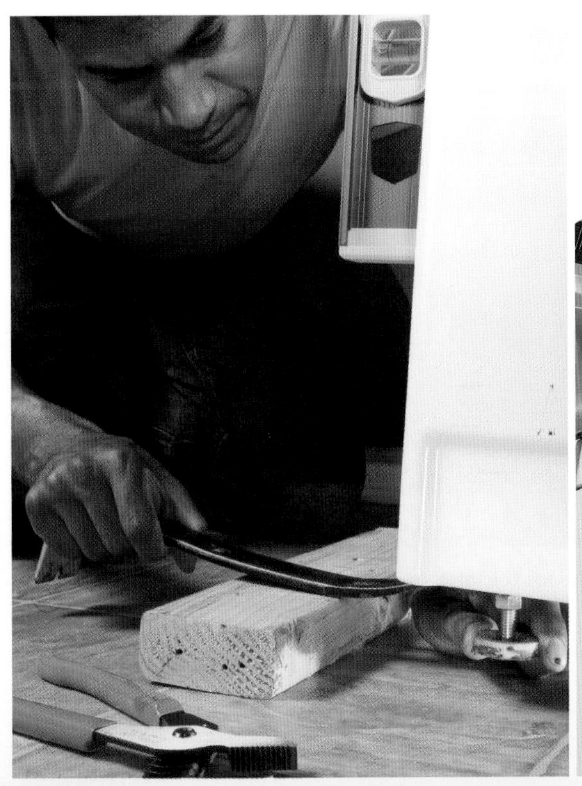

Fix an icemaker

When an icemaker stops working or produces only tiny cubes, it's usually because the water supply is partially or completely blocked. To find and fix the blockage, check out three common trouble spots:

First, check the water inlet tube for ice

The tube that supplies water to your icemaker can get plugged with ice when the water pressure is low. The trickling water freezes and plugs the tube before it reaches the icemaker.

Second, unblock the saddle valve

Most icemakers are connected to the household water supply by a "saddle" valve. One problem with saddle valves is that the needle hole in the pipe can clog. Fortunately, that blockage is easy to clear once you locate the saddle valve (Photo 3). If you have an unfinished basement, you'll probably find a tube beneath the fridge that leads to the valve. Otherwise, look under your kitchen sink.

Third, replace the water inlet valve

At the back of your fridge, there's a small electric "inlet valve" that turns the water supply to the icemaker on and off. Before you replace the valve, make sure water is flowing to it: Turn off the water at the saddle valve (Photo 3) and disconnect the supply tube from the inlet valve (see Photo 4). Hold the tube over a bucket and have a helper turn on the saddle valve. If water flows out of the tube, the water supply is fine and chances are the inlet valve is bad.

pro tip

Turn the water back on and check for leaks *before* you push the fridge back into place.

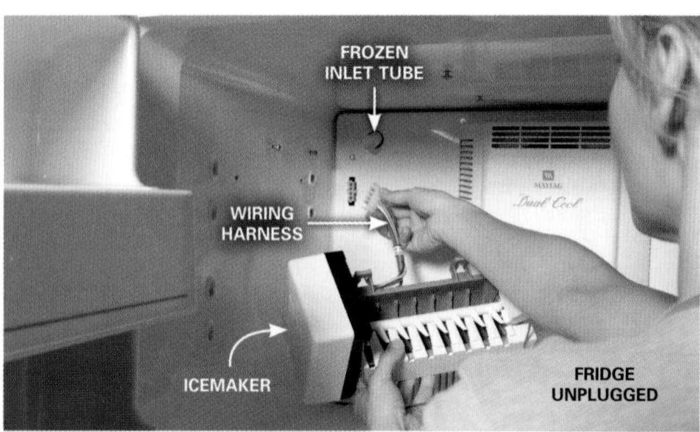

1 **Remove the screws that hold the icemaker in place. Unplug the wiring harness and remove the icemaker to expose the water inlet tube.**

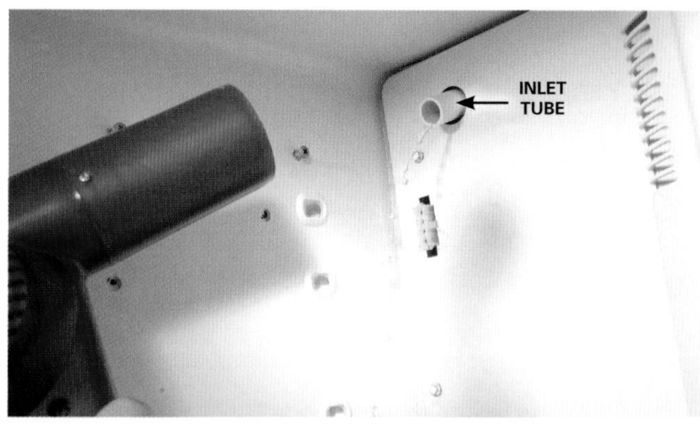

2 **Melt the ice in the water inlet tube with a hair dryer. Don't stop until water stops dripping from the tube.**

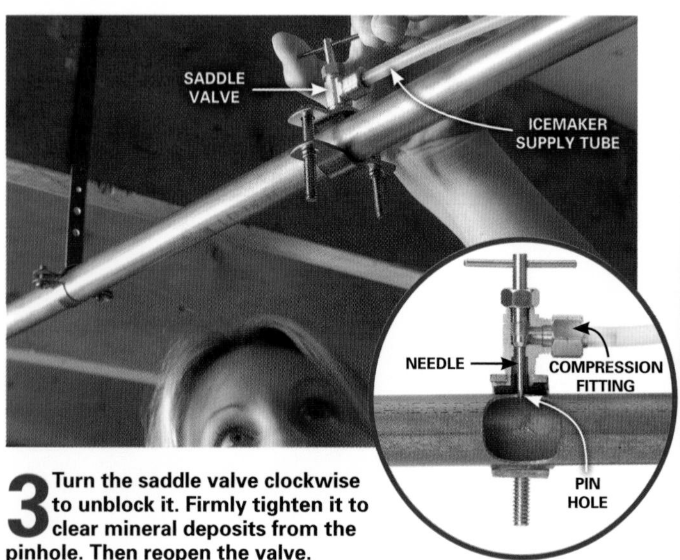

3 **Turn the saddle valve clockwise to unblock it. Firmly tighten it to clear mineral deposits from the pinhole. Then reopen the valve.**

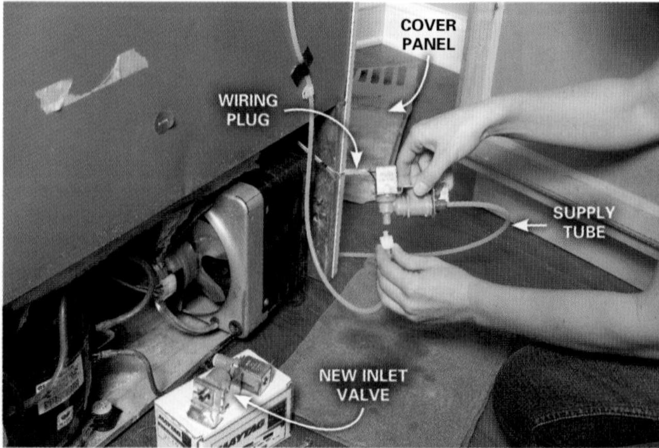

4 **Replace the inlet valve. Unscrew the cover panel and remove the screws that hold the valve in place. Unplug the wiring and unscrew the nuts that connect the water lines. Reverse these steps to install the new valve.**

Fix a leaking fridge

The water supply lines that serve icemakers or water dispensers can leak and make pools under the fridge. But a fridge without these features can create water problems too. Every fridge produces water in the form of condensation and melting ice. When the system that deals with this water fails, you can end up with puddles inside and outside of the fridge.

First, check the water supply line

If your fridge has an icemaker or water dispenser, pull out the fridge and look for a leak. If there's a leak at the inlet valve (see "Fix an Icemaker"), tighten the compression nuts. If the plastic or copper tube is leaking, replace it. Tubing is usually connected to the saddle valve and inlet valve with screw-on compression fittings.

Second, level the fridge

Water drains into a pan under the fridge where it evaporates. If your fridge is badly tilted, water can spill out of the pan. Leveling the fridge solves this problem (Photos 1 and 2).

Third, clear the drain tube

If the drain tube in the freezer gets plugged, water leaks into the compartment below or onto the floor. To unplug it, first remove the cover panel (Photo 3). In some models, you have to unscrew the floor panel too. Use a hair dryer to melt any ice buildup. Sop away the melt water with a sponge. Then clean up around the drain hole. Blow air through the tube to clear it. Any tube that fits tightly into the hole will work. You can also use a tire pump or air compressor (turn the pressure down to 30 psi).

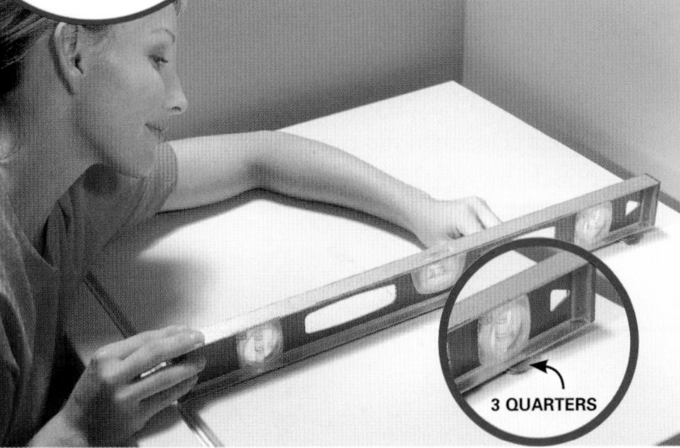

1 Adjust the fridge so it's level from side to side and tilted backward. Stack quarters near the back and set a 2-ft. level on them. When the bubble shows level, the tilt is correct.

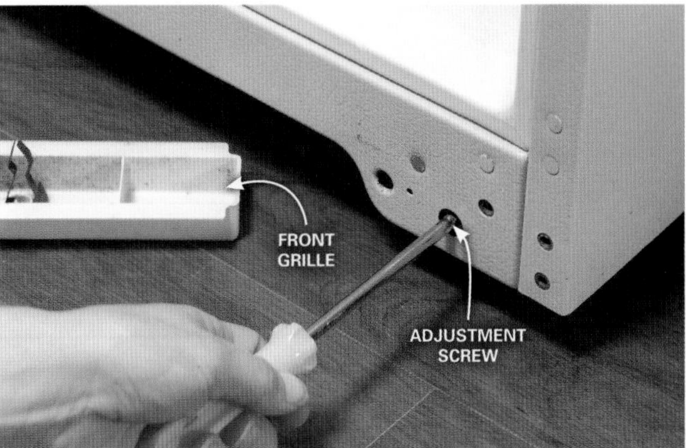

2 Pull off the front cover grille to level or tilt the fridge. Turn adjustment screws to raise or lower the front corners of the fridge.

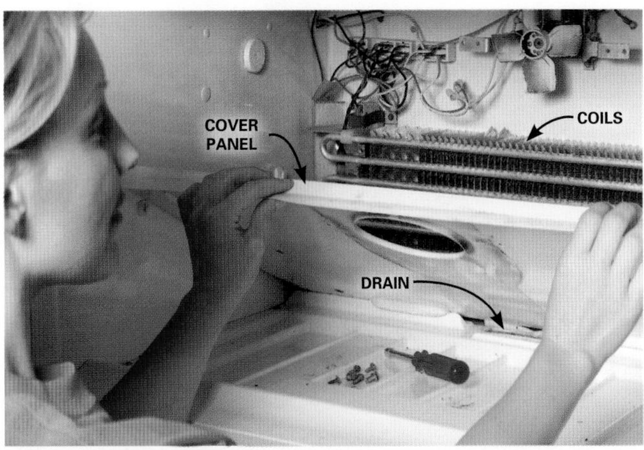

3 Remove the screws that hold the back cover panel in place. On some models, you have to pry out plastic screw covers with a putty knife to expose the screws.

4 Insert a tube in the drain hole and blow out any debris. Pour a cup of water into the tube to make sure it drains before you replace the cover panel.

Restore cooling power to a fridge or freezer

There are lots of malfunctions that can take the chill out of your fridge. One common cause of suddenly soft ice cream or warm juice is a simple loss of electricity. If the light doesn't come on when you open the fridge door, make sure the fridge is plugged in and check the breaker panel. If the fridge runs but doesn't get cold enough, chances are one of these fixes will restore the chill:

pro tip

Finding fridge parts

To get the right part for your refrigerator, you'll need the model number, which is usually stamped on a tag inside the fridge. If you can't find it anywhere on or inside the fridge, check your owner's manual.

First, check the thermostat and vents

The temperature control dial inside the fridge is sometimes irresistible to curious kids. Make sure it hasn't been turned way down. Also make sure the vents in the fridge and freezer compartment aren't blocked by food containers—these vents supply the flow of frigid air.

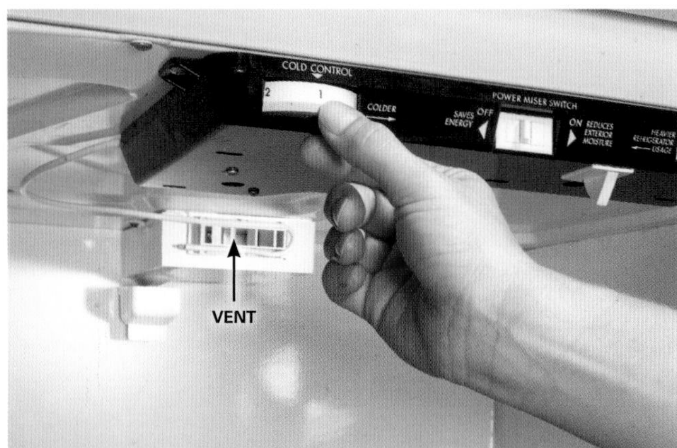

1 **Adjust the temperature control dial. Also make sure the vents inside the fridge or freezer compartment aren't blocked by containers.**

Second, clean the coils

In order for your fridge to create a chill, air has to flow freely through the condenser coils. On most older refrigerators, these coils are on the backside. Cereal boxes on top of the fridge or grocery bags stuffed behind it can reduce the needed airflow. Most newer refrigerators have coils underneath, where they can get blocked by trash and plugged with dust.

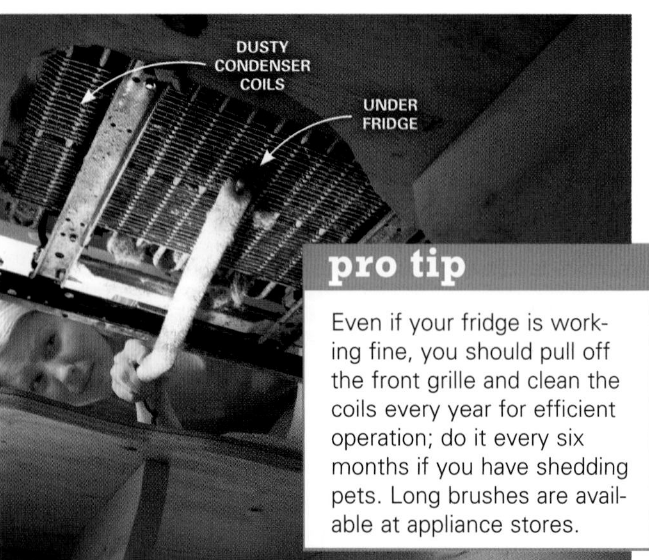

pro tip

Even if your fridge is working fine, you should pull off the front grille and clean the coils every year for efficient operation; do it every six months if you have shedding pets. Long brushes are available at appliance stores.

2 **Clean the coils so air can flow through them. Pull dust and fur balls from beneath and between coils with a long brush.**

Third, free up the condenser fan

Coils on the back of a fridge create their own airflow as they heat up. Models with coils underneath have a fan to push air through them. Dust buildup can slow the fan; wads of paper or other trash can stop it altogether.

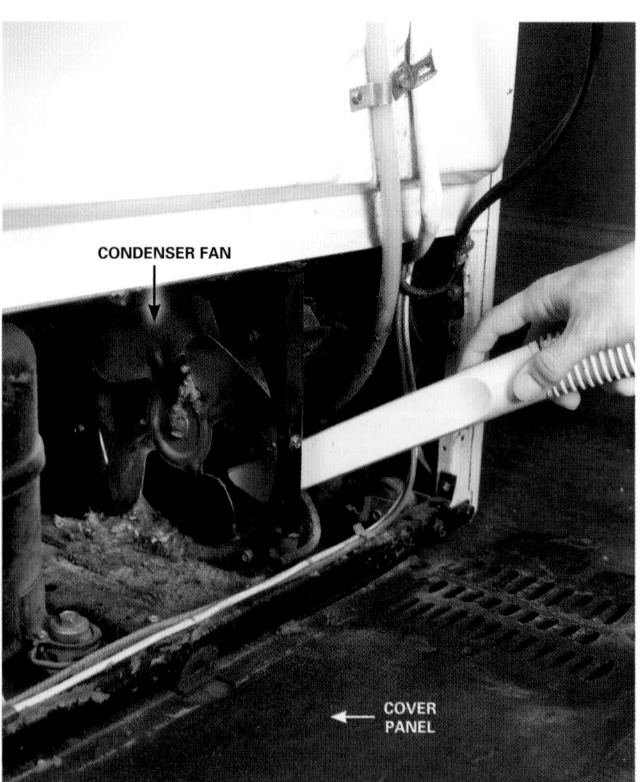

3 **Pull out the fridge and unscrew the cover panel. Vacuum the fan. Then start the refrigerator to make sure the fan turns freely.**

Quiet a noisy fridge

Refrigerator noise comes from either the compressor under the fridge, the condenser fan motor under the fridge, or the evaporator fan motor inside the freezer. Open the freezer door while the fridge is running. If the noise doesn't get louder when you open the freezer, pull out the fridge. Most refrigerators have a condenser fan motor. Unscrew the back cover and listen—you'll be able to tell whether the noise is coming from the fan or the compressor. The best cure for a loud compressor is usually a new fridge.

If the sound gets louder when you open the freezer, the evaporator fan motor is the noisy culprit. This motor is easy to replace. Your fan may not look exactly like the fan we show here, but the basic steps are the same (Photos 1 and 2). Start by unscrewing the back cover panel in the freezer compartment. To install the new fan, just reverse your steps.

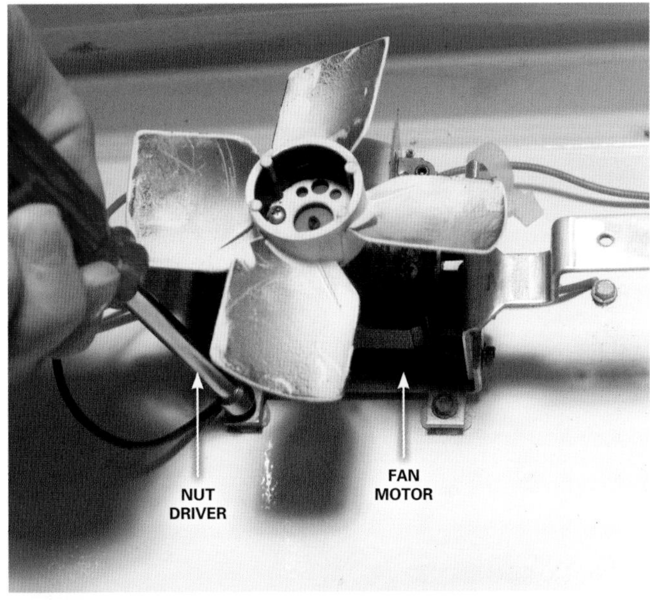

1 **Unscrew the fan from the rear wall of the freezer and unplug the wires. With some models, you'll need a socket set or nut driver to remove the fan.**

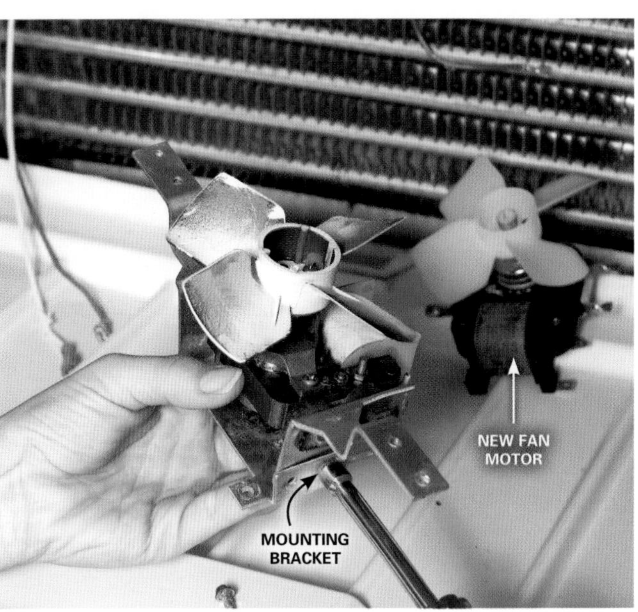

2 **Remove the fan motor from its mounting bracket. Fasten the new fan to the mounting bracket, reconnect the wires and screw the new fan into place.**

instant fix

Clear the freezer vents

These little vents on frost-free fridges allow air to circulate in the freezer (see right). Don't block them or let crumbs or twist ties get sucked in around the evaporator fan or clog the drain tube. To help save energy, keep your freezer about three-quarters full to retain cold air. But don't pack it any fuller—the air needs to circulate.

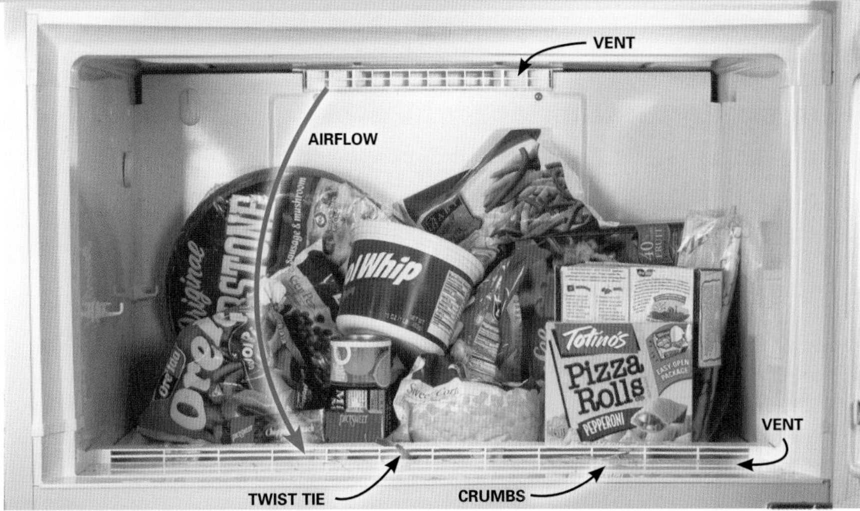

Clear food packages away from the vent openings and clean the air return so crumbs and twist ties don't clog them.

instant fix

Deodorize a dishwasher

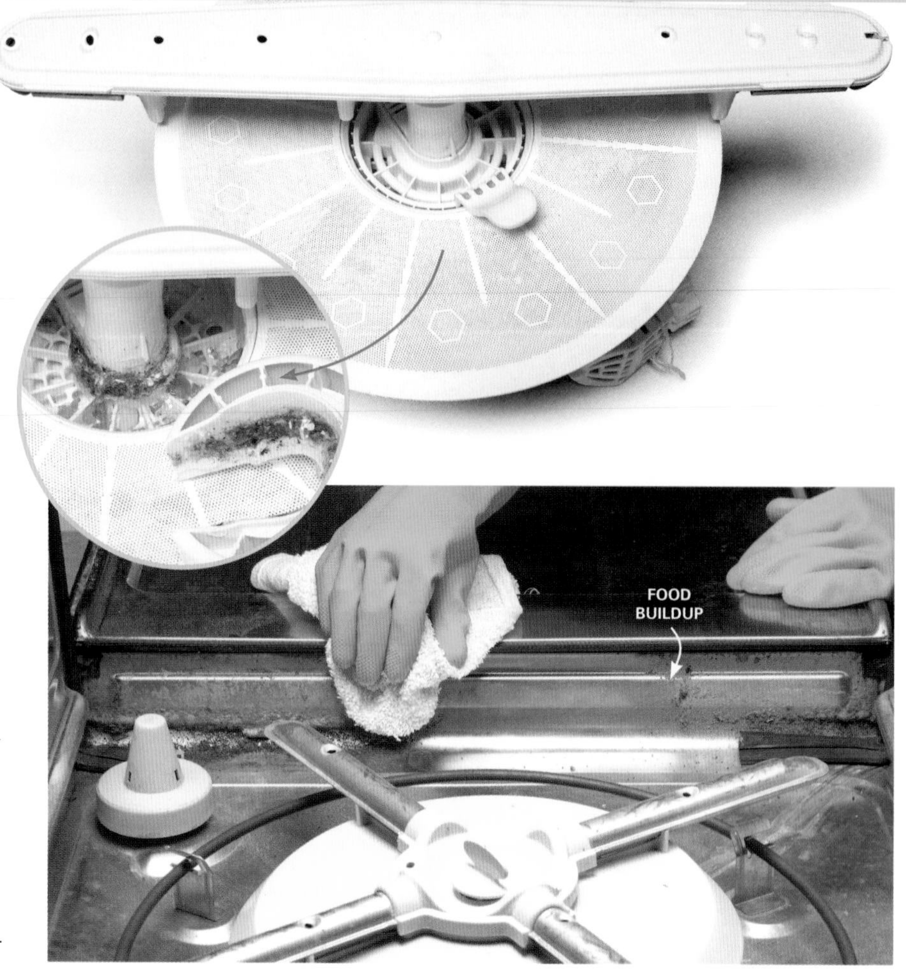

First, don't use bleach. It's very corrosive to metal parts and doesn't solve the root problem. The smell comes from bacteria that feed on trapped food and grease in the strainer screen at the bottom of the machine, in the jets in the sprayer arms and along the bottom edge of the door.

Start by cleaning and rinsing out the screen at the bottom of the tub. Next, clean out any food lodged in the ports of the sprayer arm (top photo). Then clean off the bottom edge of the door and the metal lip area that sits below the door (bottom photo). You'll be surprised at how much crud is there.

Once you've cleaned those areas, throw in a bottle of dishwasher cleaner and disinfectant and run a full cycle with no dishes or dishwashing detergent. Keep those critical areas clean in the future and your stinking problem won't come back.

Clean out food buildup. Tip the door down all the way and spray the bottom edge and lip area with cleaner/degreaser spray. Let it soak for a while, then scrub it clean. Repeat anytime you see buildup.

pro tip

Don't wreck the floor when you pull out the fridge

Nine times out of ten, you can pull out a fridge without any damage to the floor. But a sideways skid or a grain of sand caught under a wheel can scar any floor.

At the very least, lay down a cardboard runway before dragging out your fridge. For the ultimate floor protection, use 1/8-in. hardboard (about $6 for a 4 x 8 sheet at home centers). A pair of shims create a ramp for easier pulling.

Fix a bottom-freezer refrigerator leak

If you discover water on your kitchen floor near the refrigerator, first check for leaks in the water line to the icemaker. If the water line and valve are dry, chances are you have a clogged evaporator drain line. The water is from frost and ice buildup on the evaporator coil that melts off during the defrost cycle. Normally this water just drains into a pan in the bottom of the refrigerator. Then, the condenser fan motor blows warm air across the pan and the water simply evaporates.

But if the drain line clogs, the water overflows and seeps down the interior walls of the freezer and onto the floor. You can fix the problem yourself in just a few hours and save a $125 service call. All you need is a pair of tweezers and a short piece of flexible 1/4-in. O.D. tubing from any hardware store. Here's how to remove the clog.

To reach the drain, you'll first have to remove the access panel from the back of your bottom freezer. This refrigerator has been cut so you can see where all the components are. But every refrigerator is different, so search online for instructions on how to remove the access panel on your particular refrigerator.

Start by removing all the frozen food from the freezer. Put it in a cooler. Then remove the freezer drawer and slides (Photo 1). Next remove the access panel (Photo 2). Clean debris from the evaporator gutter and drain (Photo 3). Then pour hot water into the gutter to melt the ice and snake the drain with the tubing (Photo 4). Then flush water through it again. If it flows, you're done and can reassemble everything. If it still doesn't flow, call a pro.

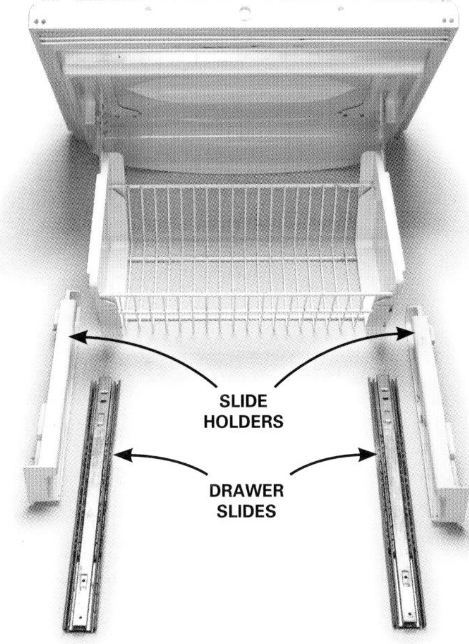

1 REMOVE THESE COMPONENTS FIRST **Pull the freezer door all the way out and lift if off the slides. If the slides prevent you from removing the access panel, unscrew or unsnap them and remove them. If the drawer slide retainers block access to the access panel, remove the screws and lift off the retainers.**

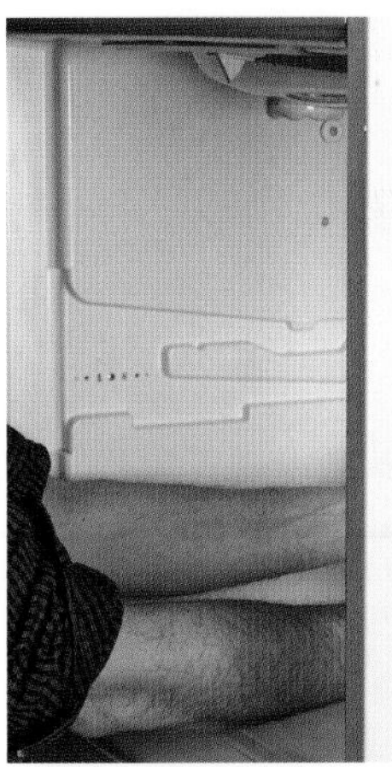
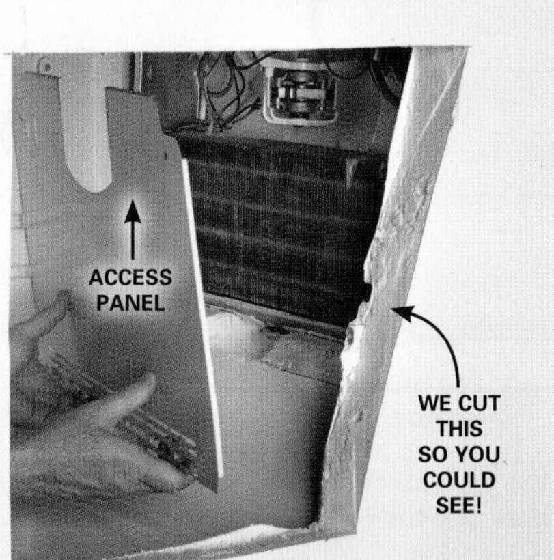

2 REMOVE THE ACCESS PANEL **Use a nut driver to remove the access-panel retaining screws and pull the panel forward. Disconnect any lights or sensors attached to the panel. Then set the panel aside.**

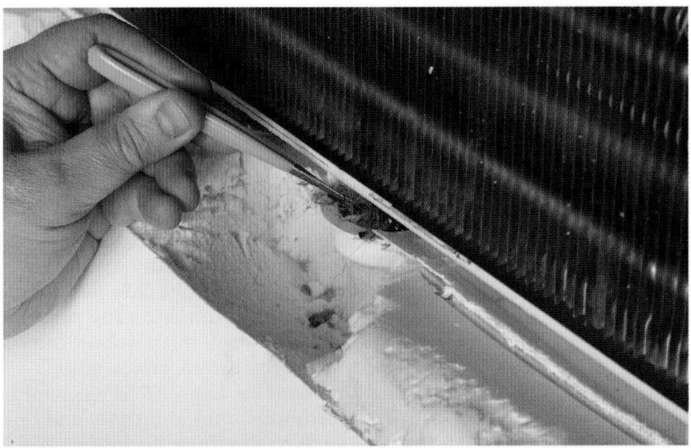

3 REMOVE DRAIN DEBRIS **Pluck the clog out of the drain with a pair of tweezers.**

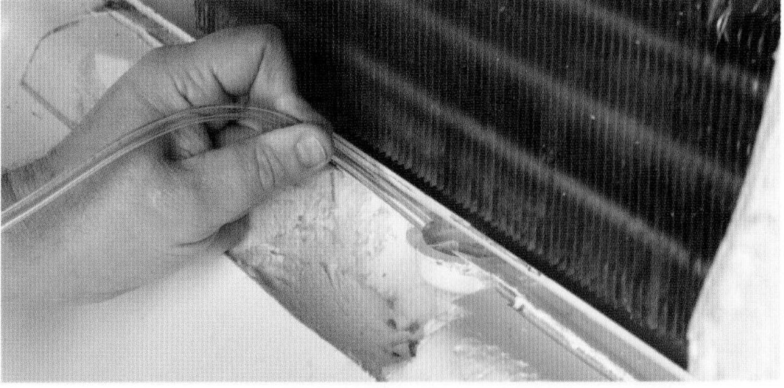

4 SNAKE THE DRAIN **Thread flexible 1/4-in. tubing down the drain and rotate it as you push it to break the clog. Stop pushing when you hear it hit the drain pan under the refrigerator. Flush the drain with hot water and make sure it all goes into the drain pan (remove the bottom front grille and shine a flashlight through the opening to see the drain pan).**

Check the ignition system on a gas range

Switches, control modules or igniters can go bad on a stove with electronic ignition. Use the following guide to test these devices.

Check that the stove is plugged in, there is power to the outlet and the circuit breaker hasn't tripped. Spark ignition stoves need electricity to power the igniters. If your oven light turns on, you have power.

Test if the switch (Photo 1) is at fault by turning a functioning burner to the "Light" position while simultaneously turning the one that's not working to "Light." If the burner that wasn't working now comes on, the burner has a bad switch. See Photo 1 for instructions on replacing a switch.

One at a time, turn each burner dial to "Light" for three seconds, then off again. Watch the igniters to see if they spark while you're doing this. (Turning off the kitchen lights may help you see them.) Replace the module (Photo 2) if none of the igniters spark.

Call in a pro to test the igniters. Igniters rarely fail, but they are difficult to test.

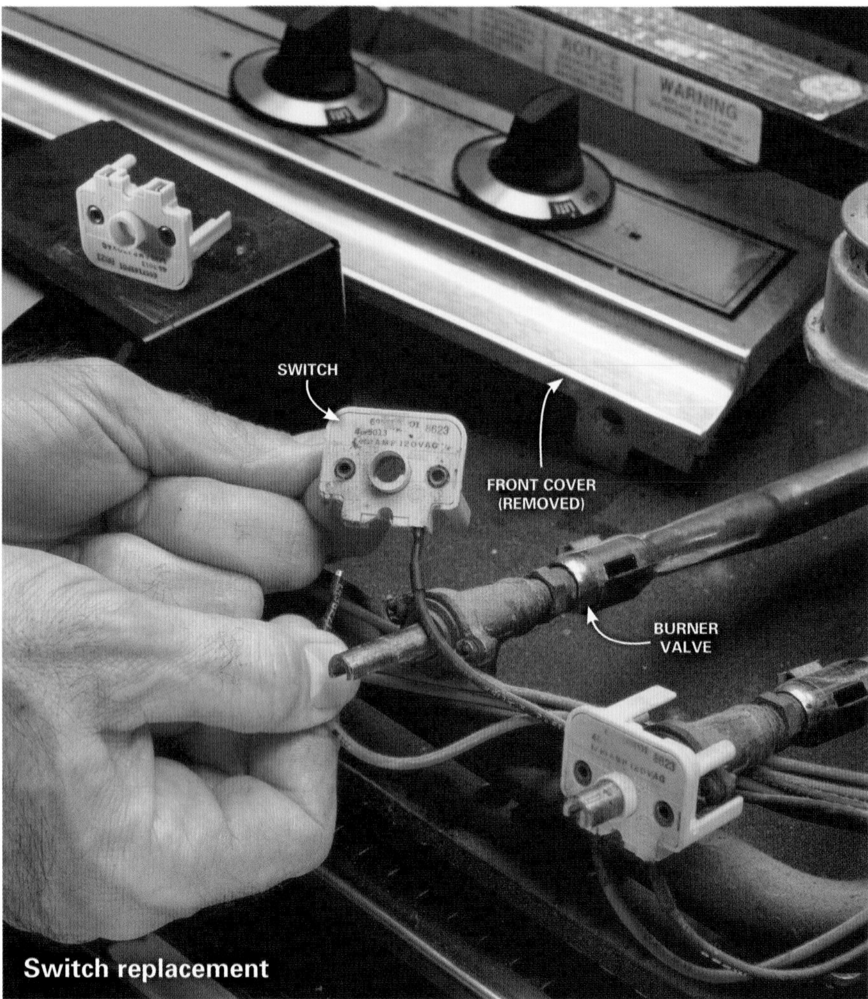

1 Pull off the burner dials and remove any screws that secure the front cover. Remove the cover. Slide the wires off the terminals and insert them into the new switch in the same location. Some connections have a pressure clamp to secure the wire (not shown). Release the wire by shoving a small screwdriver into the slot and prying. Screw in the new switch and reinstall the cover.

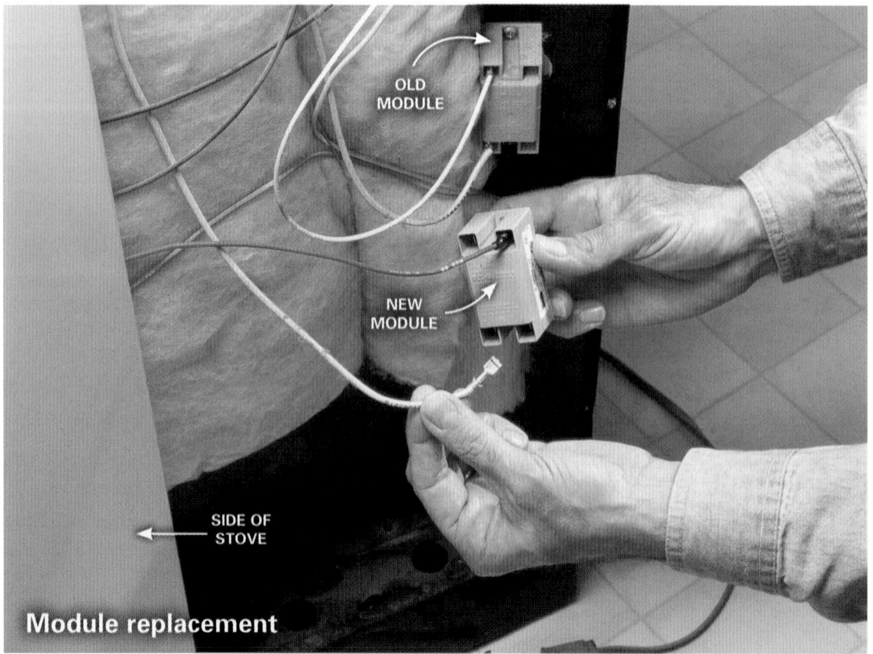

2 Locate the module by tracing the switch wires back to the source. The module is a little box about 2 x 2 x 3 in. The location on the stove will vary. Ours was behind the right side panel. It can be taken off by removing the screws and sliding it forward. If it's not on the side or behind the stove, check your owner's manual for help. Slide the wires off their terminals, one at a time, and transfer each to the new module so you don't mix them up. Remove the screws that secure the old module to the stove body and screw the new one in place.

instant fix

Repair an electric burner

caution

Always unplug your electric range before removing a burner.

If your range has a burner that's not working, chances are you can fix it without any special tools. To diagnose a burner problem, go through the steps in order. If the burners still don't work, call a service professional for help. Our list should take care of 95 percent of the problems that could occur with a burner. If you see burned wires, have a pro look at the range. It could indicate a bigger problem.

Check the burner for wear. If it's pitted and scorched (Photo 1), replace it.

Check the connections for a solid contact (Photo 2).

Remove a functioning burner of the same size and try it in the socket that's not working. If that burner works, replace the bad burner with a new one.

Inspect the burner socket. If it's charred or scorched, replace it (Photo 3). There are two main types of wire connections. Sockets have either screw connections (Photo 3) or wire leads that you attach to the range wiring with the supplied ceramic wire connectors.

1 Compare the nonfunctioning burner with the other burners. If it looks pitted and scorched, unplug the range, then slip the burner out of its socket and replace it. To remove a burner, simply lift it slightly and pull the prongs from the socket. You may have to wiggle it slightly to get the prongs to release. Some burners are held by a screw that you must remove.

2 Wiggle the burner in the socket. If it's loose in the socket, pull it out and spread the burner terminals slightly for a tighter connection. Do this gently—the metal is fragile and you don't want to crack the heating element! Then clean the socket with a wire brush. Reinstall the burner, plug the stove back in and test the results.

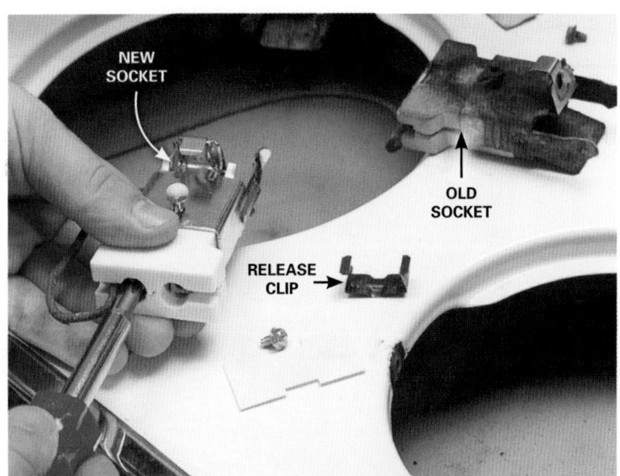

3 Replace a scorched socket by removing the screws that secure it to the range top. Then unscrew the range wires and screw them to the terminals on the new socket.

pro tip

Before you call for repair

With any appliance problem, check the power supply first. Make sure it's plugged in and that the circuit breaker hasn't tripped.

Troubleshoot a gas oven

Before you open your wallet and call a professional to repair your oven:

■ Reset your "time cook" function if your oven has one. They are often set wrong and prevent the stove from coming on. Service pros see this problem often, much to the homeowner's embarrassment!

■ Make sure the stove is plugged in and you have power to the outlet. Electronic ignition systems and some standing pilots need electricity to operate.

■ Check the oven ignition fuse (Photo 1). You'll need your owner's manual to locate it.

■ Check the pilot, if your oven has one (Photo 2). If it's out, clean and relight it according to the manufacturer's directions. If you're unsure how, call a service pro.

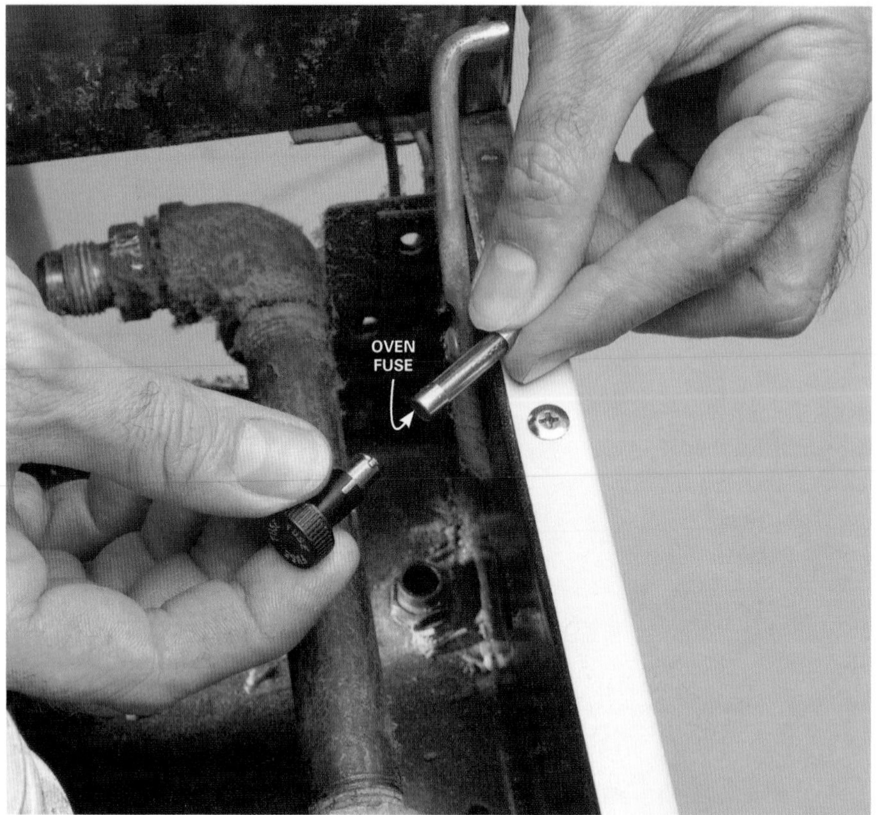

1 Check your owner's manual to see if your oven ignition system has a fuse. This one was located under the cooktop, though locations vary. Replace it with the same size fuse if the fuse element is burned.

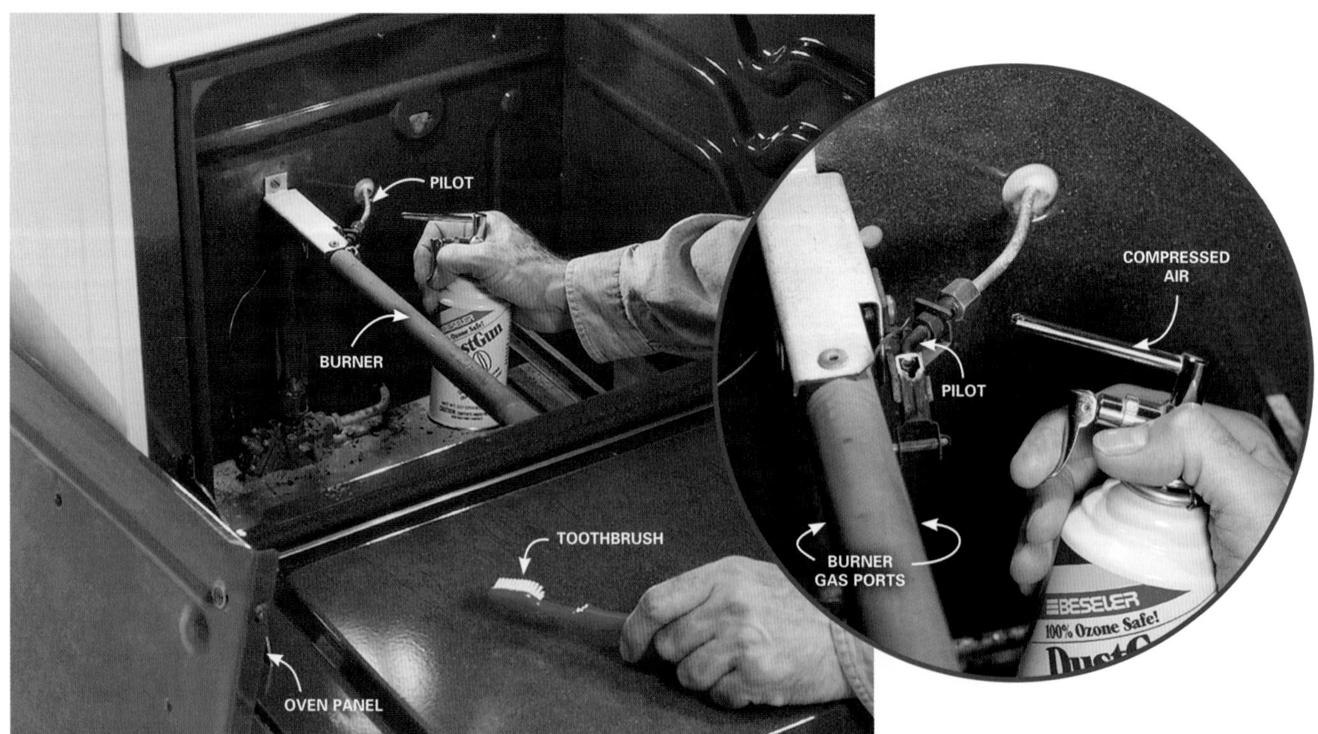

2 Check to see if the pilot is lit (standing pilot only). It's accessible under the panel in the oven or from underneath. If it's not lit, clean it as you would the cooktop pilot (Photo 2, p. 145). Also clean the tube or slit under the burner that connects the pilot to the gas ports on the opposite side of the burner. A burst of compressed air helps clear the soot. Light the pilot.

Clean the burner assembly on a gas range

Clean the burner assembly the same way for both spark ignition stoves and standing pilots. You'll need a small-diameter brush. We purchased a tube brush from a drugstore. Appliance parts stores have them too. If you have sealed burners, you're limited to cleaning only the burner ports (Photo 3). The other parts are sealed so they won't get clogged.

Set the assembly in place and try your burners. If they still won't ignite and you own a spark ignition stove, go to Step 3. If you have a standing pilot, raise or lower the flame height slightly by turning a small setscrew located on the small gas line feeding the pilot. Consult your owner's manual or call a pro to help find this screw and to tell you the proper setting for your range.

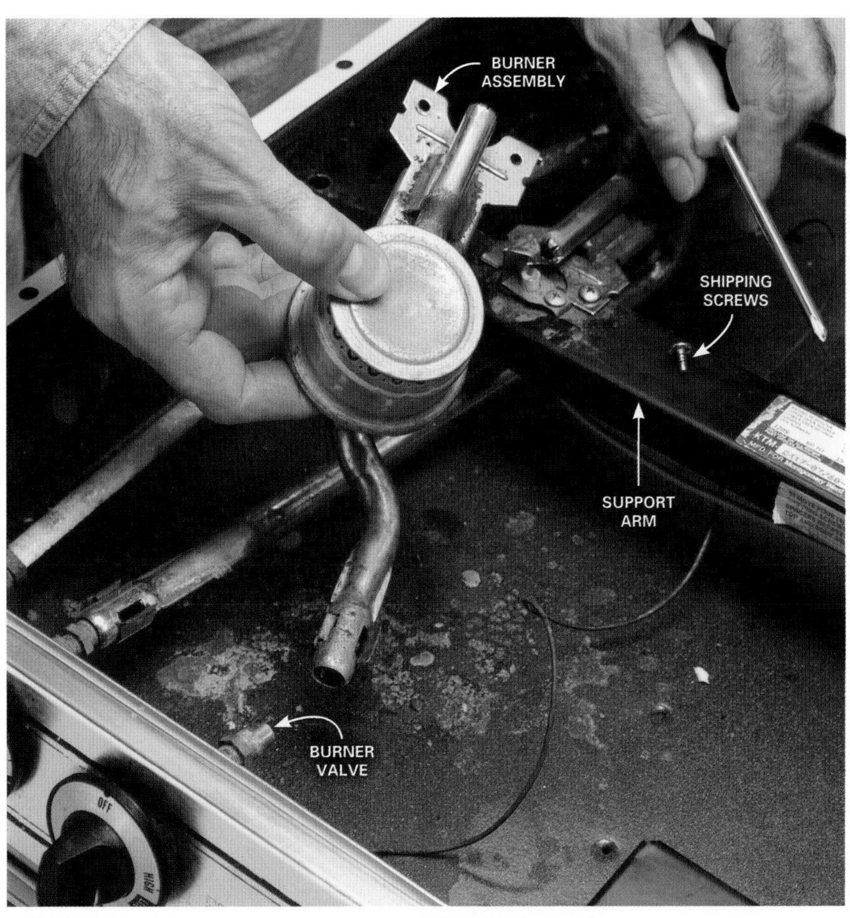

1 Lift the burner assembly off the support arm as you slide it away from the burner valve port. It just rests there. Remove the shipping screws if they're still in place. (You don't have to reinstall them.) Your burner assembly may look different from this one, but you can clean all the components the same way.

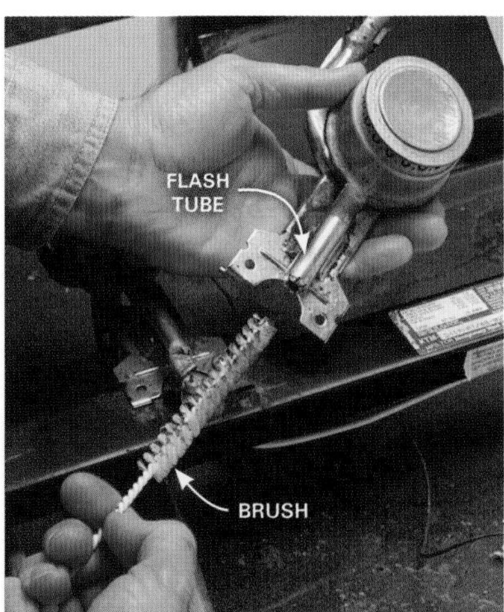

2 Shove the brush into the flash tube to clear gunk and dust. Although some pros use water and degreasers to clean the burner assembly, we don't recommend them because they could cause rust.

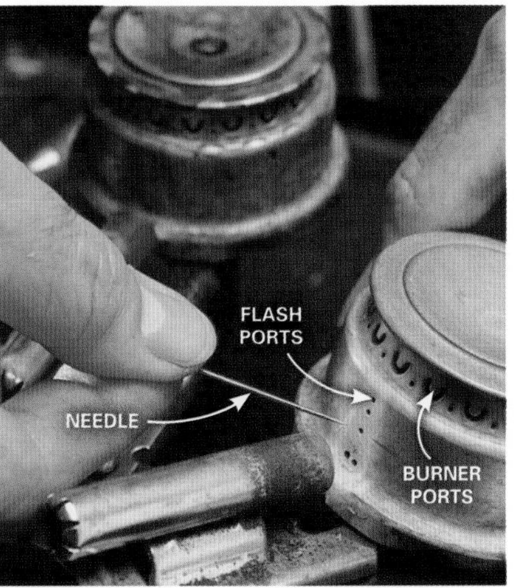

3 Clear all the flash ports with a needle, then do the same to the burner ports. Brush away any debris with a toothbrush.

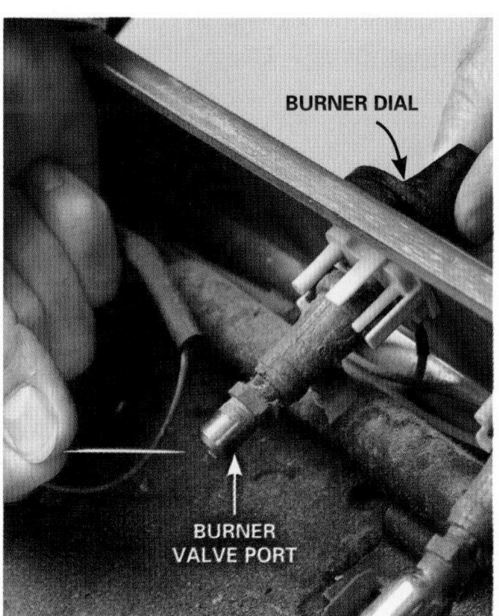

4 Stick the needle in the burner valve port a few times to clear any debris.

instant fix

Adjust your oven temperature setting

If the temperature in your oven doesn't match your temperature setting, or if your new oven just doesn't cook like your old one, you can recalibrate the temperature setting. The instructions for adjusting the temperature are in your instruction manual. If you don't have a manual, ask the manufacturer to send you one or go online and search for a downloadable version. Enter your oven's model number along with the words "instruction manual" in the search box and you're sure to find what you need.

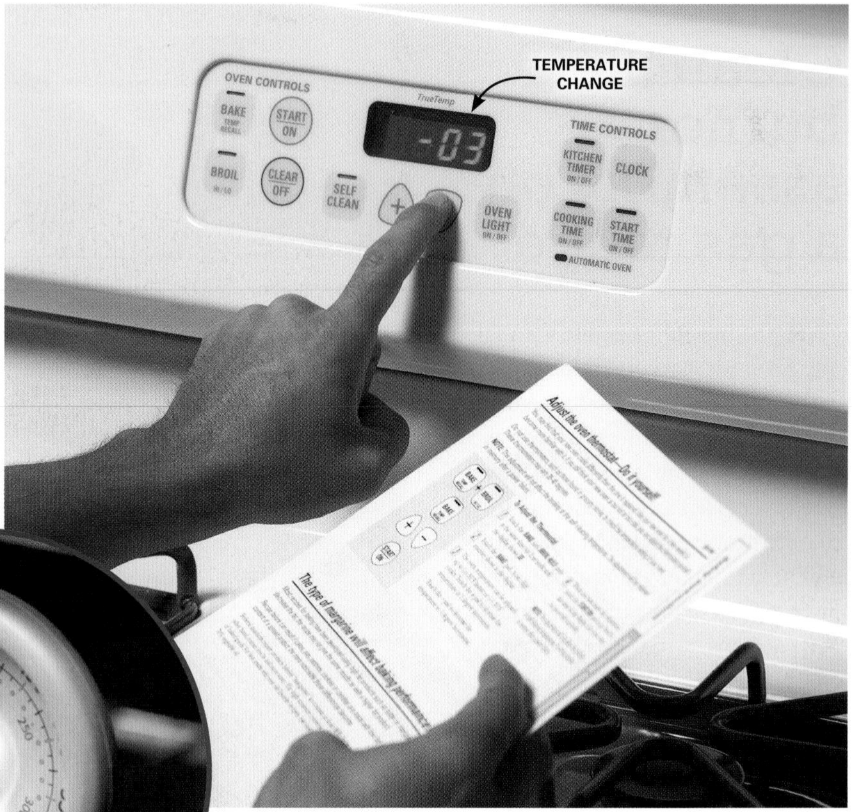

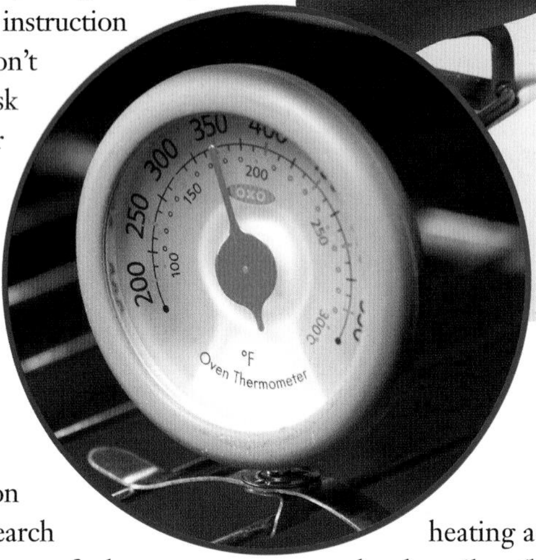

You'll need a good-quality oven thermometer to see if your oven is heating accurately. Check local retailers (kitchen and department stores tend to carry good ones) or buy one online. Place the thermometer on the center shelf and wait for the oven to maintain a constant temperature. Then use the procedure outlined in your manual to match the temperature setting to the thermometer reading.

Adjust the temperature setting. On this GE oven, you press the "bake" and "broil" buttons simultaneously, and then press "bake" to enter the temperature-adjusting mode. Then you keep pressing the "+" or "- " button to coordinate the thermostat with the actual oven temperature.

pro tip

Don't slam the lid

If you're in the habit of slamming your washing machine lid shut, your appliance repair person wants to say "Thanks!" Dropping the lid, rather than closing it gently, eventually wrecks the lid switch—and provides easy money for appliance technicians.

If your washing machine fills with water, but won't agitate or spin, it's too late. Replacing the switch yourself is a simple job on most machines; just unscrew it, unplug it and install the new one.

instant fix

Fix a slow-filling washer

If your washing machine fills with a slow trickle, you might need a fill/inlet valve. But chances are you have a simpler problem: plugged inlet screens. These screens catch debris in the water supply and protect a washer's internal parts. Often, screens clog after a remodeling project or after work by city crews on water mains. Any work on water lines can loosen sediment in pipes and lead to plugged screens.

Cleaning the screens is a simple job. The only tricky part is removing the screens without wrecking them (Photo 1). Don't just yank them out. Gently squeeze and twist as you pull. You'll distort the screens a little, but you can mold them back into shape with your fingers.

If your screens are cemented in place by mineral deposits, you may not be able to remove them without damage. A new pair of screens will cost just a few bucks at an appliance parts store. Clean the screens with running water or blow out debris with an air compressor. You may have to pick and scrape away stubborn particles with a utility knife.

pro tip

Check your washer supply hoses, too. Some contain screens that can be removed and cleaned just like inlet screens.

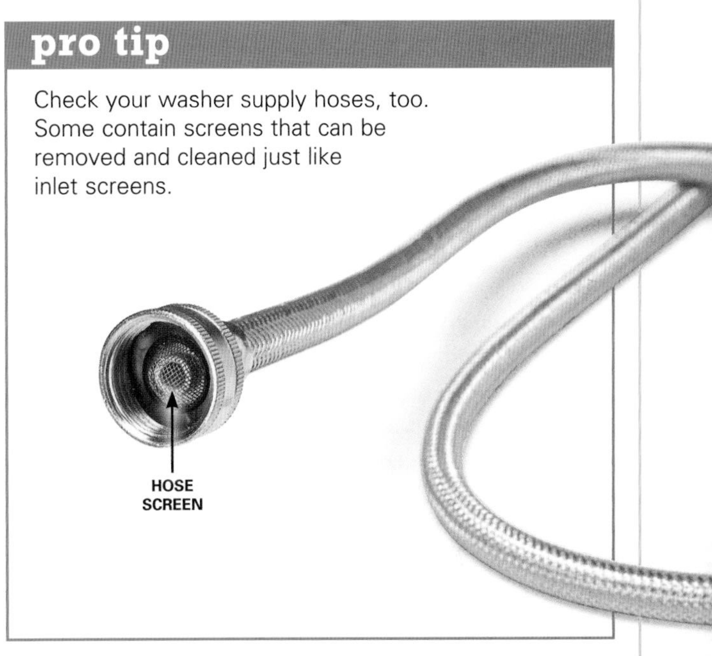

1 **Turn off the hot and cold water supplies and disconnect the hoses. Use a pair of needle-nose pliers to gently remove the screens for cleaning.**

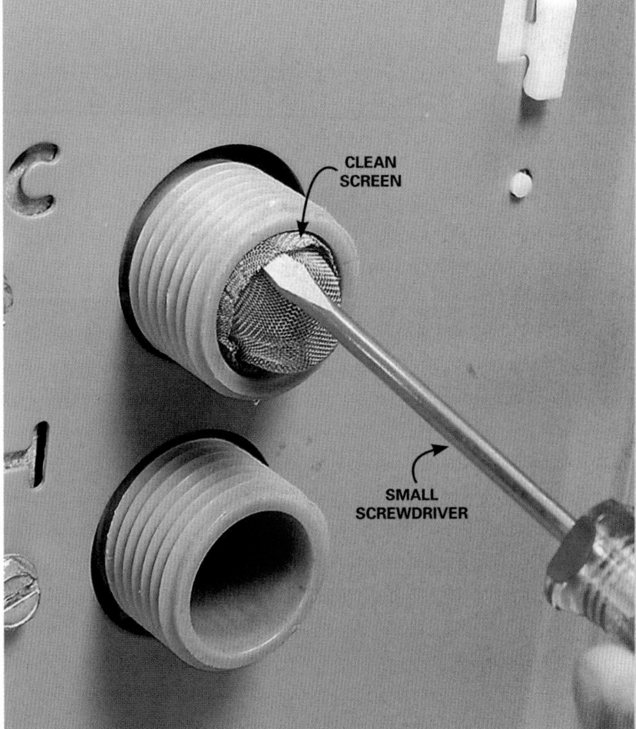

2 **Work the screen back into the inlet by pressing around the rim of the screen with a small screwdriver. Reconnect the hoses, turn on the water and check for leaks.**

Replace a noisy bath fan

If the bath fan in your home is more than 20 years old, chances are it's pretty loud. A loud fan may be good for masking bathroom noise, but the jet engine roar is downright annoying the rest of the time. Worse yet, your old bath fan may not be moving enough air to keep your bathroom free of mold and mildew.

Newer-style bath fans, on the other hand, are so quiet you can hardly hear them running, and they cost very little to operate. It's easier than you think to swap out that noisy, inefficient bath fan, especially if you choose one that's designed to be installed without ripping out the bathroom ceiling.

Of the many replacement models to choose from, we picked the NuTone No. RN110 Ultra Pro Series ($160 at supplyhouse.com) because the fan can be installed from inside the bathroom. It's not the quietest model available, but at 0.6 sones (about 25 decibels), it's a huge improvement over the old 4-sone (about 60 decibels) fan we're replacing. If you can locate a joist, cut drywall and handle basic electrical work, you can do the whole job in about two hours and save about $200 on the installation. You'll need a stud finder, a drywall saw, a drill and screws, and aluminum duct tape.

Buy the right size for your bathroom

There's no such thing as a "one-size-fits-all" bath fan. For bathrooms up to 100 sq. ft., calculate the required cubic feet per minute (cfm) by multiplying the room's length x width x height. Multiply that result by .13 and round up to the nearest 10. Example: 10 ft. wide x 9 ft. long x 9 ft. high x .13 = 105. Round up to 110 and buy a 110-cfm bath fan. For bathrooms larger than 100 sq. ft., simply add up the cfm requirements for each of these plumbing fixtures: toilet, 50 cfm; shower, 50 cfm; bathtub, 50 cfm; jetted tub, 100 cfm.

Turn off the power before proceeding

You'll have to remove the power cable from the old unit and connect it to the new fan. This must be done with the power off. Don't rely on turning off the fan switch; flip the breaker as well. Then double-check that the power is off with a voltage sniffer. If you're not comfortable working with electricity, hire an electrician to remove and connect the wires.

Find the joists and duct and enlarge the opening

Most bath fans are mounted to a ceiling joist with the duct running parallel to the joist. Start by locating the direction of your ceiling joists (Photo 1). Then locate the damper (you may have to remove the fan motor and

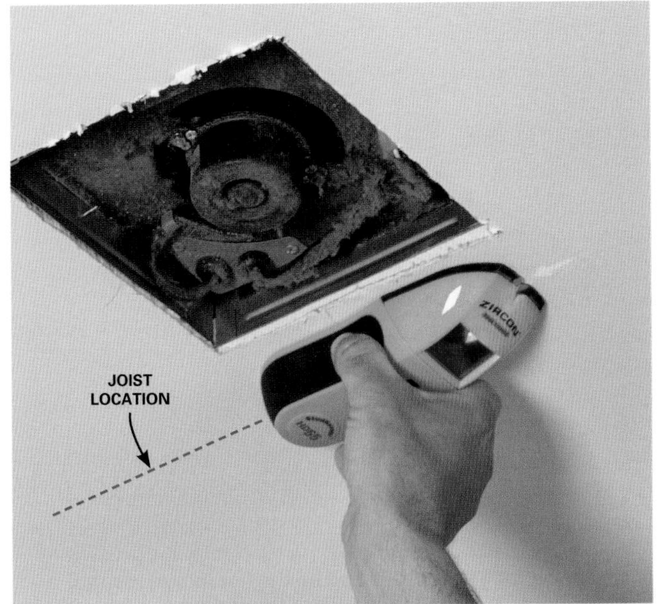

1 FIND THE JOISTS Slide a stud finder along the ceiling until you find the joist nearest the old fan. Mark the location. Then find the joist on the opposite side of the fan.

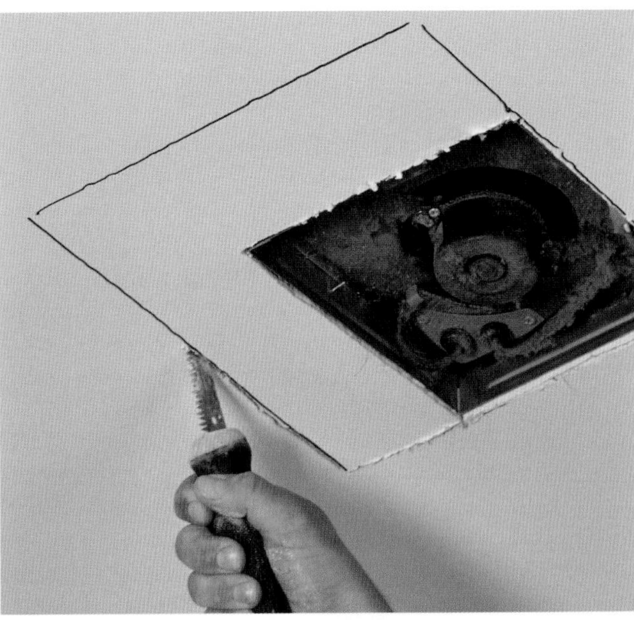

2 MARK AND CUT THE CEILING OPENING Using the template provided, trace the new opening onto the ceiling. Then cut along the lines using a drywall saw. Cut shallower strokes around the flexible duct so you don't puncture it.

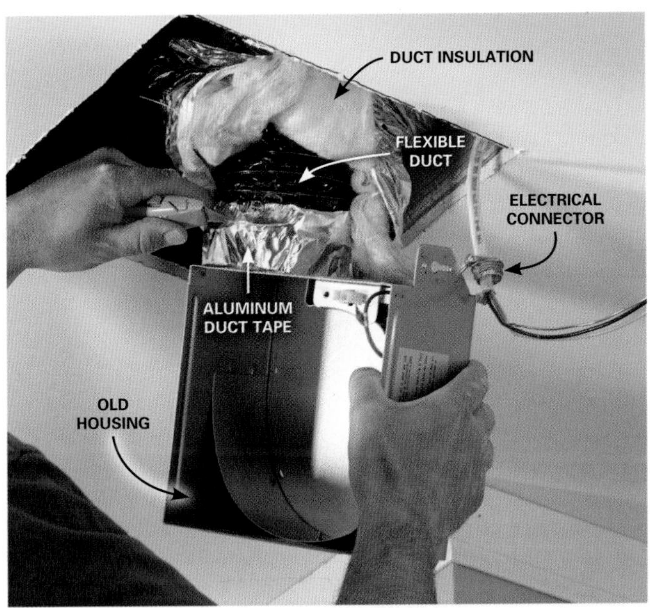

3 DISCONNECT AND REMOVE OLD PARTS Unscrew the old fan housing from the joist. Then disconnect the electrical cable from the housing. Finally, slice through the duct sealing tape with a utility knife and disconnect the duct.

4 MOUNT THE BRACKET Slide the bracket through the opening and extend it so it contacts the joists on each side of the opening. Secure both sides to the joists with drywall screws.

You may have to go into your attic

The installation we show here is all done from inside a bath with a floor above it. However, if you're replacing a bath fan in a bathroom with an accessible attic above it, you have the option of doing some of the work from up there. Use your judgment. You may save some mess by going into the attic and moving the insulation aside before you remove the old fan. Then rearrange the insulation after the installation is done. Or, eliminate the second trip by making the electrical and vent connections at the same time.

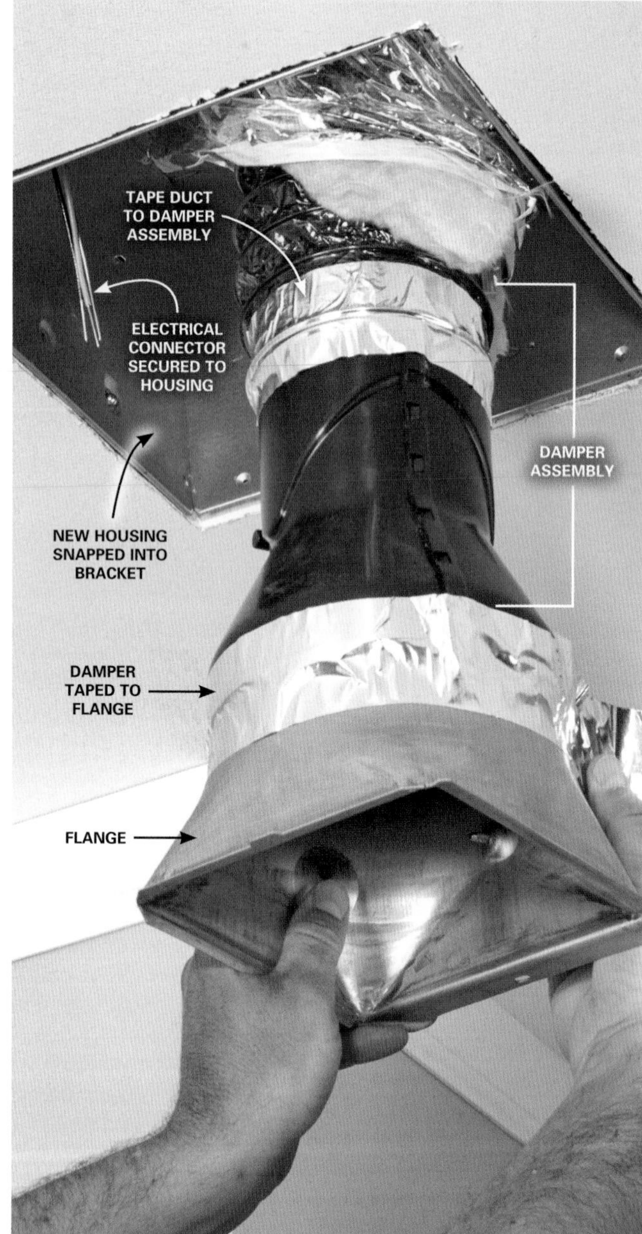

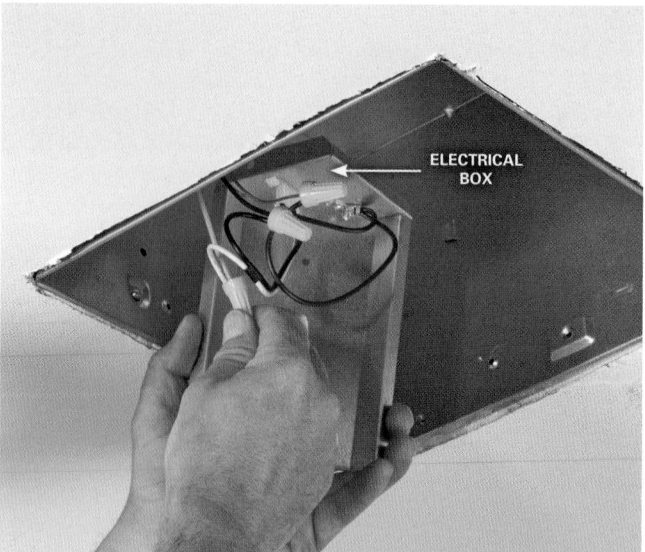

6 CONNECT THE WIRES Secure the hot (black), neutral (white) and ground (green/bare copper) wires with wire nuts. Then slide the metal electrical box into place in the housing and attach it with the screw provided.

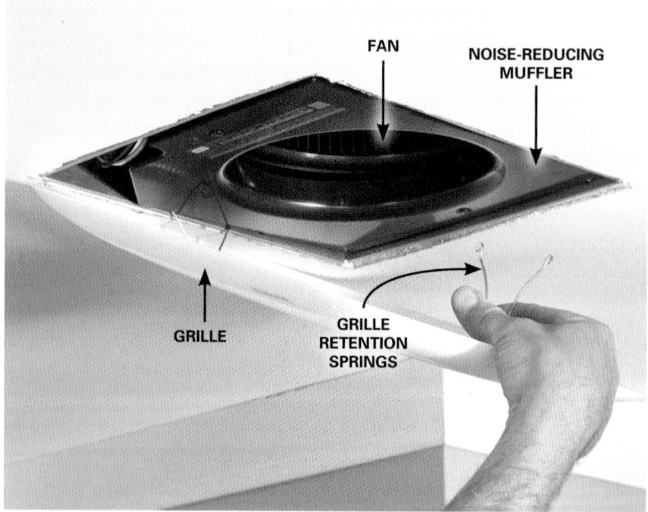

5 CONNECT THE DUCT Pull the old duct through the housing and into the room. Then tape the duct to the damper assembly. Slide the damper onto the flange and secure with aluminum duct tape. Push the duct, damper and flange back into the ceiling and secure the flange to the housing using the screw provided.

7 INSTALL THE FAN AND GRILLE Slide the fan assembly into the housing until it snaps in place. Secure with screws. Plug the electrical connector into the electrical box mounted earlier. Then screw in the noise-reducing muffler. Squeeze the grille springs and snap the grille into place.

blade from the housing). That'll tell you where the duct lies in the ceiling. Mark the duct location. Then enlarge the opening (Photo 2).

Remove and replace the housing, duct and fan

With the opening now enlarged, you'll have room to disconnect the old duct, electrical cable and old housing (Photo 3). Install and secure the new mounting frame (Photo 4). Connect the electrical cable to the new housing and snap the housing into the frame so the duct opening is facing the existing duct. Then connect the duct, damper and flange using aluminum duct tape (Photo 5). Finish the rough-in by connecting the power wires and ground to the electrical box provided (Photo 6).

Then simply slide the fan into the housing and add the muffler and grille (Photo 7). Turn on the power and test. Apply a bead of fire-resistant (intumescent) caulk around the fan housing and drywall to prevent moisture intrusion into the attic.

instant fix

Stop washing machine walk

If your washer makes loud thumping noises and is moving across the floor when it's in spin cycle, it probably needs to be leveled.

Push the machine back into position if it has moved across the floor. Adjust the front legs to make the machine level across the front and from front to back (Photo 1). The legs can usually be turned by hand after the locking nut at the top of the threads is turned down, but if the threads are rusted, use a wrench.

After leveling, lock the leg into place with the locking nut (Photo 2).

Most washing machines have self-adjusting rear legs that level from side to side, but dirt, lint and rust may keep them from working properly. If the back isn't level, tip the washing machine up a few inches and then set it back down so the weight of the machine loosens the legs. If the machine still doesn't level out, the self-leveling support may be rusted against the washing machine frame. Tip the machine off the ground, then break the self-leveling support loose by tapping the legs (Photo 3).

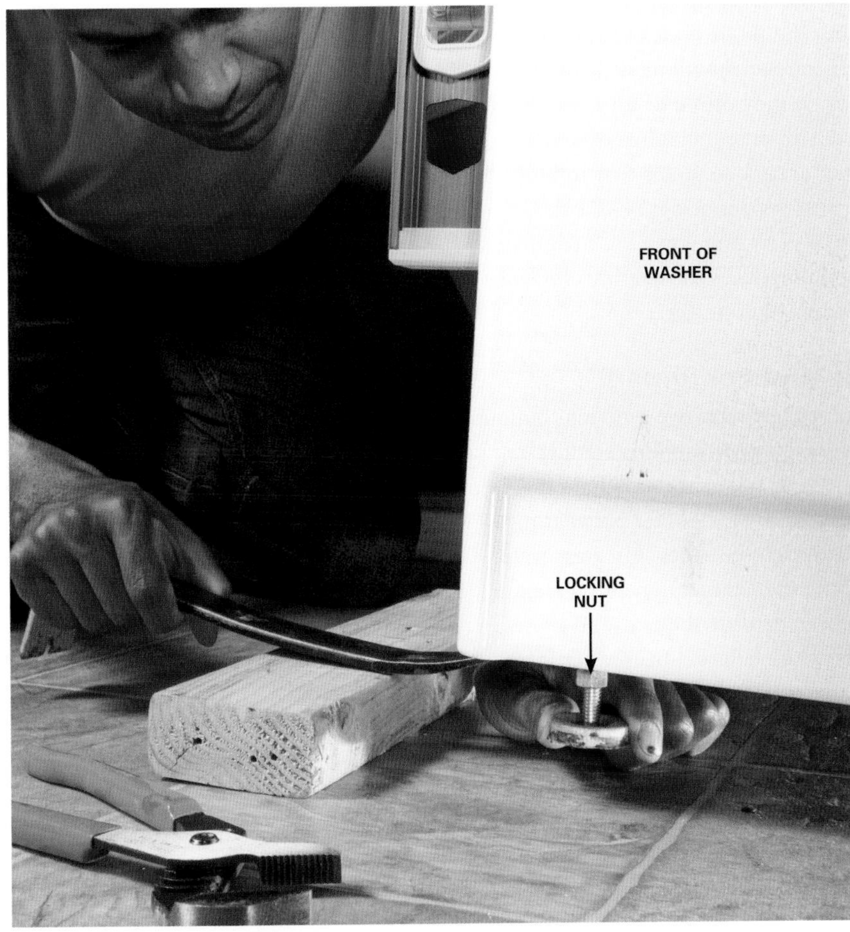

1 Lift the machine slightly with a pry bar to take the weight off the front legs, then turn the legs until the side of the washer is plumb.

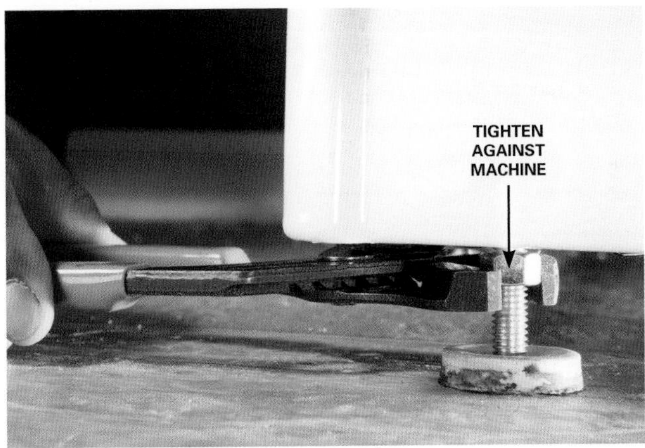

2 Tighten the locking nut up against the frame of the washing machine to keep the leg from turning.

3 If the rear leveling mechanism is frozen with rust, tap the legs a few times with pliers or a hammer to break it free.

Flush a water heater

Have you flushed your water heater lately? This boring but important chore should be done at least once a year to remove sediment that accumulates on the bottom of the tank. That's especially true if you live in a hard-water area. The task is easy to blow off because it's out of sight—but skipping it is costing you a lot. Sediment buildup reduces the heating efficiency of your water heater.

All about sediment

One sign of excessive sediment buildup is a popping or rumbling sound coming from your water heater. That's the sound of steam bubbles percolating up through the muck. On a gas water heater, the sediment creates hot spots that can damage the tank and cause premature failure. On an electric water heater, sediment buildup can cause the lower heating element to fail. So flushing offers a payback in lower energy bills and extended heater life.

However, if you've never flushed your water heater, or haven't done it in years, you could be in for a nasty surprise. As soon as you open the drain valve, the sediment will likely clog it and prevent you from closing the valve all the way after it's drained. Then you'll have sediment buildup and a leaking water heater. We'll show you the best way to drain the sediment out of even the most neglected heater and save a $200 service call. You'll need about $40 in plumbing parts from a home center, a garden hose, a wet vacuum, pliers and a pipe wrench.

Buy the parts

Not only will an old drain clog up, but you won't be able to suck debris through its small opening. The key is to build a new drain valve with a 3/4-in. full-port brass ball valve with threaded ends ($12), a 3-in. x 3/4-in. galvanized nipple ($1.50), and a 3/4-in. MIP x G.H. garden hose adapter (one choice is the BrassCraft/Plumbshop No. HU22-12-12TP; $8).

Then build a shop vacuum adapter. If your shop vacuum has a 2-1/2-in. hose, buy a converter to reduce it to 1-1/4-in. (the Shop Vac No. 9068500, $8, is one option). Then assemble a vacuum hose-to-plumbing adapter (Photo 1) with a 1-1/4-in. x 1-1/2-in. female PVC trap adapter, a 3/4-in. MIP x 1/2-in. barb fitting, a second 3/4-in. x 3-in. nipple and a 24-in. piece of 1/2-in. I.D. vinyl tubing (about $10 for these parts).

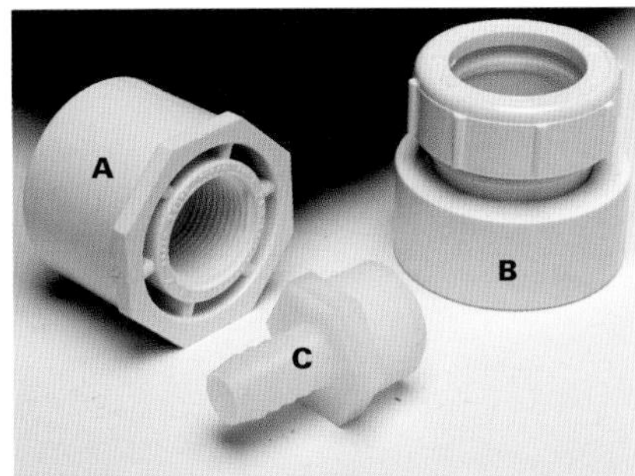

1 BUILD A SHOP VACUUM ADAPTER Glue a 1-1/2-in. PVC x 3/4-in. FIP adapter (A) onto a female PVC trap adapter (B). This allows you to attach your vacuum to 3/4-in. pipe (see below). The barbed fitting (C) connects to tubing (Photo 4).

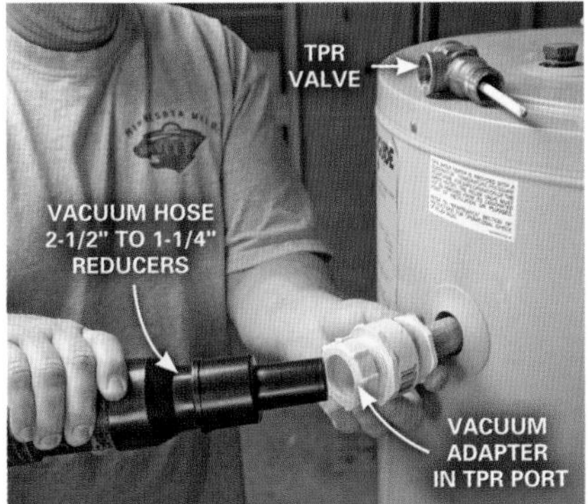

2 APPLY SUCTION Remove the temperature pressure release valve and screw in the vacuum adapter. Attach the shop vacuum hose and fire up the vacuum.

3 SWAP VALVES Unscrew the old drain valve and install the full-port valve (closed position). Attach one end of the garden hose to the valve and run the other end into a colander and on to the floor drain.

4 SUCK OUT THE SEDIMENT Remove the full-port valve and suck out the remaining sediment with your shop vacuum adapter and vinyl tubing.

Start the draining process

Shut off the gas or electricity to the water heater and open a hot water faucet and let it run full blast for about 10 minutes to reduce the water temperature in the tank. Then shut off the cold water valve at the top of the tank and attach a garden hose to the existing drain valve and route it to a floor drain. (Use a kitchen colander to catch the sediment so it doesn't clog the floor drain.) Then open a hot water faucet on an upper floor and the water heater drain valve. Let the tank drain until sediment clogs the valve and reduces the flow. Then close the upstairs hot water faucet and water heater drain valve.

Next, remove the clogged drain valve and swap in the new full-port valve. But first, remove the blow-off tube and the temperature pressure release (TPR) valve and apply suction to the tank so you won't get soaked when you yank the old drain valve (Photo 2). Then swap the valves (Photo 3). Remove the vacuum hose from the TPR port and finish draining the tank.

YUCK! This is what the sediment looks like.

Most of the sediment will flush out through the full-port valve. To remove the rest, open the cold water valve at the top of the tank in short bursts to blast it toward the drain. If you still can't get the last bit out, try vacuuming it (Photo 4).

When you're done, close the ball valve and leave it in place. But remove the lever handle to prevent accidental opening. Then reinstall the TPR valve and blow-off tube. Refill the water heater and turn on the gas or electricity, and you'll be back in hot water without all the noise.

Fix a water heater pilot light

No hot water? If you have a natural or propane gas water heater, chances are the pilot has gone out. The pilot is a small flame that ignites the gas burner on your water heater (photo above). When it goes out, first try relighting it, following the directions on the water heater label. If the pilot doesn't relight, or if it goes out right after lighting, by far the most common cause is a bad thermocouple (photo right). The good news: You can usually replace a thermocouple in less than an hour. You'll get your hot water going without waiting for a pro to show up, and save the cost of a service call.

To replace the thermocouple, follow the photo series. Be sure to turn off the shutoff valve in the gas line (Photo 1, inset); that is, one quarter turn so that the handle is at a right angle to the pipe. Since working room is tight around the burner, we recommend that you simply unscrew the three nuts at the control valve and pull out the entire burner assembly. You'll see either a slot or clips that hold it in place (Photo 2). Then either unscrew the thermocouple end or pull it out (depending on the water heater) and take it with you to an appliance parts store to find a match. Position it exactly like the old one. When relit,

A thermocouple senses the heat of the pilot and allows gas to flow to the burner. A bad thermocouple will shut off gas to both the pilot and the burner.

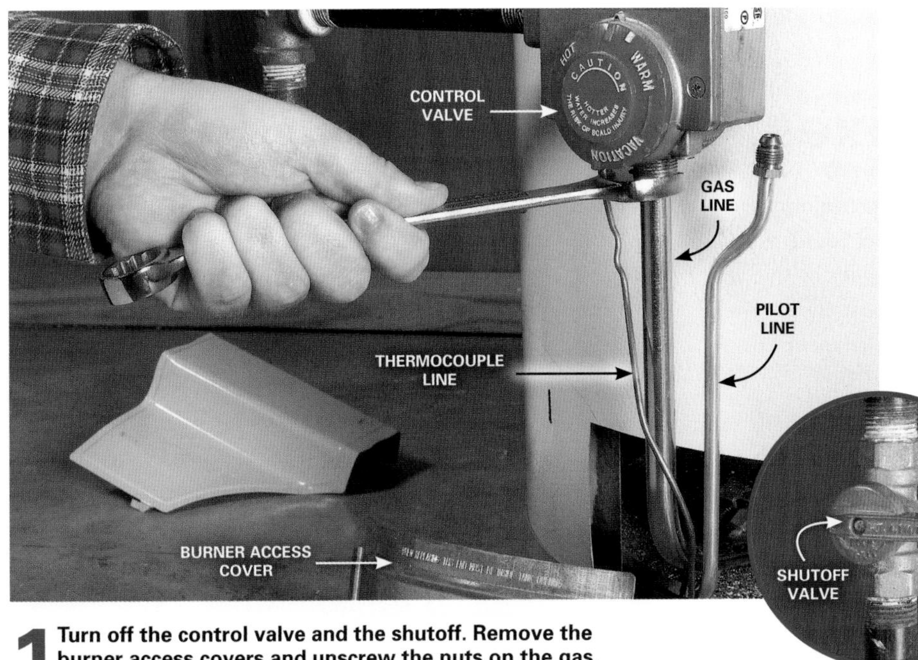

1 **Turn off the control valve and the shutoff. Remove the burner access covers and unscrew the nuts on the gas, pilot and thermocouple lines.**

BURNER
SLOT

2 **Pull out the burner assembly. Pull out the old thermocouple. Buy a new one that matches the old one in size and length.**

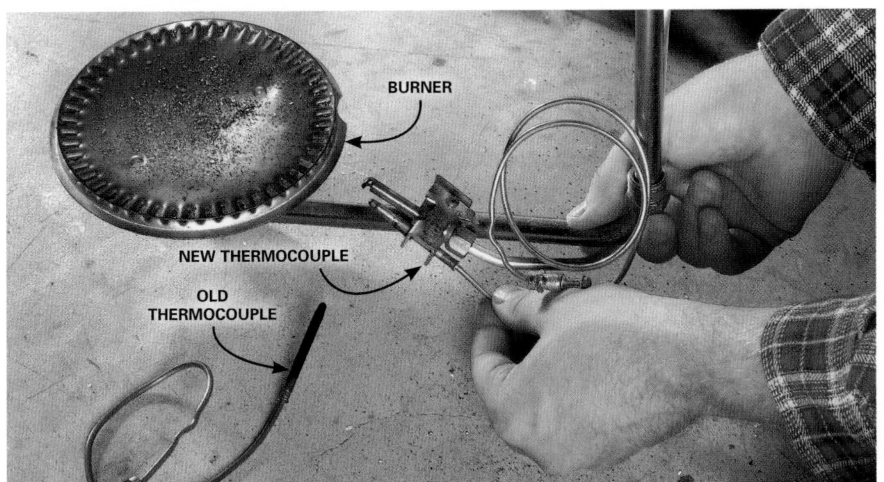

3 **Install the new thermocouple exactly like the old, slide the burner assembly back in and reattach the three lines to the control valve.**

caution

You should not be able to smell gas during this operation (except for a slight whiff when you remove the gas lines). If you do, leave the house and call your gas utility.

the pilot flame should wrap around the thermocouple bulb.

To reattach the three lines to the gas valve, thread the nuts into place with your fingers and hand-tighten them. Then snug them up with a quarter to half revolution with a wrench. The metals are soft, so don't overtighten. Be sure to test for gas leaks. You must have the pilot lit and the burner on for this test so that gas is flowing through the large tube. Reopen the shutoff valve, relight the pilot, then turn the control valve to "on." When the gas burner comes on, use a 50/50 dish soap/water mix to test the screw joints for air bubbles that indicate leaks.

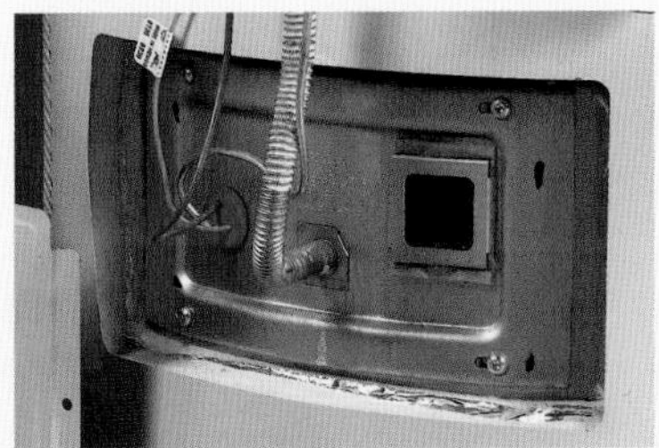

note: **Some gas water heaters have a "closed" burner chamber, which is difficult to access. We recommend that you call a service pro to fix this type. Also, some gas water heaters don't have pilots. Let the pros fix these as well.**

Instant air conditioner fixes

Chances are that if you've neglected a spring checkup, your air conditioner isn't cooling nearly as well as it could. A year's worth of dirt and debris clogging the cooling fins, a low coolant level, a dirty blower fan filter and a number of other simple problems can significantly reduce the efficiency of your air conditioner and wear it out faster.

You can't do everything; only a pro can check the coolant level. But you can easily handle most of the routine cleaning chores and save the cost to have a pro do them.

Here you'll see how to clean the outdoor unit (called the condenser) and the accessible parts of the indoor unit (called the evaporator). All the steps are simple and straightforward and will take you only a few hours total. You don't need any special skills, tools or experience. If you aren't familiar with air conditioners and furnaces/blowers, don't worry. See Figure A on p. 158 to become familiar with how an air conditioner works and the parts of the system.

You may have a different type of central air conditioner than we show here—a heat pump system, for example, or a unit mounted horizontally in the attic. However, you can still carry out most maintenance procedures because each system will have a condenser outside and an evaporator inside. Use the owner's manual for your particular model to help navigate any differences from the one shown in our photos. And call in a pro every two or three years to check electrical parts and the coolant level.

Cleaning the condenser

Clean your outdoor unit on a day that's at least 60 degrees F. That's about the minimum temperature at which you can test your air conditioner to make sure it's working. The condenser usually sits in an inconspicuous spot next to your house. You'll see two copper tubes running to it, one bare

1 Turn off the electrical power to the condenser unit at the outdoor shutoff. Either pull out a block or move a switch to the "Off" position. If uncertain, turn off the power to the AC at the main electrical panel.

2 Vacuum grass clippings, leaves and other debris from the exterior fins with a soft brush attachment. Clear away all bushes, weeds and grass within 2 ft. of the condenser.

3 **Realign bent or crushed fins with gentle pressure from a dinner knife. Don't insert the knife more than 1/2 in.**

4 **Unscrew the top grille. Lift out the fan and carefully set it aside without stressing the electrical wires. Pull out any leaves and wipe the interior surfaces clean with a damp cloth.**

5 **Spray the fins using moderate water pressure from a hose nozzle. Direct the spray from the inside out. Reinstall the fan.**

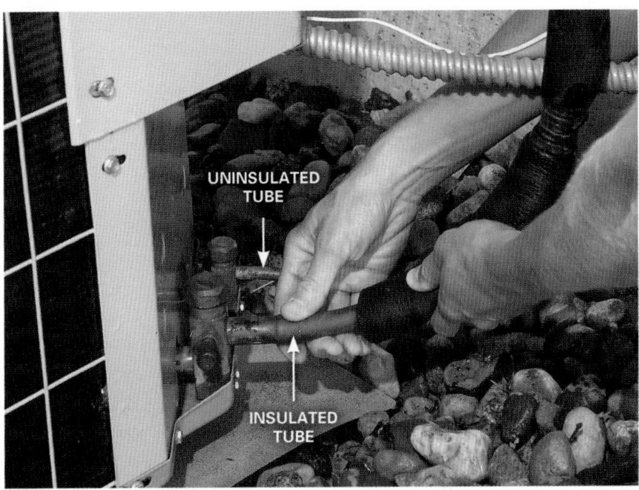

6 **Turn the power back on, then set the house thermostat to "Cool" so the compressor comes on. After 10 minutes, feel the insulated tube. It should feel cool. The uninsulated tube should feel warm.**

and the other encased in a foam sleeve. If you have a heat pump, both tubes will be covered by foam sleeves.

Your primary job here is to clean the condenser fins, which are fine metallic blades that surround the unit. They get dirty because a central fan sucks air through them, pulling in dust, dead leaves, dead grass and the worst culprit—floating "cotton" from cottonwood trees and dandelions. The debris blocks the airflow and reduces the unit's cooling ability.

Always begin by shutting off the electrical power to the unit. Normally you'll find a shutoff nearby. It may be a switch in a box, a pull lever or a fuse block that you pull out (Photo 1). Look for the "On-Off" markings.

Vacuum the fins clean with a soft brush (Photo 2); they're fragile and easily bent or crushed. On many units you'll have to unscrew and lift off a metal box to get at them. Check your owner's manual for directions and lift off the box carefully to avoid bumping the fins. Occasionally you'll find fins that have been bent. You can buy a special set of fin combs at an appliance parts store to straighten them. Minor straightening can be done with a blunt dinner knife (Photo 3). If large areas of fins are crushed, have a pro straighten them during a routine service call.

Then unscrew the fan to gain access to the interior of the condenser. You can't completely remove it because its wiring is connected to the unit. Depending on how much play the wires give you, you might need a helper to hold it while you vacuum debris from the inside. (Sometimes mice like to overwinter there!)

pro tip

Call for service before the first heat wave, when the pros become swamped with repair calls!

Figure A
Parts of a central air conditioner

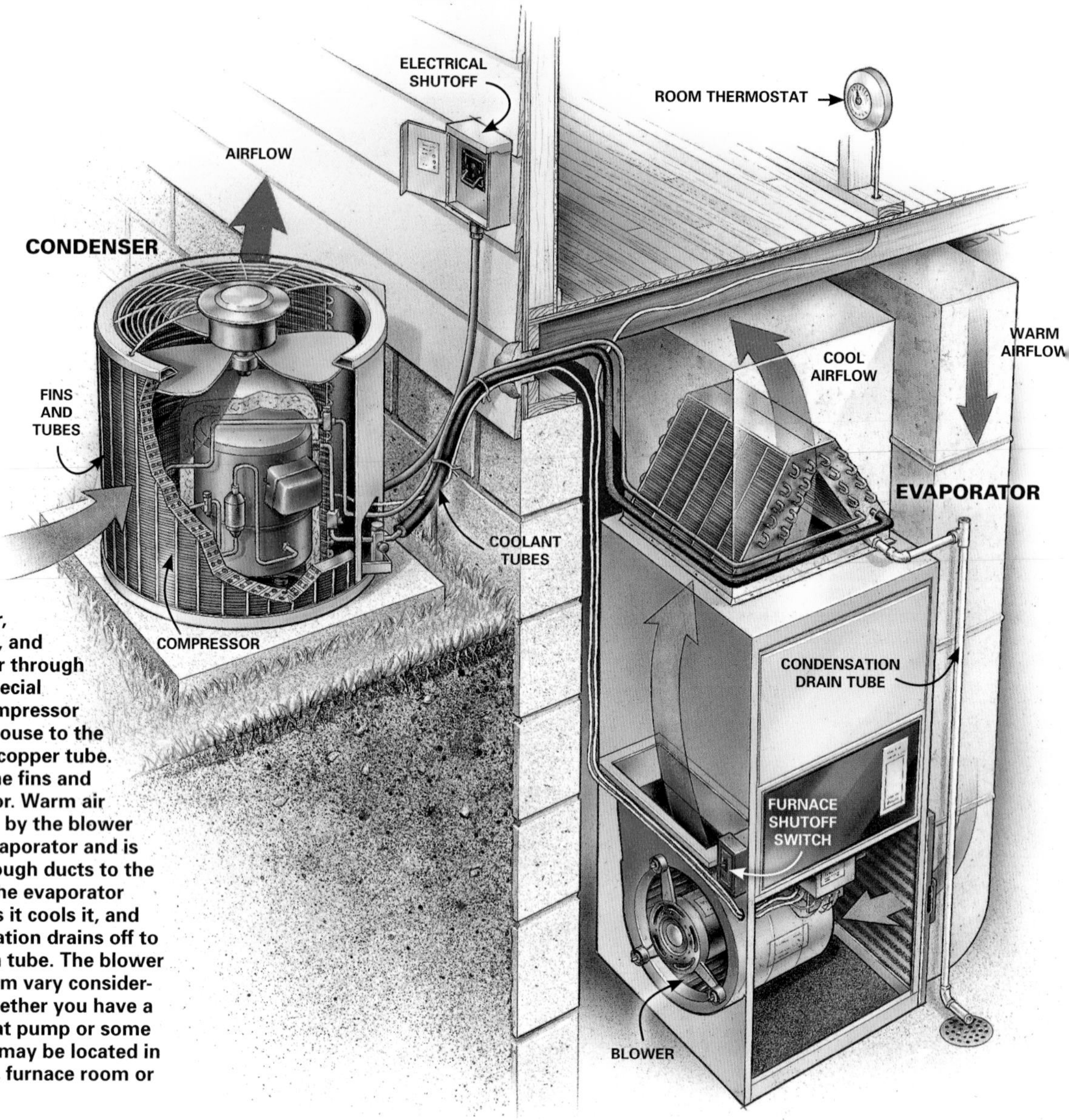

How it works:
The outside unit, called the condenser, contains a compressor, cooling fins and tubes, and a fan. The fan sucks air through the fins and cools a special coolant, which the compressor then pumps into the house to the evaporator through a copper tube.

The coolant chills the fins and tubes of the evaporator. Warm air drawn from the house by the blower passes through the evaporator and is cooled and blown through ducts to the rooms in the house. The evaporator dehumidifies the air as it cools it, and the resulting condensation drains off to a floor drain through a tube. The blower unit and ducting system vary considerably depending on whether you have a furnace (shown), a heat pump or some other arrangement. It may be located in the basement, garage, furnace room or attic.

After you hose off the fins (Photo 5), check the fan motor for lubrication ports. Most newer motors have sealed bearings (the one shown does) and can't be lubricated. Check your owner's manual to be sure. If you find ports, add five drops of electric motor oil (at hardware stores or appliance parts stores). Don't use penetrating oil or all-purpose oil. They're not designed for long-term lubrication and can actually harm the bearings.

If you have an old air conditioner, you might have a belt-driven compressor in the bottom of the unit. Look for lubrication ports on this as well. The compressors on newer air conditioners are completely enclosed and won't need lubrication.

Restarting procedure

In most cases, you can simply restore power to the outside unit and move inside to finish the maintenance. However, the compressors are surprisingly fragile and some require special start-up procedures under two conditions. (Others have built-in electronic controls that handle the start-up, but unless you know that yours has these controls, follow these procedures.)

1. If the power to your unit has been off for more than four hours:

■ Move the switch from "Cool" to "Off" at your inside thermostat.

■ Turn the power back on and let the unit sit for 24 hours. (The compressor has a heating element that warms the internal lubricant.)

■ Switch the thermostat back to "Cool."

2. If you switched the unit off while the compressor was running:

■ Wait at least five minutes before switching it back on. (The compressor needs to decompress before restarting.)

With the air conditioner running, make sure it's actually working by touching the coolant tubes (Photo 6). This is a crude test. Only a pro with proper instruments can tell if the coolant is at the level for peak efficiency. But keep a sharp eye out for dark drip marks on the bottom of the case and beneath the tube joints. This indicates an oil leak and a potential coolant leak as well. Call in a pro if you spot this problem. Don't tighten a joint to try to stop a leak yourself. Overtightening can make the problem worse.

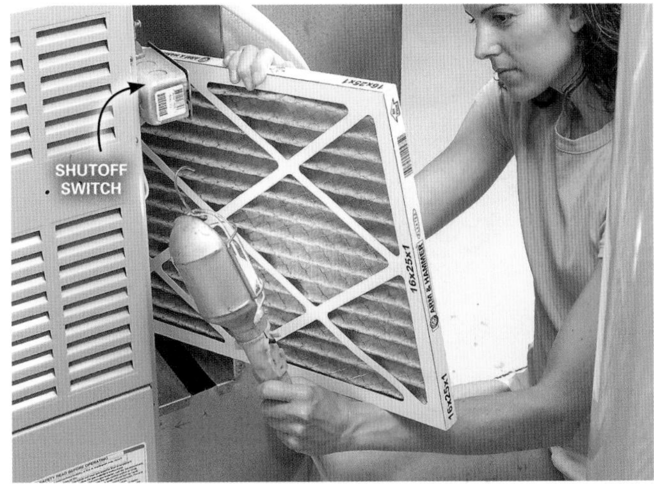

7 **Turn off the power to the furnace at a nearby switch or at the main panel. Then pull out the furnace filter and check it for dirt buildup. Change it if necessary.**

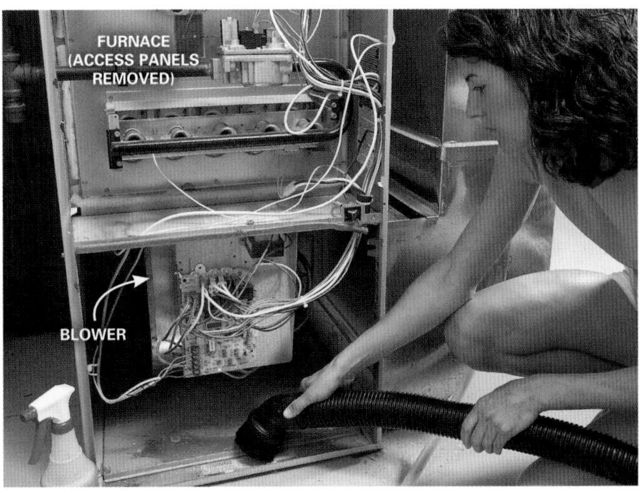

8 **Open the blower compartment and vacuum up the dust. Check the motor for lubrication ports. If it has them, squeeze five drops of electric motor oil into each.**

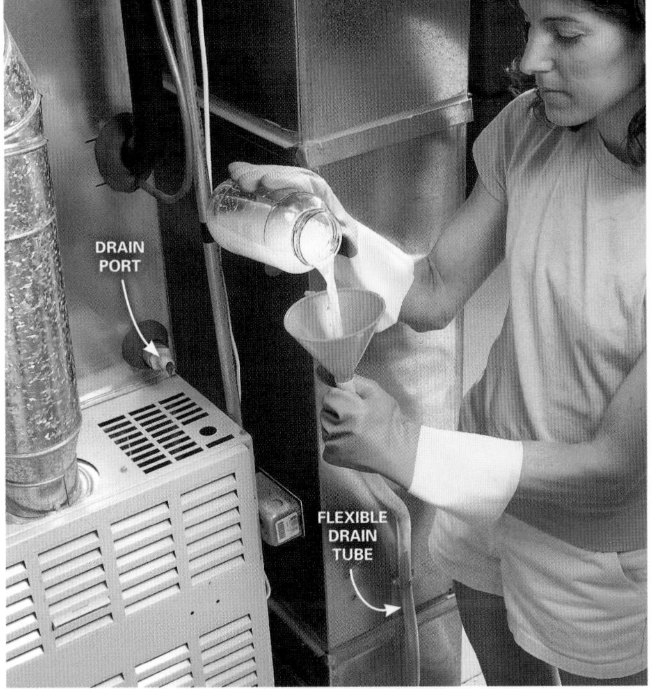

9 **Pull off the plastic condensation drain tube and check it for algae growth. Clean it by pouring a bleach/water solution (1:16 ratio) through the tube to flush the line. Or simply replace the tube.**

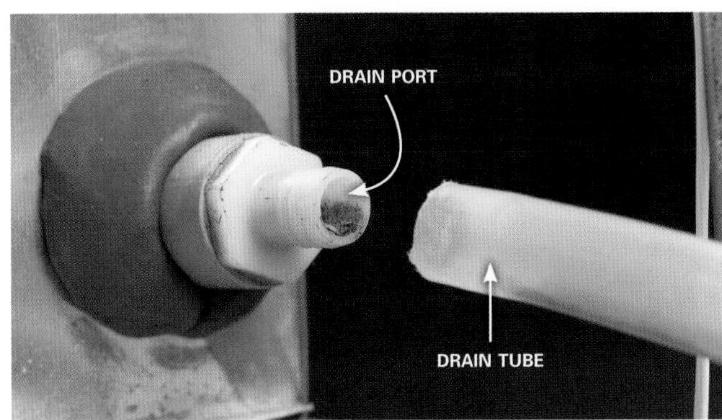

10 **Poke a pipe cleaner into the drain port and clean out any debris. Reinstall the drain tube and turn the power back on.**

Clean the indoor unit

The evaporator usually sits in an inaccessible spot inside a metal duct downstream from the blower (Figure A). If you can get to it, gently vacuum its fins (from the blower side) with a soft brush as you did with the condenser.

However, the best way to keep it clean is to keep the airstream from the blower clean. This means annually vacuuming out the blower compartment and changing the filter whenever it's dirty (Photos 7 and 8).

Begin by turning off the power to the furnace or blower. Usually you'll find a simple toggle switch nearby in a metal box (Photo 7); otherwise turn the power off at the main panel. If you have trouble opening the blower unit or finding the filter, check your owner's manual for help. The manual will also list the filter type, but if it's your first time, take the old one with you when buying a new one to make sure you get the right size. Be sure to keep the power to the blower off whenever you remove the filter. Otherwise you'll blow dust into the evaporator fins.

The manual will also tell you where to find the oil ports on the blower, if it has any. The blower compartments on newer furnaces and heat pumps are so tight that you often can't lubricate the blower without removing it. If that's the case, have a pro do it during a routine maintenance checkup.

The evaporator fins dehumidify the air as they cool it, so you'll find a tube to drain the condensation. The water collects in a pan and drains out the side (Figure A). Most tubes are flexible plastic and are easy to pull off and clean (Photos 9 and 10). But if they're rigid plastic, you'll probably have to unscrew or cut off with a saw to check. Reglue rigid tubes using a coupling, or replace them with flexible plastic tubes.

Chapter six

WALLS & CEILINGS

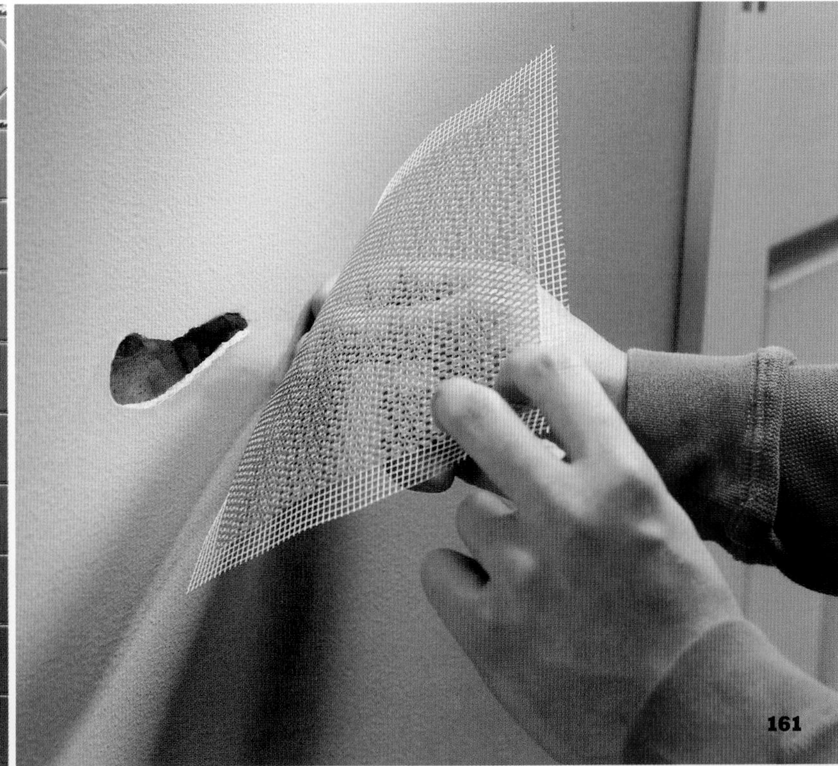

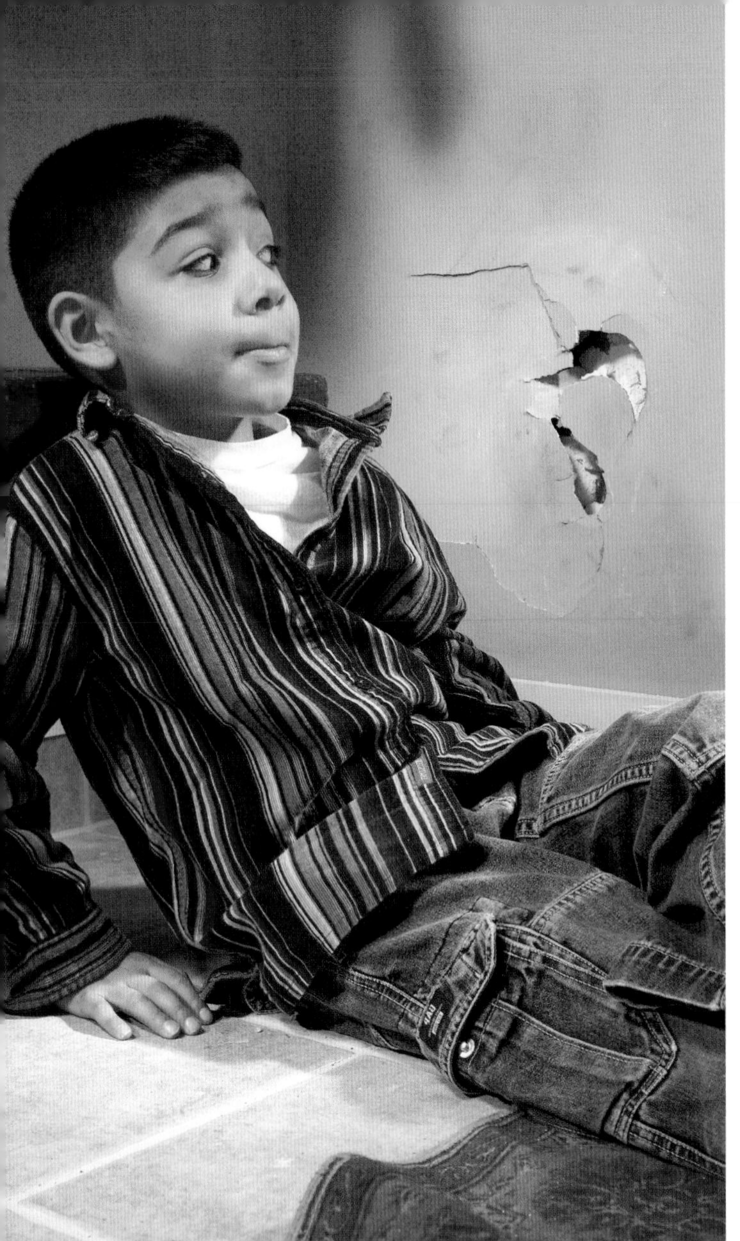

Patch large holes

Don't melt down if a doorknob, misguided chair or an impromptu hockey game knocks a big hole in your wall. With a little patience, even a novice can complete a near-invisible repair. While the total time commitment isn't great, the process stretches over three to four days to allow coats of drywall compound and paint to dry.

Before cutting out the damaged area, check the wall for obstructions. Often you'll find a wire, pipe or duct (Photo 1). If so, work carefully around them with a drywall or keyhole saw. Or make a shallow cut by repeatedly scoring the line with a sharp utility knife.

It's easier to add backer board than to try to cut the drywall over studs (Photo 2). Cut the backer boards about 4 in. longer than the height of the hole. Pine or other soft wood works well. Hold them tight to the backside of the drywall when fastening them. Hold the boards carefully so the screw points won't prick your fingers if they pop out the back side. The drywall screws will draw the boards in tight. Sink the screwheads slightly below the drywall surface.

Measure the thickness of the drywall (most likely 1/2 in.), and look for a large enough scrap from a damaged piece at a home center, rather than buy a full 4 x 8-ft. sheet. Cut it to size and screw it into place, spacing the screws every 6 in.

Taping the edges of the patch to make it invisible is the trickiest part of the job (Photos 3 and 4). Buy a gallon tub of drywall compound and a roll of paper tape. You can use mesh tape, but it isn't as strong. If you have a lot of repairs, also buy a sack of 20-minute setting compound. It hardens

ELECTRICAL CABLE
STUD LOCATION
DRYWALL SAW

1 Draw a rectangle around the break with a straightedge or square. Look or put your hand through the break to feel for wires or other obstructions. Then cut out the section with a drywall saw or utility knife.

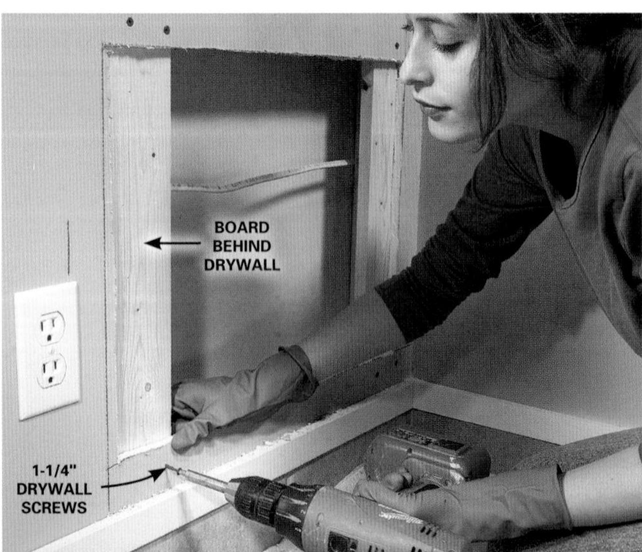

2 Insert 1x4 backer boards at each end of the hole and drive a pair of 1-1/4 in. drywall screws through the drywall into the boards to anchor them. Fit and screw a drywall patch to the boards.

3 Lay a 1/8-in. thick bed of drywall compound over the joints and press paper tape into the compound with a flexible 6-in. knife. Immediately apply a thin layer of compound on top of the tape. Allow to dry.

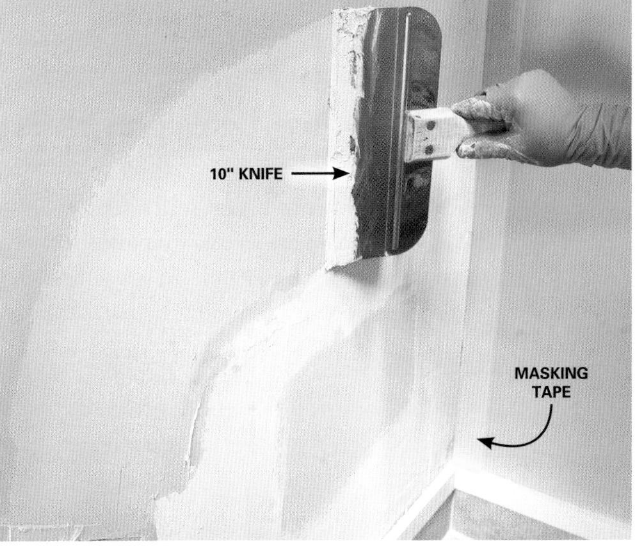

4 Apply a second coat of compound, drawing it at least 6 in. beyond the edge of the first coat to taper the edges of the repair. Let dry, then add a third coat to smooth any remaining uneven areas.

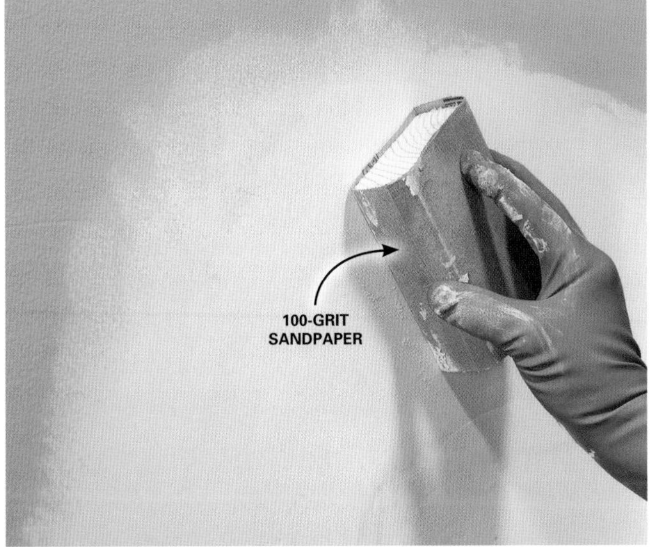

5 Sand the dry compound lightly with 100-grit sandpaper to remove ridges and blend edges. Prime and paint.

Setting compound for fast fixes

Setting-type joint compound is a great product for filling deep holes and gaps and for your first taping coat because, unlike regular joint compound, it hardens quickly without shrinking. That means less time spent filling. And you can apply a second coat of compound as soon as the first hardens. You don't have to wait for it to dry completely.

For most repairs, buy the lightweight type that hardens in 20 minutes. It comes as a powder in sacks. Mix only what you can use in about 10 minutes. It hardens quickly, often in your pan if you're too slow! Completely clean your pan and knife before mixing a new batch. Otherwise it'll harden even faster! To avoid clogging the sink drain, throw leftover compound into the trash.

quickly and doesn't shrink, so it's ideal for filling cracks and gaps before applying the joint tape. For smoothest results, also pick up flexible 6- and 10-in. taping knives.

Apply a coat of compound and tape to each joint (Photo 3). Thin the compound a bit with water to help embed the tape. Smooth the tape with the 6-in. knife, pulling out from the center toward each end. Squeeze some, but not all, of the compound out from under the tape so you don't create a big hump on the wall. Immediately apply a light coating to the topside of the tape, tapering it out onto the wall.

The second and third coats are to blend and smooth the taped joints so they'll be invisible when painted. After each coat is dry, set a straightedge against the wall to check for obvious dips and bumps. Knock off bumps and ridges with your taping knife. Add more coats as needed. Then sand, prime and paint.

pro tip

When cutting out damage, leave a few inches of drywall at corners so you won't have to spread taping compound onto adjacent walls or ceilings and repaint them as well!

Fix small holes and nail pops

Small holes caused by screws or hooks, wall fasteners or drywall fasteners that pop up are simple to repair, but again time consuming because you almost always have to repaint the walls. Nail pops are common and particularly irritating, because you're likely to have more than one. But drywall screws sometimes pop up too, as a result of damp framing that dries out and shrinks during the first year or two in new construction.

The first step of the fix is to drive nails back down using a nail set (Photo 1). If you have screws, dig the drywall compound from their heads with a utility knife and turn them in tight with a screwdriver.

Then dimple the hole slightly concave with a hammer to indent any raised edges. But take care not to crush the drywall core. In addition, cut away any paper tears with a sharp utility knife. This is a good technique to use with old wall fasteners as well. It's usually easier to tap them into the wall slightly rather than pull them out.

Two coats of drywall compound, applied with two swipes of the knife in a "+" pattern, should fill the holes (Photo 3). The first coat will shrink a bit, leaving a slightly smaller dent to be filled by the second coat. Scrape the excess off the surrounding wall so you don't build up a hump. Sand lightly to blend with the surrounding wall.

Be sure to prime the spot. Otherwise the topcoat will absorb into the patch and make the area look different from the surrounding paint. And use a roller when priming to help raise the surface texture to match the surrounding wall.

1 Drive a popped nail below the surface of the drywall with a hammer and a nail set. Cut away loose joint compound and paper shreds.

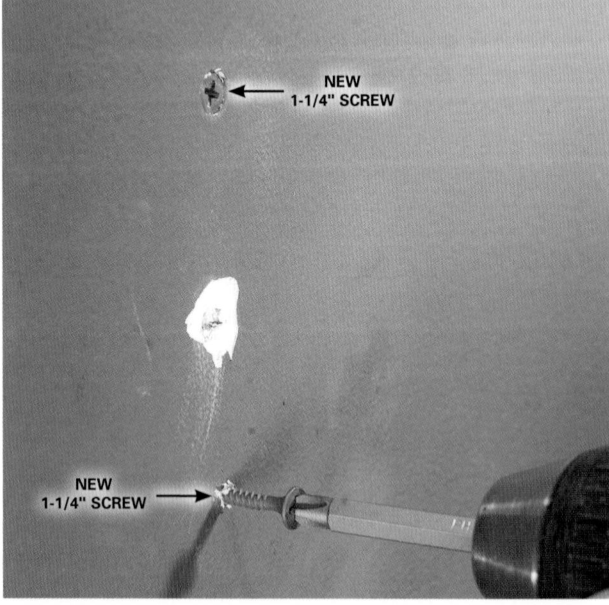

2 Drive drywall screws about 1-1/2 in. above and below the popped nail. Sink the screwhead just below the surface of the drywall.

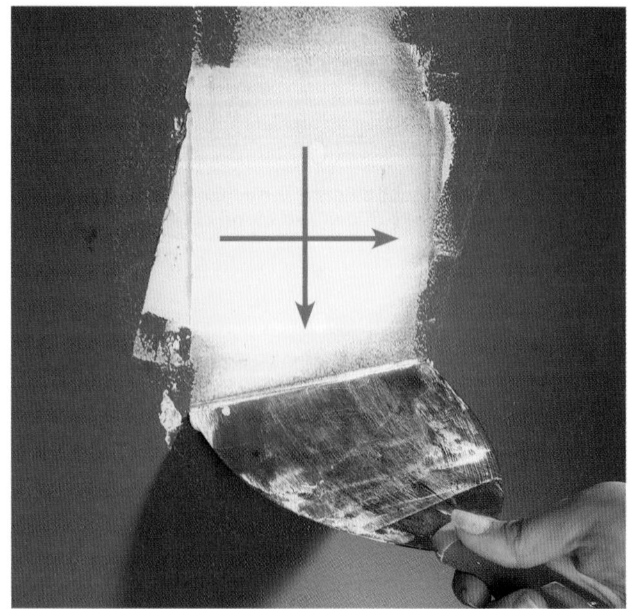

3 Fill the holes with joint compound, swiping first across the holes, then down. Let dry, apply a second coat, then sand, prime and paint.

Repair cracked corners

Every home settles unevenly as it ages. This sometimes causes inside corners to crack or ripple. Often the crack will run from floor to ceiling. Once you spot this problem, watch it for two to three months for continued movement and fix it after all movement stops.

The key to renewing the strength of the corner is to remove all loose tape and drywall compound (Photo 1). If the drywall below has crumbled, cut it away with your utility knife and fill the gap with setting compound.

Retape the joint. Crease the paper tape down the middle so it fits into the corner easily (Photo 2).

It's difficult to spread compound smoothly on one side of the corner without marring the other side. The trick is to apply compound for the second and third coats only on one side at a time. Let the one side dry, then do the other side.

Finally, buy a fine-grit sanding sponge to smooth the corners (Photo 4). It'll do a nice job without gouging.

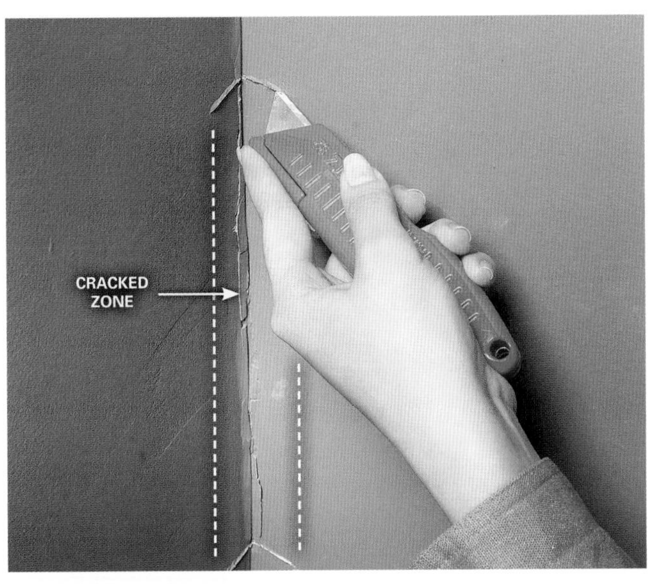

1 **Cut through the tape at the ends of the cracked area and slice, scrape and tear away all loose tape and compound.**

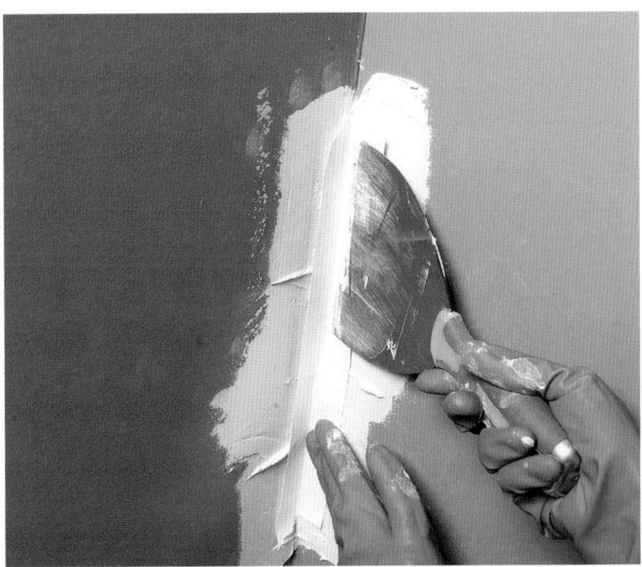

2 **Apply a 1/8-in. layer of joint compound, then fold and press paper tape into it. Stroke the length of the tape, squeezing compound out on both sides. Let dry.**

3 **Apply second and third coats to smooth the joint, tapering the compound about 6 in. out. Let one side dry before applying compound to the other side.**

4 **Lightly sand the finished repair using a fine-grit sanding sponge to make a crisp corner. Prime and paint to match the existing wall.**

Patch drywall fast

The traditional method of repairing holes in walls is to square the hole, put wood backing behind it, cut and screw on a drywall patch, and then tape the edges. Aluminum patches, available at home centers and paint and hardware stores, give the same results with much less work. The patches, which come in various sizes, are stiff enough to span holes and thin enough to disappear after taping and painting.

Select a patch large enough to overlap the hole on all sides by an inch, then stick the patch on (Photo 1). Patches can be cut or overlapped as needed.

Trowel on the first coat of joint compound over the patch, spreading the compound flat enough to see the outline of the mesh through it (Photo 2).

Allow the compound to dry overnight, then apply a wider second coat (Photo 3), followed by a final, third coat after the second coat dries. Spread the compound in thin coats extending 8 to 12 in. beyond the patch in all directions.

After the final coat has dried, sand, prime and paint.

1 **Clean off broken edges and tears around the hole. Then cover the hole entirely with the patch, sticky side toward the wall.**

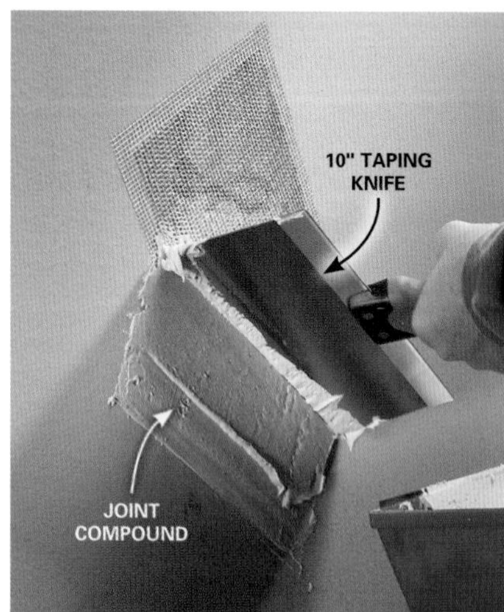

2 **Spread the first coat of joint compound over the patch with a wide taping knife. Let it dry overnight.**

3 **When it's dry, recoat the patch and then feather out the compound on all sides to make the patch blend in.**

4 **Sand the patched area with a sanding sponge until it feels smooth and even.**

Repair a drywall crack

As homes settle, cracks may radiate from the corners of doors and windows. Whether your walls are made of plaster or drywall, you can repair the cracks in two steps over a day or two—and get the area ready to sand and paint. Use paper tape; it's stronger than fiberglass tape for wall repairs. For cracks more than 1/4 in. deep, clean out the loose material and use a quick-setting crack filler like Durabond to build up the area level with the wall. Then use the steps shown in Photos 2 and 3 to fix it.

1 **Cut a V-notch through the full length of the crack, 1/8 to 1/4 in. deep, removing all loose wall material. Protect woodwork with masking tape.**

2 **Embed paper tape in joint compound using a 6-in. taping blade. To avoid trapping air bubbles under the tape, moisten the paper tape with water, lay it over the crack and squeeze excess compound and air from underneath with the blade. Apply an additional thin layer of compound and feather it off 2 in. on both sides of the tape. Let dry.**

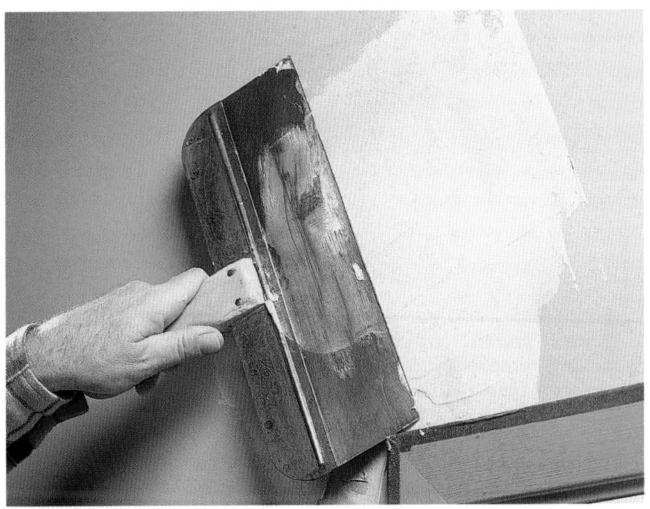

3 **Apply a second (and third, if necessary) coat of compound, smoothing it out 6 to 7 in. on both sides of the joint. Smooth the compound to a thin, even coat using long, continuous strokes with a 12-in. taping blade. Allow the repair to dry thoroughly, sand it smooth (avoid exposing the tape) and paint it.**

instant fix

Dust catcher

Minimize the mess when you're cutting or drilling a hole in drywall. Tape a bag below the work zone to catch the dust. Use an easy-release tape to avoid wall damage.

Counterattack closet mildew

For mildew, a dark, damp closet is paradise. Closet doors keep out light and block ventilation. That lack of air movement keeps closets from drying out after damp spells. In closets that adjoin exterior walls, heated air can't flow in, so wall surfaces stay cold and moisture condenses on them. Whatever the cause, here's how to deal with mildew:

1 Kill mildew with a mix of one part bleach to three parts warm water. Scrub with a sponge, but don't worry if you can't completely remove the dark stains. Let the surface dry completely before priming.

2 Cover the area with a stain-blocking primer. If you don't use a stain blocker, mildew stains can "bleed" through the paint. Use a primer that resists mildew (check the label).

Preventive measures keep mildew from coming back

Mildew is a tough enemy, but these strategies can discourage or even defeat it permanently:

- **Add mildewcide to paint, or use paint that already contains mildewcide (check the label).**
- **Cut closet humidity with a chemical dehumidifier (available at home centers). These nontoxic products absorb moisture from the air. All you have to do is place the open container in your closet. Depending on humidity, the chemical will work for two to four weeks before you have to replace it.**
- **Leave closet doors open to improve ventilation. Better yet, replace solid doors with louvered doors that allow airflow even when closed.**

Patch a water-stained popcorn ceiling

When water leaks onto a drywall ceiling, ugly coffee-colored stains usually appear. Sometimes the ceiling texture will become saturated and start to flake off. Repairing small damaged areas of typical "popcorn" ceiling texture is easy when you use a special texture patch available in an aerosol spray can at home centers and hardware stores.

Once the ceiling is dry, remove any flaking texture (Photo 1). Wear a dust mask and safety glasses to protect yourself from falling debris. Spraying the stain blocker and ceiling texture are messy, so tarp off a work area as shown in Photo 2. Many aerosol paints don't spray well upside down, but the stain-blocking primer in Photo 3 is designed to spray up. Applying the ceiling texture (Photo 4) is the trickiest part of the whole project. The texture comes out fast and the propellant dissipates quickly. You'll only get about four seconds of spray per can. The texture repair is designed to match the original texture color, but you might have to repaint the entire ceiling to completely hide the patch.

pro tip

Buy two cans of spray texture and use one to practice on a sheet of cardboard.

1 Lay down a tarp and scrape off all the loose, flaking texture with a putty knife. Hold a scrap of cardboard underneath the damaged area to catch the falling flakes.

caution

If you have ceiling texture applied before 1978, it may contain asbestos. This mineral can be hazardous if it becomes airborne, so call your local health department to learn safe procedures for removal and disposal.

2 Pin a plastic tarp around all four sides of the patching area (stay 1 ft. away from the damage), and let the tarp hang at least 4 ft. down.

3 Spray stain-blocking primer over the water-damaged area and let it completely dry. Specialized products like the one shown are designed to spray up.

4 Shake the can of texture for a couple of minutes, and then screw the nozzle onto the valve stem. Hold the can 9 to 14 in. away from the ceiling. Squeeze the trigger with quick half-second bursts while sweeping the can over the damaged area. Allow the texture to dry for 24 hours before painting.

Recaulk your tub surround

Have your kids asked you if they can use the moldy caulk around the tub for a "Grow your own penicillin" science project?

If so, it's time to dig out the old stuff, and using our tips, recaulk your tub like a pro. A good seal will help prevent water from slowly seeping into the walls and causing loose tiles and rot.

Recaulking a tub doesn't require fancy tools or materials. Just round up a scraper and a tool for digging into gaps (a painter's 5-in-1 tool will do both), as well as a caulk gun and caulk.

Tub-and-tile caulk or sealant is available in 10.5-oz. rigid tubes (for caulk guns) and 6.5-oz. squeeze tubes. While the squeeze tubes are nice for small jobs or tight spots, a caulk gun offers greater control. One 10.5-oz. tube is usually enough to seal a standard-size tub and surround, and seal around the fixtures.

caution

Don't use metal scrapers or razors on a fiberglass or acrylic tub. Instead, use a plastic putty knife. If the old caulk is really tough, soften it with a caulk softener.

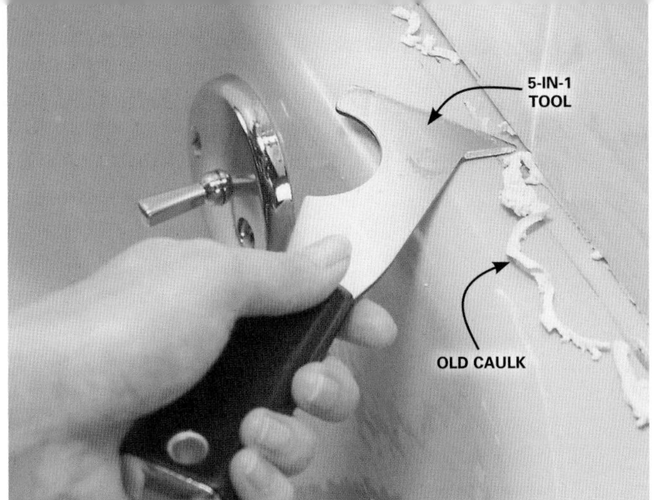

1 Remove the caulk carefully (the tub enamel and tile both can chip) with a scraper. Dig it out of the gaps with an ice pick, a flat-blade screwdriver, or our favorite, a 5-in-1 tool.

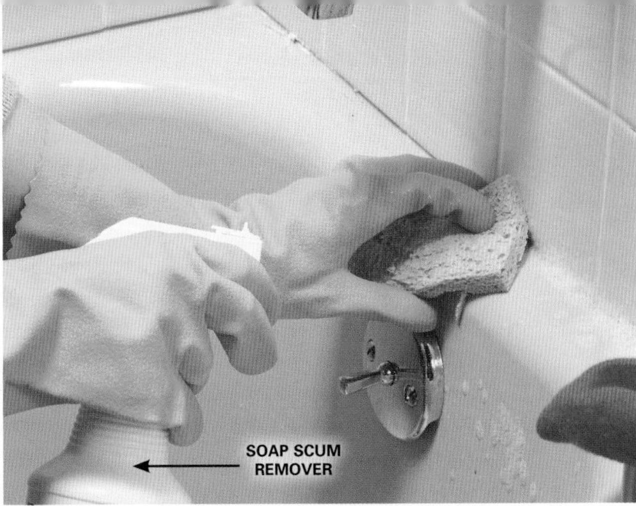

2 Clean the area thoroughly with a strong soap scum remover that contains bleach. Allow the corner surfaces to dry completely before applying any caulk. **tip:** Remove gray marks left by metal tools with a mild auto polishing compound.

3 Apply the caulk in a thin continuous bead (about 3/16 in.). It's easier to add a bit more, if necessary, than to wipe away sticky excess. Work in increments of about 3 ft. to give yourself plenty of time to smooth the bead before it begins to skin over.

4 Smooth the bead and push the caulk into the gaps with the tip of your finger. When applying silicone, keep your finger dry and have plenty of dry paper towels handy to wipe excess from your finger. When applying a "water cleanup" product, keep a damp towel handy and occasionally wet your finger as you smooth the bead.

pro tip

Recaulking

TEST THE CAULK. Most caulks and sealants have a shelf life of one to two years, but few companies bother to supply a freshness date. So take the time to test the product on a nonporous surface, such as a spare tile or a clean piece of glass, to be sure it will flow smoothly, adhere and cure. If the caulk is not fresh, you could recaulk your entire bathroom only to find that the caulk, which should begin curing in a few hours, is still not cured after three days.

REPLACE SILICONE WITH SILICONE. Nothing else will stick to silicone, or where silicone has been, but more silicone. To find out if the old caulk is silicone, clean off a section of the old caulk, let it dry, and try sticking Scotch tape to it. If the tape doesn't stick, the caulk is probably silicone.

FILL THE TUB. Bathtubs sometimes sink a bit when they're full, so before you caulk, fill the tub with water and leave it full until the bead has cured. This will help keep a sealed joint from cracking when weight is applied.

For hard-to-reach places, such as around the tub spout or behind sinks, use a piece of 1/4-in. flexible tubing as a nozzle extension.

Regrout a shower

By itself, the tile in a shower enclosure is almost maintenance free. With an occasional wipe-down, it can look good for years. Grout, however, is a different story—eventually it's going to break down. Large cracks and crumbly chunks are alarming, but smaller fractures can be trouble too. Fractures, and stains that won't wash out, may indicate spots where water is wicking in and working its way behind the tiles. Sooner or later, that water will weaken the adhesive that's holding the tile or cause rot in the walls. When that happens, the only solution is to tear out the tile and start from scratch.

The good news is that if you catch it in time, you can quickly and easily give tiled surfaces a new lease on life—and a fresh look—by applying a new layer of grout. You don't need previous tile experience; regrouting is mostly grunt work.

In some cases, you can finish the job in a few hours, but to be safe, give yourself a weekend. If you start on Saturday morning, you should be able to take a shower on Monday.

Choosing the right tools and grout

Before you begin digging into that old grout, make sure you have all the tools and materials you'll need to finish the job. To help make sense of what you'll need, think of this project in three parts: scraping and cleaning, regrouting and cleanup.

When you're choosing grout-removal tools, stick with steel to be safe. Many special grout scrapers equipped with

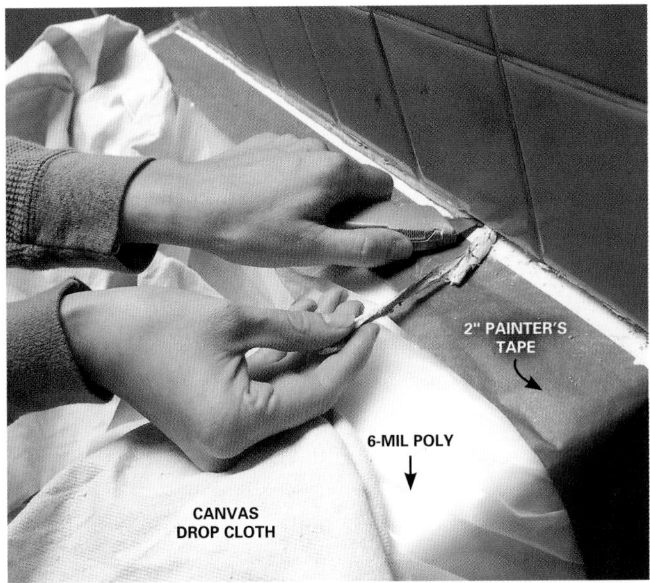

1 **Slice along each edge of the caulk/wall joint with a sharp utility knife. Pull out the old caulk.**

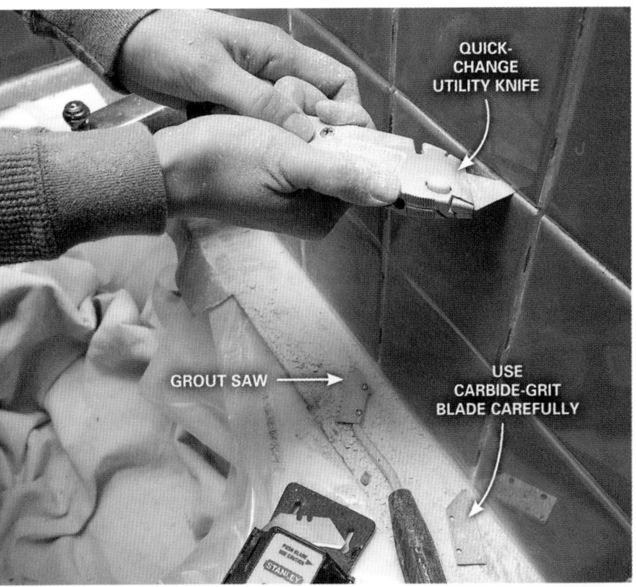

2 **Scratch out at least 1/8 in. of grout from all the horizontal and vertical lines with a utility knife or grout saw. Change blades often.**

carbide tips work well and stay sharp for a long time, but if you slip, the carbide can damage your tile or tub. Steel utility knife blades, on the other hand, may dull quickly, but they're less likely to scratch the tile. Buy a knife with easy-to-change blades, and also buy plenty of spare blades. They're ideal for cleaning out narrow joints. A grout saw (Photo 2) with a notched steel blade is also handy for snagging chunks of grout.

As for grout, buy a 10-lb. bag—you may have some left over, but that's better than running out. Grout comes in two forms: unsanded and sanded. Your choice depends on the width of the gaps between the tiles. For joints up to 1/8 in., choose the unsanded variety. For wider joints, choose sanded to avoid cracking. Whatever type you need, look for a "polymer-modified" mix. The extra ingredients help prevent future cracking and staining. It's almost impossible to match new grout to old, but don't worry. By scratching out the topmost layer from all the grout lines and adding new, you'll get a fresh, consistent color.

To apply the grout, buy a rubber grout float and a grout sponge. In case the grout starts hardening too quickly, you'll also want to buy a plastic scouring pad. Last, buy a tube of tub-and-tile caulk that matches the grout color.

pro tip

When you're shopping for grout, stick with brands that offer color-matching caulks. Factory-matched caulk/grout combinations blend almost perfectly.

Slice out caulk and scratch out grout

Before you begin your attack, take a minute to protect your tub against scratches and debris that can clog your drain (Photo 1). Tape a layer of plastic sheeting to your tub's top edge. Next, lay a drop cloth on top of the plastic to protect the tub and cushion your knees. Then remove the faucet hardware or protect it with masking tape.

Getting rid of the old caulk and grout requires plenty of elbow grease, but it's not difficult work, especially if you take your time. Begin by cutting out the old caulk (Photo 1) and then move on to the grout (Photo 2). When you're using a utility knife, switch blades as soon as the edge stops digging and starts skating on the grout (Photo 2). At times, you may have more success with the

3 **Clean out all of the dust and loose debris from the grout joints using a stiff brush and vacuum.**

grout saw. Whatever tool you choose, the goal remains the same: to remove about 1/8 in. from the top (or more, if the grout comes out easily).

When you're done, remove dust and debris, which can weaken the bond between the tile and the new grout (Photo 3).

Mix the grout and pack the joints

Once the grout is mixed, the clock starts ticking toward the moment when it will harden on the wall…or in the bucket. Pro tilers can mix and use a 10-lb. bag of grout before it hardens, but to play it safe, mix up a few cups at a time and work in sections. A smaller batch will allow you plenty of time to apply it and clean the excess from one wall at a time. When you run out, rinse the container before mixing a new batch.

Before you make a batch from a bag, shake the bag to redistribute any pigment and Portland cement that might have settled out in shipment. After it's been dry mixed, scoop out a few cups (one cup equals about a half pound) into a bucket. The instructions on the bag indicate how much water to add per pound of mix. To ensure a strong mix, start with about three-quarters of the specified amount of water and gradually pour in just enough to make the grout spreadable. Aim for a fairly stiff consistency, somewhere between cake icing and peanut butter (Photo 4, inset). Don't worry if the grout looks a little lumpy. After it's mixed, allow it to sit, or slake, for 10 minutes. During this time, the remaining dry specks will absorb moisture. Give the grout one last stir (restirring also keeps the mix from hardening in your bucket) and it's ready for application.

Focus on one wall at a time. Scoop out a dollop and press it out across the tiles at a 45-degree angle (Photo 5). It's OK to be messy. The goal is to pack as much grout into the joints as you can. Press hard and work the float in several directions.

Immediately after you fill the joints, rake off the excess grout. Hold the float on edge, like a snowplow, and cut off most of the excess (Photo 6). Move the float across the joints diagonally to prevent the edge from dipping into the joints and pulling out too much grout. Work quickly before the grout starts to harden.

The time between scraping and sponging varies from job to job. Depending on your mix, the humidity or the

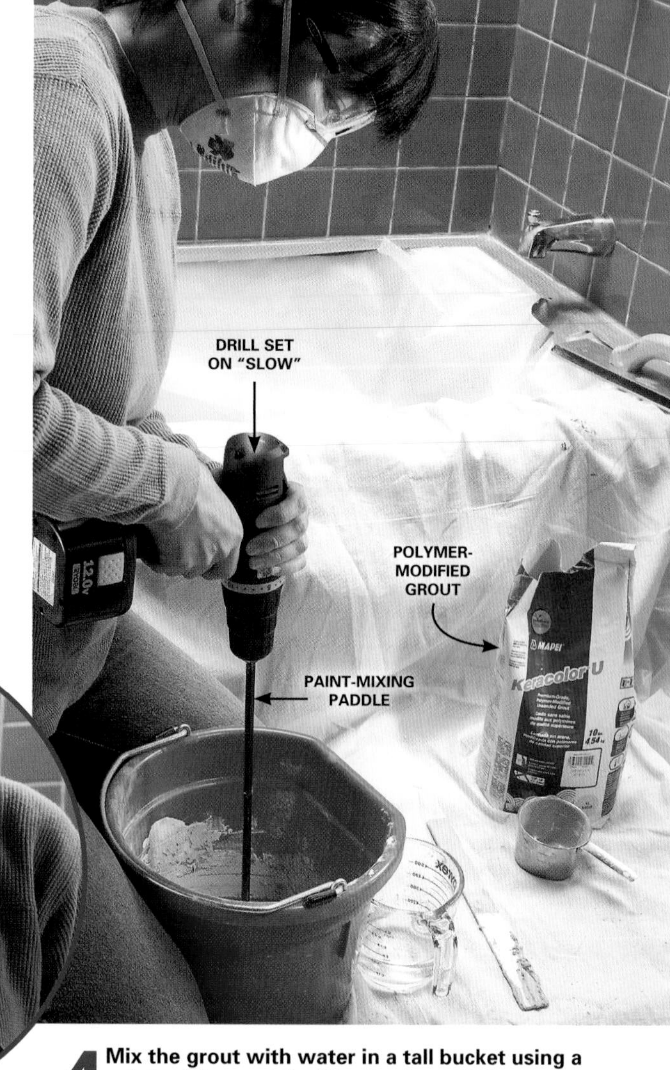

4 **Mix the grout with water in a tall bucket using a paint-mixing paddle. Mix slowly until the grout becomes a thick paste.**

5 **Spread grout at an angle to the grout lines with a rubber float. Press hard on the float to pack the joints full of grout.**

6 **Scrape off excess grout by tipping the float on edge and pushing it diagonally across the tile. Work quickly.**

7 **Wipe off the excess grout with a damp sponge as soon as the grout lines are firm. To keep the rinse water clean, dip the sponge in the "dirty" bucket and wring it out. Then dip it in the "clean" bucket and wring it over the dirty bucket.**

temperature, the grout may take anywhere from five to 20 minutes to firm up. Begin sponging as soon as the grout feels firm and no longer sticks to your finger.

Using a well-wrung tile sponge, wipe away the bulk of the unwanted grout with short, gentle, circular strokes (Photo 7). Turn the sponge so that you're using a clean edge with each pass. Rinse and wring it out in the "dirty" bucket, then dip the sponge in a "clean" bucket, and finally wring it out again in the "dirty" bucket. This two-bucket technique helps keep your sponge and rinse water clean so that you can remove grout more effectively. Wring out as much water as possible. Too much water can pull cement and pigment from your fresh grout lines.

In addition to wiping away the excess, the sponge works for fine-tuning the shape of your grout lines. To shave down any high spots and make the lines slightly convex, run the sponge across the joint until the grout lines appear uniform. (If you find a low spot, use your finger to rub in a little extra grout.)

Finally, scrape out any globs of grout that may have gotten into the joints you intend to caulk (Photo 8). This includes all corners and the tub/tile joint. You could do this chore later, but it's a lot easier now, before the grout is rock hard.

The sponge-wiped walls may look clean at first, but as the surface moisture evaporates, the remaining grout particles will create a light haze. Give the grout an hour or two to dry, then buff off any residual haze with a soft towel (Photo 9).

pro tip

You can buy a cheap grout float for less than $5. But spend a few bucks more. A better float will scrape off excess grout more cleanly. And that will save you lots of sponge work.

8 **Scrape grout out of the inside corners and tub/tile joint so that you can seal these joints with caulk later on.**

9 **Buff the haze off the tile after the grout dries (several hours). Use an old terry cloth towel.**

10 **Apply painter's tape to control your caulk lines. Apply the caulk, smooth the joint with your finger and immediately remove the tape.**

Finish up with neat caulk joints

Let the grout dry overnight before applying the caulk along the tub/tile joint and inside corners. For clean, precise caulk lines, run painter's tape along the inside corner and at the tub/tile joint (Photo 10). Just remember to remove the tape as soon as you finish smoothing. If you wait too long, the caulk will skin over or stick to the tape and you'll pull out the caulk when you try to remove the tape. Depending on the caulk, your bath should be ready for an inaugural shower in 24 hours.

To reduce mold growth, seal grout lines for extra stain and water resistance. Give the grout a week or two to cure completely before sealing. Remember that sealers wear off in time, so you'll need to reapply it every year or so. If you don't want to apply a sealer, wiping your walls down with a squeegee after each use works almost as well.

pro tip

When you cut the caulk tube's spout, cut close to the tip. That leaves a smaller hole in the spout—and a smaller hole means neater caulking.

3 solutions for a popcorn ceiling

Millions of homes have "popcorn" texture applied to ceilings. And while it does a pretty decent job of masking small imperfections in old plaster and drywall, this texture is a little out of fashion and notorious for trapping dust and cobwebs. It's also tough to make a good-looking repair with it. There's good news, however: You've got some options for dealing with an old popcorn ceiling.

1 Cover it with drywall

It's not an easy project, but there are some good reasons to consider installing drywall directly over your popcorn ceiling (and some good reasons not to).

Pros:

■ **No texture to scrape off.** Scraping, even wet-scraping, is hard, messy work. And if the popcorn texture is painted, it'll be even harder to scrape off.

■ **Lower asbestos risk.** Popcorn texture applied before 1980 might contain asbestos, which poses a lung cancer danger if disturbed and inhaled. Covering the ceiling with drywall minimizes your risk because there's no scraping involved.

■ **No repairs to make.** If you have problems like flaking texture, stains, cracks or holes in your ceiling, you can skip trying to fix all those things by covering them up. Hanging new drywall over the old ceiling gives you a fresh start!

Cons:

■ **It's a big job.** Drywall is heavy, and lugging full sheets around—especially up and down stairs—is hard work. Plus, most of the work you'll be doing is overhead, so be ready for a sore neck and shoulders. Applying tape and joint compound to seams also takes skill and practice to master.

■ **It's time consuming.** There's the time needed to hang the drywall, plus the time it takes to apply the tape and joint compound. It can easily take you a week to finish one room.

■ **Finishing requires skill.** Screwing the drywall to the ceiling might seem easy enough, but making your seams look good is another story. Applying tape and joint compound is a bit of an art. Remember, this is your ceiling! And ceiling flaws are much more visible than wall flaws.

■ **It costs money.** For a 12 x 12-ft. room, your cost will be about $160 for all the materials, including drywall, joint compound, paint and the rental fee for a drywall lift.

pro tip

Covering a ceiling is a big job, and taping drywall — especially on a ceiling — takes skill. So even if you think you can do it yourself, it's a good idea to get a bid from a pro to know how much money your hard work will save. Costs vary widely by region, but expect to pay $600 to $1,800 for a 12 x 12-ft. room.

Other key considerations for drywall

- **Do you have the time? You'll need a week or more to get the drywall hung, the seams taped and several coats of joint compound on and sanded. And it might take you even more time if you're a drywall newbie. Plus, don't forget you'll still have to paint the ceiling when you're done.**
- **Tight on space? Ever try to maneuver a full sheet of drywall up a narrow staircase, around a corner and into a small room? Cutting it into smaller pieces is an option, but that means you'll have more seams to tape and finish.**
- **Existing crown molding? If you have crown molding on the ceiling, you'll have to remove it before installing new drywall and reinstall it afterward. That's not a big deal, but it's one more thing you'll have to do. The good news about crown molding, however, is that you won't have to mud and tape along the perimeter of the room because the crown molding will cover the seams between the ceiling and the walls.**

2 Cover it with wood

Installing tongue-and-groove (T&G) planks on a ceiling is another good way to hide popcorn texture. Most of what you'll find in home centers and lumberyards is 1x6 or 1x8 pine or spruce, although you can special-order other kinds. And if you're working solo, it's a lot easier to handle T&G boards than 4 x 8-ft. or 4 x 12-ft. sheets of drywall. To see how to install T&G boards on a ceiling, visit familyhandyman.com and search for "tongue and groove."

Pros:

■ **It's easier to install than drywall.** Since T&G planks are much smaller than 8-ft. or 12-ft. sheets of drywall, you'll have an easier time installing them, especially if you're working alone. And because you'll be covering the old ceiling, you won't have to worry about asbestos or patching and painting the drywall or plaster.

Cons:

■ **Cost.** Wood isn't cheap. A single 1x8 pine T&G plank costs about $9. Covering a 12 x 12-ft. ceiling will cost at least $200.
■ **Tools.** Cutting and installing T&G boards requires several power tools (miter saw, router, pneumatic finish nailer and a compressor). Altogether, those tools will cost at least $600.

3 Scrape it off

Scraping off popcorn texture is a lot of work, but totally doable and worth the effort if your ceiling is in decent shape and you're not afraid to get dirty.

Pros:

- Less work than covering with wood or drywall. However, if the ceiling has been painted, water won't penetrate easily and you might have to dry-scrape it first—a tough and dusty job.
- Wet popcorn often comes off easily. Plus, if you mist the popcorn texture with water and scrape it off while it's still wet, you'll practically eliminate airborne dust).

Cons:

- Risk of asbestos exposure. Any popcorn texture applied to a ceiling before 1980 might have asbestos in it. Scraping releases asbestos fibers into the air, which can be inhaled and cause lung cancer.
- Repairs. After scraping, you might be left with lots of gouges, dings, loose drywall tape and other imperfections that you'll have to repair after you remove all the texture. And as with taping and mudding drywall, it takes time and skill to fix them.

Knockdown texture: A slick solution for an imperfect finish

Whether you cover your ceiling with new drywall or scrape off the texture, you're going to be left with some mudding and taping to do. And unless you're really good at it, getting a smooth ceiling will be slow or difficult or both. Instead, considering applying "knockdown texture." You basically spray texture from a hopper onto the bare drywall and knock down the high spots with a big squeegee. Your ceiling won't be perfectly smooth, but the texture hides small imperfections and looks more up to date than popcorn.

For step-by-step instructions on how to install drywall over a popcorn ceiling or how to apply knockdown texture, visit familyhandyman.com and search for "popcorn" and "knock-down texture."

6 tips for a neater paint job

1 Move furnishings for easy access to the walls and ceiling

Cramped working conditions lead to messy accidents. Every painter has stepped in a paint pan or kicked over a pail while squeezing a ladder past the couch. If you can't move furniture and other big stuff completely out of the room, stack it up. Set upholstered chairs upside down on the sofa. Cover the dining room tabletop with cardboard so you can set chairs on top of it. But don't let your stack become an obstacle. Get out your ladder and roller and make a dry run to be sure you can easily reach all parts of the ceiling. In some cases, two smaller stacks with space for a ladder between them is better than one. Maintain a generous workspace of at least 3 ft. between the stack and the walls. Cover your furniture stack with plastic. Even if you're careful, some drips and splatters are likely. A couple of bands of duct tape will keep the plastic in place and hold the stack together if you bump into it.

caution

Turn off the power to the room before removing cover plates. With the plates removed, live terminals inside the box are exposed.

2 Remove cover plates, then tape over switches and outlets

Paint slopped on electrical cover plates, switches and outlets looks tacky. Don't try to paint around them. Removing cover plates takes just a few seconds and makes for a faster, neater job. Grab a small bucket to hold all the odds and ends you'll take off the walls. Unscrew cover plates and then shield each switch or outlet with 2-in. wide masking tape. Also remove curtain hardware, picture hooks, grilles that cover duct openings and anything else that might get in your way. The thermostat is one exception—it's easier to wrap it with masking tape than to remove and reinstall it.

3 Shelter baseboard with overhanging tape

Don't waste time by completely covering baseboard with several strips of tape. A single overhanging strip of wide tape will catch roller splatters just as the roof overhang on your house keeps rain off the siding. Use 1-1/2 in. tape for narrow baseboard, 2-in. tape for wider baseboard. Tape won't stay stuck to dusty surfaces, so wipe down all your trim before masking. To minimize paint seepage under the tape, press the tape down hard by running a flexible putty knife over it.

4 Use wide tape and plastic to protect doors and windows

Paint rollers throw off a mist of paint that speckles everything below. Here's the quickest way to protect doors and windows: When you tape around door and window trim to protect the woodwork, use tape that's wide enough to project at least 1/2 in. from the trim. That way, you can stick light plastic to the protruding tape—there's no need to tape the perimeter of the plastic separately. For doors, slit the plastic with a utility knife so you can walk through.

5 Mask off sensitive wiring and tuck it in the box

A little paint in the wrong place can cripple the connections that serve a landline phone or television. To protect phone jacks without disconnecting all those tiny wires, unscrew the faceplate and cover the front with masking tape. Then mask the terminals on the back side of the plate. Slip the plate into the junction box. Disconnect coaxial cable from its plate and tape the cable's connector.

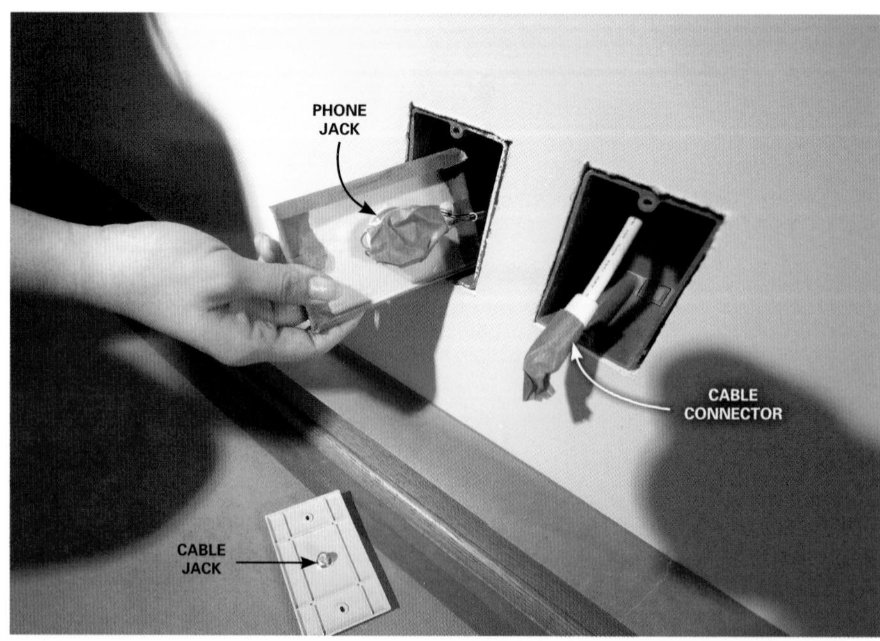

TEMPORARY HANGING WIRE

Hang and bag light fixtures

Painting a ceiling is a cinch—except for the light fixture. Here's how to get it out of your way: First remove any glass parts, including the bulbs (make sure the power is off). Unfasten the fixture, usually by removing a couple of screws. Then hook one end of a wire through the fixture and the other to the junction box. Make sure your hanger wire—not the electrical wire—supports the fixture. Then slip a plastic bag over the fixture.

Dealing with chandeliers and pendants is even easier. The decorative plate at the ceiling is usually held up by a ring nut. Just unscrew the nut and the plate will slide down over the chain or tube. There's no need to support the fixture with wire.

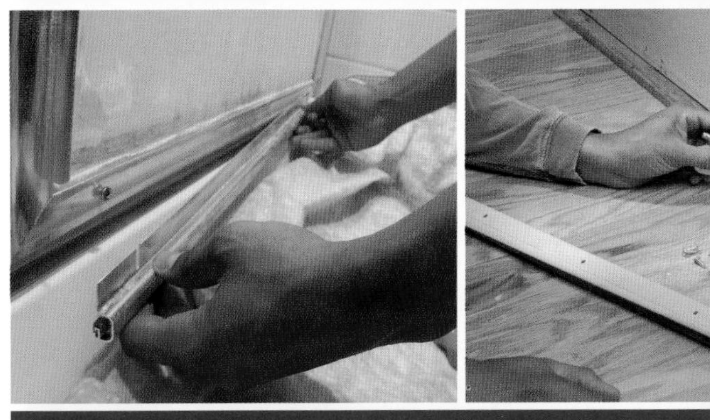

Chapter **seven**

DOORS & WINDOWS

Cures for a sticking door

The standard prescription for a sticking door is to plane the rubbing edge so that it swings freely. This always solves the problem, but it's a major hassle. You have to remove the door and lug it out to the garage. When the planing is done, you have to refinish the planed edge. Before you go to all that trouble, try the three shortcuts described here. In most cases, one of them will cure your sticking door.

1 Tighten all the hinge screws

Screws magically work themselves loose over the years. If your door rubs near the top or drags on the floor, use a screwdriver, not a drill, to tighten the screws (photo right). With a drill, you're more likely to overtighten the screw and strip the screw holes or chew up the screwheads. If you find one that's already stripped, try these fixes: Replace stripped-jamb screws with 3-in. screws. These long screws run through the jamb and into the framing behind it (bottom photo). If the screw hole is stripped in a solid door, predrill with a 1/8-in. bit and drive in a screw that's an inch longer than the original. If you have a hollow-core door, reinforce the screw hole. Dip toothpicks or wood splinters in glue and use them to fill the screw hole. Then drive in the original screw.

Tighten the hinge screws in both the door and the jamb. Snug them firmly, using a screwdriver rather than a drill to avoid stripping the screw holes.

2 Adjust a hinge

Door hinges aren't truly adjustable. But by driving a long screw through the jamb and into the wall framing, you can draw the hinge and jamb toward the framing and slightly reposition the door (photo right). Before you drive a screw, close the door to determine exactly where it rubs against the jamb. If it rubs near the top of the side jamb (which is most common), draw in the upper hinge. If the door rubs at the lower side jamb or head jamb, draw in the bottom hinge. If the door rubs all along the side jamb, draw in all the hinges. Often, you can move the door up to 1/8 in. with this method.

To use this technique, remove a screw near the middle of the hinge (rather than the top or bottom screw). Drive in the 3-in. screw with a drill. When the screw is snug against the hinge, give the screw another quarter turn. Close the door to check the fit. Continue tightening and checking until the door no longer sticks. Keep an eye on the door trim as you tighten—if you begin to create gaps at the trim joints, stop. It's rare, but you might find that you can't draw in a hinge at all because the jamb is already tight against the framing or shims.

Run a 3-in. screw through the jamb and into the wall framing to draw the hinge inward.

3 Draw in the jamb

This is really just another version of the hinge adjustment described above. By driving a long screw through the "latch" side of the jamb (rather than the hinge side), you can often draw in the jamb and give the door a little extra space (photo right). Try this only if drawing in the hinges doesn't work; it leaves you with a large screwhead hole to cover. Countersink the screwhead with a countersink bit. Drive a screw near the middle of the area where the door is rubbing. You may need to add a second screw. Tighten screws gradually and watch the trim to make sure you don't open joints. Cover the screwheads with wood filler and then sand and paint or stain the filler to match.

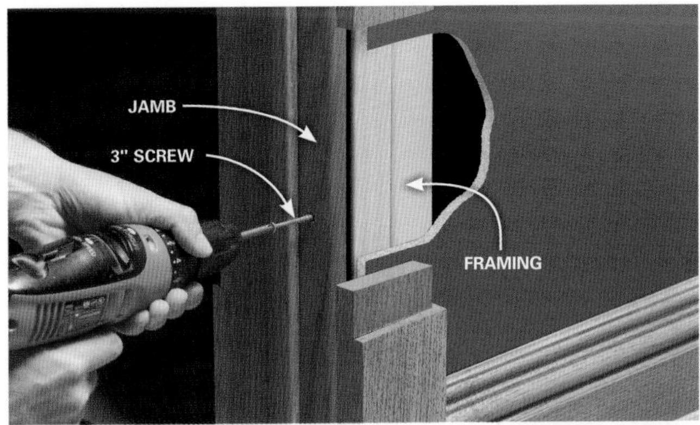

Predrill a 1/8-in. hole and create a recess for the screwhead with a countersink bit. Then drive a 3-in. screw into the wall framing to draw in the jamb.

4 Plane the door with a belt sander

If your door still sticks after you've tried tightening and driving screws, you'll have to plane it. Start by scribing the door where it rubs against the side or top of the jamb (Photo 1). A carpenter's compass is the best tool for this. Then remove the door. The best tool for "planing" the door isn't a plane, but a belt sander (Photo 2). You could also do the job with a hand plane or an electric planer. Begin with a 50-grit sanding belt. This coarse belt removes wood fast. Keep the sander moving so you don't grind a hole in one spot. Some older doors have a beveled edge, but don't accidentally create a bevel if the door didn't originally have one (Photo 3). When you're about 1/16 in. away from the scribe line, switch to an 80-grit belt and sand to the line. Finally, use a 120-grit belt to smooth the door's edge.

If you sand the area around the mortise that holds the door latch, you might end up with a latch that protrudes. Solve this problem by deepening the mortise with a sharp chisel. The belt sander will leave sharp corners on the edge of the door. Round them slightly by making a couple of passes with 120-grit paper.

COMPASS

1 Scribe the door. Set the pencil tip and compass point 1/8 in. apart and run the point along the jamb. Masking tape makes the pencil line easy to see.

2 Remove the excess wood with a belt sander. Sand right up to the line, but not into it.

3 Stop sanding occasionally to make sure that you're sanding squarely and not creating a beveled edge. Remove the excess wood with a belt sander. Sand right up to the line, but not into it.

Hang the door back on its hinges to check the fit. Don't be surprised if you have to remove the door and sand off some more. If there's a 1/8-in. gap between the door and the jamb, you're ready to paint or stain the sanded edge. You can remove the door or finish it in place (Photo 4). If the top or bottom edges of the door are unfinished, paint or varnish them. A coat of varnish limits shrinking and swelling because it slows moisture movement in and out of wood.

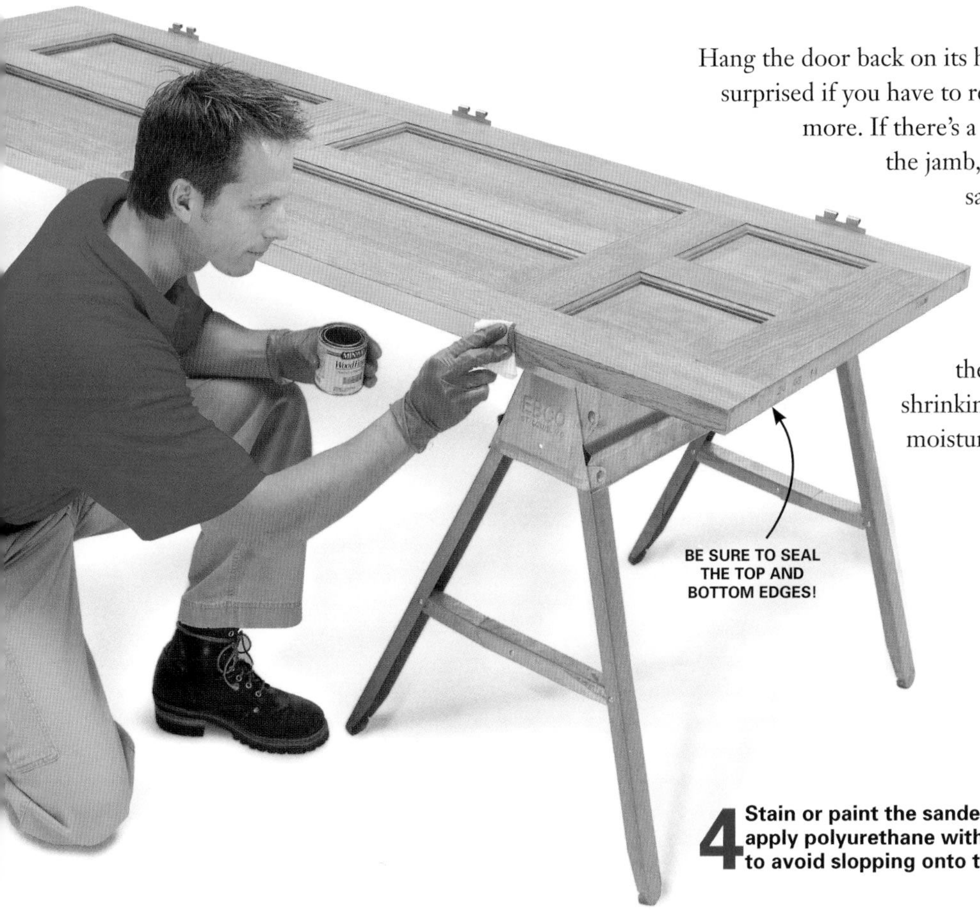

BE SURE TO SEAL THE TOP AND BOTTOM EDGES!

pro tip

Wipe-on polyurethane lets you neatly coat the edge of the door without slopping finish onto the front or back.

4 Stain or paint the sanded edge. When varnishing the edge, apply polyurethane with a lint-free rag rather than a brush to avoid slopping onto the door's face.

Pro tips for removing and rehanging doors

- **If you plan to remove the knob and latch, do it before you remove the door. They're easier to remove when the door is standing upright.**
- **Support the swing end of the door with shims. Just slip them under the door; don't force them in tight. The shims keep the swing end from dropping as you remove the hinge pins.**
- **Tap pins up and out of the hinge knuckles with a long screw, bolt or screwdriver.**
- **Remove the bottom pin first and the top pin last. Be ready to catch the door as you remove the top pin.**
- **Hinge pins can be stubborn, but resist the urge to give them a hard whack. Hard blows go off course and dent woodwork.**
- **If you find that the hinge knuckles won't slip back together, loosen the screws on one hinge a little. The hinge leaf will move slightly and mesh with its partner. Tighten the screws when the door is in place.**

Bifold door fixes

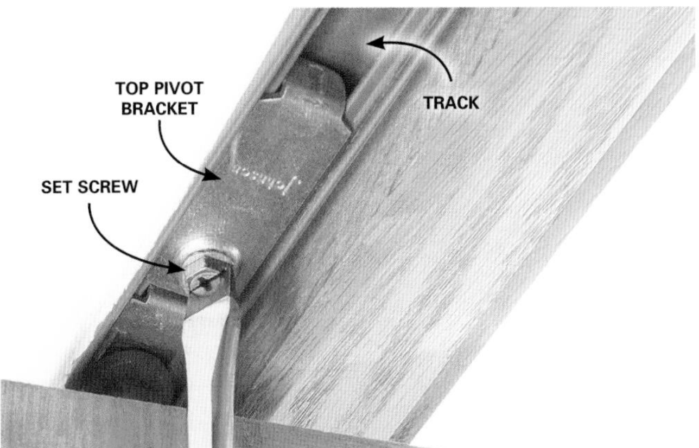

1 **Loosen the top pivot bracket setscrew with a screwdriver. Slide the bracket in the track until the door is parallel to the jamb. Tighten the setscrew firmly.**

2 **Tighten a loose bottom bracket with 1-1/2 in. screws driven through the drywall into the framing. Avoid screwing through the carpeting if possible.**

1 Adjust a door that sticks

Are you frustrated with a bifold door that doesn't close smoothly, or never opens without sticking, scraping or binding? Chances are it's out of alignment in the door frame. The fix is usually simple and often takes less than 10 minutes.

First, close the door and look along the edge of the door as it lines up with the frame (opening photo). The door edge and frame should line up nice and parallel. Even if it's off by only 1/4 in., the door will probably bind. Most often the problem is a loosened top pivot and bracket, which allowed the door to slip sideways out of alignment (Photo 1). Open the door and then loosen the setscrew for the top bracket slightly with a screwdriver. Then close it again. Push or pull the top of the closed door to align its edge parallel to the frame. Close the door to check for smooth operation and to see how the doors meet. Open the door gently so the pivot doesn't slip, then tighten the setscrew. You may have to repeat these steps a few times with both doors to get the "perfect" result.

If the door binds against the lower part of the frame, check the bottom pivot and bracket next. (Look for a worn edge on the door and scrape marks on the door frame.) The bottom pivot often loosens and slips. Either raise the door slightly to shift the pivot in or out, or loosen the setscrew and shift the bracket seat (Photo 2), depending on the type of hardware you have. Sometimes the entire bracket comes loose because the mounting screws are stripped, broken or missing (Photo 2). You'll need to remove the door to fix these. Test the door for smooth, non-binding operation by opening and closing it several times. You may have to readjust the top pivot bracket to make the door parallel to the frame again.

The top roller guide rarely needs attention, but make sure that it runs smoothly in the track. Apply a light coating of wax or silicone spray to eliminate any sticking.

2 Tighten a loose knob

You can fix that wiggly knob so it won't come loose again! Simply put a drop of epoxy into the knob hole before reattaching the knob. And add a washer under the screw-head inside, if the screwhead is pulling into the door. Allow the epoxy to set up for 24 hours before use.

pro tip

Before making any other repairs, make sure that the hinges joining the bifold doors are screwed on tight.

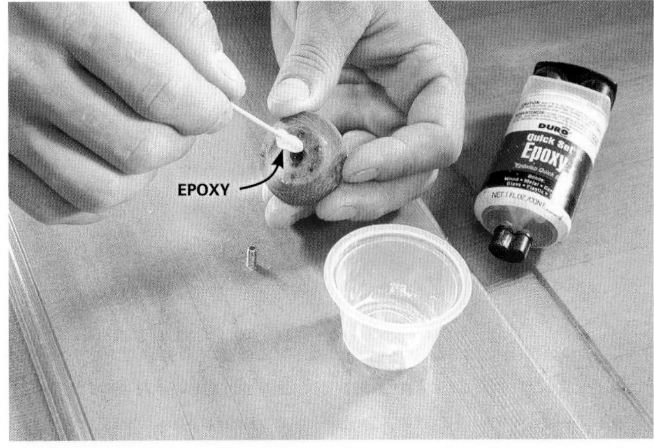

Add a drop of epoxy to repair a loose door pull. Screw it on and allow it to set for 24 hours before use.

3 Trim a door that binds on carpet

Adding carpet or changing to a thicker pile may cause the bottom of a bifold door to scrape and bind along the floor. First try to raise the door to clear the carpet using the bottom pivot adjustment. But usually you have to trim off the door bottom.

The easiest way to measure a bifold door for cutting is with the door slightly opened. A half inch of clearance is adequate (Photo 1).

Removing a bifold door doesn't always go as smoothly as Photo 2 shows. Sometimes the top pivot doesn't compress enough to free the bottom pivot. Turn the bottom pivot height adjustment to lower it, if possible. Or gently lift the door off the lower bracket with a flat pry bar. As a last resort, loosen the top pivot bracket setscrew and slide the top away from the door frame.

To replace the door, follow the steps in Photo 2 in reverse order. Check for proper alignment.

Lay the door face down on a worktable. Cut from the backside of the door to leave a clean cut on the front. You can reduce splintering by first scoring the cutting line (Photo 3) and, using a guide, sawing slightly to the outside of it (Photo 4). Bevel the cut edges with 100-grit sandpaper (Photo 5).

Cutting the door will shorten the bottom pivot hole. You may have to redrill to deepen it.

Extend the bottom pivot the same amount as the door was shortened, using the height adjustment screw.

2 **Open the door completely and lift it to compress the top pivot spring (1). Swing the door bottom out from the bottom bracket (2). Pull the door down and out of the top pivot bracket.**

1 **Measure up 1/2 in. from the highest point on the new carpeting and mark the door.**

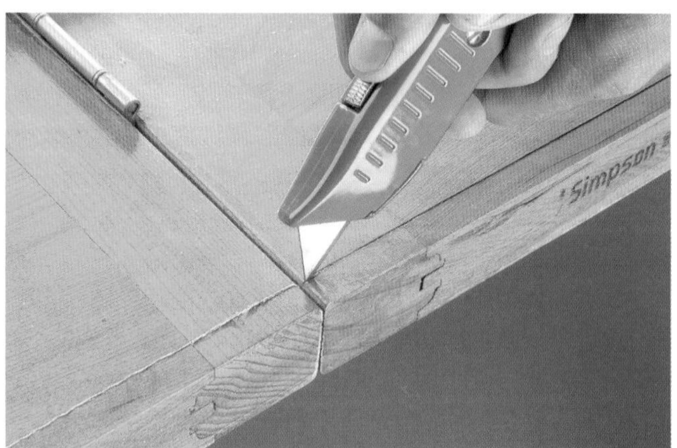

3 **Mark the cutting line on the back side of the door and then score the line with a utility knife to reduce splintering.**

Replacement parts

If you need to replace worn, broken or missing parts, look for exact replacements at home centers or hardware stores. If you can't find what you need, be creative. If the parts are basically the same size and shape, they should work fine. You may need to redrill the pivot holes to fit a larger pivot, or plug and redrill to fit a smaller one.

Top rollers

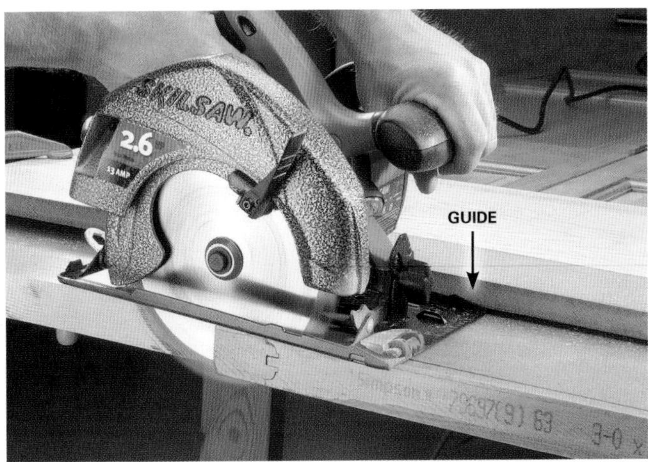

4 Clamp a cutting guide to the door, mount a crosscut-type blade in your saw and cut slightly to the outside of the line.

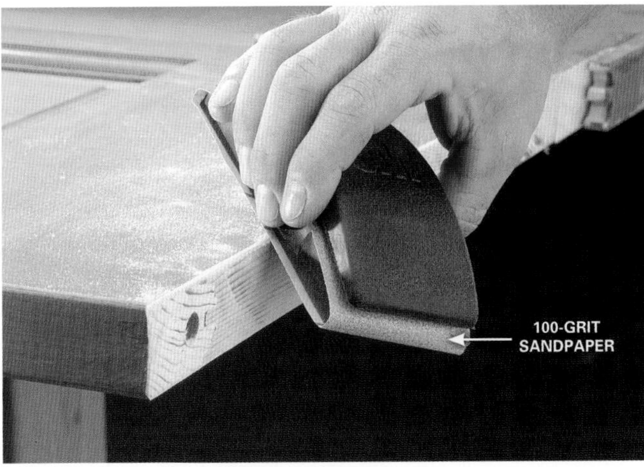

5 Knock the sharp edges off the fresh cut with sandpaper. Add a coat of sealer to the raw edge to prevent swelling. Remount the door.

4 Fix a busted bifold door pivot

Often, heavily used bifold doors wobble and don't work because the top pivot has broken loose. But that's easy to fix because home centers carry various plates and brackets to reinforce the pivot. To install one, grab the closed bifold door with both hands and lift up while you pull the bottom pivot free of the floor bracket. (To make reinstallation easier, first mark where the bottom pin sits in the floor bracket.) Set the door on a workbench or on sawhorses and remove the pivot (Photo 1). After you secure the pivot (Photo 2), rehang the door by aligning the top pivot with its bracket, lifting the door and setting the bottom pivot back into the floor bracket.

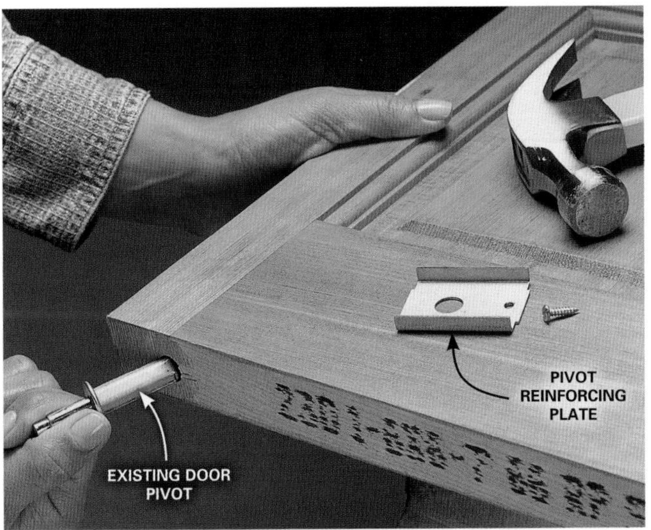

1 Remove the bifold door and pull the top pivot from the top edge.

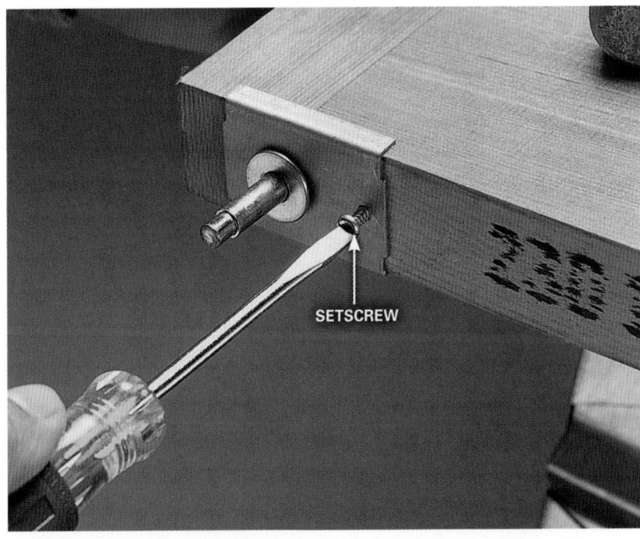

2 Center the reinforcing plate over the pivot hole with the setscrew hole pointing toward the center of the door. Lightly tap the plate in place with a hammer. Secure it with the enclosed setscrew, and reinsert the pivot.

Top pivots

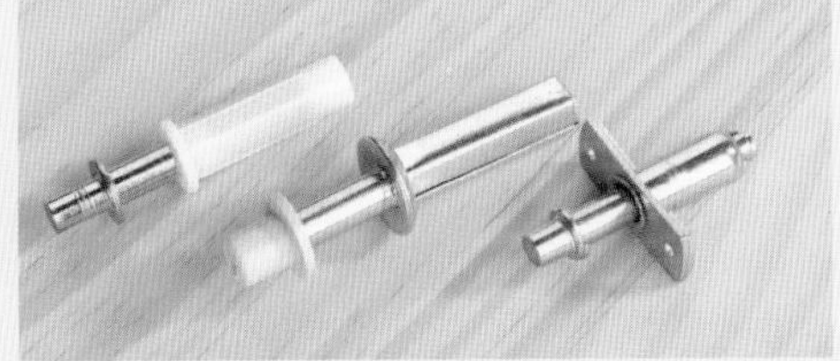

Bottom pivots and brackets

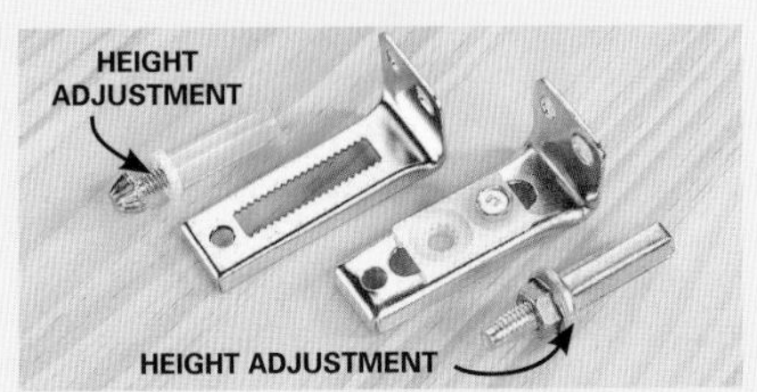

A new window in one day

The kitchen in our new house featured a garden window that was stealing useful cabinet and countertop space. We didn't like its exterior look either, and ultimately my wife, Steph, decided to take the lead on replacing it. Doing it herself saved our family about $1,200, and with my help she got it done in just a day. At first she thought she was biting off more than she could chew, but she quickly realized that—like most carpentry jobs—window replacement is just a matter of following simple steps. Here's how to do it. — Mike Berner, associate editor

1 REMOVE THE TRIM Cut the caulk around the trim and the window. Pry the trim away from the window and the siding. Remove the trim from the inside of the house as well.

2 PULL OUT THE OLD WINDOW Remove the screws or nails that hold the window in the opening. If the window still doesn't budge, there may be foam, more caulk or hidden screws keeping it in place. Work a reciprocating saw blade between the window and the framing and cut around the window, then wiggle the window out of the opening.

Where to start

Before you can shop for a new window, you need to know the size of the "rough opening," the framed opening the window jamb sits inside. So your first step is to remove the window's trim on the inside of the house and measure the opening.

You could take those measurements to a lumberyard or home center and order a custom window or a replacement window that fits inside the existing window jamb. But we went with a simple stock window, one that was available on a shelf at the home center.

With a stock window, we were limited by size and style options, but for us, that wasn't a problem. We wanted a smaller window for space to install more countertops and cabinets when we remodel the kitchen. There's some extra work involved in adjusting the opening, but we took this path for a few reasons:

- Save Money: We found a good-quality window for $200. A similar custom-sized window would have cost us twice as much.
- Save Time: The last time I ordered custom-sized windows, it took six weeks to get my hands on them. We chose our window, took it home and got to work, all on the same day.

3 FRAME THE NEW ROUGH OPENING The new rough opening needs to be 1 in. wider and 1 in. taller than the new window. That allows space for leveling the window and insulating around it. We first raised and leveled the sill and added cripple studs. Then we added trimmer studs to make the rough opening the size we needed. Make sure the trimmers are plumb and there's enough blocking for sheathing.

4 PATCH IN THE SHEATHING Cover the framing with exterior-rated plywood or OSB. Our job required only a 2 x 4-ft. sheet of 3/4-in. CDX plywood. Steph cut it to size and screwed it into the framing with 2-in. coated screws. Then she capped the sill by nailing on a piece of cedar siding (Photo 5), giving it an outward slope. If any water gets in, the slope will send it back out.

5 TUCK IN TAR PAPER We used tar paper as a water-resistant barrier (WRB). Newer houses might have house wrap material, which will work the same way. Start at the bottom and overlap the existing WRB. Then cover the sides, followed by the top, always overlapping the previous layer and tucking the WRB underneath the siding as best you can.

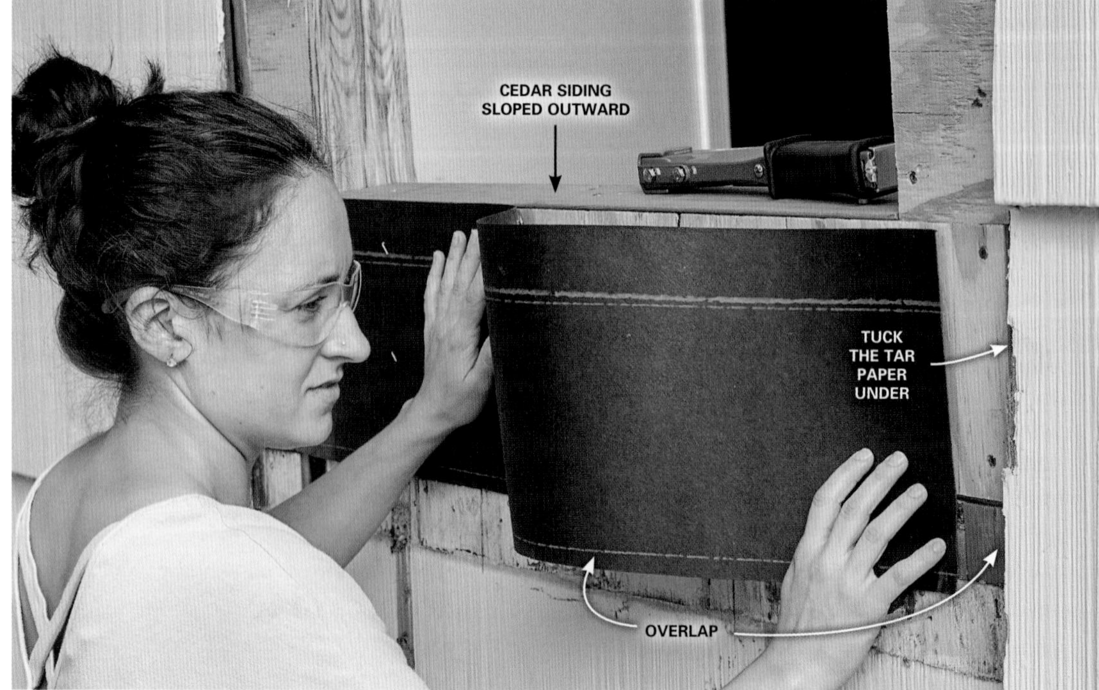

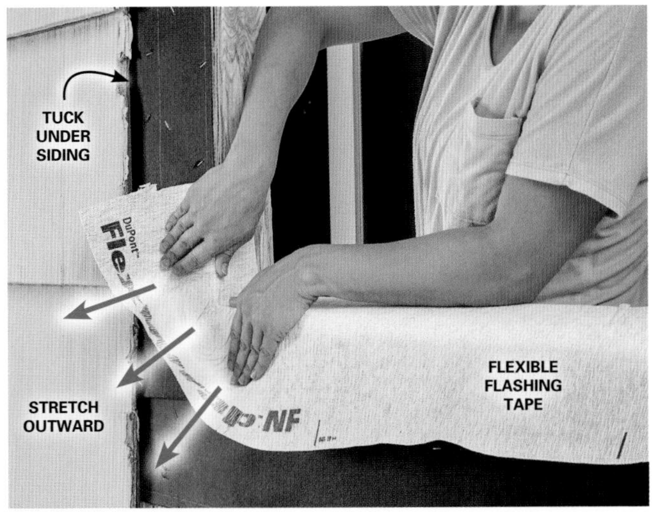

6 FORM THE WINDOW PAN The window pan protects wood from any water that might enter around the window. Cut flexible flashing tape 12 in. wider than the window opening, peel off the backing and lay the tape on the sill without stretching it. Starting from the middle, press the tape into the corners then up the sides. Fold it over the sill and stretch the tape around the corner. Many window installers don't cover the side or top corners with flashing tape, but I always add the extra layer of protection. I wrap 4-in.-wide flashing tape over the side corners, then the top. When all the tape is on, roll over it with a J-roller.

7 APPLY SEALANT TO THE WINDOW To make the connection watertight, apply a continuous bead of sealant along the side and top flanges. Be sure the bead goes right over the nail holes; penetrations through the tape must be sealed well. Don't seal the bottom flange; if water gets in, it must have a way out.

8 PLACE THE WINDOW Rest the bottom of the window on the sill, then tilt the window up and into place. You'll need a helper waiting inside to center the window. Next, the helper will raise the window with a few shims and adjust them to make sure the bottom of the window is level. When it's level and centered, drive a nail in the very bottom hole on each side flange.

9 PLUMB AND SQUARE THE WINDOW Hold the window in place with a few sets of shims on both sides of the window, a pair that holds the top and one toward the bottom. Adjust the shims so the sides of the window are plumb. Once the bottom is level and the sides are plumb, drive a nail into the top hole of each side flange. The real test is how the window operates; don't nail it off until it operates smoothly.

10 NAIL THE FLANGE When you've centered the window and it's level and plumb and operates smoothly, drive nails in all the holes on the top and sides. Don't nail the bottom flange. Then install the drip cap that came with the window.

11 COVER NAIL PENETRATIONS As an added measure against water intrusion, cover nails in the flange with flashing tape. Start with the sides and extend the tape a few inches past the bottom and top nail flanges. Then cover the top flange, making sure it overlaps the tape covering the sides.

12 INSTALL Z-FLASHING AND TRIM Install Z-flashing above the top piece of trim. It should be cut to the same length and tucked under the water-resistant barrier (tar paper or house wrap) and will shed water over the trim. Then install the trim using coated trim screws.

13 REPLACE THE SIDING Our siding is double-course cedar shakes, which we were able to match easily. Caulk around the window and trim using a high-quality exterior sealant. Then paint the siding.

1 **"Unzip" the old, damaged weather stripping, pulling it through the brads that hold it in.**

Stop drafts around doors

Here's an easy way to keep heat from slipping out your doors, too. Take 30 minutes and replace the weather stripping and door sweeps around your steel entry doors. Plan to do this project on a warm day since you'll have to remove the doors. Steel doors use a compression-style strip for the hinge side and a magnetic one for the knob side and the top. But look at the door and confirm the style of weather stripping on all three sides and the type of door sweep before you head to the store. You'll find replacement weather stripping in a variety of lengths and colors at home centers and hardware stores.

To remove the door, close it and use a hammer and a pin punch or a thin nail to tap out the door hinge pins. Turn the knob, open the door slightly and lift it off the hinges. When you rip out the old weather stripping, you might find that it's tacked into place with small brads from the manufacturer. Leave them in place after removing the old weather stripping or you'll damage the doorjamb. Then shear off the shanks inside the groove with an old chisel (Photo 2) or drive them deeper into the groove with a screwdriver. Press the new magnetic weather stripping firmly into the groove on the knob side and top of the door frame and do the same with the compression strip along the hinge side. To ensure that the strips won't pull out, pin them with a few 1-in. brads, especially in the magnetic strips (Photo 3).

The sweep on the door bottom is even easier to replace. Pry or slide out the old sweep. Run a bead of caulk along the bottom edge of the door, tap the sweep into place and then staple it at the ends (Photo 4). While you're at it, you might as well do a quick fine-tune of the adjustable threshold. Adjust all four screws until the door opens and closes without too much drag and any drafts have been eliminated (look for light between the sweep and the threshold with the door closed). Turn the screws clockwise to lower the threshold and counterclockwise to raise it (Photo 5).

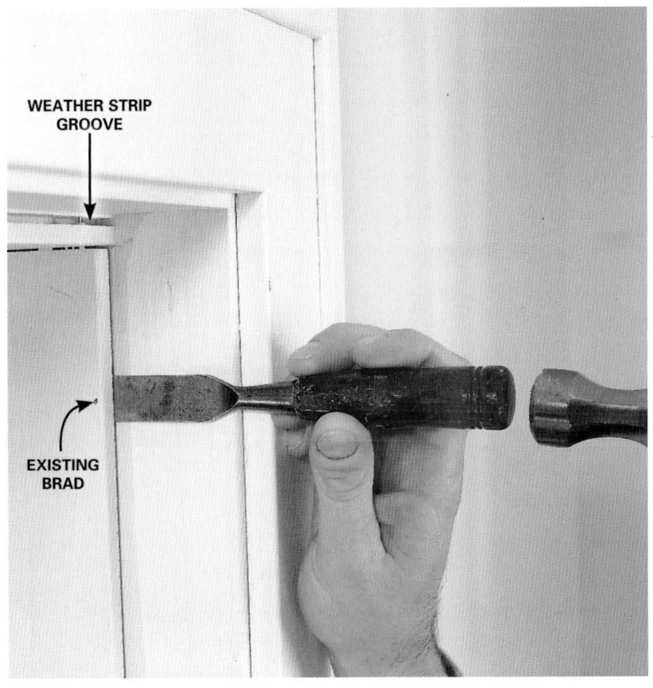

2 **Cut off the old brads or push them all the way back into the groove with an old chisel.**

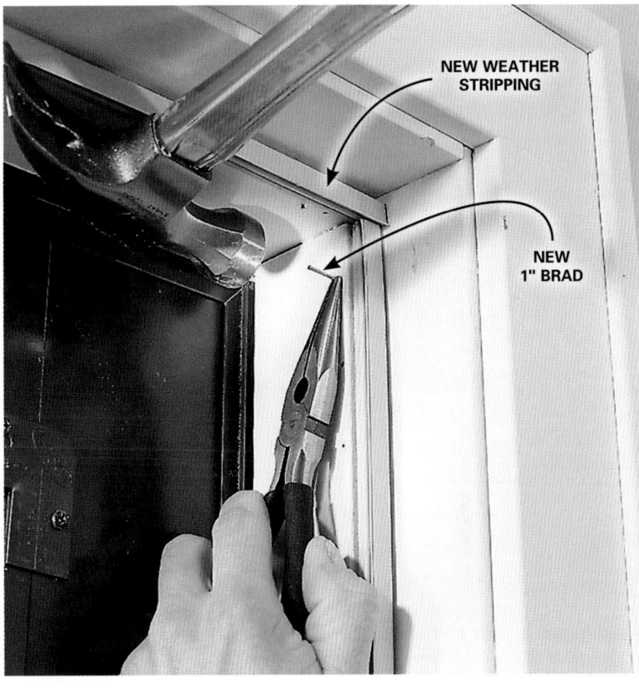

3 **Cut the new weather stripping to length and reinstall it, pinning it with new brads positioned near the old ones.**

4 **Peel out the old door sweep and caulk the ends of the door frame. Tap in the replacement sweep and staple the ends with 1/2-in. staples or the fasteners provided with the sweep.**

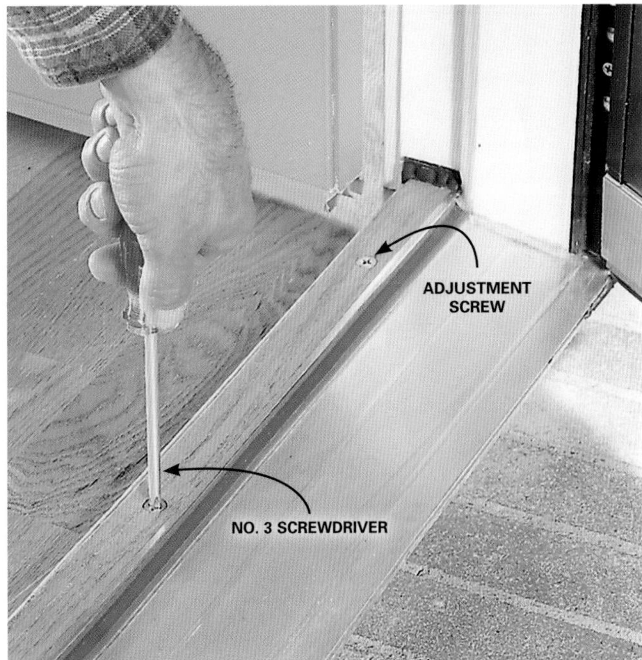

5 **Adjust the door threshold with a No. 3 Phillips screwdriver. Move it up or down until the door closes smoothly with no light seeping through.**

Repair split trim

Rather than replacing the trim, use the fix shown in Photos 1 and 2 to repair it in place. To ensure a proper glue bond, leave the spring clamp on the molding overnight.

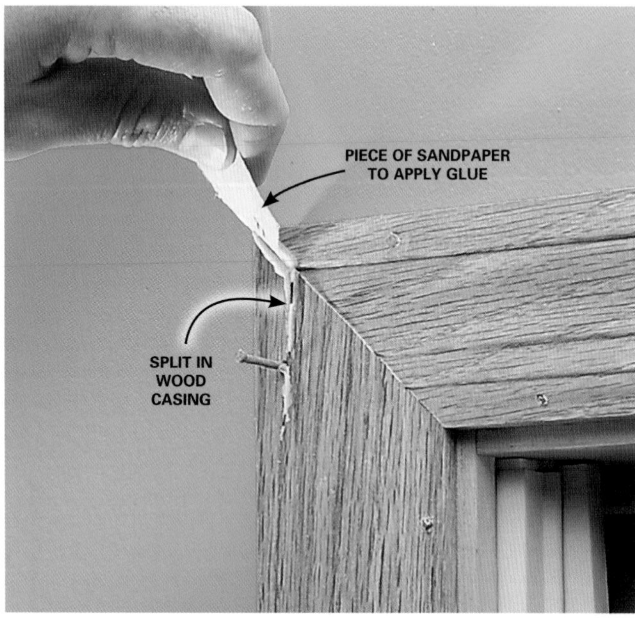

1 **Insert a thin applicator (like sandpaper) smeared with wood glue deep into the wood crack. Don't move the nail that caused the split. Instead, use it to wedge the crack open so you can apply glue deep inside the crack.**

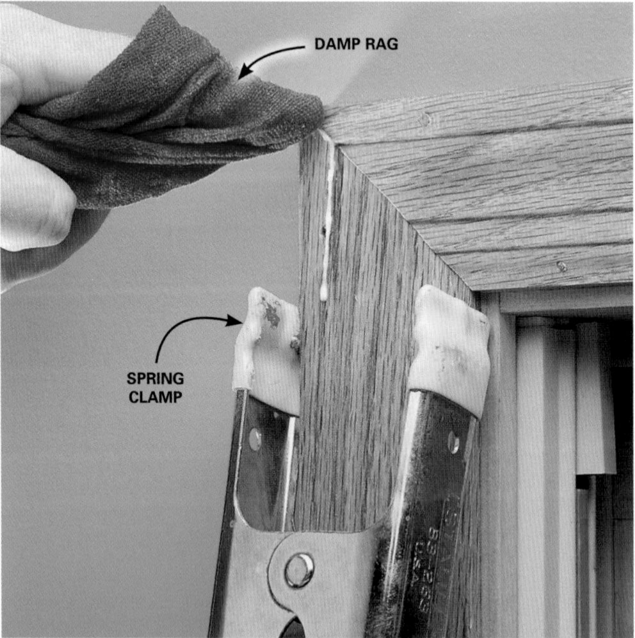

2 **Apply a spring clamp across the top of the molding once the nail is pulled. Using a damp cloth, wipe off all excess wet glue. Once the glue has dried, drill a 3/32-in. hole next to the original nail hole, install an 8d finish nail and set the nail-head. If a gap remains in the tip of the split molding (at the top of the miter joint), drill a 1/16-in. hole on the side of that molding and carefully drive a 1-in. long brad-size nail to close the gap.**

Silence a squeaky hinge

A little petroleum jelly will rid the hinge of that annoying wail. The jelly works its way into the hinge and adheres well, so it won't run off and make a mess like other lubricants.

Photos 1 and 2 show how to punch out a hinge pin and grease it up. After all the hinges have been lubricated, open and close the door a few times to work the petroleum jelly into the hinge joints.

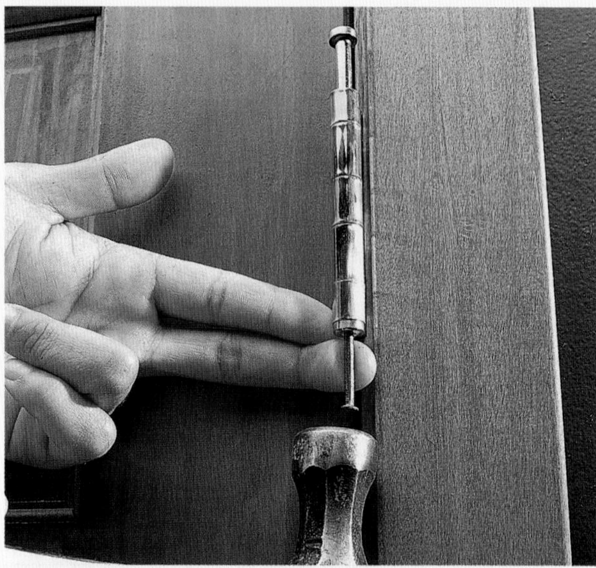

1 **Loosen each hinge pin by tapping a nail up from underneath. Once the pin is loose, pull it out (lift up on the door handle to relieve pressure if the pin binds). Keep the door closed and work on one hinge at a time.**

2 **Lightly coat the hinge pin with petroleum jelly and dab a little in the top of the pin slot. Reinsert the pin and wipe off any excess.**

Free up a sticking dead bolt

You use your dead bolt every day without giving a thought to maintenance. But one of these days, it's going to fight back and refuse to open. Don't panic; it's just crying for a few shots of lube. You can get it working again with dry Teflon lube spray. It's a better choice than graphite because it sprays on wet to soak into the lock mechanism. The solvent evaporates, leaving behind a dry, slippery powder. Start by lubing the lock cylinder (Photo 1). If that doesn't free it, you'll need to lube the bolt mechanism (Photo 2).

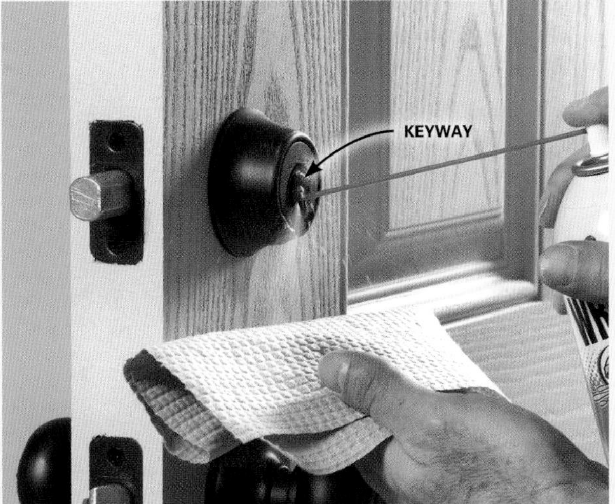

1 Shoot the keyway. Leave the lock cylinder on the door and spray inside the keyway. Then insert your key and twist it several times to work in the lube.

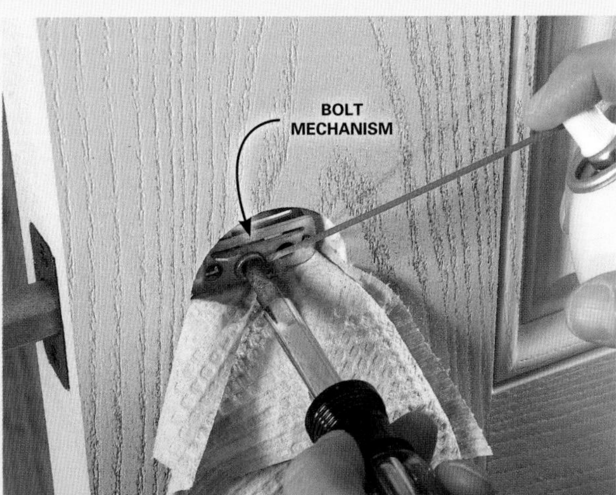

2 Shoot the bolt. Remove the two screws that hold the lock cylinder and pull it from the door. Then saturate the bolt mechanism with the spray lube and twist it back and forth with a flat-blade screwdriver. Reinstall the lock cylinder and you're good to go.

Fix a loose hinge

Over time, many doors get heavy use, causing the hinge screws to strip out and the hinges to loosen. Once this happens, the door ceases to swing smoothly and may require lifting and pushing to get it closed because of the binding hinge. If you get teed off at a door hinge that frequently comes loose because the screws don't hold anymore, grab a hammer, knife, wood glue and your golf bag for a quick fix.

Completely remove the loose hinge from the door and frame. Remove only one hinge at a time so you don't have to take the door down. (If you have several hinges with stripped screws, however, you may want to remove the entire door.)

Locate the stripped screw holes and repair with golf tees as shown in Photos 1 and 2. Once the hole is plugged, reattach the hinge and screws. Screwing through the golf tee will cause it to expand and tighten the hinge even more, restoring your doors to proper working condition.

1 Unscrew the loose hinge. Squirt wood glue on a golf tee and tap it into the stripped hole until tight. Let the glue dry for an hour.

2 Cut the golf tee flush with the door frame using a sharp utility knife, then screw the hinge back in place.

Adjust a dragging shower door

If the sliding doors on your shower or bathtub don't glide smoothly, repair them soon. A door that drags on the lower track will eventually do permanent damage to both the door and the track. A dragging roller at the top of the door will wear and require replacement.

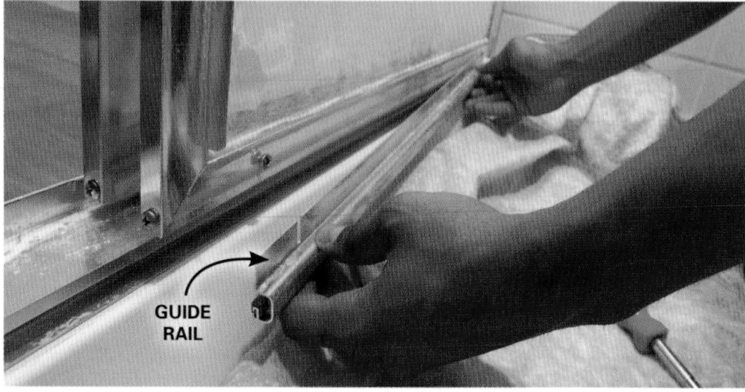

1 Unscrew the guide at the lower edge of the sliding door. Protect the shower or tub from scratches with a drop cloth.

2 Lift the door out of its track inside the upper rail. Tilt each door in or out to remove it. Wipe both tracks clean.

First, make sure the rollers on both doors are riding on the tracks inside the upper rail. Sometimes, one roller falls out of the track and the bottom edge of the door skids along the lower rail. In that case, you only have to lift the door and guide the roller back onto the track.

If an off-track roller isn't the problem, you'll have to remove the doors to adjust and possibly replace the rollers. Many doors have a small plastic guide at the middle of the lower rail. To remove this type of guide, just remove a single screw. Others have a guide rail screwed to the door (Photo 1).

With the guide removed, lift the doors out of their tracks (Photo 2). Then make sure the rollers turn easily. If not, apply a little silicone spray lubricant. Some lubricants can harm plastic, so check the label. If the lubricant doesn't do the trick, replace the rollers. Most home centers and some hardware stores carry replacements. Take an old roller with you to find a match. In many cases, you can use a replacement that's slightly larger or smaller than the original. But be sure to check the original and replacement edges match—either rounded or flat.

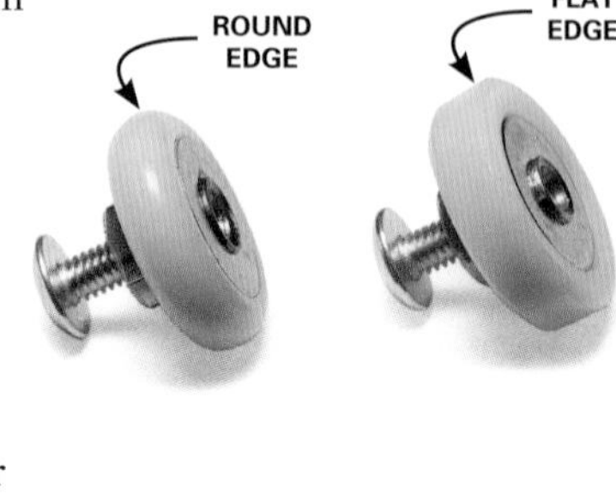

Screw the new rollers into place and rehang the doors. You'll probably have to remove the doors once or twice to adjust the rollers for smooth operation (Photo 3).

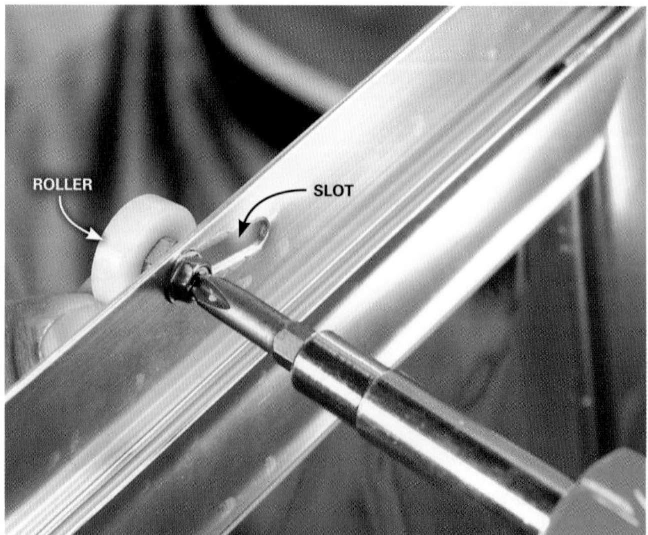

3 Raise or lower each door by repositioning the roller in its slanted slot. Loosen the screw to move the roller.

Patch dents in a metal door

Steel entry and service doors provide years of reliable service but will get dinged and dented. Hiding the dents is just like taping and sanding drywall except the patching material is a little thicker and tougher.

The easiest way to fill in the dents is with a premixed patching or glazing compound designed for steel doors. It's available at home centers and hardware stores. For a heavy-duty fix, use a two-part auto body filler. It's available at auto parts stores.

Apply both fillers in the same manner. Carefully prepare the surface of the door, patch the dent and sand it smooth as shown in Photos 1 – 3 (deep dents may require a second coat after the first one dries). Prime the patch and repaint the entire door to hide all evidence of patching.

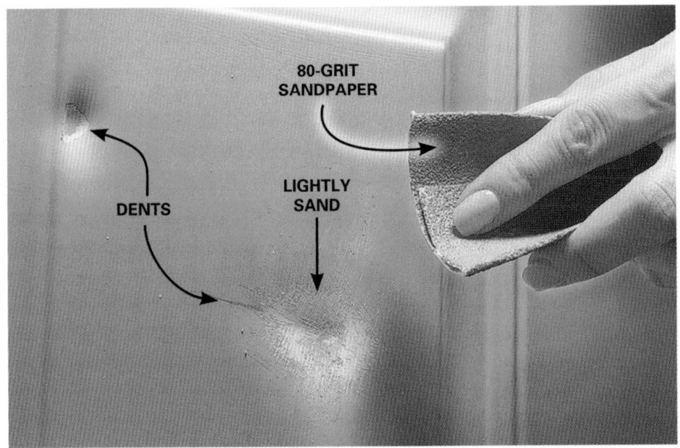

1 **Scrub dirt off the door with detergent, then rinse and dry the area. Lightly sand the dented area with 80-grit sandpaper to help the patching compound bond, then wipe clean.**

2 **Press patching compound into the dent with a small putty knife, then smooth and feather out the edges as if you're spreading drywall mud.**

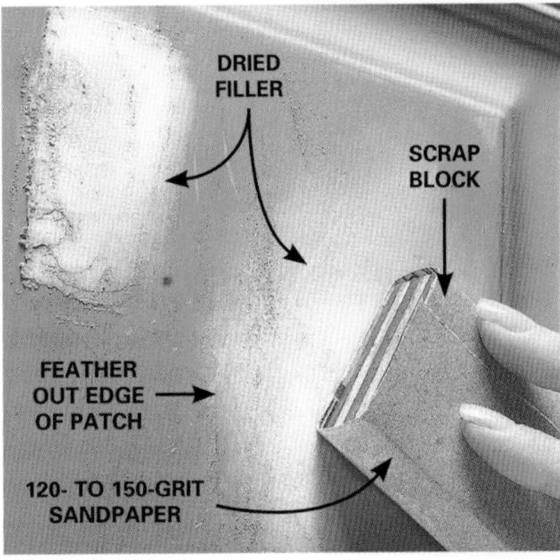

3 **Sand the area flat after the filler dries using 120-grit sandpaper wrapped around a flat block. Switch to 150-grit sandpaper to smooth out the edges of the patch.**

instant fix

Align a patio screen door

There you are, balancing a tray full of burgers fresh from the grill, struggling to open the sticking patio screen door. Badly aligned rollers cause the screen door to bind and stick when it's opened or closed. Eventually this stresses the corner joints of the door, and if they open or loosen up, the door is shot. But you can adjust the door to run smoothly in minutes with just a screwdriver.

You'll find two adjustment screws at the bottom of the door, one at each end, that lift and lower separate rollers. Inspect the rollers for damage. First lower the door to the track (Photo 1), then raise it evenly (Photo 2).

Still runs rough? Clean the track. Chances are, leaves, grit or other debris is clogging it.

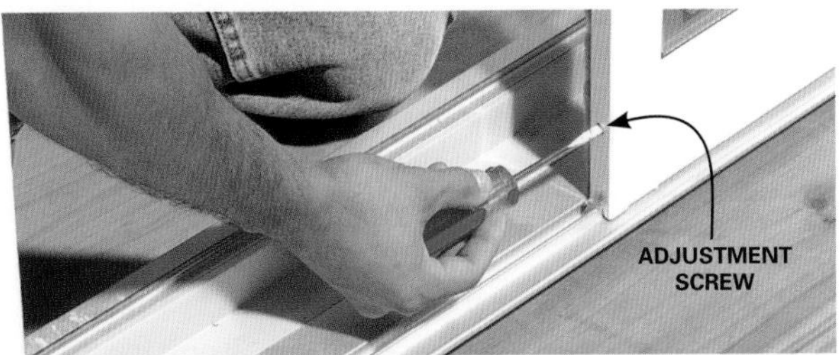

1 **Turn the adjustment screws counterclockwise and lower the door frame until it rests on the track.**

2 **Raise one roller until it lifts the door off the track approximately 1/4 in. Slowly raise the second roller on the other end until the gap between the bottom of the door and the track is even. Make sure there's a gap between the top of the screen frame and the upper track as well.**

Fix a sliding patio door

Years of dirt, exposure to the elements and hard use can turn sliding doors into sticking doors, but the problem is usually easy to fix.

Start with a good cleaning. Scrub caked dirt and grime out of the track with a stiff brush and soapy water. If the door still doesn't slide smoothly, the rollers under the door either need adjusting or are shot.

Locate the two adjusting screws at the bottom of the door (on the face or edge of the door) and pry off the trim caps that cover the screws. If one side looks lower, raise it until the door looks even on the track (Photo 1). If the door still sticks, turn both screws a quarter turn to raise the whole door. Then slide the door just short of the jamb and be sure the gap is even.

If the door still doesn't glide smoothly, you'll have to remove the door and examine the rollers. Get help for this—the door is heavy! Unscrew the stop molding on the inside of the jamb (Photo 2). Be sure to hold the door in place once the stop is removed—if you forget and walk away for a moment, the door will fall in, requiring a much bigger repair! Tilt the door back (Photo 3) and set it on sawhorses. Inspect the rollers for problems. If they're full of dirt and debris, give them a good cleaning and a few drops of lubricant and see if they spin freely. However, if the rollers are worn, cracked or bent, remove them (Photo 4) and replace them with a new pair.

You can order rollers and other door parts through lumberyards and home centers or online. Look for the door manufacturer's name on the edge of the door or the hardware manufacturer's name on the roller.

1 Lift or lower the door on the track with a screwdriver or Allen wrench. Raise it just enough to clear the track and roll smoothly.

2 Remove the screws that hold the stop molding. Cut the paint or varnish line on the room side of the stop molding so it pulls off cleanly.

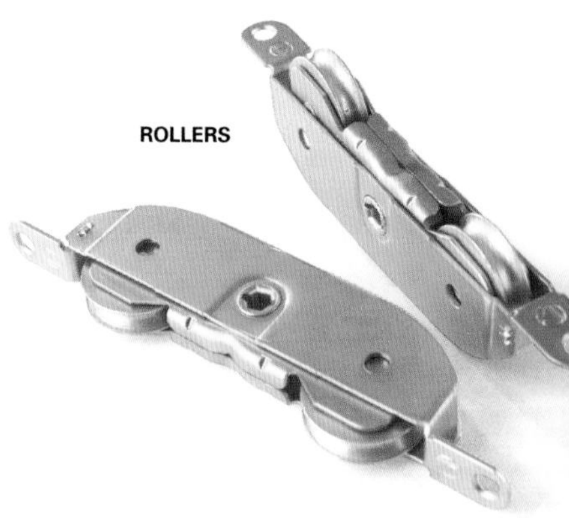

3 Grip the door by the edges and tip it about a foot into the room. Lift it up and out of the track one edge at a time.

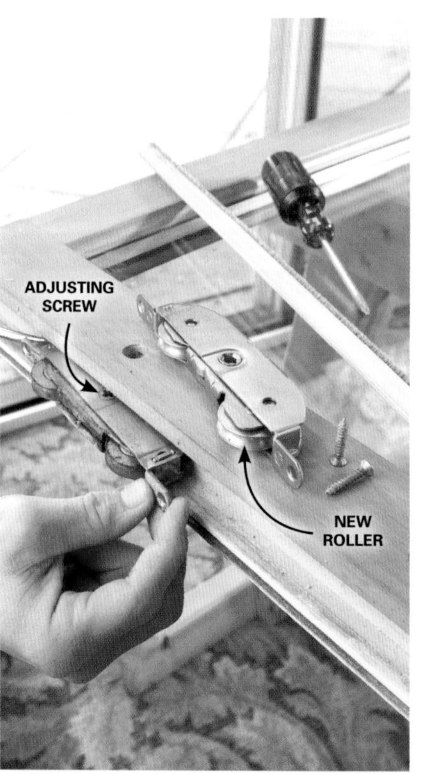

4 Unscrew and pry out the screws that hold the roller in, then carefully lever it out with a screwdriver. Clean or replace the rollers.

Replace your weather strip

Older wood doors usually rely on a non-adjustable threshold to keep the weather out. If your old door doesn't seal tight against the threshold, you're wasting energy. You could screw a surface-applied weather strip to the face of the door, but a door-bottom weather strip is a less obtrusive way to create a good seal.

The door bottom we're using is available at most home centers and hardware stores. If you can't find a door bottom that's smooth on one side, you can slice off the barbed flanges from bottoms designed for steel or fiberglass doors.

Cut the bottom of the door to allow enough (but not too much) clearance to install the new door bottom. The goal is to create an even 3/8-in. space between the top of the existing threshold and the bottom of the door. Close the door and measure the largest gap between the door and the threshold. If the gap is less than 3/8 in., calculate how much you'll have to cut off the bottom to equal 3/8 in. Mark this distance on the door at the point you measured. Then use a scribing tool to extend a mark across the bottom of the door (Photo 1).

Remove the hinge pins and move the door to a set of sawhorses. Mount a sharp blade in your circular saw and cut along the line. Protect the surface of the door with masking tape. If you have a veneered door, score along the line with a sharp utility knife before sawing it to avoid chipping the veneer.

Cut the door-bottom weather strip about 1/8 in. shorter than the width of the door and tack it to the bottom of the door with a staple gun. Rehang the door to test the fit. If it's too snug, remove the weather strip and trim a bit more from the door. When the fit is perfect, remove the staples and mount the weather strip (Photo 2).

1 Scribe a line on the door 3/8 in. above the top of the threshold. Remove the door and carefully cut along the line with a circular saw.

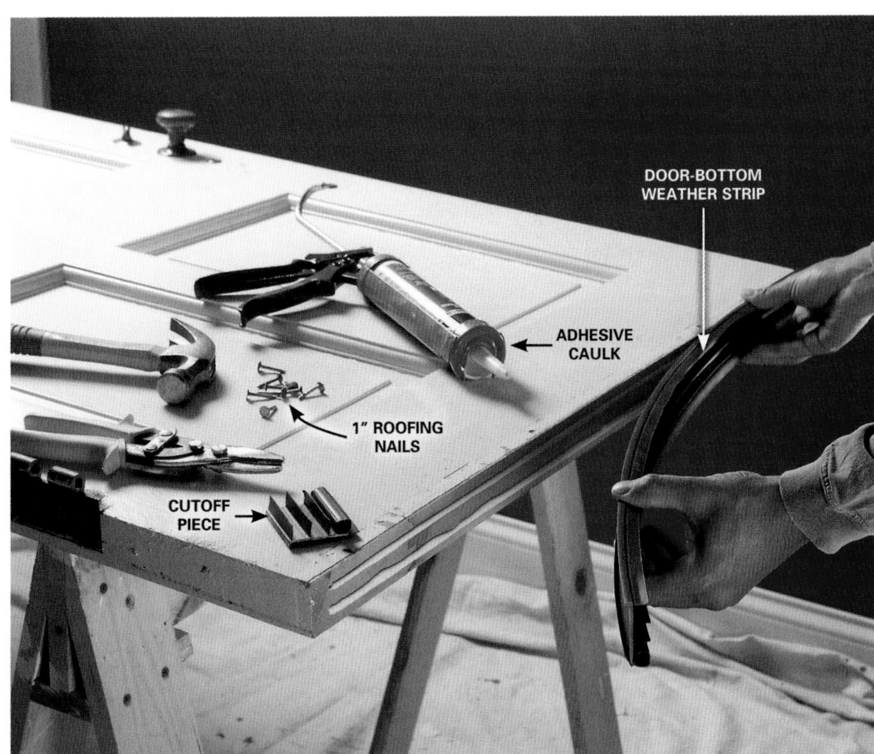

2 Cut the door bottom to length with a tin snips or utility knife. Apply two parallel beads of adhesive caulk the length of the door and nail the door bottom to the door.

6 slick window fixes

If you're thinking about replacing your casement windows because they're drafty, fogged up or just hard to open, consider this: You can fix most of the problems yourself for a fraction of the cost of new windows—and it won't take you more than an hour or two per window.

We'll walk you through the fixes for the most common casement window problems. (Casement windows are the type that swing like doors.) You won't need any specialty tools, and the materials are available from most window manufacturers or online window supply companies.

Although your windows may look different from the ones shown here, the techniques for removing the sash and fixing problems are similar.

1 Replace a subborn crank operator

If the splines on the crank operator shaft are worn or broken off, or the gears don't turn easily or at all, then it's time to replace the crank operator.

You don't need the make, model or serial number of the crank operator. You just need a picture. Snap a photo, email it to a hardware supply company and the company will sell you a new one. You can also look at online catalogs to find an operator that matches yours.

To replace the operator, first take the crank arm off the sash. Most crank arms slip out of a notch on the guide track on the sash (Photo 1). Others are pried off with a flathead screwdriver, or a channel is unscrewed from along the bottom of the sash. If the operator also contains a split arm operator, unhook that, too (Photo 2).

1 **Open the window until the crank arm bushing is aligned with the guide track notch. Push down on the arm to pop the bushing out of the track.**

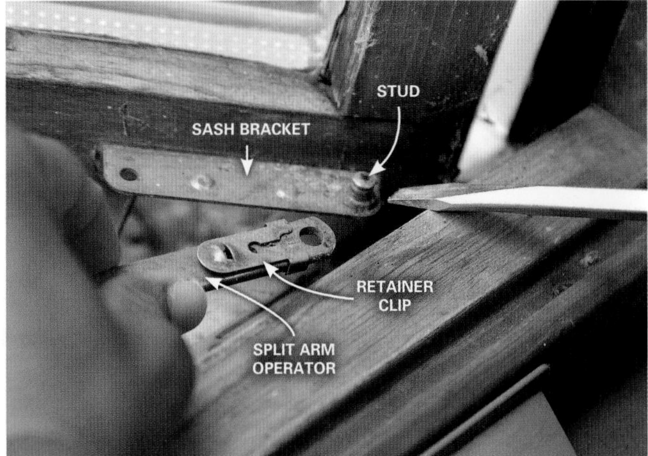

2 **Slide back the retainer clip on the arm and pry the arm off the stud on the sash bracket with a screwdriver.**

Slide or pry off the operator cover. If you have a removable cover, cut along the casement cover with a utility knife to slice through any paint or stain that seals it on the window jamb. Remove the trim screws along the top of the casement cover. Gently pry the cover loose (Photo 3). Be careful—the cover can easily break! Unscrew the crank operator. Set the new operator in place, aligning it with the existing screw holes, and screw it to the jamb. If the cover isn't removable, crank operator screws will be accessible on the exterior of the window.

Figure A
Casement window operation

When you turn the handle, the operator moves the crank arm and the split arm operator. The split arm operator then opens the window sash. Casement window operators come in several styles.

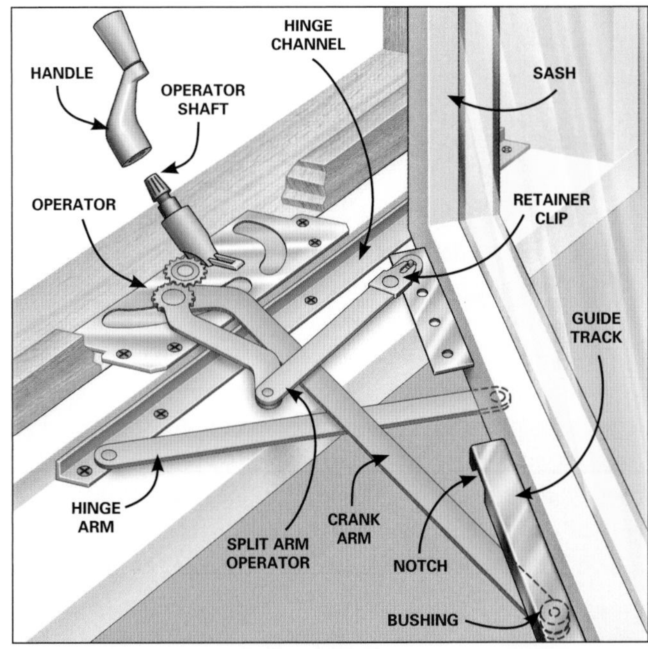

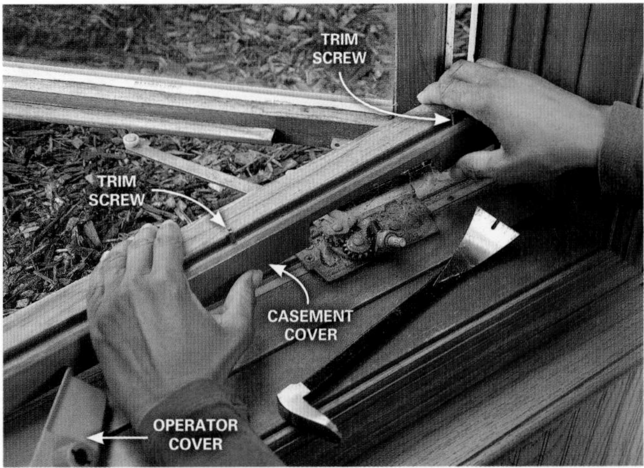

3 **Lift off the casement cover to expose the crank operator. Remove the screws, take out the crank operator and replace it.**

2 Fix a stripped crank handle

If you turn your window handle and nothing happens, the gears on your handle, crank operator shaft or both are probably stripped. Take off the handle and look for signs of wear. If the teeth are worn, replace the handle. If the shaft is worn, you can replace the whole operator (see the next fix). But here's a home remedy to try first.

Start by backing out the setscrew to remove the handle (some newer handles don't have setscrews and simply pull off—and this fix won't work). If you have a folding handle, mark where the setscrew is on the operator shaft when the window is closed and the handle is folded up. Remove the handle and file the shaft so the setscrew can lock onto the shaft (photo right). The metal is tough; it'll take about 15 minutes to get a flat side. Or use a rotary tool with a grinder bit to speed up the job. Vacuum the shavings out of the operator so they won't harm the moving parts.

SETSCREW

Reattach the handle with a longer setscrew (available at hardware stores). If you open and close the window a lot, this fix may not hold up in the long run.

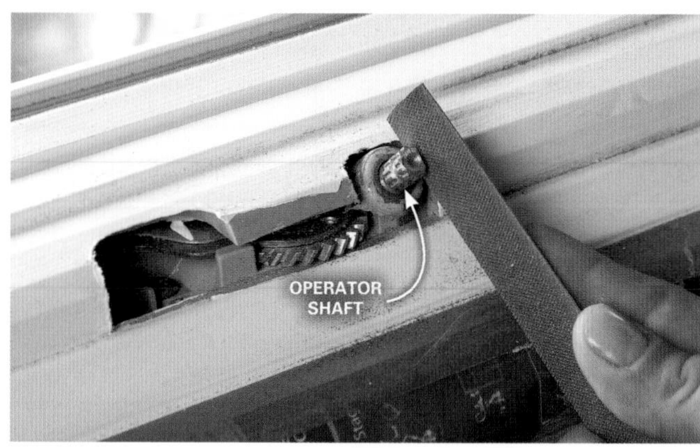

File a flat spot on the operator shaft, then insert a longer setscrew into the handle. The flat side lets the setscrew lock onto the shaft.

3 Replace a fogged sash

If you have broken glass or fogging (condensation between the glass panes), you'll have to replace the glass or the entire sash. If the sash is in good shape (not warped or cracked), you can sometimes replace just the glass. Call your window manufacturer to see whether glass replacement is an option and if a fogged window is covered under your warranty. You'll need the information that's etched into the corner of the glass and the sash dimensions.

Contact a glass repair specialist to have only the glass replaced. Or you can replace the sash yourself. Order it through the manufacturer.

To replace the sash, first remove the old one. You take this sash off by removing the hinge screws (Photo 1). For sashes that slide out, see Photos 1 and 2, p. 211. Remove any hardware from the damaged sash and install it on the new sash (this sash doesn't require any hardware).

Install the new sash by sliding it onto the hinge arms, then screw it to the hinges (Photo 2).

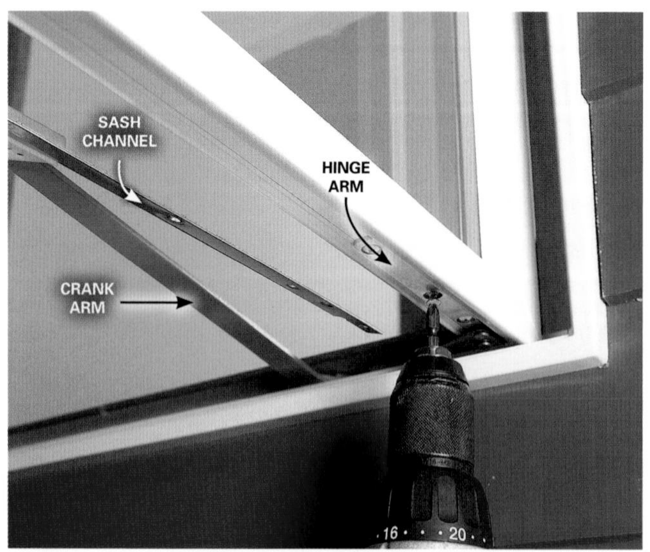

1 Take off the sash by removing the screws in the channel and the hinge arms. Then slide the sash off the hinge arms.

2 Align the sash lip with the hinge arms, then slide the sash onto the hinges. Insert screws to fasten the sash in place.

4 Fix a sticking window

If you have a window that drags against the frame when you open it, close the window and examine it from the outside. The sash should fit squarely and be centered in the frame. If not, you can adjust the position of the sash by slightly moving the hinge channel. (If the window is centered and square but still drags, see the next fix.)

1 **Open the sash and disconnect the crank arm. Pry the split arm operator off the top and the bottom of the sash with a screwdriver (the hinge arms easily pop off).**

2 **Slide the hinge shoes out of the hinge channels at the top and bottom of the window to remove the sash.**

You can move the channel at the top or the bottom of the window, depending on where the sash is dragging (but don't move both channels). Start by taking out the sash (Photos 1 and 2). If the hinge arm is screwed to the sash, see Photo 1.

Mark the hinge channel location on the frame, then unscrew the channel. Fill the screw holes with epoxy (for vinyl windows) or wood filler (for wood windows). Filling the holes keeps the screws from realigning with their old locations when you reinstall the channel. Scrape the filled holes smooth before the epoxy sets. Place the channel back on the jamb, about 1/8 in. over from the mark (move the channel away from the side of the sash that's dragging), drill 1/8-in. pilot holes and then reinstall it (Photo 3).

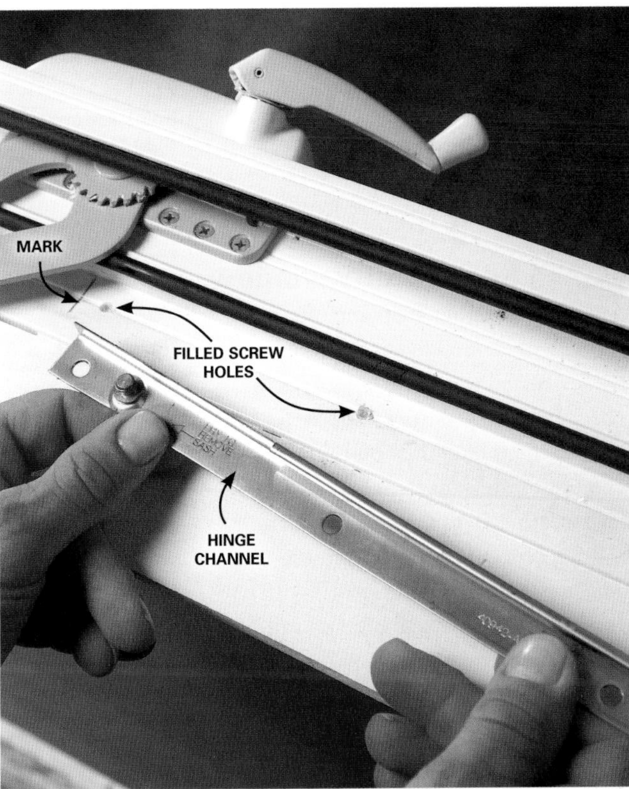

3 **Set the hinge channel in place, slightly over from its former location. Drill new holes, then screw it to the jamb.**

pro tip

Sometimes, spray lubricant can make stubborn hardware operate smoothly. But be sure to choose a product that's labeled "dry lubricant"— it won't leave any oil film that leads to dirt buildup.

5 Replace a sagging hinge

Over time, hinge arms that support heavy windows can start to sag, causing the sash to hit the frame in the lower corner that's opposite the hinge. First make sure the window sash is square and centered in the window opening. If it's not, see the previous fix. To eliminate drag in a window that fits squarely, replace the hinge arms at the top and the bottom of the window. You can buy the hinges at window hardware supply stores.

Remove the sash from the window. The hinge arms are located near a corner or in the middle of the window frame. Unscrew the hinge arms from the window, then install the new ones in the same locations (photo left).

Align the new hinge arm with the screw holes and fasten it into place. If the screw holes are stripped out, fill them with toothpicks dipped in wood glue, let the glue dry, then cut the toothpicks flush.

6 Seal a drafty window

Weather stripping often becomes loose, worn or distorted when the sash drags or when the strip gets sticky and attaches itself to the frame, then pulls loose when the sash is opened. Windows have weather strip on the sash, frame or both. Regardless of its location, the steps for removing and replacing it are the same. Weather stripping is available from your window manufacturer. The window brand and glass manufacturer date are etched in the corner of the glass or in the aluminum spacer between the glass panes. You'll also need the height and width of your sash (take these measurements yourself).

If the weather strip is in good shape and loose in only a few places, like the corners, apply a dab of polyurethane sealant to the groove and press the weather strip into place. Otherwise, replace the entire weather strip. First remove the sash and set it on a work surface so you can access all four sides. If the weather strip is one continuous piece, cut it apart at the corners with a utility knife.

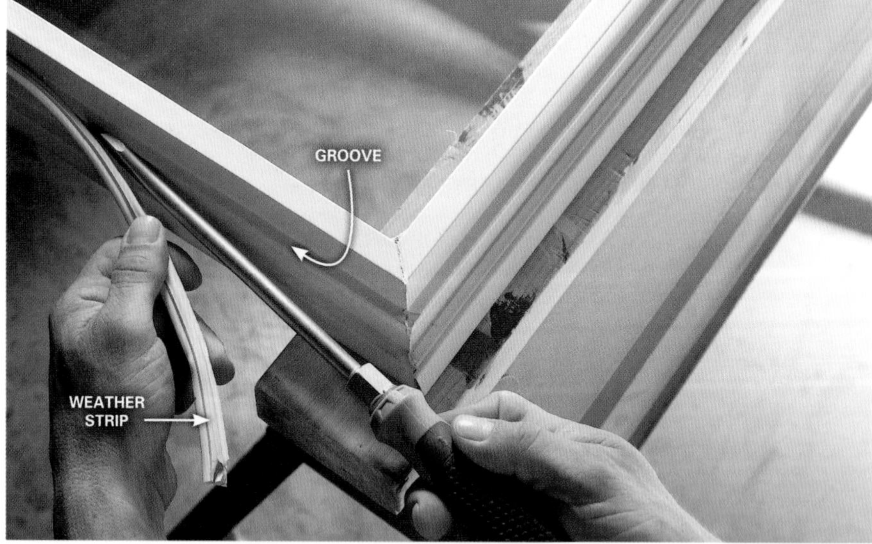

Work the old weather strip out of the groove gently to avoid tearing it and leaving the spline stuck in the groove.

Starting at a corner, pull the weather strip loose from the sash. If the spline tears off and remains stuck in the groove, make a hook from stiff wire to dig it out.

Work the new weather strip into the groove, starting at a corner. You'll hear it click as the strip slides into the groove.

pro tip

If the window is stuck shut, it's likely that the weather strip is sticking. After you muscle it open, spray silicone lubricant on a rag and wipe it on the weather stripping. Don't use oily lubricants; they attract dust.

Replace a broken sash cord

Older double-hung windows have sashes that move up and down in channels. The sash position is controlled by counterweights concealed behind the side jambs. If a cord breaks, you can fix it as shown.

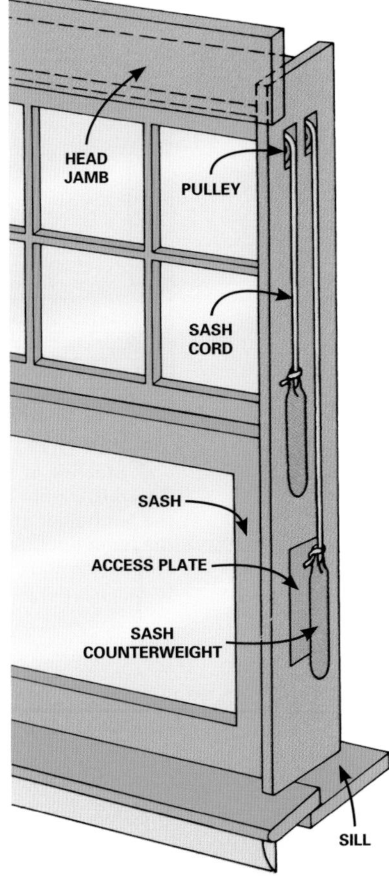

Inner view

The sash weights are held by sash cords that run over a pulley and are attached to each side of each sash.

1 Unscrew or pry out inner stop using a putty knife or pry bar. If you have metal weather stripping, carefully remove and save it. Pull bottom sash out from frame. Remove knotted sash cord (or chain) from channel in side of window sash.

2 Unscrew or pry out the access plate in the jamb to expose the weights. The plate must come out at an angle, not straight out. If the plate is painted stuck, score around it with a utility knife. If it's still stuck, attach a drywall screw in the center and pull out with pliers.

3 Pull out the weights and broken cord. The new cord should be the same thickness as the old. To help feed the cord, use a piece of strong string. Tie a bent nail to one end of string to serve as a weight and direct it over the pulley. Firmly tie other string end to new cord.

4 Feed cord over pulley, pull it down and tie it to the old weight. Rest sash on the sill, pull cord down until weight bumps pulley, and thread cord through channel on the side of the sash. Cut cord 2 in. longer than the sash channel. Tie a tight knot in the cord end and push in the hole at the bottom of the sash channel. Replace sash and inner stop.

1 REMOVE THE SASH Push in on the jamb liner while you pull out on the top corner of the sash. Release the opposite side using the same technique. Then pivot the sash downward and tilt it sideways to remove it.

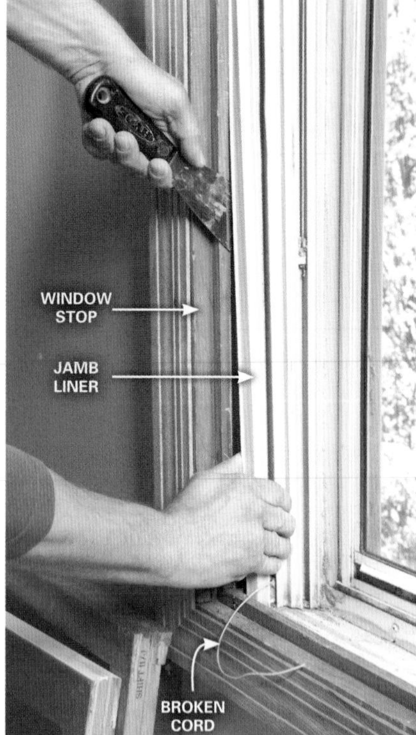

2 PRY OUT THE JAMB LINER
Starting at the bottom, wedge a stiff putty knife into the crack between the jamb liner and the window stop. Pry the jamb liner flange out from under the stop. Then slide the putty knife upward to release the jamb liner.

Fix a broken window jamb liner

Modern double-hung windows (the upper and lower window sashes slide up and down past each other) don't use pulleys and sash weights to support the sash (the moving part of the window). Instead they have liners on each side that contain a spring assembly. If your sash won't stay in the raised position, chances are that some part of the jamb liner hardware is broken. You might be able to spot a broken cord or other sign of the problem by looking closely as you open and close the window. If you determine that the jamb liner mechanism is broken, you can fix it by replacing both jamb liners.

The first step is to find a source for the new jamb liners. The original manufacturer is the best source of replacement parts. If you don't know what brand your window is and can't find a label, search online for a window repair parts specialist that can help you. Companies like Blaine Window Hardware at blainewindow.com (301) 797-6500) can identify the jamb liner and send you new ones. Snap several pictures of your jamb liner, showing the end profile and any identifying marks and show or send them to the parts supplier. Temporarily reinstall the old jamb liner and sash to secure the house while you're waiting for the new parts to arrive.

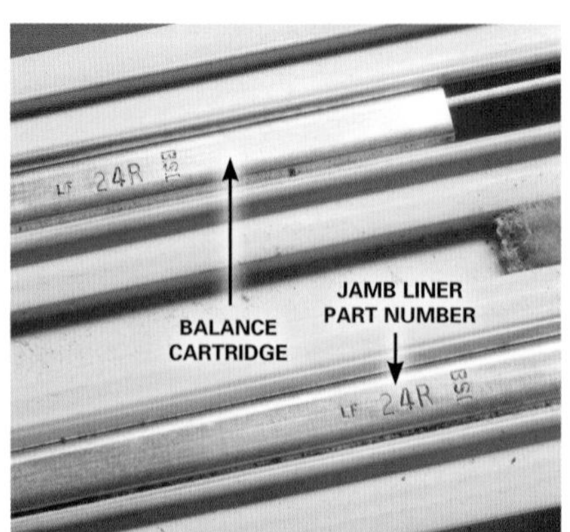

3 Find the information you'll need to order new jamb liners stamped on the metal balance cartridges.

The photos show how to remove a common type of jamb liner on a Marvin window. Photo 3 shows where to find the information you'll need to order a new Marvin jamb liner. Start by tilting out the sash (Photo 1). Then remove the jamb liner (Photo 2). If you're handy and want to save money, you can repair the jamb liner instead of replacing it. To see how, go to familyhandyman.com and search for "window repair."

Replace a window screen

Installing heavy-duty screen is a lot easier than training your pet to stop pushing and clawing at the door or window. Keep in mind that heavy screen has one drawback: It blocks sunlight and your view more than standard screen.

Heavy-duty screen is installed just like any other screen. If your screen is in a wooden frame, you'll have to carefully remove moldings and pry out staples to remove the old screen. Then staple the new screen into place, stretching it tight as you go. Replacing screen in a metal frame may look more complex, but it's actually faster and easier. All you need are scissors, a utility knife, clamps, a nail set, a spline roller and spline. Spline comes in three sizes; take a piece of the old spline to the home center to match the thickness. These replacement steps take about 15 minutes.

1 **Pull out the old spline and remove the old screen. Cut a new piece of screen about 4 in. wider and longer than the old one. Also cut four pieces of new spline, making each a couple of inches longer than the sides of the frame.**

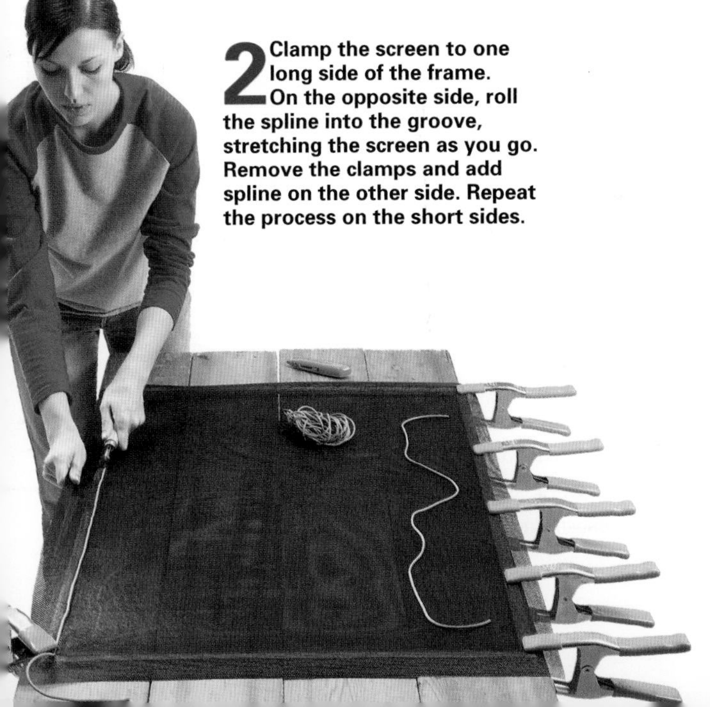

2 **Clamp the screen to one long side of the frame. On the opposite side, roll the spline into the groove, stretching the screen as you go. Remove the clamps and add spline on the other side. Repeat the process on the short sides.**

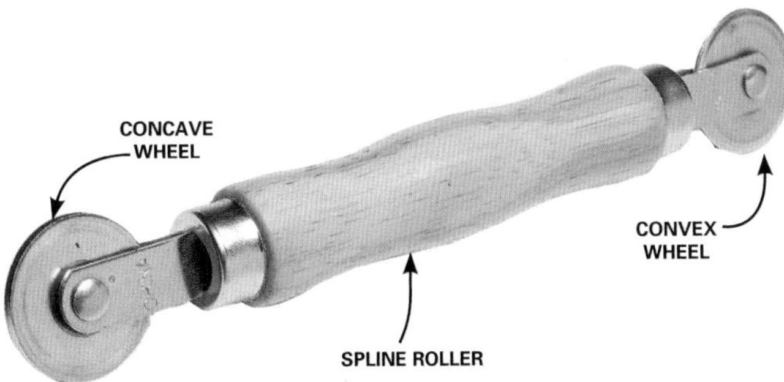

3 **A spline roller has a concave wheel and a convex wheel. Use the concave end first. When all four splines are in place, roll them again, this time with the convex wheel.**

4 **Trim off the excess screen with a utility knife. Put a sharp new blade in the knife and pull it carefully along the spline.**

Safety first

We won't show you how to deal with problems involving a high-tension torsion spring—the type mounted on a rod over your door that acts as a counter-balance and determines how much effort it takes you to raise and lower the door. These springs are dangerous. Some manufacturers, such as Clopay and Wayne Dalton, now have do-it-yourself–friendly systems that can be adjusted with a power drill. Unless you have this type of system, and the instruction manual, hire a professional. Adjusting or replacing extension springs—the type mounted on each side of your door by the tracks—or the cables connected to them can also be dangerous and should be left to trained professionals.

You can adjust safety systems yourself, particularly the automatic reversal mechanism, but leave repairs to pros. Don't take chances when it comes to safety.

Garage door tune-up

When you hear the words "tune-up" and "garage" in the same sentence, you probably think of your car, motorcycle or lawn mower. But there's a different type of tune-up, one that's simple to perform and can extend the life of the "equipment" by up to five years: a garage door tune-up.

Squeaking and grinding noises, rough operation and poorly reacting safety mechanisms are sure signs your door needs attention. Here we'll show you how to maintain and inspect your garage door to ensure it will work smoothly and safely. The garage door in our example is a 16-ft.-wide steel door with an overhead torsion spring and automatic opener. Your door might be slightly different, but most of the maintenance steps described here will be the same.

1 Lubricate the hinges, rollers and tracks

Oiling the moving parts on your door will help it operate more smoothly and more quietly. Make sure to:

- Apply two drops of regular household oil (such as 3-in-One) in each seam of every hinge. Apply the oil on top so it can work its way down and lubricate the entire seam.
- Apply two drops in each seam of each roller mount bracket on the door, and a drop or two on the ends of each roller pin.
- Apply six drops of oil on the roller track. To ensure that all the rollers come in contact with the lubricated section, apply the oil about 1 ft. from the curve in the track. **Note:** Do NOT oil the track if your door has nylon rollers; certain oils can soften, gum up and ruin nylon rollers.

After you've oiled all the parts, use the automatic opener to raise and lower the door a few times to help distribute the oil.

pro tip

Wipe away any grease buildup on the rollers and roller pins before lubricating the door. Grease combines with sand and grit to form a sludge that acts as an abrasive and eats away at the rollers.

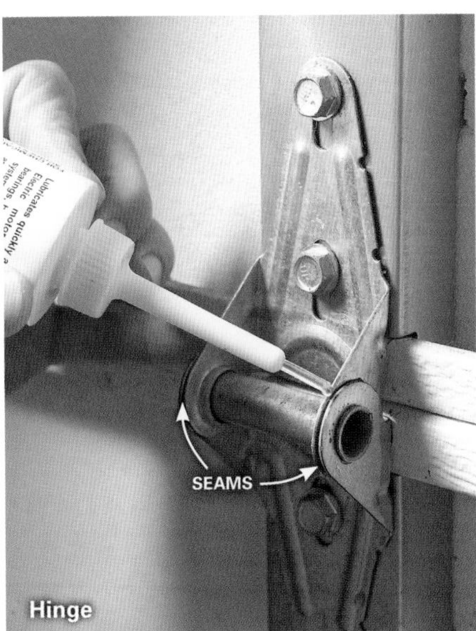

Hinge

Roller bracket and pin

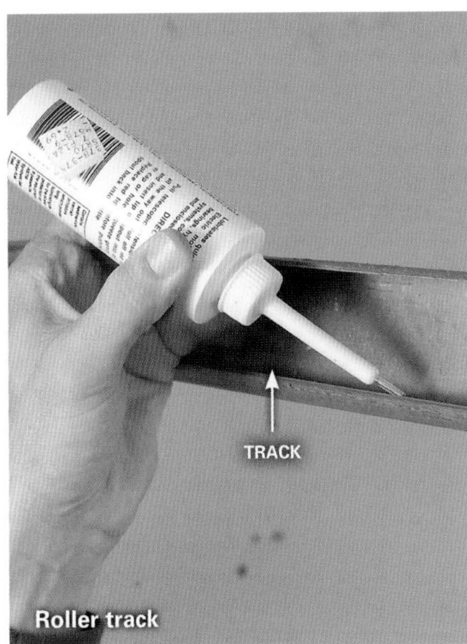

Roller track

2 Check cables and cable connection points for wear

Cables can fray and break in two places: along their length and at the ends where they connect to the roller brackets and spring mechanism. Inspect your cables; hire a professional to replace frayed cables immediately.

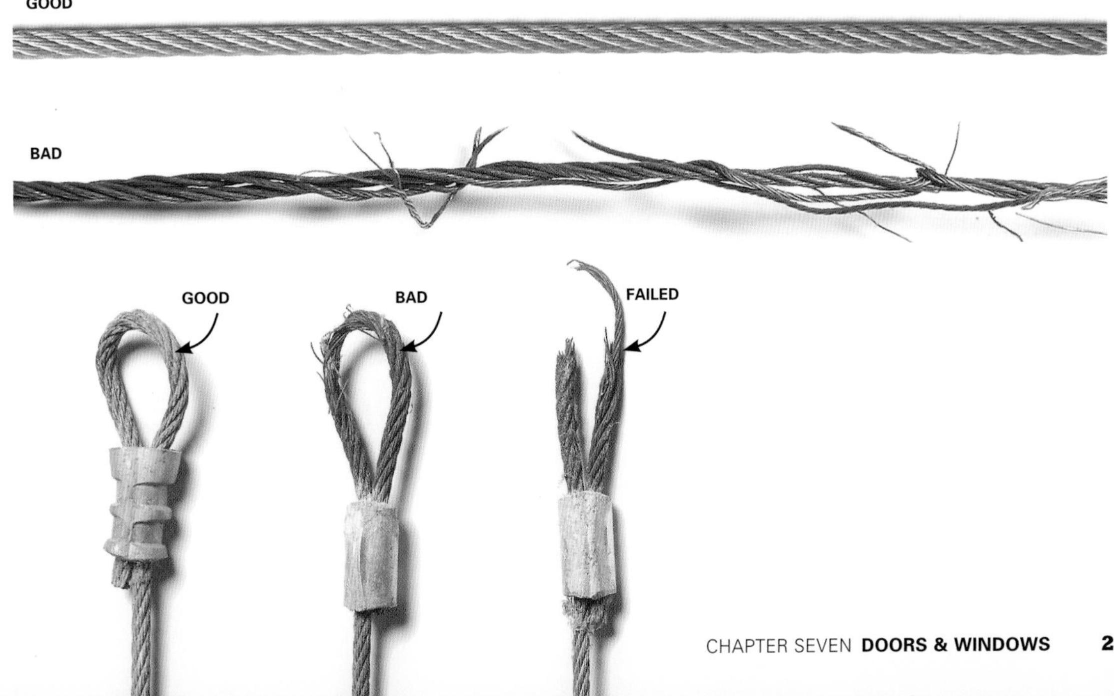

3 Check the door for balance

With the garage door in the closed position, disengage the door from the automatic opener by pulling down on the emergency release handle. Manually open the door halfway and let go. If the door is balanced properly, it should stay in the halfway position or creep down slowly.

If the door closes quickly or if you have to pull it down hard from the halfway position, it isn't properly balanced and will overstress the automatic opener. Hire a garage door professional to adjust the spring tension.

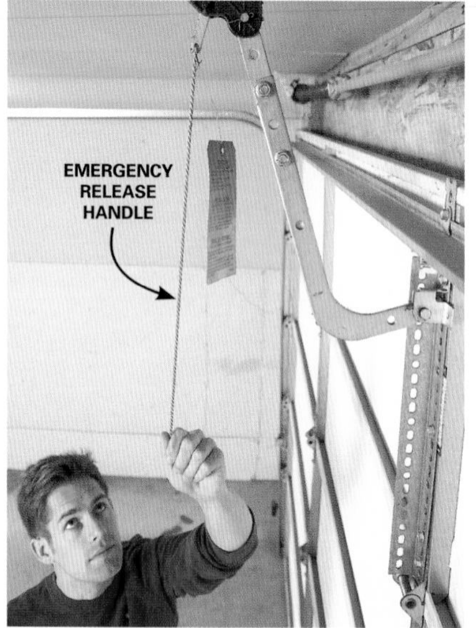

pro tip

Manually operated doors have brackets and locking tongues (one on each side) that are operated by cables connected to the exterior handle (inset). If your door has an automatic opener, remove the brackets; if these locks are accidentally engaged while the opener is trying to open the door, you could damage the door or opener.

4 Replace worn weather seals

The elements, age and rodents (who rarely use the automatic opener) can all take their toll on the weatherstripping around the door, particularly the weather seal along the bottom. If you can see gaps at the bottom of the door when it's closed, replace the seal.

Most metal doors have two channels along the lower edge that the weather seal slides into. To replace the seal, first use a screwdriver to open the channels on their ends (they've usually been pinched to secure the existing seals in place) and slide the old seal out. Wipe the channels clean, lubricate them with dish soap or silicone spray, then slide the new seal into place. This process is *much* easier if you have a helper.

5 Tighten bolts on garage door and garage track brackets

Tighten the bolts that connect the hinges to the door and those that secure the mounting brackets to the garage framework. Bolts on steel doors (like the one shown) rarely loosen; those on wood doors tend to loosen and should be examined and tightened regularly.

6 Lubricate the cable connections and springs

While you shouldn't attempt to replace or adjust cables or springs, you should lubricate them:

■ Apply one or two drops where the two cables connect to the bottom roller mount brackets. This is also a good time to check the cable for wear (see p. 217).

■ Run a bead of oil along the top of the torsion spring. The oil will eventually work its way down, coating the spring and preventing corrosion.

TORSION SPRING

CABLE

BOTTOM ROLLER BRACKET

7 Check the safety reversal features

Today's garage doors and openers include several safety features. To check the safety reversal system, set a 2x4 flat on the ground centered in the opening as shown. Close the door using the opener. When the door contacts the 2x4, it should reverse itself and open.

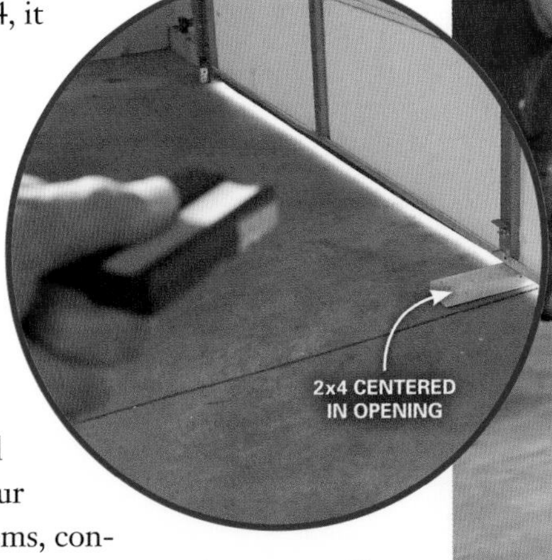

To check the safety reversal sensors, start closing the door with the automatic opener, then wave your hand between the safety reversal sensors (photo above). The door should reverse and reopen.

If your door fails either test, read the opener owner's manual for adjustment guidelines. If your adjustments don't fix the problems, consult a trained professional to repair or replace the opener. If your opener lacks these safety features altogether, replace it.

2x4 CENTERED IN OPENING

SAFETY REVERSING SENSORS

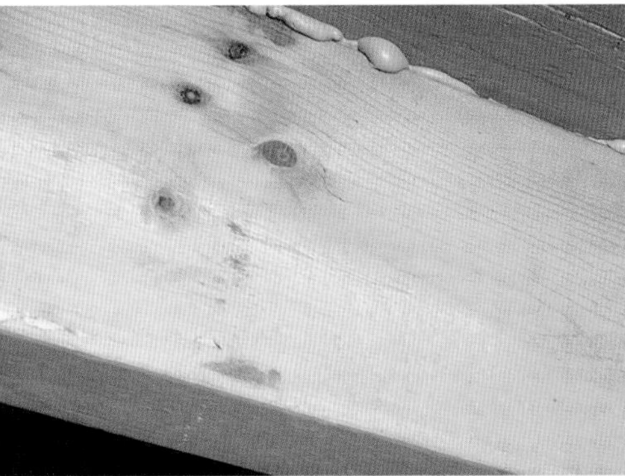

Chapter **eight**

FLOORS & FLOOR COVERINGS

Patch damaged carpet

You can patch a small hole, tear or burn using techniques that will make the repair virtually invisible. You'll need a small "plug" of carpet that matches the damaged piece. If you don't have a remnant, you can steal a piece from inside a closet or underneath a piece of furniture you never intend to move. (This may sound extreme, but it's a lot cheaper than replacing the entire carpet.)

If you have a "plush"-type carpet with a flat surface and no pattern, you can make a repair that's absolutely invisible. If your carpet has a color pattern, a textured surface design or looped yarn, you'll have to be fussier when you cut the plug, and the repair may be visible (but you're probably the only one who will notice it). Before starting this repair, buy a carpet knife that has replaceable blades. You'll also need a roll of one-sided carpet tape.

Cut out the damage and a matching plug

Be sure the area you're working in is well lit. To mark the area you'll cut out, part the carpet fibers around the damage as if you were parting your hair (Photo 1). Keep the part lines at least 1/2 in. from the damaged spot. Cut along the parts using a sharp, new blade in your carpet knife (Photo 2).

Next, cut a replacement plug, using the cutout as a template. To start, make a first cut in the replacement material, using a straightedge to guide your carpet knife. Then set the cutout on the replacement material with one edge aligned along that first cut. When you lay the cutout on top of the replacement material, make sure their naps are running in the same direction. You can tell which direction the nap is running by rubbing your hand over the carpeting and watching which way the fibers fall or stand up. Once you have the cutout lined up correctly, part the fibers around the three uncut sides just as you did before.

Cut along the parts and test-fit the plug in the cutout hole, making sure the nap of the plug matches the nap of the surrounding carpet. If the plug is a little too big, trim off a single row of fibers with sharp scissors (old, dull scissors will tear the fibers).

1 **Part the carpet fibers with a Phillips screwdriver. The parts mark your cutting lines and let you cut the backing without cutting or tearing the fibers.**

2 **Cut through the carpet backing. Make the cuts as straight as you can and avoid cutting completely through the carpet pad.**

3 **Test-fit all the pieces of carpet tape before you stick them in place permanently. Mark a square on the carpet pad to help align each piece later.**

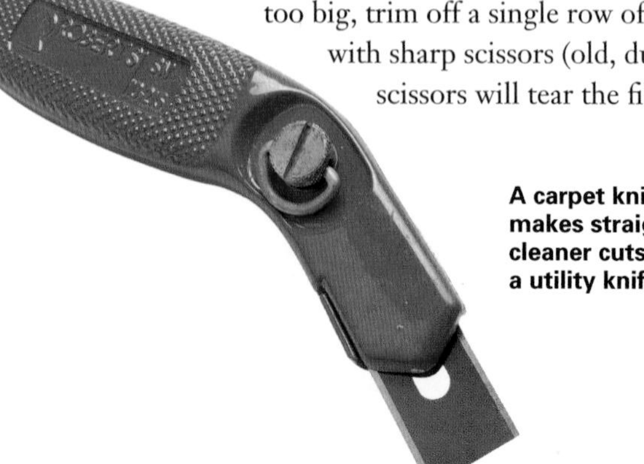

A carpet knife makes straighter, cleaner cuts than a utility knife.

4 **Peel off the tape's backing and set each piece in place, sticky side up. Don't let the super-sticky tape touch the carpet backing—or anything else—until it's in position.**

5 **Set the plug tightly against one side of the hole. Then lower the other edges into place, holding back the surrounding fibers. Press the plug into the tape with your fingers, then with a carpet tractor.**

Prepare the hole for the new plug

Cut pieces of carpet tape and position them in the hole without removing the backing (Photo 3). Cut the ends of the tape diagonally so the pieces will frame the hole without overlapping. The tricky part is getting the tape positioned so it's halfway under the plug and halfway under the surrounding carpet. A helper makes this easier.

After marking their positions in the hole, remove the pieces from the hole and carefully (this is sticky stuff!) remove the protective backing from the tape. While pulling the carpeting up with one hand, slip the tape pieces back into the prepared hole one piece at a time (Photo 4). Be sure the edges of the tape line up with your markings.

Insert the plug

Now you're ready to fit the new plug into the hole. Pull the fibers of the surrounding carpet back from the edges. Push one side of the plug lightly onto the tape to make sure it's set exactly right—you really only have one shot at this (Photo 5). After you're sure the plug is placed correctly, use your fingers to work in the direction of the nap all the way around the hole as you press the plug down firmly onto each side of the tape.

A carpet tractor will do the best job of meshing the fibers, but a seam roller or even a rolling pin would work too. Place a telephone book on top of the plug overnight. Trim any fibers sticking up with sharp scissors. You'll be surprised how "invisible" this repair is once you're finished. You can vacuum and clean your carpeting as you normally would, and this repair should last as long as your carpet does.

pro tip

Be sure to choose heavy-duty tape reinforced with mesh, not the thin, flimsy version or the "hot-melt" type that requires a special iron to apply.

A carpet tractor will mesh the fibers and make the repair invisible.

Rescue wet carpet

When carpet gets soaked, you have to act fast. The longer it stays soggy, the more likely it is to stretch out, discolor or get moldy. If a large area is waterlogged, complete replacement may be the best option. But if only a corner or a small room is soaked, you can save the carpet with just a couple of hours of work.

Tear out the soggy pad

First, go to the corner nearest the wet area, grab the carpet with pliers and pull the carpet off the tack strip. Continue pulling the carpet off the tack strip by hand until you can fold back the entire wet section. Run a fan or two to dry the carpet.

Wet carpet pad is like a big sponge. You have to get rid of it ASAP. Cut around the wet area with a utility knife. Make straight cuts so you have straight seams when you patch in the new pad. If the pad is glued to a concrete floor, scrape it up with a floor scraper (Photo 1). If the pad is stapled to a wood subfloor, just pull up chunks of pad and pry or pull out the staples if you have just a few. For faster removal on a larger area, use a floor scraper. Have garbage bags handy to prevent drips on the carpeting. Wet pad is heavy. Don't fill the bags so full that you can't haul them out without wrecking your back!

A floor scraper is the best tool for removing old adhesive or staples.

Wipe up any water on the floor, then flop the wet carpet back into place. Drying it flat and in place helps the carpet retain its shape. Run fans until the floor and carpet are completely dry. This can take a couple of days.

Patch in the new pad

Measure the area of pad you need to replace and take a piece of the old pad to a flooring store or home center to find similar replacement pad. The color doesn't matter, but the new pad must be the same thickness and density as the old pad. Some stores will cut the pad to the size you need.

Fasten the pad to a concrete floor with carpet pad adhesive and duct-tape the seams together (Photo 2). On a wood subfloor, all you need is a staple gun and 5/16-in. staples. Use a utility knife to trim off any pad covering the tack strip.

Reattach the carpet

As you refasten the carpet to the tack strip, you need to stretch it toward the wall. If you're dealing with a corner or a small area, you can use a knee kicker alone. Starting at one end of the loose carpet, set the head of the kicker about 2 in. from the tack strip and nudge the carpet tight against the wall. Force the carpet into the tack strip with a stiff putty knife. Also tuck the edge of the carpet into the space between the wall and the tack strip with a putty knife. Continue along the wall, moving the kicker over about a few inches each time.

If you're dealing with a larger area of carpet or if the carpet has stretched out of shape, bubbled or wrinkled after getting wet, you'll need to rent a power stretcher to restretch the carpet.

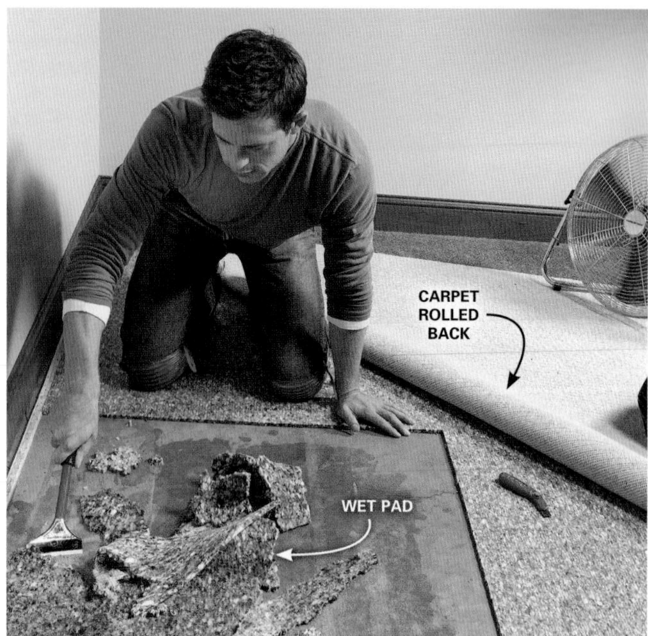

1 Dry out wet carpet right away. Fold back the carpet and start a fan. Cut around the soaked section of pad and scrape it up.

2 Dry out wet carpet right away. Fold back the carpet and start a fan. Cut around the soaked section of pad and scrape it up.

Eliminate floor squeaks from above

Typically, squeaks occur when wood elements move and rub against nails. The solution is to use screws to tightly pull together the wood pieces. However, this is tough if you can't get at the floor from below.

The strategy: Locate the squeak, find the nearest joist, and tighten the flooring to the joist or subfloor with a trim-head screw driven through the floor from above.

Locating the squeak and the joists

Walk back and forth across the floor and do some detective work to find the spot that's squeaking. Kneel down near the squeak and have another person walk across the floor. Use a piece of masking tape to mark its probable location. Next, locate the joist nearest to your mark.

- If there are floor heating registers, pull the register out and probe along the edge of the metal ductwork. Usually these floor registers are installed next to a joist.
- Probe through the carpet and subfloor using a finish nail as a drill bit; it won't grab the carpet fibers like a twist bit.
- Sometimes the joint between plank flooring pieces is wide enough for a 1/16-in. twist drill bit to squeeze through. Drill through the subfloor along this joint and probe with the bit to locate the joist.
- Once you find a joist, it's a good bet that the rest are spaced 16 in. on center (although sometimes 19-1/4 in. or 24 in. on center). Lay a tape measure out from the known joist to locate the others.

Eliminate the squeak

Drive a trim-head screw through the flooring and into the joist. If you're working on carpet, just drive it right through. Go slowly so that carpet fibers won't grab and wind onto the screw threads. On hardwood, first drill a clearance hole through the hardwood plank, followed by a 1/8-in.-deep countersunk hole the size of the screw head. Drive the trim screw tight and then putty the screw hole.

If the squeak's gone, mission accomplished. If not, drive another screw into the joist several inches away. Still squeaks? Try another spot off to the side of the joist. Because you're literally working in the dark, this is a real hit-or-miss process. If you're up to three or four attempts and you're still not victorious, sit back and reassess how important this "squeak mission" is to you—especially if you have a beautiful hardwood floor.

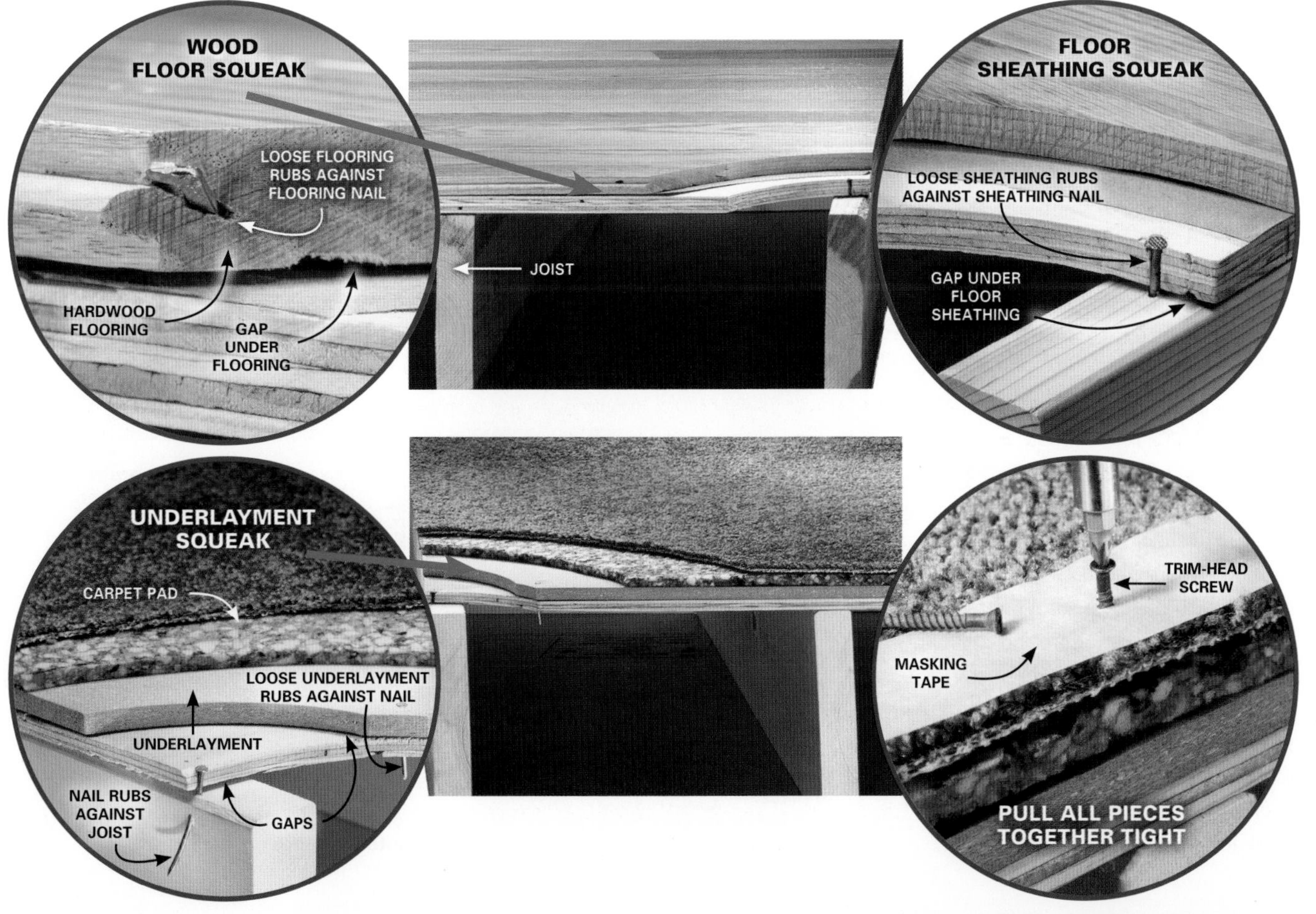

instant fix

Stop squeaks with shims

Floor squeaks are caused by wood rubbing against a nail, other wood, or even ductwork and piping. Finding the squeak can be difficult, but if the squeaking floor is open from below, you're in luck. You'll have several options to stop it.

To locate the source of the squeak, have a helper spring up and down on the squeaky area while you listen and watch for subfloor movement from below. Also look for loose nails or subfloor seams rubbing against each other. It doesn't take much movement to cause a squeak, especially since your floor amplifies the sound like a giant soundboard.

Finding the exact cause of the squeak, and then choosing the best remedy, isn't always a simple task. Don't be surprised if you have to try several solutions before you stop it for good. Look for gaps between a joist and the subfloor first. Plug in a drop light and examine the area closely; a gap or movement may not be obvious.

If you spot a gap, use the wood shim solution to stop floor movement. Shims are available at any home center or lumberyard. Push a pair of shims in lightly (Photo 1). If you drive them in, you'll widen the gap and potentially create a new squeak. Adding construction adhesive before final assembly makes the fix permanent while filling in irregularities between the wood surfaces.

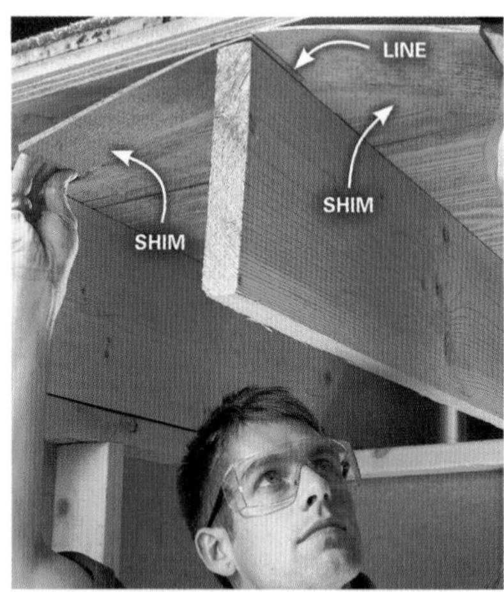

1 Slide a pair of shims into the gap for a snug fit. Draw a line on each shim to mark the depth. Don't wedge the gap wider.

2 Add a bead of construction adhesive to both sides of each shim. Shove shims back into the gap. Align to the depth line.

3 Score the excess shim two or three times with a sharp utility knife and snap it off. Keep off the floor for four hours while the adhesive hardens.

Block squeaky joints

Once in a while, movement in a subfloor joint will cause a squeak. You can stop it by screwing and gluing 2x8 blocking under the joint to give it solid support (Photos 1 and 2). First angle-screw through the blocking, up into the joists, to ensure a tight fit. But be sure to drive additional nails or screws to anchor the block. Otherwise it might work loose and cause more squeaks!

1 Cut 2x8 blocking to fit snugly between joists. Add construction adhesive to the top and slide it into place.

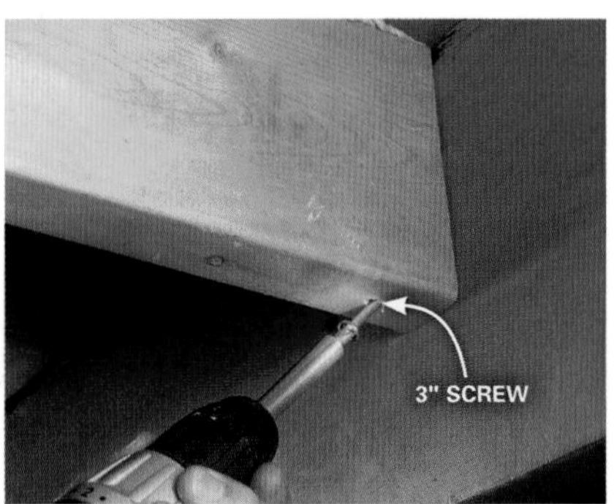

2 Predrill angled pilot holes with a 1/8-in. bit. Drive 3-in. wood screws to force the block snug against the subfloor seam. Drive an additional pair of screws (or 16d nails) through the joist into the block on each end.

Stop squeaks with screws

A solid wood floor is usually fastened with hundreds of nails, so squeaks often occur as the floor ages. But some squeaks aren't caused by nails; they come from one edge of a board rubbing on another. A simple "first" solution is to dust the squeaky area of your floor with talcum powder, working it into the cracks. The talc reduces friction and may solve the problem, at least for one season. **Note:** Talc can be slippery. Wipe off the excess.

For a more permanent solution, however, you'll usually have to screw the subfloor to the wood flooring from below. Drill a 1/8-in. pilot hole about 1/2 in. less than the thickness of the entire floor, and buy screws 1/4 in. shorter than the floor thickness so they won't penetrate the surface. You can find your floor thickness by either removing a floor register and measuring the floor where the duct comes through, or by drilling a small hole in an out-of-the-way corner and measuring with a nail.

To maintain a safe margin, mark the desired drilling depth on the drill bit with masking tape. Space your screws about every 6 in. in the area of the squeak. Have someone stand on the floor above while you drive the screws. Set the heads flush with the subfloor. Sinking the head into the subfloor could cause the screw point to break through the finished floor surface.

Mark the depth of the pilot hole on a 1/8-in. drill bit with tape. The depth should be 1/2 in. less than the floor thickness. Drill pilot holes 4 to 8 in. apart. Drive No. 8 wood screws flush to subfloor.

instant fix

Stop squeaks with construction adhesive

Sometimes the gapping between the subfloor and joist is too narrow, too irregular or too widespread for shims to be effective. Or perhaps you can't pinpoint the exact source of the squeak. A good solution is to use a bead of construction adhesive to glue the wood together. You don't have to press the gaps closed; construction adhesive fills the space and hardens. The key is to force it as far as possible into the gaps without widening them. Work both sides of the joist for a strong, lasting connection. And glue nearby joists as well in case you can't find the exact squeak source. Keep off the floor for a day until the glue hardens.

caution

Construction adhesive contains a strong solvent. Wear a respirator with an organic vapor cartridge when working in closely confined areas.

Squeeze a thick bead of construction adhesive into the crack along both sides of the squeaky joist and subfloor. Apply adhesive to adjacent joist/subfloor joints as well.

The easiest flooring ever

Luxury vinyl is a beautiful, tough alternative to tile or hardwood flooring. Luxury vinyl tile (LVT) resembles stone or ceramic tile; luxury vinyl plank (LVP) mimics hardwood boards. Both can be installed over many types of flooring, so you may not have to deal with the cost and hassle of removing the old floor at all. With these tips from our expert, you can install luxury vinyl over an existing floor at a fraction of the cost in just a few hours.

TONGUE

GROOVE

Choosing the right tile

Interlocking is easy

The tongue-and-groove design makes it easy to snap the tiles into place. Working from left to right, the short ends angle in first. Then tip the opposite end downward, lift and angle the long edge into the previous tiles and push them together.

WEAR LAYER The wear layer on luxury vinyl is 8 to 28 mils thick. This layer protects the decorative layer from scratches to keep it looking like new. Thicker is generally better, but your lifestyle matters more. If you wear socks around the house, 8-mil will be plenty; if you have three kids and two dogs, go for a thicker wear layer.

DECORATIVE LAYER From modern tile and stone to rustic wood designs, LVP and LVT come in many styles to fit any room around the house, 8-mil will be plenty; if you have three kids and two dogs, go for a thicker wear layer.

RIGID CORE Some luxury vinyl has a rigid core to provide extra durability and better sound blocking. The thicker rigid core, however, requires a flatter surface to avoid bridging low spots.

INTEGRATED PAD Some vinyl tiles come with a built-in pad attached to the bottom of each tile to provide cushion underfoot. This eliminates the need for a separate underlayment.

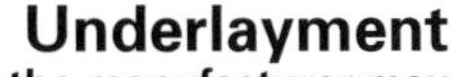

Underlayment

If a tile doesn't come with a built-in pad, the manufacturer may recommend a cushion of underlayment. It acts as a pad for a softer landing, provides a vapor barrier and may reduce sound. It can also prevent some imperfections in the existing floor from telegraphing through the tile. Without underlayment, things like screw head holes, uneven seams, small high spots and even tiny grains of sand can lead to wear marks.

Install over almost anything:

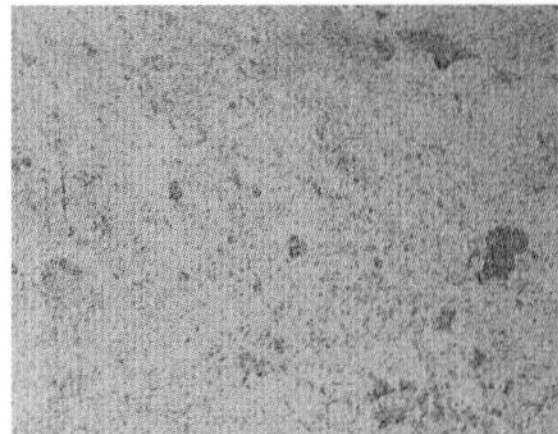

CONCRETE If it's flat and smooth, you're good to go. If the surface is pitted or rough, either grind it smooth or cover it with self-leveling compound.

OSB/PLYWOOD Fill any gaps and screw holes with a patching compound and sand down high spots.

SHEET VINYL Make sure seams are sound. If they're not, adhere them to the subfloor before moving on.

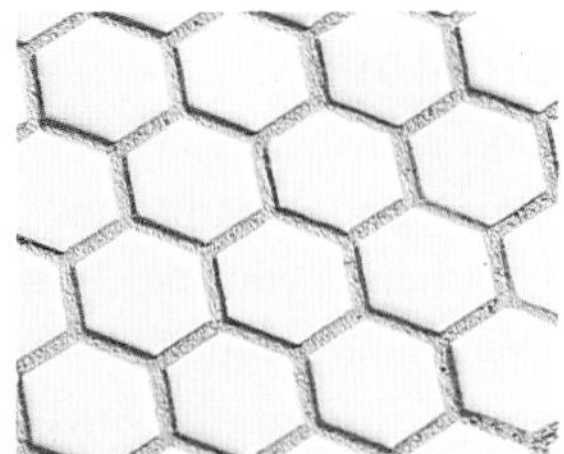

TILE Avoid installing luxury vinyl over grouted tile. If removing the tile isn't an option, your best bet is to pour a self-leveling compound.

Plan and prepare

Spread samples all over the room

The samples will look different throughout the day. Before you buy your flooring, place samples around the room to see how they look in different light conditions.

Acclimate the tiles

Vinyl shrinks and expands slightly as the temperature changes, so let it assume room temperature before installing it. With the tiles packed together, that can take several hours. To speed up acclimation, get the tiles out of the box.

Shuffle the tiles

Each style consists of a limited number of unique designs. To get a good random pattern, mix tiles from several different boxes. Open your boxes and pull from the top of each to make new stacks. You can cross two things off your list by doing this when you unpack the tile.

Clean the old floor

Don't leave even a tiny grain of sand on the old floor before you install the new one. It might "telegraph" through the vinyl and cause a wear mark, especially with thinner luxury vinyl.

BUY ALL THE TILE AT ONCE Tile is produced in large batches, or "lots." Within the lots, all the tiles will be consistent, but each lot may vary slightly in size and color. Buying all the tile you need at one time will give you a better shot at getting tiles in the same lot. Double-check the batch, lot or dye number, and make sure all the boxes match.

CHECK YOUR SUBSTRATE Use a level or straightedge to find out how flat your substrate is. Check several areas in different directions for low spots. Measure the biggest gap between the floor and the straightedge and check it against the manufacturer's specifications. For this tile, the manufacturer says the floor should be flat to within 3/16 in. over 10 ft. If the gap is bigger than what the manufacturer recommends, you'll need to address this before moving on. *See your options at right.*

Dealing with high spots and low spots

Trowel floor patching compound to fill small low spots. For larger areas, cover the entire floor with a self-leveling compound. An added benefit of using self-leveling compound is that you can also determine exactly where the top of the flooring will finish, eliminating some bulky transitions.

PLAN THE LAYOUT To avoid skinny rows along walls or cabinets, connect tiles to span the room until you can't fit a full-width tile. If the distance between the last row of tile and the wall is less than half the width of a tile, you'll want to shift the first row. You could measure the width of the space and figure out how the tiles will land along the walls, but it's best to trust your eyes and not your tape measure.

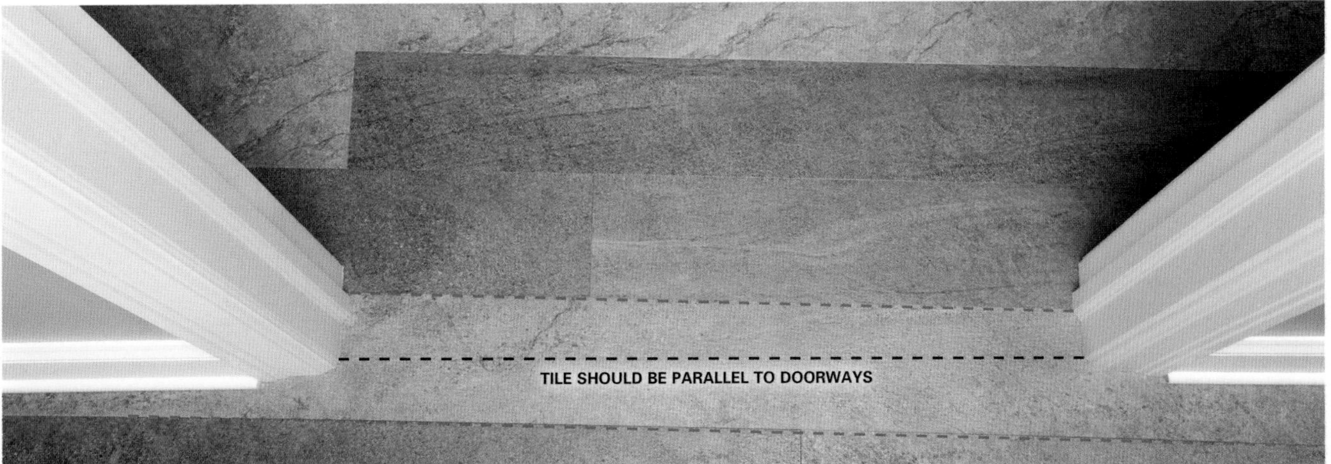

EXPECT OUT-OF-SQUARE ROOMS Many rooms aren't perfectly square, and it's easy to notice planks or tiles that are cut with a taper (wider at one end than the other) especially if the wall is particularly long. Crooked flooring is obvious at doorways. If you see the tiles don't line up with the door, guests will too. Shift the layout so it's crooked somewhere less visible.

Installation tips

START ROWS WITH CUTOFFS You'll end each row by cutting the last tile to fit. Instead of wasting the leftover cutoff, make it the beginning of the next row.

Change levels with transition molding

Transition molding is used to cover the cut ends of vinyl and to make up for height differences when meeting a different type of flooring. There are three common options:

Reducer strip
For transitioning vinyl floor to another floor of a different height.

T-Molding
For a smooth transition between floor surfaces that are about the same height.

End cap
For transitioning from vinyl floor to carpet. Also used to terminate vinyl flooring into an exterior door.

LEAVE A GAP UNDER SHOE MOLDING Pinching the flooring down with shoe mold won't allow for expansion and contraction and could cause buckling or separation at the seams. Use a 1/32-in. tile spacer or shim under the shoe to create a small gap. Be sure to nail the shoe into the baseboard, not down through the vinyl.

STAGGER THE SEAMS There's no set rule for staggering seams in vinyl planks, but if you lay your planks down and the seams end up creating a pattern, you'll notice it every time you walk on the floor. Avoid forming "H" and stair-step patterns. If you make sure seams don't line up for four or five rows, your eye will be unlikely to spot a pattern.

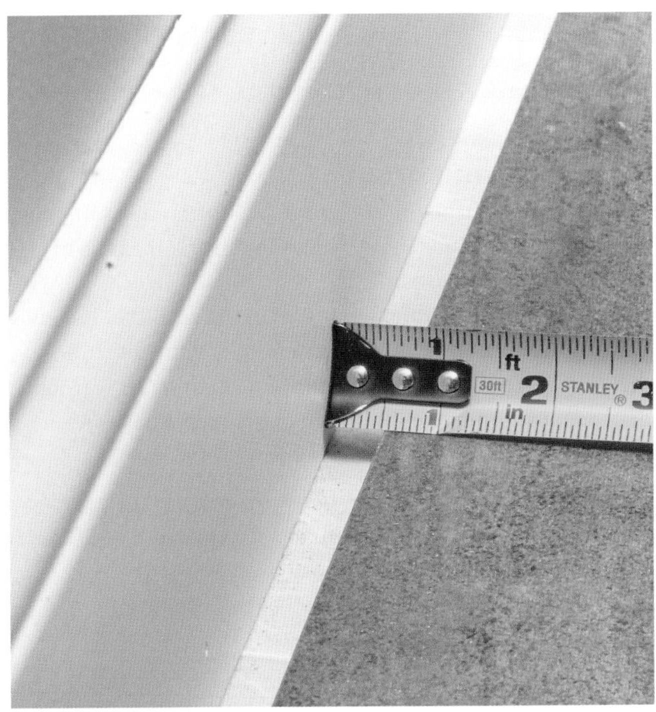

LEAVE A GAP It's surprising how much vinyl can expand or shrink with changing temperatures. A gap at the edges will ensure you won't ever come home to a buckled floor. Check with the manufacturer to see what it recommends for your tile.

MARK WITH A SCRAP Instead of using a tape measure to transfer measurements to the tile, use some scrap. Align the tile you want to cut where it will snap in, placing it on top of the previous row. Use a full-width scrap (cut the tongue off) against the wall and scribe the tile.

INSTALL THE PLANKS IN REVERSE Being able to install vinyl tile backward is a real time-saver and makes going through doorways and installing tile under cabinets a snap. Assemble the row first, then tip the tongue underneath the groove on the previous row and pull them tight.

HEAT AND BEND If you run into a situation where you need to bend the tile to get it to fit under a doorjamb or toe-kick, make the tile more flexible with a heat gun. Be careful not to scorch the face of the tile.

Replace a damaged tile

When a tile chips or breaks, the only way to fix it is to replace it. The total repair time will be around two hours, spread over a couple of days. Most of your time will be spent on the first day removing the damaged tile, the grout and the old adhesive and then installing the new tile. The final step (done a day or two later) is regrouting around the new tile.

Matching the tile and grout

If you're lucky, you'll have some extra tiles. If you don't have extras, visit some tile stores. You might be able to find a close match. If you can't find anything close, you can get creative and replace a few more tiles to make a new pattern.

Matching the grout can be a bit tricky, even though tile stores carry a wide range of colors. For the best match, take a piece of the old grout with you to the tile store.

Adhesives and grout

Whether the damaged tile is on the floor or on the wall, the repair steps are similar. The main difference is the type of adhesive and grout used.

For floor tiles, use thin-set mortar as the adhesive. It comes in a powder that you mix with water. Follow the directions on the package for the correct mixture consistency. To regrout floor tile, use sanded grout. For wall tile repairs, use pre-mixed mastic adhesive and non-sanded grout.

pro tip

Mix some grout before you start the project to make sure the color matches. Grout changes color as it dries and you may find you'll need to do some color adjusting by mixing two colors.

COLD CHISEL

DAMAGED TILE

1 **Remove the damaged tile with a cold chisel and hammer. Start at the edge of the tile, in the grout. Ceramic tile is brittle—small pieces will fly! Wear safety glasses and gloves. Be careful not to chip the surrounding tiles.**

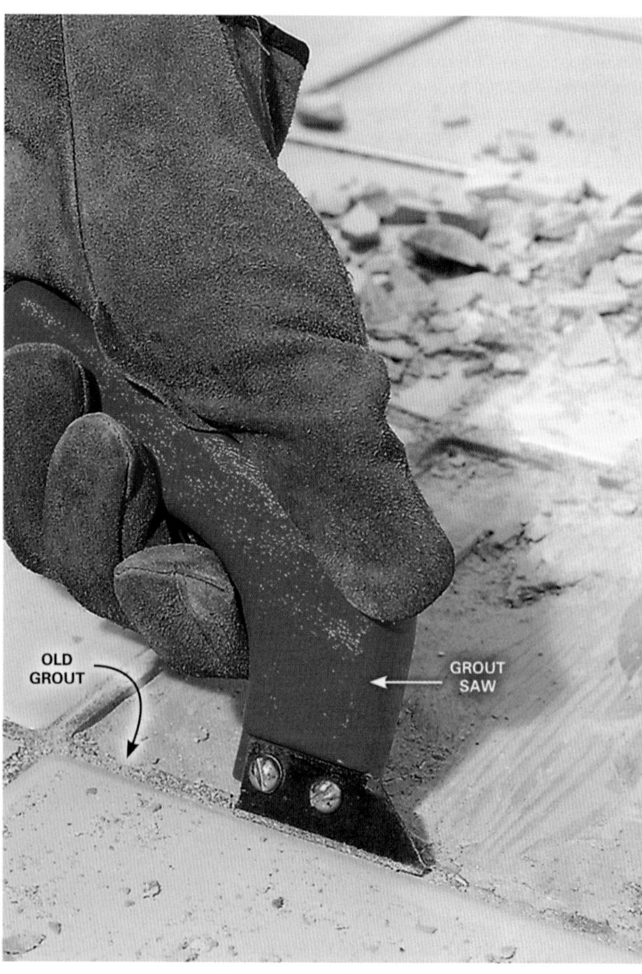

2 **Remove the old grout with a grout saw. Some of the grout can be chipped out with the chisel; however, you'll need to saw away all of the old grout to ensure a proper fit for the new tile.**

Always check the adhesive package for the required drying time before applying the new grout. If you rush the regrouting step and the tile shifts, you'll need to start over. Lastly, seal the grout with grout sealer, available from the tile dealer.

All of the specialized products, including the grout saw (Photo 2), grout float (Photo 6) and adhesive trowel are sold at tile stores.

3 **Scrape off the old adhesive with a cold chisel. Get rid of as much as possible so the new tile will adhere properly and lie flat. Scraping is the best way to remove old adhesive. Don't use a heat gun or solvent unless you want a big mess.**

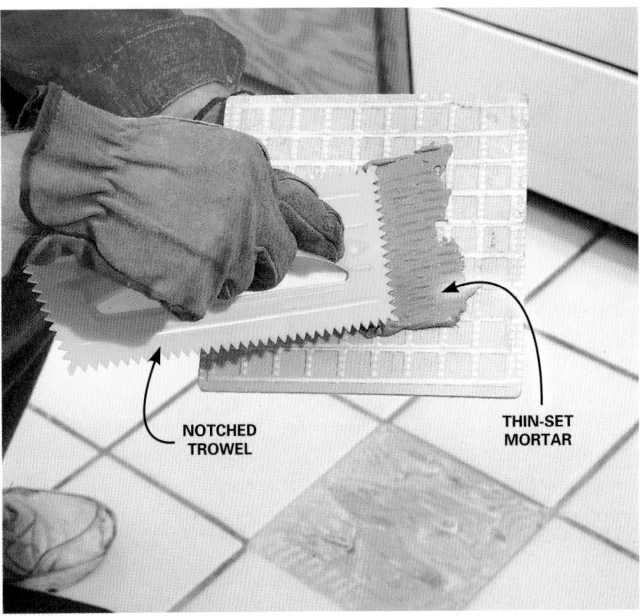

4 **Apply the adhesive (thin-set mortar for a floor tile) with a notched trowel on the back of the tile. Be sure to spread the adhesive out to the edges. Don't skimp on the adhesive: Too little will make the tile sit lower than the surrounding tiles. Any excess adhesive will ooze out and can be removed after the next step.**

5 **Place the tile, making sure that the grout lines are even with the adjacent tiles. To set the tile firmly into the adhesive, use a short length of wood and gently tap it with a hammer. If the tile is lower than the surrounding tiles, simply remove it, apply additional adhesive and then reset the tile. Scrape out any excess adhesive from between the tiles with a screwdriver. Once the tile is set, stay off it until the adhesive is dry, usually 24 hours.**

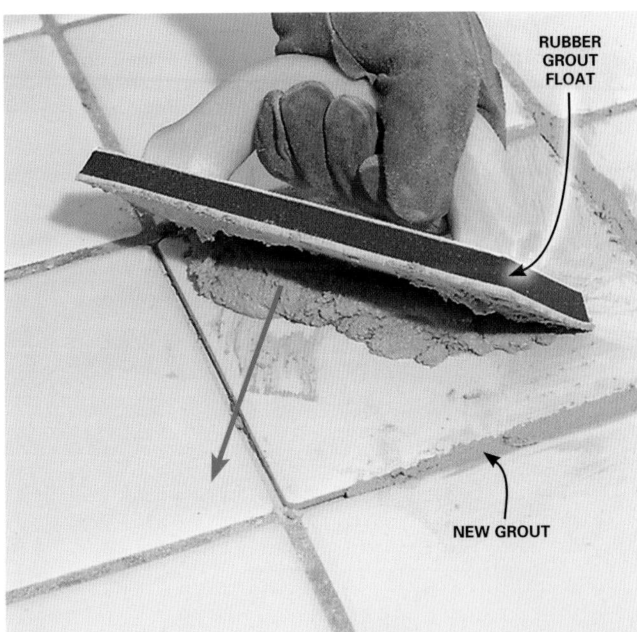

6 **Spread the grout using a rubber grout float. Hold the float at a 45-degree angle to the tile. Move the grout in both directions at an angle to the grout lines to make sure it fills the gaps between the tiles. Let the grout set for about 10 minutes and then wipe the area with a damp grout sponge. A grout sponge has rounded corners and is the best way to shape the grout lines. Once the grout has dried, usually overnight, wipe off any residue with a soft cloth.**

Replace a laminate floor plank

You can fix minor chips and scratches in a laminate floor with filler products from the home center. But if the damage is severe, you have to replace the plank (you did save a few from the installation, right?). It's a job you can do yourself in about two hours. In addition to a spare plank, you'll need a circular saw, hammer and chisel, router or table saw, drill and wood glue.

Some flooring experts recommend removing the base molding and unsnapping and numbering every plank until you get to the damaged portion. That works if the damaged plank is close to the wall. But trust us, if the damaged section is more than a few rows out from the wall, it's actually faster to just cut it out. If your laminate floor is glued together, the unsnapping routine won't work at all. See "Removing Glued Planks," p. 237.

Start by drawing a cutting line 1-1/2 in. in from all four edges of the plank. Drill a 3/8-in. relief hole at each corner of the cutting line and again 1/4 in. in from each corner of the plank.

Cut out the center section with a circular saw, cutting from hole to hole (Photo 1). Next, cut from the center section into each corner, stopping at the drilled hole (Photo 2). Finally, cut a relief cut from the center section out toward the seam of each plank. Tap a chisel into each relief cut to break out the uncut portion. Then remove all the cut pieces.

The new plank has a groove at one end and one side, as well

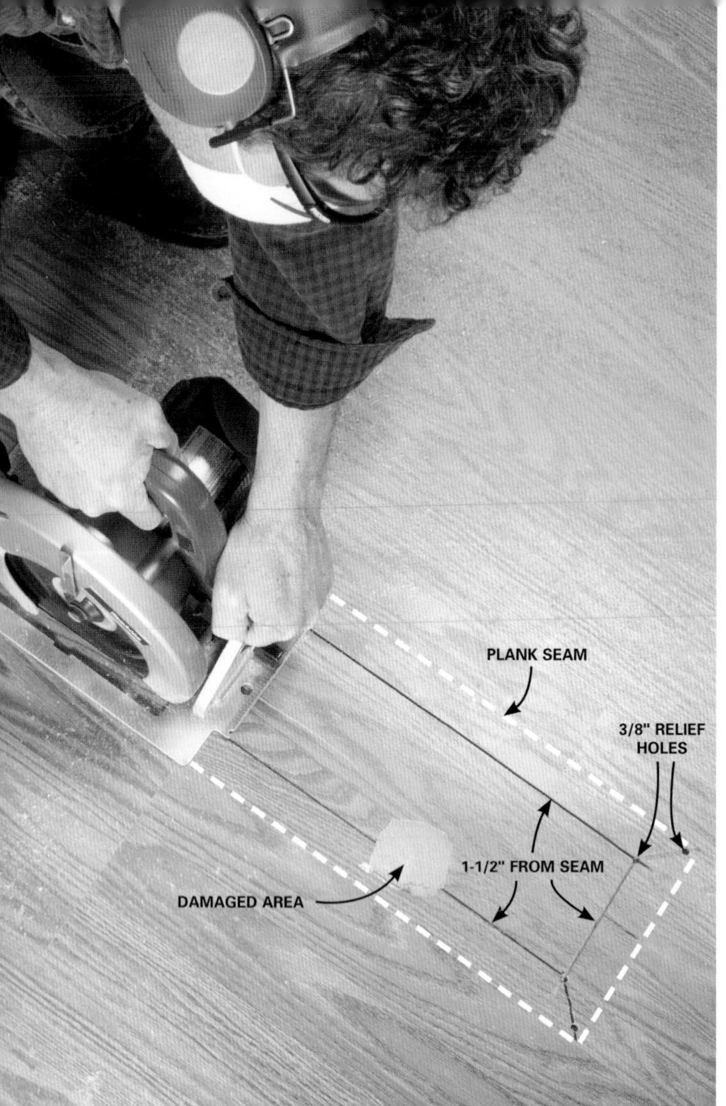

1 Remove the center section. Set the depth of your circular saw a tad deeper than the floor thickness. Then lift the blade guard and dip the blade into the cutting line.

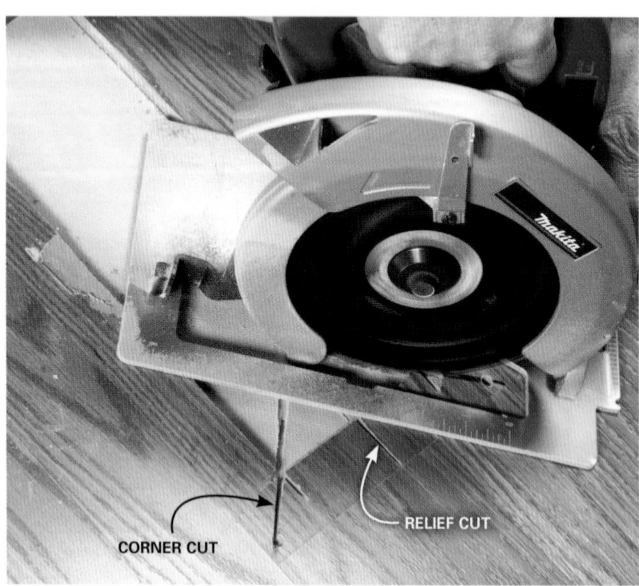

2 Cut to the corners. Cut from the center section to the drilled hole in each corner—but no farther! Break out the remainder with a chisel.

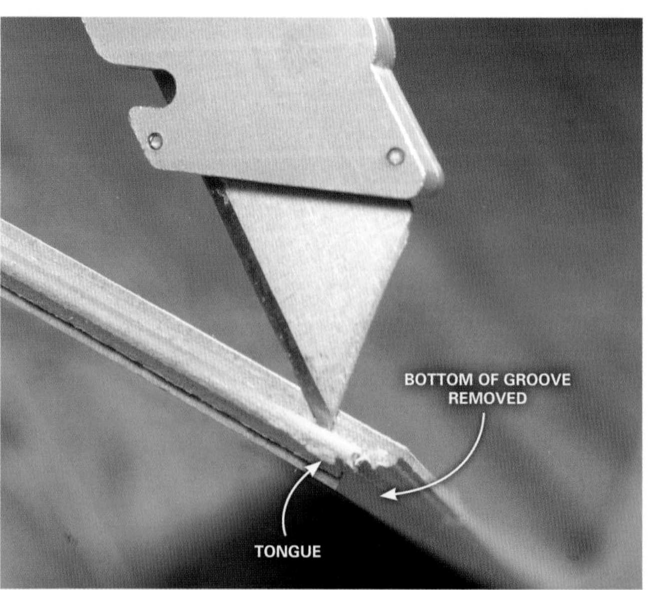

3 Remove the bottom lip. Score the tongue several times with a utility knife. Then snap it off with pliers. Shave off any remaining scraps with your knife.

pro tip

Removing glued planks

Most of the early laminate floors were fastened with glue. But that doesn't mean you can't do an "in-place" patch on those floors too. Follow all the cutting directions shown for a snap-together floor. Then use pliers to break the glue bond (Photo 1). Clean off the old glue (Photo 2) and lay in the new plank.

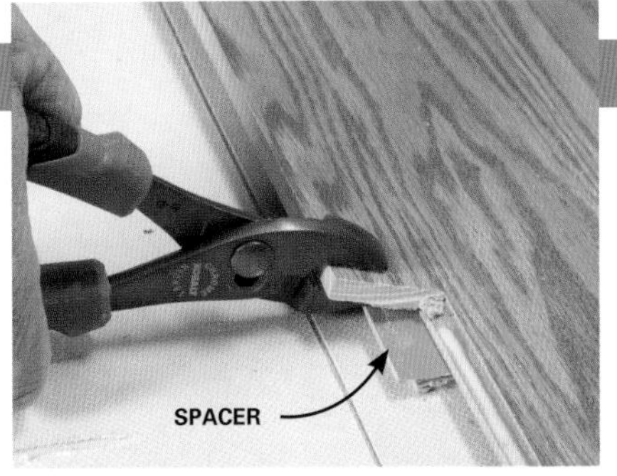

1 Raise the floor to gain leverage. Slip a dowel or scrap piece of flooring under the seam. Grab the section with pliers and tilt it down until the glued seam cracks apart. Then snap it upward to break any remaining glue.

2 The old glue has to go. Use a flat-blade screwdriver or small chisel to chip out the old glue. Get the surfaces as smooth as possible for a flush fit and a good glue bond.

as a tongue at the opposite end and side. But you can't install it until you cut off the bottom lip of both grooves and the side tongue. Use a utility knife to remove them (Photo 3). Here's a tip for cutting the groove. Stick the blade inside the groove and cut off the bottom from the inside (or use a table saw).

Apply a bead of wood glue to all four edges of the new plank. Insert the glued tongue of the new plank into the groove on the existing flooring and drop the plank into place. Wipe off any excess glue and load books on the plank until it's dry.

Stiffen a bouncy floor

Bridging, or "X-bracing," allows joists to share weight. As a footstep falls on one joist, some of the force is transferred to neighboring joists. Even if your joists already have a row of bridging at the center of the span, adding a row on each side of the existing bridging will stiffen the floor.

Begin by checking the original bridging. If any of it is loose, add some nails or screws to secure it. Add a row of new bridging at both of the one-third points of the span. If your joists span 12 ft., for example, place bridging 4 ft. and 8 ft. from the foundation wall. If there is no bridging in the center of the span, install a row there as well.

Metal bridging is available at home centers in lengths to fit between joists that are centered 16 in. or 24 in. apart.

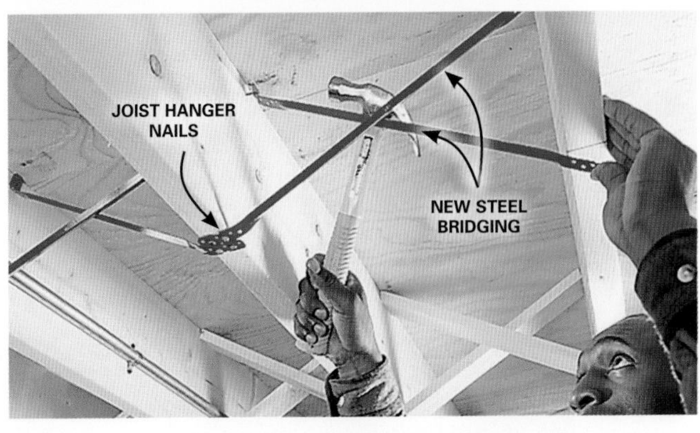

Fasten metal bridging with 1-3/8 in. joist hanger nails. Each piece of bridging requires four nails, two at each end.

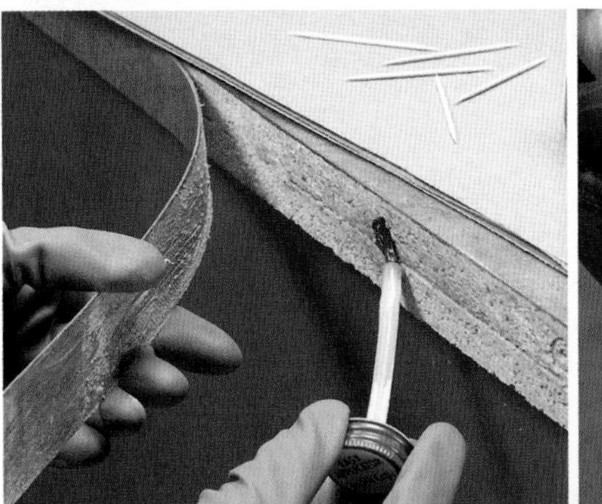

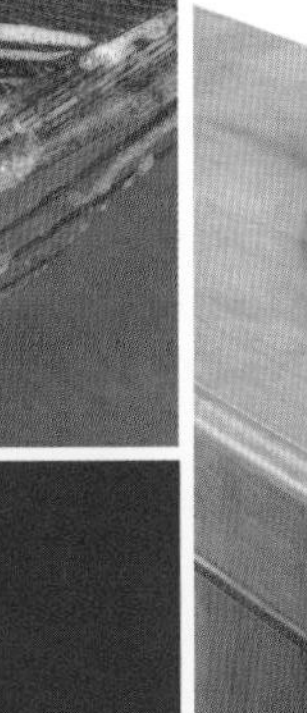

Chapter **nine**

FURNITURE & CABINETS

Refinish furniture without stripping

Stripping furniture is a messy, time-consuming process. And sometimes the results aren't as great as you had hoped. Fortunately, you don't always have to resort to stripping to restore your furniture to its original luster.

To show you an easier alternative, we enlisted Kevin Southwick, a furniture restoration specialist. We'll show you Kevin's tips for cleaning, repairing and restoring finishes without all the messy chemical strippers and tedious sanding. You'll save tons of time. And since you'll preserve the patina and character of the original finish, your furniture will retain the beauty of an antique. One word of caution, though: If you think your piece of furniture is a valuable antique, consult an expert before you do anything.

Assess the finish with mineral spirits

Before you start any repairs or touch-up, wipe on mineral spirits to help you decide what your next steps should be. The mineral spirits temporarily saturates the finish to reveal how the piece of furniture will look with nothing more than a coat of wipe-on clear finish. Don't worry; this won't harm the finish. If it looks good, all you have to do is clean the surface and apply an oil-based wipe-on finish. If the surface looks bad even when wetted with mineral spirits, you'll have to take other measures to restore the finish. We show some of these in the following steps.

Clean it up

A thorough cleaning is an important first step in any furniture renewal project. Removing decades of dirt and grime often restores much of the original luster. Kevin says it's hard to believe, but it's perfectly OK to wash furniture with soap and water.

Kevin recommends liquid Ivory dish soap mixed with water. Mix in the same proportion you would to wash dishes. Dip a sponge into the solution, wring it out, and use it to gently scrub the surface. A paintbrush works great for cleaning carvings and moldings. When you're done scrubbing with the soapy water, rinse the surface with a wrung-out sponge and clear water. Then dry it with a clean towel.

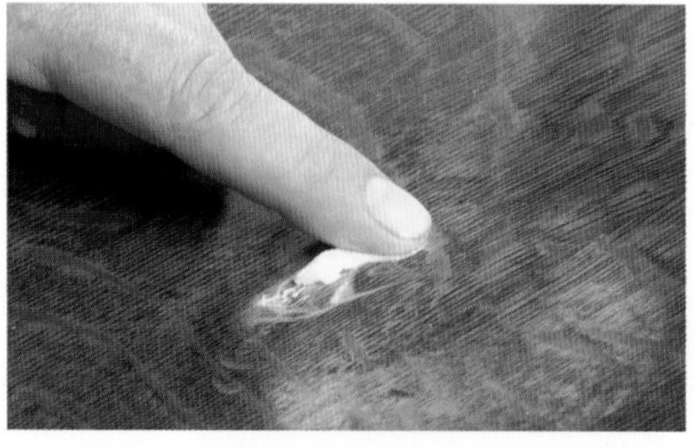

Fix white rings

White rings can be easy to get rid of, or they can be a real nightmare. First, slather the ring with petroleum jelly and let it sit overnight. The oil from the petroleum jelly will often penetrate the finish and remove the ring or at least make it less visible.

If that doesn't work, you can try a product such as Homax White Ring Remover or Liberon Ring Remover. They often work but may change the sheen. If these fixes don't work, consult a pro to see what your other options are.

Scrape paint without damaging the finish

Paint spatters are common on old furniture, and most of the time you can remove them easily without damaging the finish. Here's a trick we learned from Kevin to turn an ordinary straightedge razor into a delicate paint scraper. First, wrap a layer of masking tape around each end of the blade, and then bend the blade slightly so it's curved.

The masking tape holds the blade slightly off the surface so you can knock off paint spatters without the blade even touching the wood. Hold the blade perpendicular to the surface. The tape also keeps you from accidentally gouging the wood with the sharp corner of the blade. The curved blade allows you to adjust the depth of the scraper. If you tilt the blade a little, the curved center section will come closer to the surface to allow for removing really thin layers of paint.

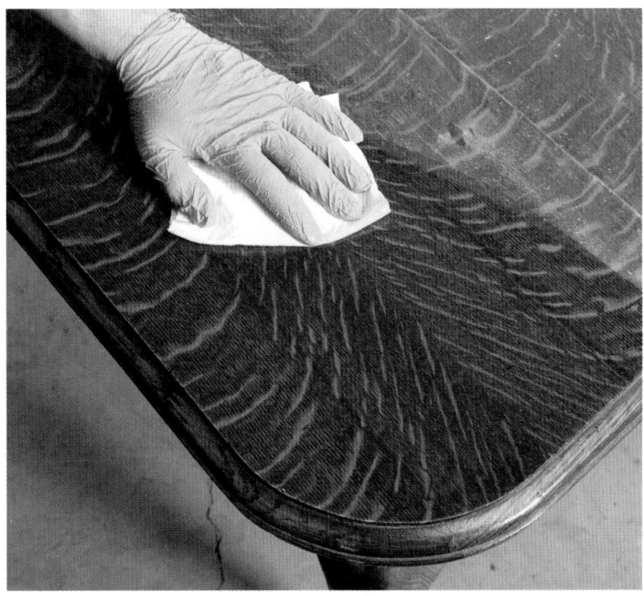

Renew the luster with wipe-on finish

The final step in your restoration project is to wipe on a coat of finish. After you clean your furniture piece and do any necessary repairs and stain touch-up, wiping on a coat of finish will restore the sheen and protect the surface. Any wipe-on finish will work—Minwax Wipe-on Poly is a common brand. But Kevin prefers a wipe-on gel finish like General Finishes Gel Topcoat Wipe On Urethane. It's thick, so it's easy to put on with a rag. One coat is usually all you need to rejuvenate an existing finish. To find a retail store near you that sells General Finishes Gel Topcoat, use the store locator at generalfinishes.com.

To apply wipe-on finish, first put some on a clean rag. Apply it in a swirling motion like you would with car wax. Then wipe off excess finish, going in the direction of the grain. Let the finish dry overnight and you'll be ready to proudly display your furniture restoration project.

Get rid of dents

You can often get rid of small dents by wetting them. The moisture swells the crushed wood fibers back to their original shape. (You can't fix cuts or gouges this way, though.)

Moisture must penetrate the wood for this to work. Finishes prevent water from penetrating, so Kevin suggests making a bunch of tiny slits with a razor blade to allow the water to penetrate. Use the corner of the blade, and keep the blade parallel to the grain direction. Next, fill the dent with water and wait until it dries. If the dent is less deep but still visible, you can repeat the process. As with most of the repairs we talk about here, the repaired surface may need a coat of wipe-on finish to look its best.

Replace missing wood with epoxy

If you discover missing veneer, chipped wood or a damaged molding, you can fix it easily with epoxy putty. Kevin showed us the process he uses, and the resulting repair is so realistic that it's hard to spot. When it's hardened, the epoxy is light colored and about the density of wood. You can shape, sand and stain it like wood too, so it blends right in. Quickwood and KwikWood are two brands of this Tootsie Roll–shaped epoxy. You'll find it at home centers and specialty woodworking stores.

To use this type of epoxy, you slice off a piece with a razor blade or utility knife and knead it in your gloved hand. When the two parts are completely blended to a consistent color and the epoxy putty starts to get sticky, it's ready to use. You'll have about five or 10 minutes to apply the epoxy to the repair before it starts to harden. That's why you should only slice off as much as you can use quickly.

1 FILL THE DAMAGE WITH EPOXY When the epoxy putty is thoroughly mixed, press it into the area to be repaired.

2 SMOOTH THE PUTTY Use your wetted finger to smooth the putty. Press the putty until it's level with the surrounding veneer.

3 ADD WOOD GRAIN On open grain wood like this oak, use a razor blade to add grain marks.

4 SAND THE EPOXY Sand carefully to avoid removing the surrounding finish. Make a detail sander by gluing sandpaper to a thin strip of wood.

Photo 1 shows how to replace missing veneer. Here are a few things you can do before the putty starts to harden to reduce the amount of sanding and shaping later. First, smooth and shape the epoxy with your finger (Photo 2). Wet it with water first to prevent the epoxy from sticking. Then use the edge of a straightedge razor to scrape the surface almost level with the surrounding veneer. If you're repairing wood with an open grain, like oak, add grain details by making little slices with a razor while the epoxy is soft (Photo 3).

After the epoxy hardens completely, which usually takes a few hours, you can sand and stain the repair. Kevin sticks self-adhesive sandpaper to tongue depressors or craft sticks to make precision sanding blocks (Photo 4) . You can also use spray adhesive or even plain wood glue to attach the sandpaper.

Blend the repair into the surrounding veneer by painting on gel stain to match the color and pattern of the existing grain. You could use stain touch-up markers, but Kevin prefers gel stain because it's thick enough to act like paint, and can be wiped off with a rag dampened in mineral spirits if you goof up or want to start over.

Choose two colors of stain that match the light and dark areas of the wood. Put a dab of both on a scrap of wood and create a range of colors by blending a bit of the two. Now you can use an artist's brush to create the grain (Photo 5). If the sheen of the patch doesn't match the rest of the wood when the stain dries, you can recoat the entire surface with wipe-on finish to even it out.

5 STAIN THE EPOXY TO MATCH Stain the patch with gel stain to match the color and pattern of the grain. Match the stain color to the light and dark areas of the wood.

Restore the color with gel stain

It's amazing what a coat of gel stain can do to restore a tired-looking piece of furniture. The cool part is that you don't need to strip the old finish for this to work. Kevin demonstrated the tip on this round oak table. The finish was worn and faded. He loaded a soft cloth with dark gel stain and worked it into the surface. Then he wiped if off with a clean cloth. It was a surprising transformation. Of course, gel stain won't eliminate dark water stains or cover bad defects, but it will hide fine scratches and color in areas where the finish has worn away.

There are other products, but Kevin prefers gel stain because he finds it easier to control the color and leave a thicker coat if necessary. Also, since it doesn't soak in quite as readily as thinner stains, gel stain is somewhat reversible. Before it dries, you can remove it with mineral spirits if you don't like the results. Gel stains offer some protection, but for a more durable finish or to even out the sheen, let the stain dry overnight and then apply a coat of wipe-on finish as shown on p. 240.

Fill small cracks

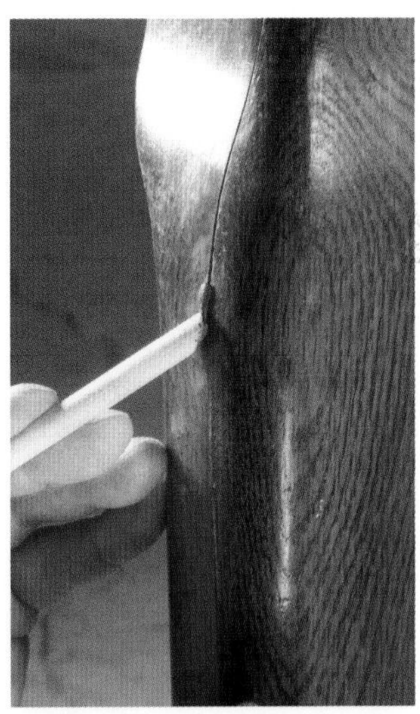

If you find nail holes or tiny cracks after applying the final finish, fill them with colored wax fill sticks, wax repair sticks or fill pencils, found at home centers and paint stores.

The directions tell you to rub the stick over the defect. But Kevin recommends breaking off a chunk and warming it up in your hands. Then shape it to fit the flaw and press it in with a smooth tool. He uses a 3/8-in. dowel with an angle on the end. For cracks, make a thin wafer, slide it into the crack and then work the wax in both directions to fill the crack. Buff with a soft cloth.

instant fix

Fix a wobbly chair

Do you have a chair with wobbly legs that rocks and rolls when you sit on it? Tighten those loose joints quickly and easily with a glue such as Wonderlok 'Em. This special glue fills gaps and forms a strong bond that'll tighten the joint. It's available at home centers and hardware stores.

Standard white and yellow glues rely on tight wood contact for a strong bond. They're not good for filling gaps, which are typical in most loose chair joints. Scrape off as much white or yellow glue as you can with the pointed end of a can opener.

This glue dries fast. Even when filling a gap, it may only take a few minutes for the glue to dry, so work quickly. If you have to fill multiple or large gaps, wrap the chair joints tightly with an old bike tire, tie-down strap or rope. Otherwise, simply hold the joint tight with downward pressure for about a minute after applying the glue.

The glue provides a virtually permanent bond in the wood joint, but it will decrease the value of fine antique pieces. Call a professional for proper antique restoration.

Attach the applicator tip to the glue bottle, stick it into the loose joint and sparingly fill the joint. Hold the joint tight for about one minute. Clean up any glue spills with nail polish remover.

Clamp irregular objects

Save those old bicycle tubes! They can be used as clamps for regluing chair legs or other irregular objects. Cut the tube on each side of the valve stem. Knot one end around a chair leg, tightly wrap the tube around the legs, and secure it with a hand clamp. The rubber can be stretched around any unusually shaped object to hold it tight until the glue dries.

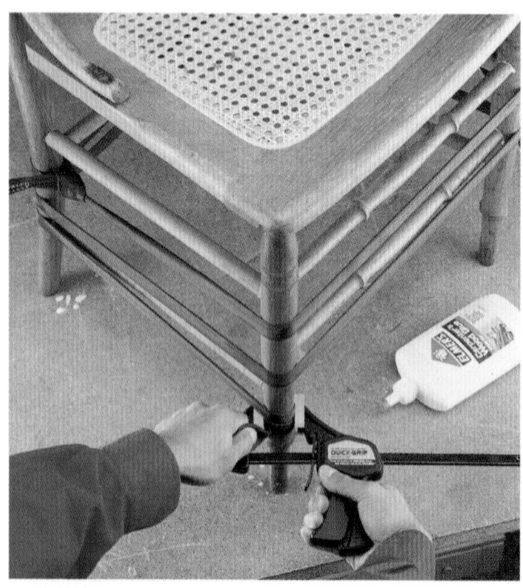

Tighten a worn joint

Some joints are just too damaged to allow for a tight glue joint, especially when repairing areas that have broken several times. One way to save the chair is to use 24-hour epoxy as both a filler and a bonding agent. Keep the joint upside down so the epoxy doesn't run out. Scrape off excess epoxy while it's still soft.

Clean the old glue from the mortise and tenon. Then fill the mortise about halfway with epoxy. Set chair leg (tenon) into mortise, align and clamp.

pro tip

If you miss a nail, you'll probably split a rung when you knock the chair apart. Don't worry. This "disaster" is easily repaired. The damage is more cosmetic than structural. Pull the nail with locking pliers and then finish disassembling the chair. Save all wood chips for regluing and clamping later, at reassembly.

Renew a wood finish in 30 minutes

If you have wood furniture that's looking dull, revive the shine with paste wax. Wax is a more durable coating than liquid furniture polish and it won't attract dust, as many polishes do. Wax will fill and hide very fine scratches, but it won't hide dents or deeper scratches.

Wax is available in several colors. Most home centers and hardware stores carry only light-colored wax, which is fine for most finishes. But don't use light wax on dark finishes that have recesses in the grain. Yellowish wax that fills the tiny crevices in the surface will look bad. (This won't happen on glossy, solid dark finishes.) You can also use dark wax to deepen the color of a finish.

Clean the wood with mineral spirits to remove grime as well as residue left by furniture polishes (Photo 1). When the mineral spirits dries, buff off any residue with a dry cloth. Then cut a rag from an old cotton T-shirt and wrap it around a walnut-sized ball of wax. As you rub with the ball, wax will ooze through the rag (Photo 2). Apply only enough wax to form a thin gloss—a heavy coat just leaves you with more wax to buff off later. If you haven't used wax before and you're working on a large piece of furniture, wax and then buff small areas no more than 3 x 3 ft.

Don't wait for the wax to dry completely and form a haze the way you would with car wax. Fully dried furniture wax is very hard to buff smooth. Wait only until the wax partially dries and begins to look dull (typically 15 to 30 minutes). Then rub the surface with a cotton cloth to remove the excess wax. The rag should glide smoothly over the wax with only a little elbow grease. If you've waited too long and can't rub out the swirls of wax, simply apply more wax, then wait and wipe again (solvent in the second coat of wax will soften the first coat).

A wax finish doesn't require any special care; simply dust with a dry or damp cloth. A wax coating will last months or even years depending on how heavily the furniture is used. When the finish again looks worn, scuffed or dirty, just clean and rewax. Don't worry about wax buildup. Each new wax job dissolves and removes much of the previous coat.

1 Clean the wood using a soft cloth dampened with mineral spirits. Open windows for ventilation.

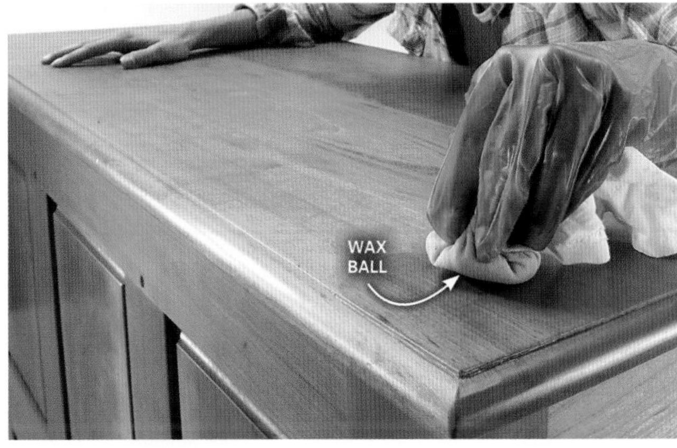

2 Wrap a ball of wax in a cloth and apply a thin, even coat of wax. Rub on the wax in a circular pattern.

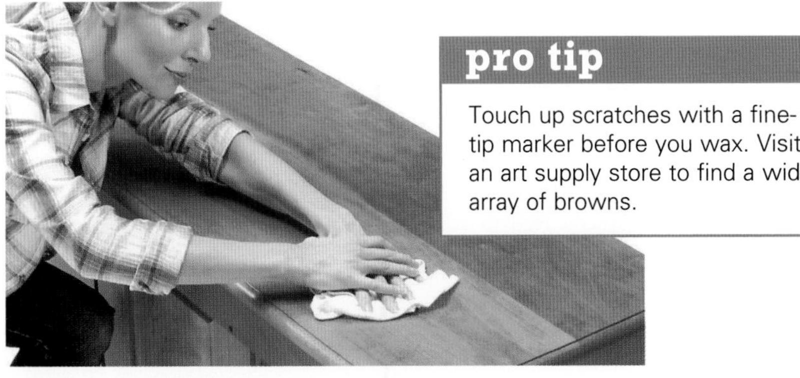

3 Wipe off the excess wax with a soft cloth. Turn and refold the cloth frequently to expose clean cloth.

pro tip

Touch up scratches with a fine-tip marker before you wax. Visit an art supply store to find a wide array of browns.

Reglue loose laminate

End caps and other laminate edges sometimes come loose and can get broken off if not reglued, but as long as the particleboard backer is in good condition, the fix is simple.

Scrape off chunks of debris or dried lumps of glue from the end cap. If the countertop is newer, first try to iron the end cap back on with a medium-hot iron to reactivate the glue. However, in most cases the loose piece will need to be reattached with contact cement.

Sand rough areas with medium-grit sandpaper, then apply the contact cement (Photo 1). Open nearby windows to dissipate the fumes from the glue. After both sides are completely coated, keep them separated with a toothpick (Photo 2) until the adhesive is tacky. Carefully rejoin the two sides, starting at the back of the glued area (Photo 3). Contact cement bonds instantly, and if the wrong areas accidentally touch, you'll have great difficulty pulling them apart.

Finally, rub away any dried glue around the edges with your finger.

1 Spread contact cement on with the applicator or a disposable natural-bristle brush, covering all edges.

2 Keep the two sides separate until the glue is dry but still a little tacky—usually in about 20 minutes.

3 Align and then push the laminate edge back against the particleboard, applying pressure with a smooth block of wood for a good bond.

Fix sagging shelves

Stocked up on canned goods, did you? Now the shelves are sagging and you're looking for a quick fix. If your cabinet has a center stile, check the back of the stile and the back of the cabinet to see if the manufacturer drilled shelf bracket holes to support the center (Figure A). They're hard to spot and often ignored by whoever installed the cabinets.

If you find predrilled holes, just buy some brackets at the hardware store and install them. That'll support the center of the shelf. If there are no holes, you have two choices: You can drill holes or you can make a "bridge" (Figures B and C).

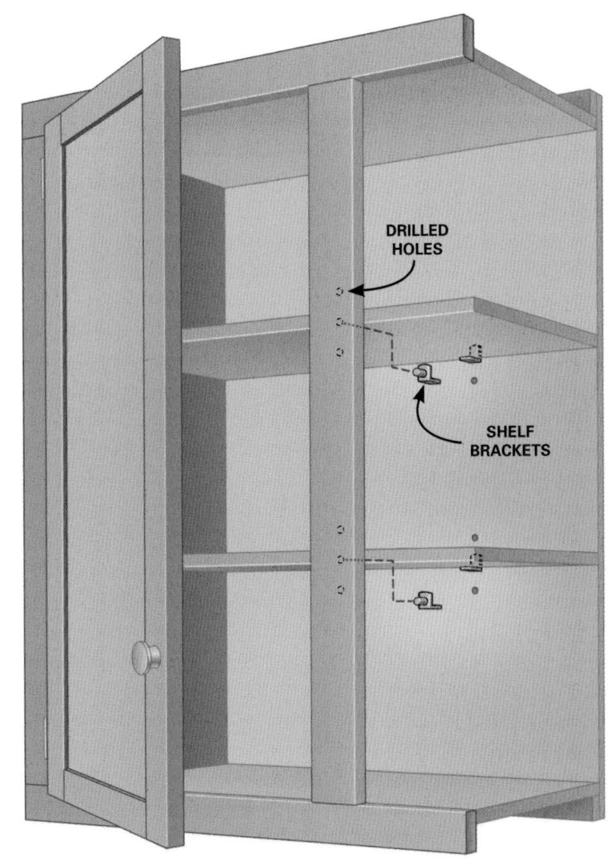

Figure A
Install brackets in predrilled holes or drill your own with a right-angle drill.

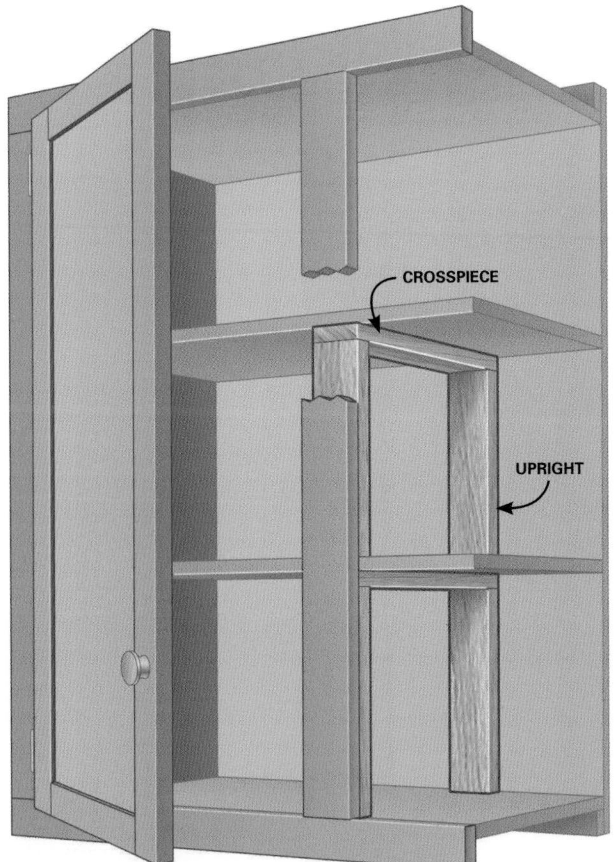

Figure B
For cabinets with a center stile, build 1x2 bridges. Nail the crosspiece on top of the uprights. Then slide the bridge into place under the shelf.

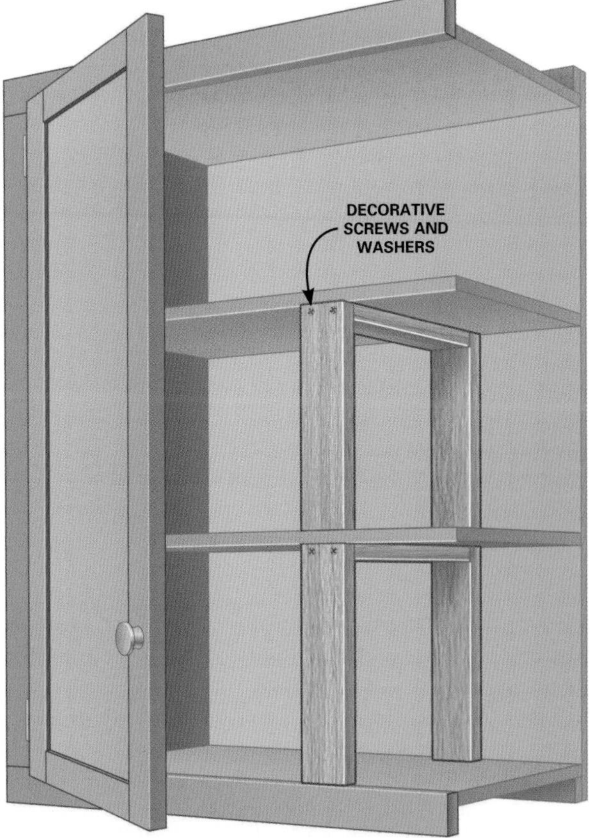

Figure C
For cabinets with no center stile, position the crosspiece between the two uprights. Secure with decorative screws and washers.

Instant cabinet fixes

Some cabinet fixes are tough, even for pros. But the most common problems are easy-peasy lemon squeezy, as the kindergartners like to say. Hit the hardware store in the morning to pick up supplies, then come home, get to work and you'll be done in time to feed your crew.

These fixes won't help with major problems like split panels on doors, but they will solve the little problems that bug you daily. Your cabinets will look and operate better—and sometimes a little satisfaction goes a long way.

1 Build a shelf that won't sag

Don't bother replacing a sagging shelf with another 1/2-in.-thick shelf or it'll end up sagging too. Instead, cut a new shelf from 3/4-in. plywood. Make it the same length and 1-1/2 in. narrower (so you can add rails). Then glue and brad nail (or clamp) 1x2 rails along the front and back of the shelf, flush with the ends. The rails give the shelf additional support so it won't sag, even if you load it up with heavy cookware. Apply a polyurethane (or other) finish to match your other shelves.

3/4" PLYWOOD

1x2 LUMBER

2 Replace worn-out drawer slides

Lubricants won't fix damaged drawer slides. They have to be replaced. This is a common problem on silverware drawers and other drawers that carry a lot of weight. Buy new slides that are the same, or nearly the same, as your old ones. Then it's just a matter of swapping them out. You'll find a limited selection of drawer slides at home centers, but there are dozens of online sources.

3 Fill in stripped screw holes

When the screws in your hinges or drawer slides turn but don't tighten, the screw hole is stripped. That can prevent doors and drawers from closing properly. Fix the problem with glue and toothpicks. Start by removing the hardware. Then apply a drop of wood glue to the ends of toothpicks and cram as many as will fit into the hole (maybe only two or three). Wipe away any glue that drips out. Let the glue dry, then use a utility knife to cut the toothpicks flush with the cabinet or drawer. Reinstall the hardware, driving the screw through the filled hole.

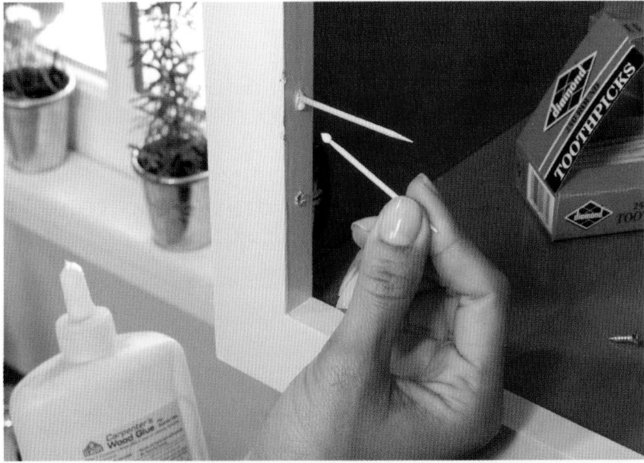

4 Adjust Euro hinges

Adjusting cabinet doors with European hinges is as easy as turning a screw or two. Hinges like this one adjust in three directions; others adjust in two. If your door is crooked—not square with the cabinet—fix that first, then raise or lower it to the same height as adjacent doors.

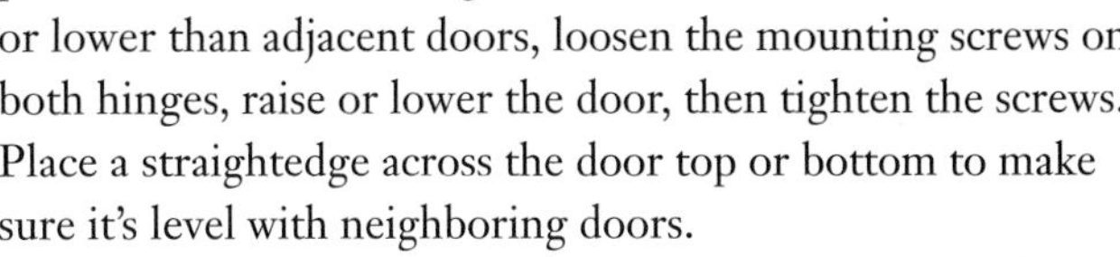

For crooked doors, adjust the side screw on one hinge, which moves the door from side to side. It's a trial-and-error process. Make a small adjustment, then close the door to check its position. If the door is higher or lower than adjacent doors, loosen the mounting screws on both hinges, raise or lower the door, then tighten the screws. Place a straightedge across the door top or bottom to make sure it's level with neighboring doors.

If the door sticks out too far from the cabinet or the hinge side brushes against the cabinet when you open the door, adjust the depth screw. Some hinges move the door as you turn the depth screw; others require you to tap the door in or out and then tighten the screw.

Door adjustments aren't as easy if you have traditional hinges. If your doors are sagging, first try tightening the screws. If the hinges are bent, replace them if you can find a match.

5 Silence banging doors with bumpers

Doors and drawers slam loudly when wood smacks against wood. That's why most have "bumpers" near the interior corners to cushion the impact and reduce the noise. But the bumpers sometimes fall off (or kids pick them off). Get new ones at home centers or online Peel off the backing and stick the bumpers in place. They're available clear or with felt, and in different thicknesses. Use bumpers the same thickness as those on adjacent doors.

BUMPER

6 Repair busted drawers

Some drawers are held together by only a few drops of glue or short brad nails. When you first notice a drawer corner coming apart, take out the drawer and fix it. And if one corner is failing, others probably will too. Save yourself future hassles by repairing all the weak corners now. Place a piece of scrap wood against a corner and lightly rap it once with a hammer. If the corner comes apart, fix it. If not, it should hold up.

To fix the corner, first remove the drawer front, if possible. Most fronts are attached by screws driven from inside the drawer. Remove any fasteners from the corner, then scrape away the old glue with a utility knife. Reglue the corner, tap the sides back together and clamp the drawer until the glue dries.

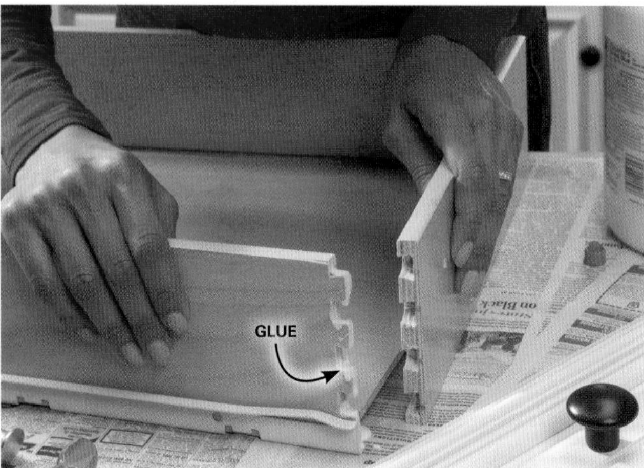

8 Glue loose knobs

Once knobs fall off your cabinets, twisting them back on won't solve the problem. They'll just keep coming loose. Use a dab of thread adhesive to keep them in place. Apply the adhesive to the screw, then attach the knob. If you decide to replace the knob later, don't worry. You can remove it with a screwdriver.

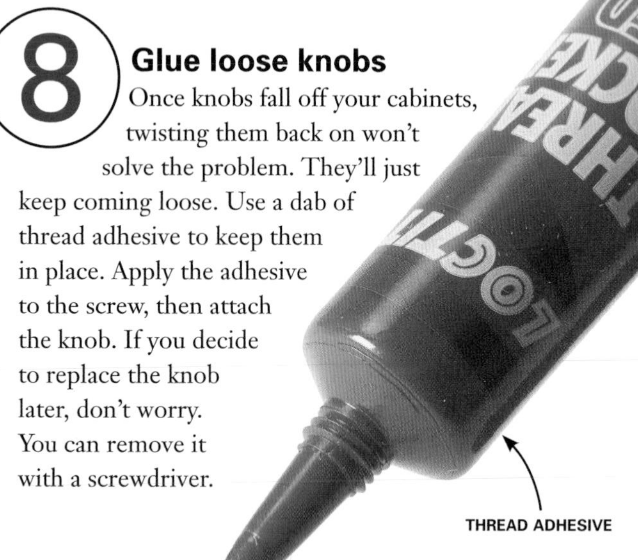

7 Renew the shine

Grease splatters and smoke can leave a film on your cabinets, dulling the finish. Wash the cabinets with a wood cleaner to bring back the luster.

Use a sponge to rub the cleaner onto the cabinets. Cleaners like Murphy's don't need to be rinsed off, which cuts your cleaning time. For stubborn grease spots, scrub lightly with the cleaner using a No. 0000 steel wool pad. Cleaning the cabinets once a year keeps them shiny and protects the finish.

9 Beef up a wimpy drawer bottom

The thin plywood used for drawer bottoms sometimes gets wavy. Stiffen up the bottoms with 1/4-in. or 3/8-in. plywood. Cut the plywood to fit over the drawer bottom, leaving about a 1/4-in. gap on each side. Apply wood glue on the drawer bottom and set the plywood over it. Set a gallon or two of paint over the plywood to hold it in place until the glue dries.

10 Add back plates to cover worn areas

Years of opening doors and drawers can wear away the finish near cabinet knobs. Instead of undertaking the time-consuming task of refinishing the cabinets, try this quick fix: Install back plates under the knobs or handles. Simply unscrew the knob or handle, slide the back plate under it, then reattach the knob or handle. Back plates are available in a wide range of styles. You can special-order them at home centers or buy them online.

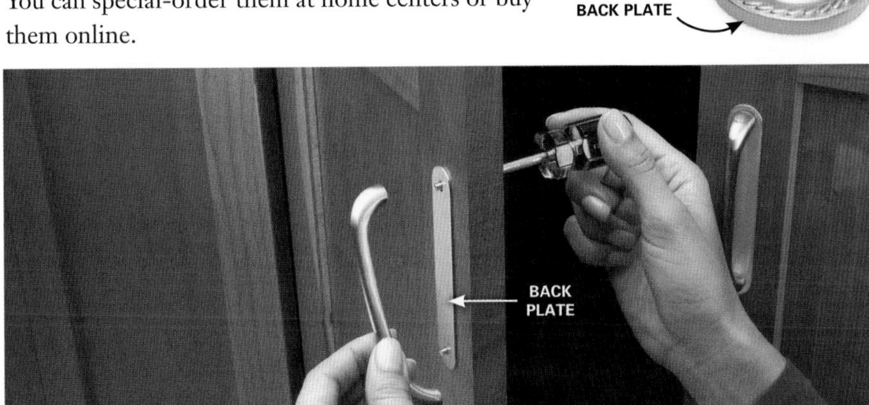

11 Fill in scratches

Use a wood fill stick to make scratches less visible. The stick fills in and colors over the scratch. Soften the stick with a hair dryer to make the application easier. Then run the stick over the scratch and wipe away any excess with a cloth. The fill probably won't be an exact match with the surrounding cabinet, but it'll be close. The sticks work on shallow and deep scratches. They're available at home centers and online.

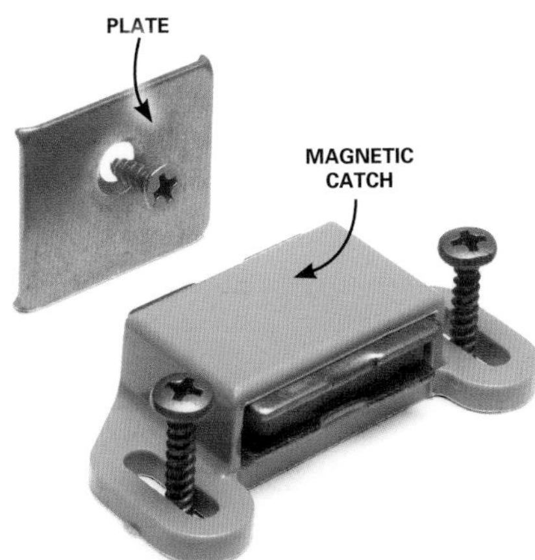

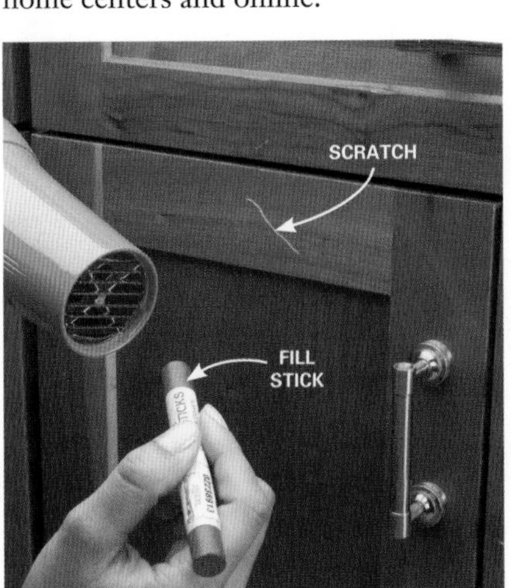

12 Pull doors shut with magnets

This trick is an oldie, but it still works. When your cabinet door is warped and won't fully close, simply install a magnetic catch at the problem area. Screw the magnetic catch to the cabinet rail or stile and the plate to the door. The magnet pulls the door closed.

13 Replace bad latches

Older cabinets sometimes have "roller catches" that hold the doors closed. If you have these and your door won't close or stay closed, loosen the screws to slide the catch forward or backward on the cabinet frame. Or replace it if it's broken. The catches are available at home centers.

14 Lubricate sticking drawers

The fix for sticking drawers is easy. First remove the drawer. Wipe the drawer slides and the cabinet track with a clean cloth to remove any debris. Then spray a dry lubricant directly on the drawer slides. It'll say "dry lubricant" on the label. Replace the drawer and slide it in and out of the cabinet several times until it glides easily. If the drawer is still hard to open, replace the drawer slides.

Dry lubricants won't leave an oily residue that attracts dirt and dust. The lubricants also work great on squeaky hinges.

Re-cover a chair seat

If you have upholstered chair seats that are stained, worn out or just plain ugly, there's no need to call a pro. You can do a first-class upholstery job yourself, even if you have zero experience. Don't worry about making mistakes; you can correct them by prying out staples and starting over.

If the chair is fairly new, you can simply cover the existing fabric with new material. But it usually makes sense to tear off the old fabric and replace the foam padding, since most foam has a life span of only five to 10 years. Many fabric stores carry foam and upholstery fabric, but for the best selection and advice, start with an upholstery store. You'll also need a can of spray adhesive, scissors, a stapler and 5/16-in. staples.

Turn the chair upside down and remove the screws that fasten the seat to the chair frame. Then tear off the old fabric with pliers and pry out the staples with a small screwdriver. If the seat is made from particleboard, you might find that it's warped, crumbling or even broken. Making a new seat is easy: Just lay the old seat on a piece of 1/2-in. plywood, trace around it and cut a new seat with a jigsaw.

Cut the foam to size with scissors. Take the wood seat outside and give the top side a light coat of spray adhesive. Position the seat carefully when you set it on the foam; the adhesive grabs instantly and you may not be able to pull it off. Cut the batting and fabric (Photo 1). Stretch the batting slightly as you staple it into place (Photo 2). Staple the fabric at the middle of all four sides and flip the seat over to make sure the pattern is centered. Tug the fabric toward the

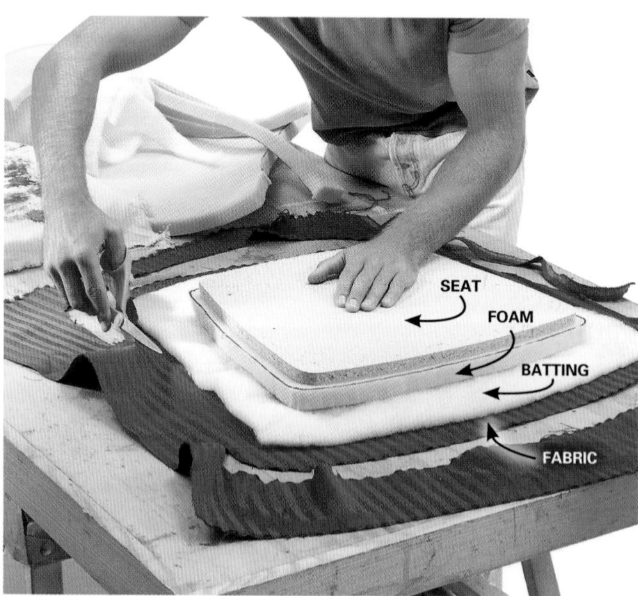

1 **Cut the foam about 1/2 in. larger than the wood seat. Cut the batting at least 2 in. larger and the fabric at least 3 in. larger.**

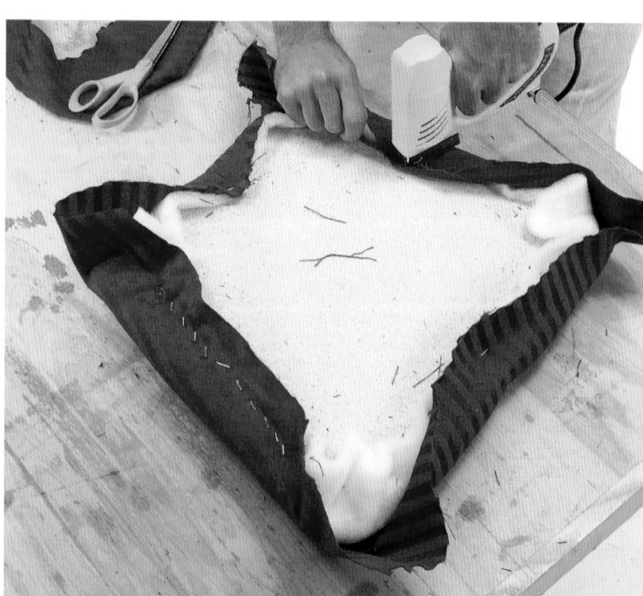

2 **Staple the fabric at the middle of each side and work toward the corners, stretching the fabric as you go. Stop about 2 in. from corners and leave the corners for last.**

3 **Create gathers in the fabric to form a smooth curve around curved corners. Work toward the corner from alternating sides. Then pull back the "ear" of fabric and staple it.**

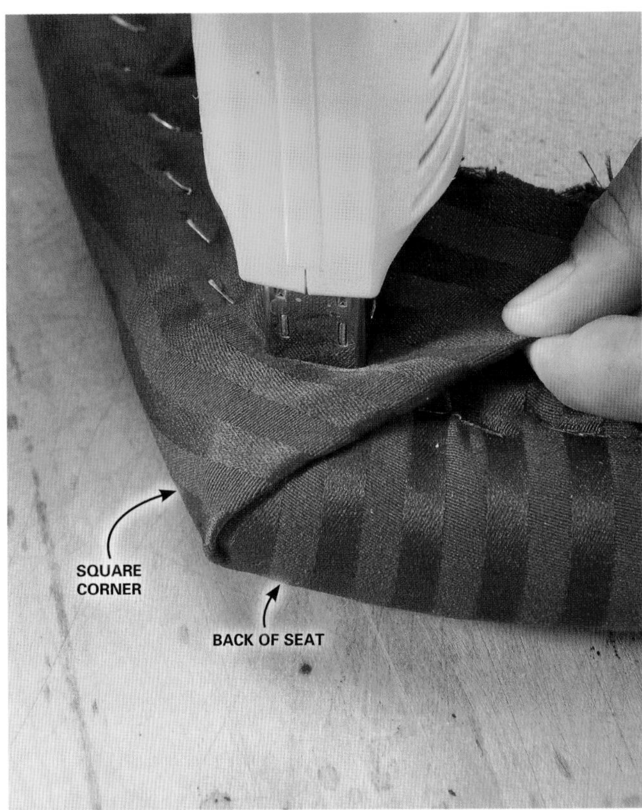

4 **Fold fabric around square corners. If your seat has square corners toward the rear, fold the fabric against the back edge of the seat, where the crease will be hidden by the chair's back.**

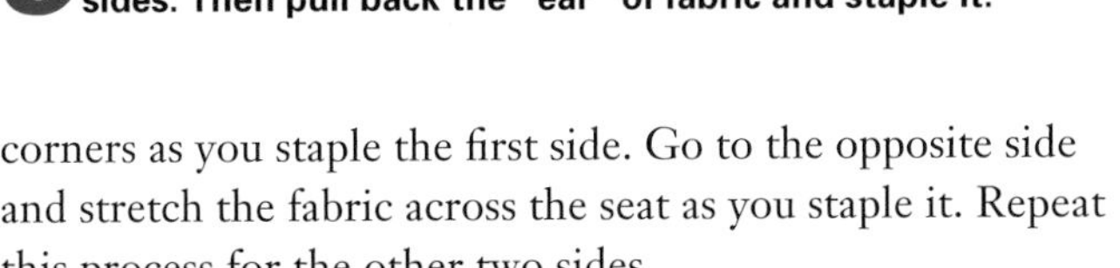

corners as you staple the first side. Go to the opposite side and stretch the fabric across the seat as you staple it. Repeat this process for the other two sides.

If your seat has rounded corners, you can wrap them so that no folds or creases are visible from above (Photo 3). If the seat has square corners, crease and fold the fabric as you would when you gift-wrap a box (Photo 4). It's usually helpful to trim away excess fabric as you work on corners.

pro tip

Before you screw the seat onto the chair, consider treating the fabric with a stain repellent if it wasn't treated at the factory.

Clean a yucky pullout cutting board

If you love the convenience of your pullout wooden cutting board but don't use it because it's stained and grungy, try this chef-approved, two-step process. Simply scour the board with a lemon and a pile of kosher salt, then apply mineral oil. The coarse kosher salt is an excellent abrasive, and the citric acid kills bacteria. When the stains are gone, rinse the board and let it dry. Mineral oil helps prevent the wood from absorbing stains.

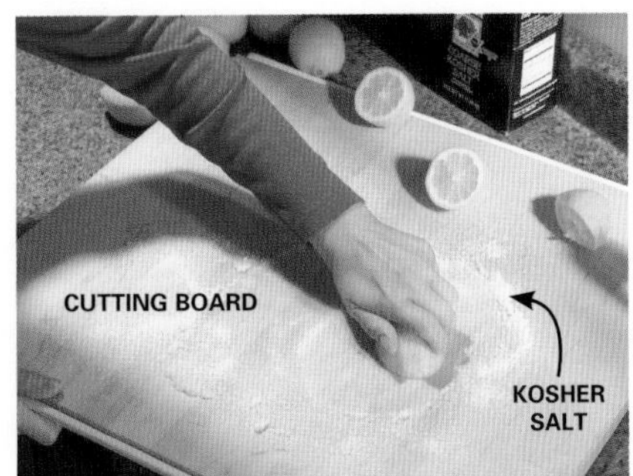

1 **Scour the cutting board with a lemon and kosher salt until the board is clean.**

2 **Apply mineral oil to the board and wipe off the excess. After a few hours, apply a second coat.**

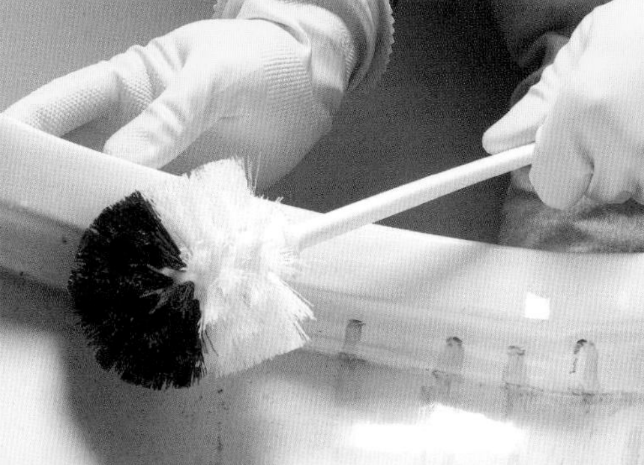

Chapter **ten**

SOLUTIONS FOR TOUGH CLEANING JOBS

Remove oil stains from concrete

You can't scrub oil and grease stains away. The trick is to draw them up out of the concrete. To do this, mix trisodium phosphate (or a TSP substitute) with water and an absorbent material to make a smooth paste. (See "Buying Absorbent Materials"). The cleaner slowly soaks into the concrete and breaks up the old oil, and the absorbent material captures it. Once the paste dries, the cleaning action stops, and you can scrape and sweep it away (Photo 3). Either throw it away or renew it with more TSP and water and reapply it for deeper cleaning. Use a nylon brush for cleanup (Photo 4). A wire brush may leave steel particles, which can cause rust stains.

pro tip

Patience is the key. Old, long-neglected stains may require two or three applications for complete removal.

ABSORBENT MATERIAL

TSP

OIL STAIN

1 **Pour 1 oz. trisodium phosphate (or TSP substitute) and a cup of water into a small bucket and mix. Add about a cup of absorbent material and mix to make a creamy paste. Wear eye protection and rubber gloves.**

PASTE

2 **Spread a 3/8-in. thick layer of the paste over the stain. Allow the paste to dry for about 24 hours.**

3 **Scrape and brush off the powdery residue and either reuse it or dump it in your trash.**

4 **Scrub the area with water and a nylon brush. Rinse with a garden hose.**

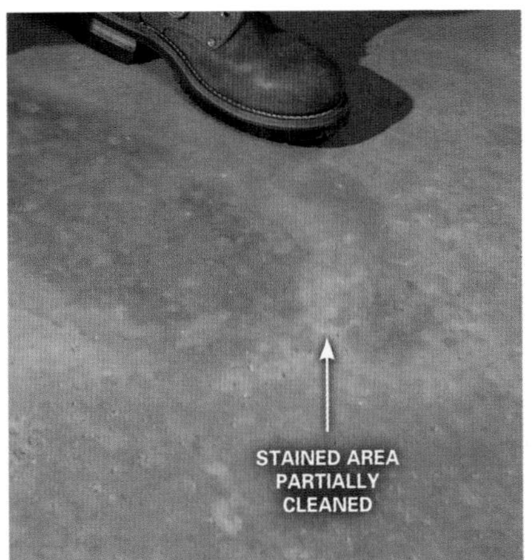

5 Compare the stained area with the surrounding concrete. Repeat the process a second (and perhaps third) time to fully remove the stain.

Buying absorbent materials

You have a variety of options for absorbent materials. For small stains, simply use baby powder or powdered talc. For larger stains, you'll need a bulk material. One good choice is diatomaceous earth, sold as a filtering agent for swimming pools. It's available from most pool supply stores.

Cat litter is also a good absorbent; however, it's too coarse to make a good paste unless you crush it into a powder. The same goes for the absorbent materials that are designed to soak up oil spills.

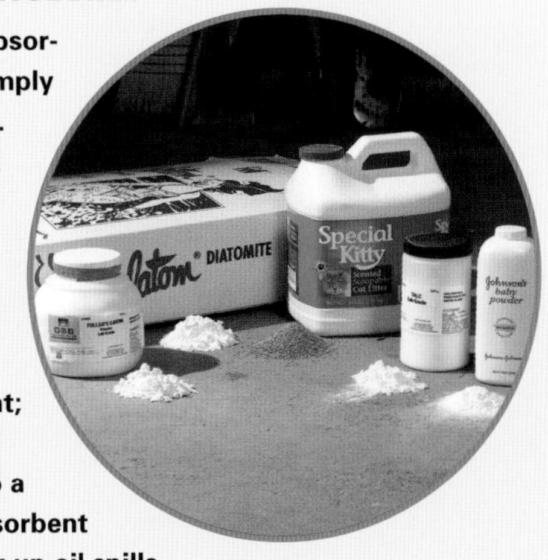

Remove paint stains from concrete

Cleaning old paint from concrete is similar to stripping paint from wood. Buy the same types of paint strippers. If you're working outdoors or in a detached garage (with the door open) and want fast results, you can use a methylene chloride–type stripper. The active ingredient will be listed on the can. Caution: Methylene chloride can be hazardous. Use only in a well-ventilated area. And wear a respirator equipped with a fresh organic vapor cartridge (Photo 1).

If you use a safer, slow-acting stripper, expect to wait several hours for it to work.

Mix absorbent material into the stripper (Photo 1). Thick strippers won't need much. You can add more paint stripper to the paste after you apply it to keep it actively working on stubborn paint. Scraping with a hard plastic scraper may also help. But let the stripper do most of the work. After scraping, let paint residue dry and toss it into the trash.

pro tip

If the stripper dries before it can soften the paint, apply more stripper and cover it with plastic.

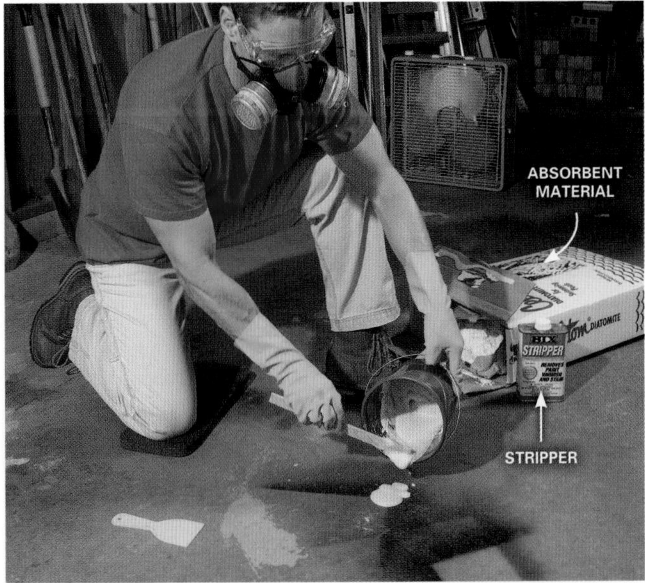

1 Add paint stripper to an absorbent material to make a creamy paste. Spread a 1/4- to 1/2-in. layer of paste over the paint stain. Then wait 10 to 20 minutes while the stripper loosens the paint stain.

2 Scrape off the paste and loosened paint with a plastic scraper. Spread a second application if necessary.

3 **Scrub area with a nylon brush, scouring powder and water to remove softened paint particles still stuck in the rough concrete.**

4 **Rinse with plenty of water. Continue scrubbing with a nylon brush to finish cleaning.**

Remove rust stains from concrete

1 **Add 1/4 cup of muriatic acid to 2 cups of water in a large, shallow plastic pan. Always pour acid into water, never water into acid. Mask nearby materials with plastic covering to protect them from splashes.**

Rust is really tough to get out, because no simple solvent will dissolve it. One effective way to remove rust from concrete is to dissolve the surface layer of concrete using a mild muriatic acid solution. (Muriatic acid is available at home centers and hardware stores.)

The acid dissolves the cement in the surface layer of concrete. You want to minimize this etching process, so start with a light application and observe the results. You'll see the solution begin bubbling almost immediately (Photo 2).

After the bubbling stops, scrub lightly with a long-handled nylon brush to see if the rust disappears.

Once the entire area is clean, thoroughly rinse it with lots of water to dilute any remaining acid and remove all traces of residue (Photo 3). Direct the rinse water away from your lawn or plants.

2 **Rinse with plenty of water. Continue scrubbing with a nylon brush to finish cleaning.**

3 **Rinse and scrub the area thoroughly, using plenty of fresh water to flush away all traces of residue.**

4 **Acid treatment leaves the surface of the concrete slightly rougher, like fine sandpaper. Once it's dry, seal your floor to reduce future staining.**

After cleaning with acid, play it safe. Thoroughly rinse your protective gear, wash your clothing and take a shower to make sure all traces are washed away.

Since each acid cleaning erodes the concrete surface, it's far better for your garage floor if you avoid the problem in the first place. Hang up wet tools and other items that'll cause rust.

A coat of sealer, paint or epoxy paint will also protect your concrete from rust and other stains. Acid washing is often the first step to applying concrete finishes. So if you've ever considered a floor coating, now is the time to do it. After acid cleaning, applying the finish will seem quick and easy by comparison. Aside from stain protection, a coating will give you an attractive, easy-to-clean surface and reduce freeze-thaw damage to concrete in cold climates.

pro tips

Acid safety

- Wear rubber boots, goggles and rubber gloves.
- Also wear a respirator with a cartridge rated for acid vapor.
- Maintain good ventilation. Open doors and windows and add a fan for better air movement (Photo 1).
- Keep a 5-gallon bucket of clean water handy to quickly wash away any spill on bare skin.
- When mixing, always pour the chemical into the water, never the water into the chemical.
- Use only glass or plastic containers (no metal).
- Cover nearby areas with plastic to protect them from splashes.
- Read the manufacturer's dilution guidelines on the label and follow them if they're different from ours (Photo 1).
- Store extra acid out of reach of children.

Remove rust from a toilet

To make your toilet bowl clean again, start with a dry bowl so water won't dilute the cleaner. To tackle difficult rust stains, skip your discount-store toilet bowl cleaner and head to the hardware store for a product containing diluted hydrochloric acid (also listed on product labels as hydrogen chloride, HCL or muriatic acid).

Be sure to use a toilet brush with stiff nylon bristles in a plastic base. Those old wire brushes scratch the bowl. Once the bowl surface becomes scratched or worn, stain removal becomes next to impossible.

Two cautions when cleaning with diluted hydrochloric acid. First, if you use an in-tank cleaner that contains bleach, remove it and flush multiple times to remove bleach residue. A combination of bleach-containing and acid-containing products (toilet cleaners) produces deadly vapors.

Second caution: Scrub slowly because droplets that splatter outside the bowl can harm carpet, tile, vinyl and your skin. Keep a rag and a bucket of water handy to wipe up spatters. Same goes for setting the bottle down on these surfaces—don't. And make sure you flush and rinse the bowl immediately.

1 Close the water shutoff valve by turning it clockwise until it stops. Flush the toilet and plunge out as much water as possible.

pro tip

Make sure you don't use a bleach-containing product on rust—it will set the stain.

2 Pour an aggressive cleaner (one containing hydrochloric acid; see "Cleaners That Work") on a plastic toilet brush and spread it over the entire bowl surface.

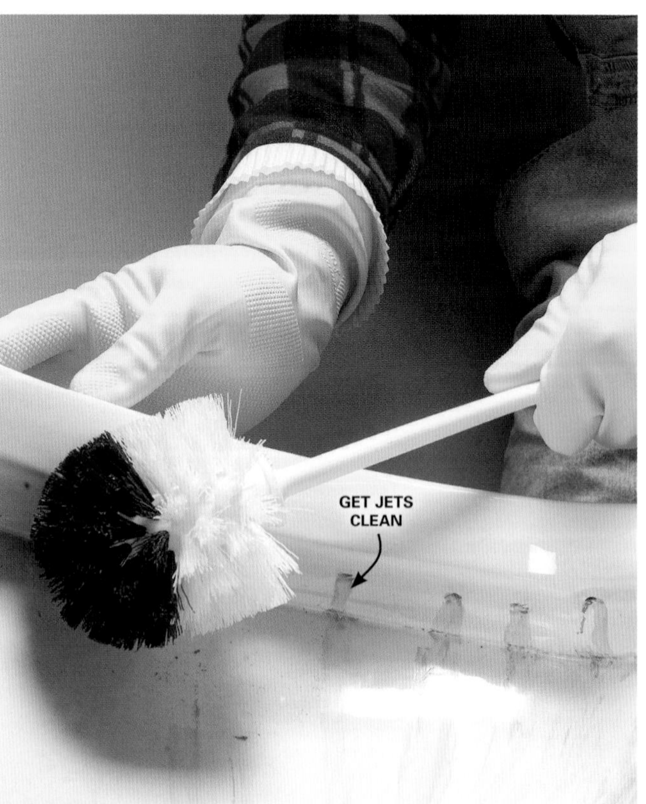

3 Force the brush tip back and forth, especially along the toilet jets (holes under rim), around the water line and on visible stains. Scrub until stains are gone, reapplying cleaner as necessary, then flush twice.

Remove mineral deposits from faucets

To remove tough mineral scale buildup on chrome faucets, use a product such as Lime-A-Way according to label directions. For weekly cleaning, an all-purpose cleaner such as Comet Bathroom or Scrubbing Bubbles will work fine.

To ensure your crusty faucet will shine again, aside from giving it a vigorous toothbrush scrubbing, apply and remove the proper cleaner as directed on its label.

caution

Read and follow the label to make sure the cleaner is safe to use on both the faucet surface and the tub, tile or sink surfaces. Do not use abrasive cleaners. Do not use all-purpose cleaners on marble or other natural stone surfaces. Buy a special stone cleaner.

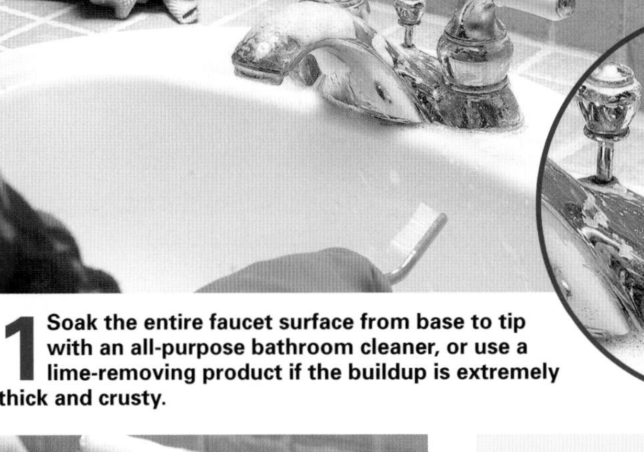

1 Soak the entire faucet surface from base to tip with an all-purpose bathroom cleaner, or use a lime-removing product if the buildup is extremely thick and crusty.

If scrubbing doesn't remove hardened mineral deposits on the aerator screen, unscrew the spout tip by turning it counterclockwise. Soak it overnight in vinegar, then scrub it with the toothbrush and flush with water before reinstalling.

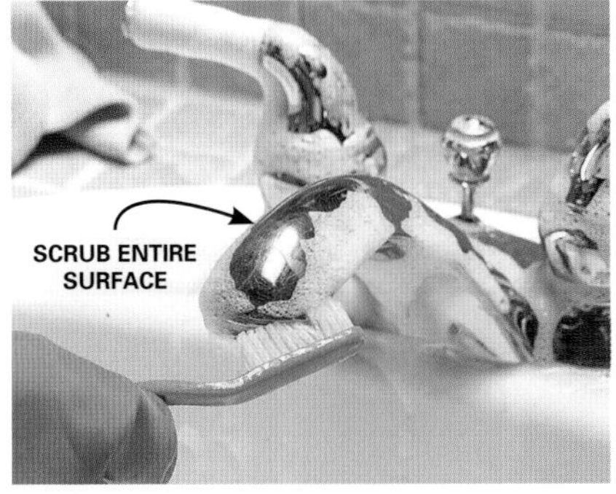

2 Scrub the surface with an old toothbrush, pushing bristles into crevices on the end of the spout (aerator and screen) and on the handles, as well as at the base of the faucet.

3 Once all deposits have been removed, rinse the cleaner off immediately by wiping the entire surface down with a dripping-wet sponge. Dry and polish with a soft cloth.

Cleaners that work

There are five basic types of cleaning chemicals: surfactants, alkalis, acids, solvents and disinfectants. Develop a basic understanding of these and you can pick the right cleaner for any job.

- **Surfactants, found in almost every cleaning product, help carry the ingredients into tiny cracks and pores. They also help loosen, emulsify (disperse in water) and suspend soils for removal.**
- **Alkalis, which have a pH higher than 7, are best at removing (neutralizing) acidic soils, which have a pH less than 7. Alkalis chew up acidic fats and oils (from hamburger grease to body oil to plain old mud), breaking them into smaller particles that can be washed away. Alkaline cleaners range from mild liquid dishwashing detergent and glass cleaner to strong lye (sodium hydroxide) drain openers and degreasers.**
- **Acids work best on neutralizing alkaline soils (tough water stains), such as lime scale, soap deposits, rust and more. Acids break stains into small particles to be washed away. Acidic cleaners range from mild (vinegar, lemon juice) to heavier cleaners such as phosphoric acid (found in toilet bowl and tub/tile cleaners) and hydrochloric or sulfuric acids (found in toilet bowl cleaners).**
- **Solvents, such as mineral spirits, work by dissolving soils rather than neutralizing them like alkalis or acids. They're distilled from petroleum or plant products and are mostly used on oily and greasy soils.**
- **Disinfectants, such as quaternary ammonium or pine oil, are added to cleaners that tout antibacterial power. They kill germs that smell, cause disease, stain clothes and spoil food.**

Remove soap scum from tile

Numerous cleaners are available to remove soap scum from tile. But if you face layers of soap scum buildup, stick with an effective bleach-containing, nonabrasive product.

Scum cleaners commonly contain bleach (sodium hypochlorite), which effectively cuts through soap scum and kills mildew. Be sure to READ THE PRODUCT LABEL and match it to the material (tile, fiberglass, etc.) being cleaned.

1 Coat the entire tiled surface (grout, caulk and all) with an all-purpose cleaner that attacks soap scum. Wait 5 to 10 minutes to allow the product to work, which saves your scrubbing elbow.

2 Remove remaining visible scum and deposits by applying light pressure with a non-scratch nylon scrubber. Reapply product to difficult areas and scrub until clean.

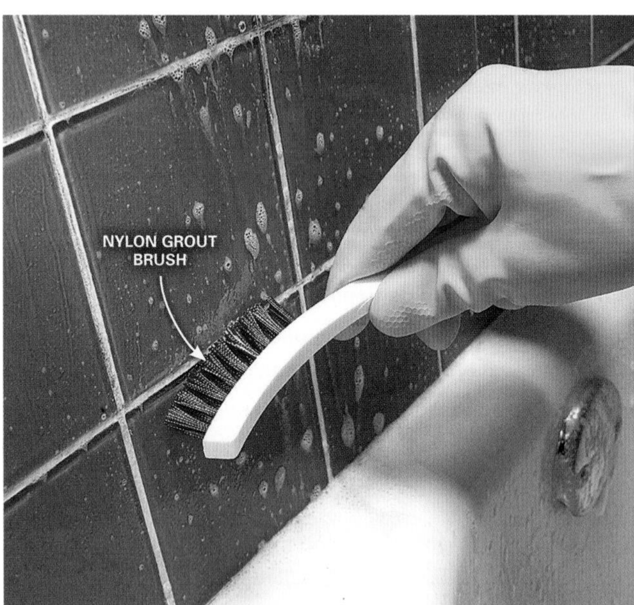

3 Remove stains and deposits on grout or caulk by lightly scrubbing back and forth with a grout brush or old toothbrush. Reapply product as needed.

4 Rinse the entire tiled surface thoroughly with a dripping-wet sponge. Push it back and forth across the top of the wall so rinse water streams to the bottom of the wall. Repeat until all cleaner is removed. Then, start at the top of the tile with a bathroom squeegee and move downward to remove as much water as possible.

instant fix

Remove any glass stain

Window manufacturers recommend abrasive cleaners for the toughest glass stains. Apply a mild abrasive such as Soft Scrub, Bar Keepers Friend or Bon Ami to a soft rag and scrub. These products usually won't scratch glass, but start in a small, inconspicuous spot just to make sure. If elbow grease alone won't do the trick, or if you have large areas to cover, use a drill and small buffing wheel (Photo 1). You can use a similar method on glass shower doors (Photo 2). An electric buffer works fast on the large surface.

1 Scrub away the toughest stains on glass with a buffing wheel and mild abrasive. When you're working near the sash, protect it with masking tape.

2 Remove shower doors and lay them flat. Buff the glass with a car polisher and mild abrasive.

Wash windows like a pro

Try washing windows with a squeegee and you'll never go back to a spray bottle and paper towels. Squeegees get your glass clear and streak-free in a fraction of the time it takes with paper towels. In this article, we'll show you the equipment you need and simple steps to follow for fast, clear results.

The keys to success are buying a good squeegee and keeping it fitted with a sharp, new rubber blade. The same high-quality window washing tools the pros use are readily available at home centers and full-service hardware stores. The whole setup costs less than $30 and will last many years. You'll need a 10- or 12-in. squeegee, a scrubber, a bucket (a 5-gallon plastic bucket will work), hand dishwashing liquid (we recommend Dawn) and a few lint-free rags or small towels.

Buy a high-quality squeegee

Buy a good squeegee and replace the blade frequently. Look for replacement blades, also called rubbers, where you buy the squeegee and pick up two

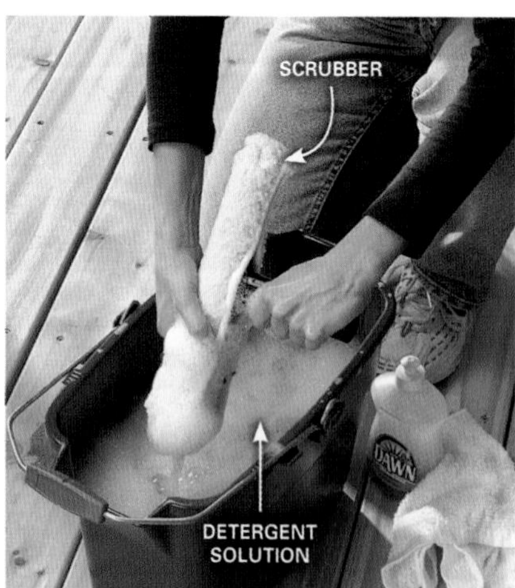

1 Dip the scrubber in a solution of 1 teaspoon dishwashing liquid to two gallons of water. Squeeze excess water from the scrubber.

2 Scrub the glass, working at all angles to clean the edges. Make sure to cover every square inch of the glass.

pro tip

When you store the squeegee, make sure nothing touches the blade.

3 Tip the squeegee so that only the corner contacts the glass. Then, starting at the top corner of the glass, clean a narrow strip of glass from top to bottom on one side. This clean strip makes it easier to start the horizontal stokes.

or three to have on hand. The pros we talked to change their squeegee blades as often as once a day. That's because you just can't do a good job if the edge of the blade becomes nicked, sliced or rounded over with use. If your squeegee leaves streaks or just isn't performing like new, don't hesitate to replace the blade (Photos 10 and 11). You can get a little more mileage out of blades that aren't nicked or sliced by simply reversing them to expose a fresh edge.

SQUEEGEE

You don't need fancy buckets or special soap. Any large bucket will do. Just add a couple of gallons of water and about a teaspoon of dishwashing liquid and you're ready to go. In warm weather, you'll get a little more working time by using cool water.

SCRUBBER

Scrubber or sponge? It's up to you. A scrubber works great and is worth buying if you have a lot of medium to large panes of glass. But a good-quality sponge is all you really need, especially if most of your windowpanes are small.

pro tip

If you're washing windows in below-freezing temps, add windshield-washing solution until the water doesn't freeze on the glass.

4 Press the squeegee blade against the glass in the upper corner and pull it steadily across the window. Concentrate on keeping the top of the squeegee in contact with the top edge of the window.

5 Wipe the blade on the clean towel in your front pocket or wipe it across the scrubber to remove dirt and excess water.

6 Begin again, with the top of the squeegee overlapping the previous stroke about 2 in. Pull the squeegee across the window at an angle to direct excess water down. Wipe and repeat.

pro tip

Microfiber rags work great for window cleaning. They're available in the cleaning section at home centers and hardware stores.

The squeegee method is easy to master

Professional window cleaners sweep the squeegee back and forth across the window in one continuous motion. But this "fanning" technique takes practice to master. Instead, the method we show allows you to get great results immediately. We're moving the squeegee horizontally across the glass (Photos 4 – 6), but vertical strokes will work too. If you work vertically, angle the squeegee to direct excess water toward the uncleaned area.

Touch up with a rag

If all goes well, a quick run around the perimeter of the glass with a clean rag will finish the job (Photo 7). If you left a squeegee track, wait a few minutes until it dries. It will often disappear. If not, you may be able to rub streaks away with a few light rubs with the clean, dry rag. But don't hesitate to simply redo the entire window. By now you're probably getting so good that it will only take a few seconds anyway.

7 Use the rag in your pocket to wipe up excess water along the bottom edge of the window. Then poke your finger into a dry spot on a separate lint-free rag and run it around the perimeter of the window to remove any remaining suds. Wipe off any streaks using a clean area of the lint-free rag. Change rags when you can't find any fresh, clean areas.

8 Wash divided-lite windows with a sponge and a small squeegee. If you can't find a small enough squeegee, you can cut off a larger one to fit your glass size. Scrub the glass with a wrung-out sponge. Then use the tip of the squeegee to clear a narrow strip at the top (same technique as Photo 3). Pull the squeegee down and wipe the perimeter.

Yes, you can use a squeegee inside the house, too

The pros do it all the time, even in houses with stained and varnished woodwork. The key is to squeeze most of the soapy water out of the scrubber to eliminate excessive dripping and running. Then rest the scrubber on the edge of the bucket rather than dropping it in the water after each window. Depending on how dirty your windows are, you may be able to wash five or 10 windows before rinsing the scrubber. Keep a rag in your pocket to wipe the squeegee and quickly clean up soapy water that runs onto the woodwork. Use a separate clean rag to wipe the perimeter of the glass.

Get your windows sparkling clean in less than 30 seconds—

9 Remove paint specks and labels with a razor blade mounted in a holder. Always use a new blade to avoid scratching the glass. Wet the window first and push the blade across once. Rinse the blade and repeat on the next section to avoid trapping debris under the blade that could scratch the glass. Don't use a razor blade on tempered glass.

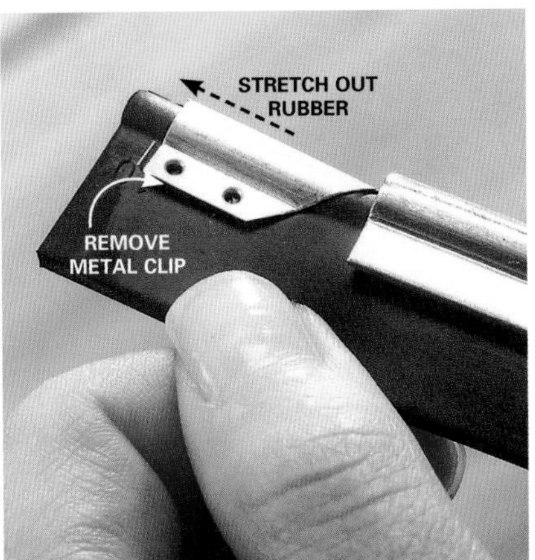

10 Change the squeegee blade if it's nicked, sliced or worn. Grab the end of the blade and stretch it out to expose the metal clip. Slide the clip off. Then slide the blade out the opposite end. Blades without clips are held by screws and the clamp on the handle.

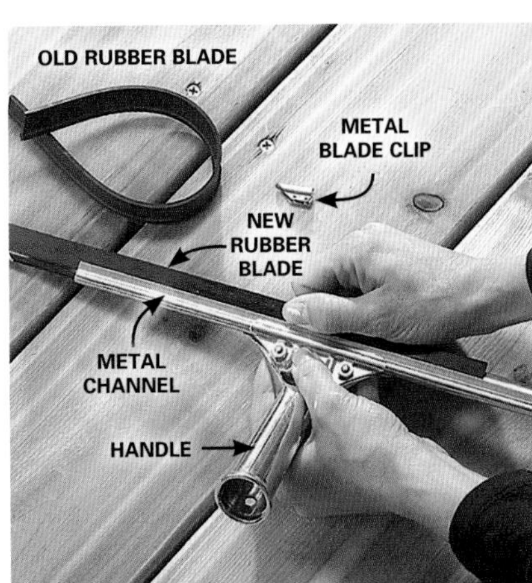

11 Slide the new blade into the metal channel. Stretch it as in Photo 10 and reinstall the metal clip. If necessary, cut the end of the blade to leave 1/8 to 3/16 in. protruding from the channel.

pro tips

For hard-to-clean windows

Dried paint, sticky labels, tree pitch and bug crud may not yield to plain soap and water. Here are a few tips for removing this tough grime.

- Scrape wetted glass with a new, sharp razor blade to remove dried paint (Photo 9).
- Remove tree pitch or bug droppings with a fine white nylon scrub pad. Wet the glass first and rub in an inconspicuous area to make sure you're not scratching the glass.
- Add 1/2 cup of ammonia per gallon of water to help remove greasy dirt.
- Loosen sticky residue left from labels or tape by soaking it with a specialty product like Goof Off. You'll find Goof Off in the paint department at hardware stores and home centers. Then scrape off the residue with a razor blade.

just scrub, squeegee and wipe!

10 tips to stop mold & mildew

Black spots growing on the wall or a dank smell in part of the house may at first seem like an unsolvable mystery, but water is always, somehow, the cause. The solution may be stopping a leak, reducing the humidity, plugging a gap in the insulation—or even just opening a closet door for better air circulation. But if you find and eliminate the water source, the mold (or mildew, which is basically the same problem) will go away.

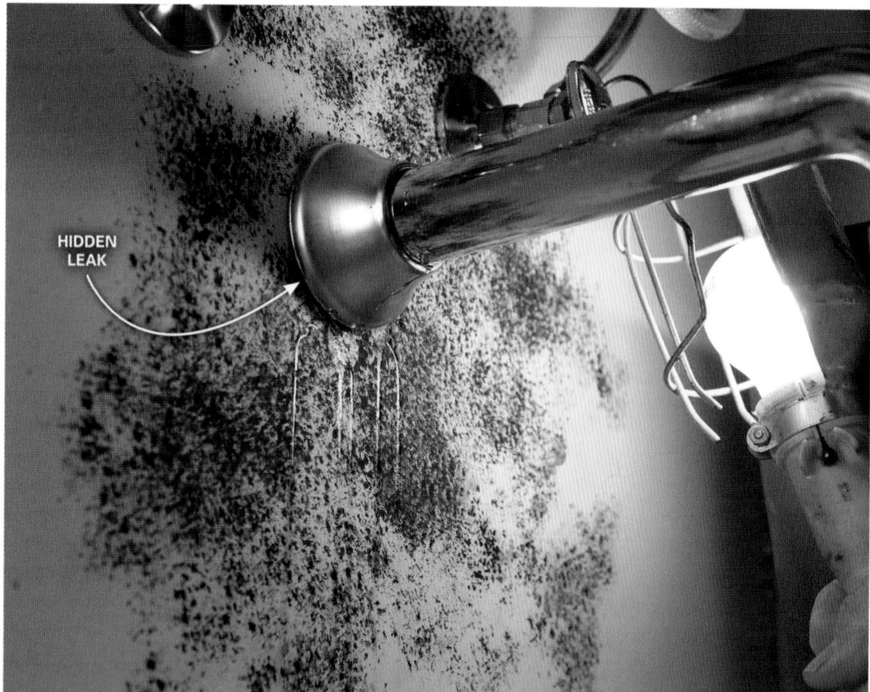

1 Check for plumbing leaks

If you see mold near water pipes, waste lines, icemaker lines or plumbing fixtures, chances are the mold is feeding off a nearby leak. Let the water run while you check the pipes and surrounding area for damp spots. Remember that water can travel in any direction—down, sideways or even up when it wicks into absorbent material like drywall—so the actual leak may be some distance from the mold.

Plumbing leaks support mold growth. Drips from this leaky sink drain keep the drywall damp, creating a perfect home for mold.

2 Don't ignore mold

Mold can be an early warning sign of a moisture problem inside walls or ceilings that could cause an expensive problem like wood rot. Avoid the temptation to just wipe the mold away and forget about it—find and stop the water source.

3 Listen to the air conditioner

If your central air conditioner cycles on and off quickly and you see mold near the diffusers, the unit may be too large for the house, causing the house air to cool before the humidity is removed. The easiest fix is to simply turn on a dehumidifier.

In air-conditioned houses, vinyl wallpaper on an exterior wall or vinyl flooring over a crawl space can also create mold. Moisture in warm air coming in from outside gets trapped behind the vinyl and condenses on the cool surface. The fix is to remove the wallpaper or insulate the crawl space with 6-mil poly and rigid insulation.

pro tip

Find out more about solving mold problems by searching thefamilyhandyman.com for "mold," "leaks," "tile," "flashing," "basement" and "humidity."

4 Look for outside leaks

If mold is growing on an exterior wall or ceiling, first look for a leak in the wall or roof. Measure from the moldy area to a reference point like a door, then find the spot on the other side of the wall or ceiling.

Closely inspect nearby vents, roof flashing, decks, window wells and anywhere wood is rotting. Look for ground sloping toward the house and downspouts emptying next to the wall. If the ground around the house gets too wet, moisture will wick into the foundation or slab and become persistent dampness.

Mold can be a warning sign. The musty odor of mold alerted homeowners to this flashing leak before wood rot could cause structural damage.

5 Inspect the ductwork

If mold forms on the ceiling under a duct or register and there's no sign of a roof leak, badly insulated ductwork may be the cause. Warm, moist air condenses and forms water on ducts carrying cold air through the attic or crawl space—just like beads of water form on a cold drink in summer. The condensation is a sign that the duct is uninsulated or missing a vapor barrier. Eventually the water saturates the insulation and drywall and mold spores (which are everywhere) take root.

In cold weather, the reverse happens. Moisture forms anywhere warm air escapes—for instance, at unsealed joints between duct sections.

Condensation can imitate leaks. Torn insulation allows condensation on this duct, causing mold on the ceiling just as a roof leak would.

6 Don't let mold make you sick

Breathing mold spores can cause asthma, allergic reactions and other health problems. Always wear an N95-rated respirator, rubber gloves and eye protection when removing mold. Seal moldy materials in plastic and wash clothes after working around mold to avoid spreading spores around the whole house. If you smell mold coming from your ducts, if your house has been flooded or you have large areas of mold (more than 10 sq. ft.), contact your local health department or a mold remediation specialist.

Three biggest causes of mold

Water leaking into the house from the roof, walls or ground.

Water leaking from pipes, plumbing fixtures or appliances.

Condensation produced when warm, moist air contacts a cool surface.

7 Is it mold or dirt?

Most mold is unmistakable, but sometimes small or largely hidden growths just make a surface look dirty.

For a quick test, dip a swab in diluted bleach (1 part bleach, 16 parts water) and dab it on the wall. If the spot quickly lightens (or keeps coming back after cleaning), assume it's mold.

Mold test kits are available that detect the presence and identify the type of mold, but they won't help determine the cause or what to do about it.

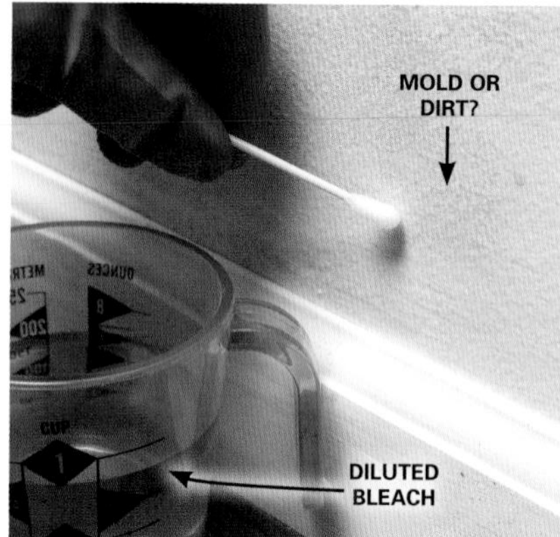

Test suspicious-looking spots with a few drops of diluted bleach to see whether it's mold or just dirt.

8 Stop mold from coming back

Once the moisture has been dried up, clean and spray the area with an antimicrobial treatment to prevent mold from coming back. In basements or other larger areas with musty odors, it may be more effective to fog the entire room. (Concrobium Mold Control is an antimicrobial treatment available at home centers and hardware stores that can be dispensed by spray or with a fogging machine. Visit concrobium.com for more information.)

If you need to build or rebuild an area where moisture has been a problem, use materials that resist mold growth and aren't affected by water. Construct walls with pressure-treated wood and rigid insulation and cover the walls with paperless drywall, which has nothing for mold to feed on. In areas where mold might grow, such as basement walls, spray the surfaces with an antimicrobial treatment. Paint walls with mildew-resistant primer and paint or add mildewcide to your paint.

MOLD-RESISTANT PRIMER

MOLD-RESISTANT PAINT

To avoid feeding mold, use paints with mildewcide and materials that mold can't feed on.

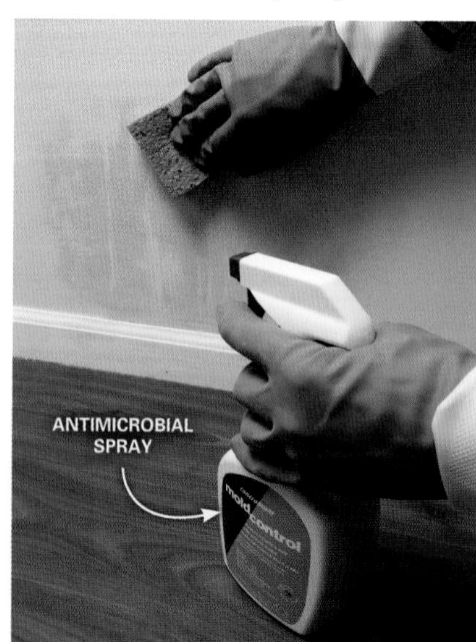

Discourage future mold growth with an antimicrobial treatment. Whole rooms can be fogged using rental equipment from home centers.

Moisture-hunting tools

If you can see or smell mold but can't find an obvious cause, you can usually pinpoint the problem with one or more of these diagnostic tools.

Moisture meters (at right; starting at $30 at hardware stores and online tool suppliers) measure the water content in building materials. If a room smells musty but has no visible mold or moisture, measure the surfaces around the room with a moisture meter. A higher-than-normal reading in one area can indicate a leak or a problem with water coming in through the foundation or floor.

Humidity gauges (above right; starting at $15 at hardware stores and online) measure the humidity in the house. Mold grows best in warm, moist environments, so keep the humidity low—below 50 percent humidity when possible.

Infrared thermometers ($40 to $120 from online tool suppliers) use an infrared beam to measure the temperature on any surface, letting you locate hot or cold spots in the walls where condensation may be occurring because of missing insulation.

Air movement indicator. This can be anything that creates smoke or vapor, like a stick of incense or a fog-making device, such as the SmokPoint fog-maker, widely used by mold remediation and insulation inspectors; $70 from zerotoys.com.) Hold it near baseboards, windows or wall penetrations to track moisture-creating drafts and air leaks.

9 Missing insulation feeds mold

Warm air seeks gaps in the insulation, and when it hits colder surfaces as it flows out of or into the house, water condenses—which then feeds mold. These spots often occur on outside walls near floors or windows, at corners and around outlets and lights. If the mold disappears after cleaning it and lowering indoor humidity with a dehumidifier or vent fan, just keep an eye on it. If it recurs, open the wall and fix the problem.

Mold on walls is often caused by condensation. This poorly insulated wall collects moisture that feeds mold.

10 Win the war against bathtub mold

Mold around the tub or shower is a different problem, since the moisture source never goes away. Bleach-type cleaners kill mold on the surface, but it usually grows back because mold is still living under the surface.

To prevent the problem, spray the wall with an antimicrobial treatment, then seal tile grout with two coats of grout sealant to keep water from wicking in.

If the mold is extensive and tiles come off, rebuild the wall with cement board tile backer and new tile.

If the wall is sound but the mold stains won't go away, you may need to regrout the area. Scrape out the caulk and stained grout, then spray the wall with antimicrobial treatment to keep buried spores from growing back. Regrout and caulk, then coat the whole wall with grout sealant.

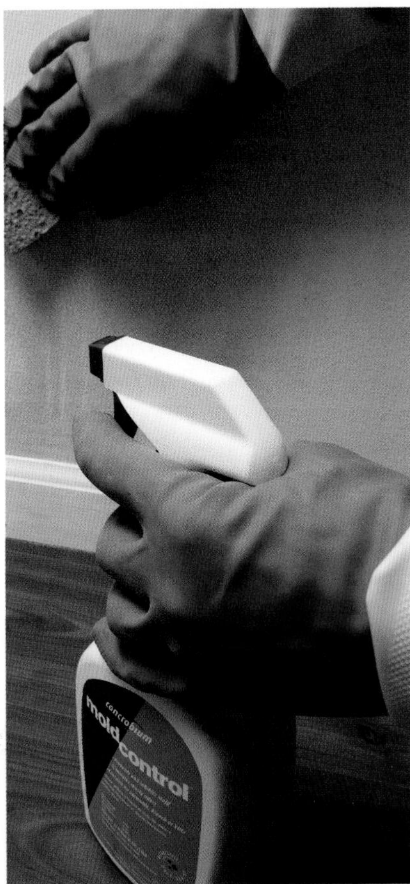

Seal tile and grout with grout sealant to keep walls from absorbing moisture and feeding mold below the surface.

Make your gas grill look like new

If your gas grill is looking old and gray and the cart is starting to rust, you're probably thinking it's time for a new grill. Sure, it would be cool to own one of those shiny new stainless steel models—if you're willing to spend $800 or more. But if the cart, base and cover of your current grill are still sound, you can whip it into like-new shape in less than a day. You just need special paint, some new accessories and elbow grease. The paint and supplies cost less than $70 at home centers. And you can pick up new handles, knobs, emblems and a new thermometer for about $40 from a local appliance parts store or online (grillparts.com is one source). You'll have to wait at least 24 hours for the paint to cure, but then you can get back to burger-flipping. Here's how to do the job.

Buy supplies

Stop at any home center and buy a bottle of heavy-duty degreaser, nitrile gloves, a respirator, a stiff-bristle scrub brush and a wire brush. Also pick up 80-grit and 120-grit sandpaper, brush-on or spray-on rust converter, primer for rusty metal and a few cans of heat-resistant paint (one choice is Krylon High Heat Max, $15). You'll also need disposable plastic sheeting, a shop vacuum, a palm sander, a bucket and a garden hose.

Clean and sand and prime

Cleaning a greasy gas grill creates quite a mess. And the last thing you want is to move the grease from the grill to your driveway or garage floor. So do the project outdoors and tarp off the entire work area. Start the job by removing the burners, grates and grease cup. Use your shop vacuum to suck up all the loose crud from the bottom of the grill and any dirt and rust from the propane tank shelf. Next, remove the knobs, emblems and thermometer (if equipped). Mix up a strong solution of degreaser using the dilution ratios listed on the label. Then grab your scrub brush and gloves and wash the entire grill (Photo 1). If you have a power washer, soak the grill with degreaser and then blast off the grease and loose paint. Rinse it with water and let it dry in the sun.

Next, mask off the wheels, gas valves, warning labels, manufacturer's nameplate and any other parts that won't be painted. Then grab your respirator and palm sander and sand the exterior (Photo 2). Pretreat the worst rust spots with a rust converter product. Once that dries, prime the rusty areas and bare metal with a primer for rusty metal (Photo 3). Let the primer dry.

Paint the grill and install the new parts

Wipe the entire grill with a tack cloth, then spray-paint it (Photo 4). Finish up by installing the new accessories (Photo 5). Remove the masking and let the paint dry for the recommended time. Then install the burners and grates and get grilling.

1 **DEGREASE THE ENTIRE GRILL** Spread degreaser inside the cover and burner area and over the entire exterior. Then scrub the entire grill with a brush. Make sure you remove grease from all the crevices.

2 **SAND AND WIRE BRUSH** Sand pitted and corroded areas with 80-grit sandpaper. Use a wire brush in the crevices to remove surface rust and chipping paint. Then switch to 120-grit sandpaper and sand the entire grill and cart.

3 **SPRAY ON PRIMER** Apply rust converter, then spray primer over the converted rust and bare metal areas. Let it "flash" for the recommended time. Then apply a second coat.

4 **APPLY THE FINISH COAT** Paint the top of the grill lid first. Then spray down each side all the way to the bottom of the cart. Paint the front of the grill last. Apply a second coat after waiting the recommended time.

5 **INSTALL NEW PARTS** Attach the new cover lift handle or knobs. Snap on the new emblems. Screw in the new thermometer.

Bonus **section**

GET RID OF PESTS!

Seal up your house to keep pests outside

Insects, spiders and rodents all have their place. OUTSIDE! It's faster and easier to keep pests out than it is to remove them. The exterior of your house is full of paths for pests to find their way in. So we called on our expert to help us find those paths and give us some tips and tools to lock pests out.

ILLUSTRATION: JOHN KEELY

Seal them out!

1 **TRIM TREES:** Overhanging branches make your roof accessible for tree-scaling pests like squirrels and chipmunks.

2 **CAP YOUR CHIMNEY:** Any vents on your roof that lead into your home should be covered with a cap and screen.

3 **SEAL VENTS:** Gable, soffit and crawl space vents need a mesh backing to keep out critters. When it's missing, these are good spots for birds and bats to call home.

4 **REMOVE STANDING WATER:** The stagnant water in rain barrels, wheelbarrows, pools and birdbaths can become a breeding ground for insects such as mosquitoes.

5 **SEAL YOUR GARAGE:** A broken garage door seal will allow pests to move into your garage Replacing it is easy.

6 **TAKE CARE OF ANTHILLS:** If the ants on your driveway don't bother you, use a perimeter spray to keep them outside. If you want them gone, use granular bait.

7 **FILL HOLES:** Use hydraulic cement to patch small holes from old conduit or cable entry points, as well as gaps and cracks in your block or concrete foundation. Use caulk for gaps and cracks around trim and siding.

8 **FLAPPER CHECK:** Make sure the flapper for your dryer vent opens easily and closes all the way.

9 **INSPECT DOOR AND WINDOW SEALS:** Check that the weather stripping and sweeps are intact, and repair them if they aren't.

10 **PROTECT YOUR GARDEN PRODUCE:** If you don't want to fence the garden, try a raised bed. If rabbits are eating your garden, sprinkle powdered fox urine around the plants.

11 **GUTTER DETERRENT:** Keep critters from clogging gutters by using a downspout guard and retractable downspout.

12 **BAG YOUR BURNERS (NOT SHOWN):** When grilling season is over, wrap the burners and any other openings to keep bugs out.

Take your time inspecting

The first step on your pest prevention patrol should be to walk around your house armed with a mirror, kneepads and a roll of masking tape. Plan to spend about an hour noting and marking spots where pests could find a way in. A good place to begin is the front door, and move your way around the house. Start low and look for cracks and holes in the foundation. Then look for gaps where the siding starts and work your way up to the roof.

Check vent flappers

Check the flappers on your dryer and range vents. They're designed to open as air gets pushed out of these appliances, but if the vents become clogged, the flappers will get stuck open. This is especially true for dryer vents. Remove any debris or lint buildup and make sure the flapper closes when the appliance isn't exhausting.

Cap the chimney and vents

Chimney caps and furnace exhaust vents are easy to seal. Chimney caps have setscrews that snug the cap to the flue pipe. PVC vent caps with mesh come in different sizes and fit right over the end of the exposed pipe.

Repair screens

If you have insects sneaking into a small tear in a window or door screen, a quick patch will do the trick.

Cut a square hole around the tear with a straightedge and a sharp utility knife. Keep the hole as small as possible and leave at least 1/2 in. of old screen next to the metal frame.

Cut a patch of fiberglass screen that will lap 1/2 in. over each edge. Lay wax paper under the window screen to keep the glue from sticking to the workbench. Apply a bead of glue around the hole, and spread the glue through the patch and window screen with a flat wooden stick.

CRACKED VENT BOOT

Quick fix for a roof boot

After years of exposure to weather, roof vent boots can dry and crack, leaving an inviting opening to the warmer air inside. Bees and other insects, as well as rain and snow, can get in and cause havoc. You don't need to replace the boot; just buy no-caulk thermoplastic flashing and slip it over the vent. They cost less than $7 at home centers.

NO-CAULK VENT FLASHING

Replace weather stripping

If your weather stripping is allowing big drafts to get through your windows and doors, chances are bugs can find a way into your house as well. Check that the weather stripping is sound and replace it if necessary. For older doors and windows, an adhesive-backed option is quick and easy. For newer doors, the weather stripping has a built-in barb that fits into a kerf on the doorjamb. Pull the old one out and press a new one in.

Caulk gaps in siding and trim

There's often a gap where two different types of building materials come together, and pests will come right in. To seal the gap, first fill it with backer rod (sold in many different sizes), then mask off a nice, clean line for caulk, squeeze it in and smooth it out.

How NOT to attract pests

- **Remove pest homes**
  Woodpiles, garbage cans, wheelbarrows full of dirt or water, and children's sand tables can all make nice homes for pests. Move them away from your home, cover them or remove them altogether.
- **Elevate your plants**
  Pests love vegetation, but if the plants are on a stand, they're a lot harder to get at. Potted plants can also collect water, which is a breeding ground for insects.
- **Tamper-proof pet food**
  Your pet isn't the only one who likes dry kibble. Don't store pet food in the bag you buy it in. When you open the bag, dump it into a sealed, tamper-proof container.
- **Upgrade porch lights**
  Ever notice the flock of insects at your front door light? It's not necessarily the light they are attracted to; it can be the heat from the bulb. Swap your incandescent bulb for an LED option that's approved for wet locations.
- **No-vacancy A/C**
  It's smart to protect your A/C unit from snow and ice during the winter. Instead of creating a nice, warm home by wrapping it with a tarp, protect it with a piece of plywood and a few bricks.
- **Pest-proof your grill**
  When you store your grill for the winter, make sure it's clean and free of grease and burnt bits of food. If the burners are removable, take them off, wrap them and plug the hose ends to keep bugs out.
- **Close the garage door**
  It's obvious, but when you're not going in or out of your garage, make sure it's closed—or you'll find yourself fostering birds, mice and squirrels.
- **Clean thrifting**
  If you like the thrill of bargain hunting, make sure you also enjoy cleaning whatever furniture or clothing you find before you bring it in. You never know where it came from or if it sat in a garage for years before someone decided to donate it.

Our favorite sealing weapons

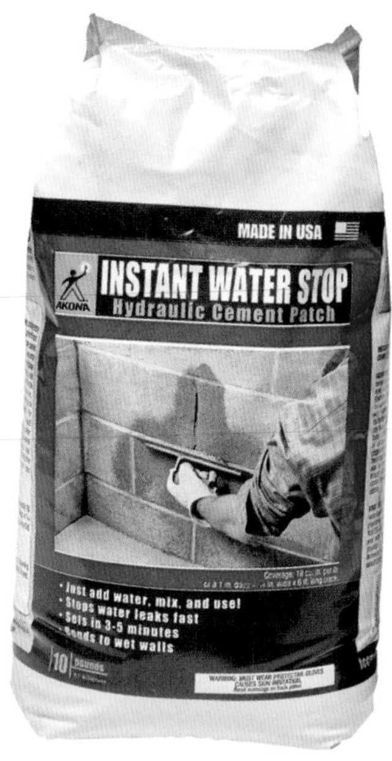

Copper and Expanding foam

Stuff a generous amount of copper mesh into the larger gaps around your home. Use a screwdriver to press it in, leaving about 1/2 in. of space to fill with expanding foam. The foam will keep out small pests, and the copper mesh will act as a second layer of defense in case the foam is chewed by pests.

Fiberglass mesh

To fill holes in your block or concrete foundation, use hydraulic cement. Regular cement shrinks as it cures, making it difficult to get a good patch. Hydraulic cement expands as it cures, so it can fill voids tightly. **Note:** After you mix hydraulic cement with water, it will start to harden after about three minutes, so mix up only what you can apply in that time.

Siding, window and door caulk

Caulk is the gold standard for filling small gaps and cracks up to about 3/8 in. deep and wide. When you're buying caulk to fill gaps outside, look for the words "paintable" and "flexible" on the tube. If you can't find a matching color, go with clear so it doesn't stand out.

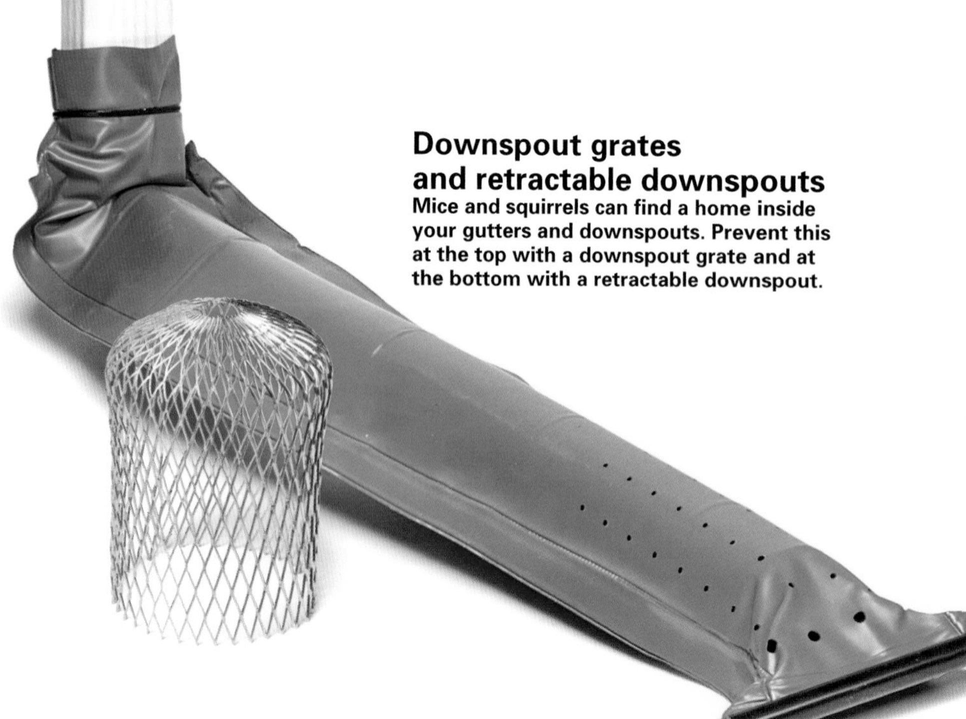

Downspout grates and retractable downspouts

Mice and squirrels can find a home inside your gutters and downspouts. Prevent this at the top with a downspout grate and at the bottom with a retractable downspout.

VIA AMAZON

Fiberglass mesh

This is the go-to screen door patch, but it's also great for attic and crawl space vents, which have larger spaces that birds and bats can get through. Most vents will have it already, but if it's missing, glue or staple a layer of mesh on the back of the vent.

Pro tips for pest control

Joe Stampley does battle with home invaders every day. And wins. Some of it is dirty work: crawling under decks, squeezing into attics, cleaning out traps and removing wasp nests. But there is a lot more to pest control than dirty work. Joe's skills in identification and prevention and his experience outsmarting pests are what really make Joe successful. To help you win the war, he opened his toolbox and shared some tricks of the trade.

MORE SMARTS = LESS CHEMICALS
"It's more practical than spraying a chemical." Joe uses chemicals as a last resort— only about 10% of the time.

IDENTIFICATION IS KEY
Understanding what you're up against is the first step to getting your pest problem under control.

MICE ARE THE WORST
Joe's toughest foes are mice. They reproduce and populate quickly, making them hard to eliminate.

Disinfectant spray + dust brush + toilet brush

Joe makes sure the area he leaves behind is cleaned up and sanitary for the homeowners. Disinfecting spray and a dust brush are the perfect tools for small droppings and other messes. He wields a toilet brush for bigger messes.

Headlamp

Frequently encountering dark spaces, cracks and crevices, Joe finds a light mandatory, and having both hands available to plug holes and set traps, priceless.

KNEEPADS

Respirator

Joe doesn't often use chemicals—only when all his other options have failed—but when he does, he protects himself with a mask and respirator. He changes the filters regularly and makes sure his mask is cleaned every day so he doesn't have to smell yesterday's cheeseburger.

Bait gun

This gun can apply bait, insecticide and rodenticide gels with pinpoint precision. Joe prefers using the bait gun because chemical sprays drift around.

SAFETY GLASSES

Latex gloves

You might think these are for protecting Joe's hands from the chemicals, and you'd be right, but they also keep scents from giving Joe away. Many pests have a strong sense of smell and run for cover when they smell humans.

Expanding foam

Joe uses window and door foam instead of foam formulated to stop pests. Anti-pest foams work, but Joe would rather avoid chemicals in areas where kids might poke and pick at foam.

Copper mesh

Forget steel wool; it can rust and crumble away. Use copper mesh instead. It will last forever, and the interlocking design makes it difficult for rodents to gnaw through and pull out of cracks.

Did you know?

Ants are the ultimate pest: They are found on every continent except Antarctica and have been around for more than 50 million years. They don't have eyelids, so they never sleep. They also snack on rodenticide without harm.

Zone Monitor

These sticky cardboard tents attract and trap insects. They allow Joe to identify the pests and know the quantity he's dealing with. And that helps him decide what to do next.

Handy stick

This is a homemade tool consisting of a hook screw and a dowel. Joe uses it to reach into small crevices and ones he'd rather not stick his hands into. And sometimes, he uses it to scoop something up off the ground to avoid bending over.

Insect bulb duster

Joe uses a bulb duster to gently apply powdered pesticides in cracks and on other surfaces. He also has one for nontoxic powders like flour or baby powder that he uses to track pests in areas where chemicals should be avoided, such as kids' rooms and daycare centers.

Brush multi-tool

Joe has fashioned this trap cleaner into his own pest multi-tool. It not only cleans out the traps he empties daily but also contains the keys for opening them.

Joe's tips for outsmarting pests

Heed the warnings on pesticides

The labels on insecticide and rodenticide products have important information on how to use them safely, including where to spray, when to spray, how much and how often. Keep yourself, your family and the environment safe by strictly following these guidelines.

Ask good questions of potential exterminators

When hiring a pest control service, ask:

- How do you plan to identify the pests?
- What removal methods do you use, and how do you keep pests out?
- When do you decide to resort to chemicals, and what products do you use?

The answers can help steer you to a professional, safety-minded company. For more info about hiring a pro, visit pestworld.org.

Don't expect instant results

Pest control is a process, not a set-it-and-forget-it solution. Joe often makes several trips to identify, monitor and solve problems. In some cases, you'll need ongoing service to keep pests from returning.

Overdo traps

Joe always puts out more than the required number of traps. If the situation calls for 15 traps, he puts out 20. This ensures that he catches all the rodents. For extra insurance, he leaves a few traps behind.

Protect other animals

When targeting pests, you can accidentally harm other animals. This is called secondary poisoning, and birds and other animals that make a snack out of pests can get caught in the crossfire. Joe uses pesticides that contain warfarin or bromethalin because they pose less risk to birds and mammals through primary and secondary poisoning.

Double up

Mice can nibble away expanding foam, and tiny insects can sneak past copper mesh. When possible, use both. Stuff in the mesh, then seal it in with foam.

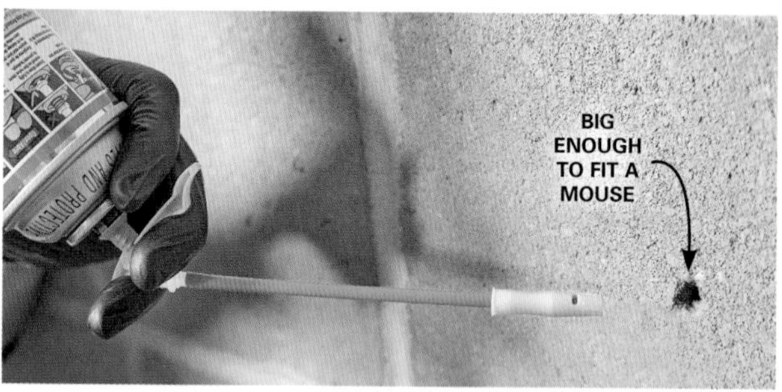

Don't skip tiny holes

Mice can fit into a hole as small as 1/4 in. If their elongated skulls can fit through, the rest can too. Plus, filling those holes will also keep bugs out.

NIKITAROYTMAN PHOTOGRAPHY/ SHUTTERSTOCK

Keep the lights off

To find pest entry points, head to the basement, crawl space or garage and keep the lights OFF. Light shining through gaps and cracks will show you where pests can get in. And you'll have better luck tracking down rodents and other pests because many are nocturnal and sensitive to light—when a light goes on, they will scurry!

BETWEEN THE MATTRESS AND THE BOX SPRING

ALONG BASEBOARD

UNDER BEDS

Safe, effective pesticide

Diatomaceous earth is harmless to humans; some brands are even considered safe for consumption (although there's no reason to eat it). Here's how it works: When insects like bedbugs or ants crawl over diatomaceous earth, this abrasive powder scratches off the waxy layer of their exoskeleton. The bugs then become desiccated and die. Joe spreads diatomaceous earth with his bulb duster under mattresses, bed frames and at the baseboard trim.

SAFER BRAND

12 simple steps to prevent pests

Sometimes it doesn't take a pest pro to keep out pests. There are many quick and easy steps you can take yourself:

- **Install a squirrel guard on your bird feeders. It will keep rodents from spilling the food and attracting more pests.**
- **Clean outdoor grills and cooking areas.**
- **Use city-issued trash bins, and if they get cracked or the lid goes missing, ask for a replacement.**
- **Move stacks of firewood away from your house. They make perfect homes for pests. If you don't want a pest nest, don't stack wood at all.**
- **Take out the trash more often.**
- **Don't store paper bags or an excess of household cleaning products under cabinets, near trash or next to your fridge.**
- **Run a dehumidifier to remove moisture.**
- **Go through your storage area twice a year and move things around. If nothing jumps out at you and you see no signs of pests, you're fine—but you probably will.**
- **Remove clutter.**
- **Eliminate standing water.**
- **Get rid of mold and bacteria.**
- **And finally, Joe says, "If you see a hole and you can plug it, plug it."**

Index